The United States and the Malaysian Economy

This is the first book to examine, in depth, US economic involvement in colonial Malaya. Exploring the relationship between the United States and the Malayan/Malaysian economy, the book concentrates on the period 1870 to 1957, with particular focus on trade flows and foreign direct investment (FDI). It surveys the reasons behind the levels of US trade and investment, and considers the impact of the presence of both British governments and businesses on the US–Malayan relationship.

The book goes on to examine the impact of US trade and investment on Malaya, with detailed analysis of the cases of three important US inward investors: Yukon Gold Company, United States Rubber Company and Ford Motor Company. The author argues that the British colonial presence provided an infrastructure that facilitated US trade and FDI flows with Malaya, although on occasion restrictive policies followed by the colonial government directed US FDI flows elsewhere. However, US FDI and trade remained constrained by Malaya's status as a low income developing country with little potential for market-oriented manufacturing investment. Nonetheless, it demonstrates that US trade and FDI has a positive impact on the Malayan economy through flows or organisational and technological capabilities. An epilogue brings the story up to date for contemporary US–Malaysian economic relations.

Overall, this book is an insightful and highly original account of the part played by US trade and investment in Malaya's economic development.

Shakila Yacob is Associate Professor in the Department of History, University of Malaya, and Deputy Director of the International Institute of Public Policy and Management. Her research interests are in the areas of international business and business history.

Routledge Studies in the Growth Economies of Asia

1 **The Changing Capital Markets of East Asia**
Edited by Ky Cao

2 **Financial Reform in China**
Edited by On Kit Tam

3 **Women and Industrialization in Asia**
Edited by Susan Horton

4 **Japan's Trade Policy**
Action or reaction?
Yumiko Mikanagi

5 **The Japanese Election System**
Three analaytical perspectives
Junichiro Wada

6 **The Economics of the Latecomers**
Catching-up, technology transfer and institutions in Germany, Japan and South Korea
Jang-Sup Shin

7 **Industrialization in Malaysia**
Import substitution and infant industry performance
Rokiah Alavi

8 **Economic Development in Twentieth Century East Asia**
The international context
Edited by Aiko Ikeo

9 **The Politics of Economic Development in Indonesia**
Contending perspectives
Edited by Ian Chalmers and Vedi R. Hadiz

10 **Studies in the Economic History of the Pacific Rim**
Edited by Sally M. Miller, A. J. H. Latham and Dennis O. Flynn

11 **Workers and the State in New Order Indonesia**
Vedi R. Hadiz

12 **The Japanese Foreign Exchange Market**
Beate Reszat

13 **Exchange Rate Policies in Emerging Asian Countries**
Edited by Stefan Collignon, Jean Pisani-Ferry and Yung Chul Park

14 **Chinese Firms and Technology in the Reform Era**
Yizheng Shi

15 **Japanese Views on Economic Development**
Diverse paths to the market
Kenichi Ohno and Izumi Ohno

16 Technological Capabilities and Export Success in Asia
Edited by Dieter Ernst, Tom Ganiatsos and Lynn Mytelka

17 Trade and Investment in China
The European experience
Edited by Roger Strange, Jim Slater and Limin Wang

18 Technology and Innovation in Japan
Policy and management for the 21st Century
Edited by Martin Hemmert and Christian Oberländer

19 Trade Policy Issues in Asian Development
Prema-chandra Athukorala

20 Economic Integration in the Asia Pacific Region
Ippei Yamazawa

21 Japan's War Economy
Edited by Erich Pauer

22 Industrial Technology Development in Malaysia
Industry and firm studies
Edited by Jomo K. S., Greg Felker and Rajah Rasiah

23 Technology, Competitiveness and the State
Malaysia's industrial technology policies
Edited by Jomo K. S. and Greg Felker

24 Corporatism and Korean Capitalism
Edited by Dennis L. McNamara

25 Japanese Science
Samuel Coleman

26 Capital and Labour in Japan
The functions of two factor markets
Toshiaki Tachibanaki and Atsuhiro Taki

27 Asia Pacific Dynamism 1550–2000
Edited by A. J. H. Latham and Heita Kawakatsu

28 The Political Economy of Development and Environment in Korea
Jae-Yong Chung and Richard J Kirkby

29 Japanese Economics and Economists since 1945
Edited by Aiko Ikeo

30 China's Entry into the World Trade Organisation
Edited by Peter Drysdale and Ligang Song

31 Hong Kong as an International Financial Centre
Emergence and development 1945–1965
Catherine R Schenk

32 Impediments to Trade in Services: Measurement and Policy Implication
Edited by Christopher Findlay and Tony Warren

33 The Japanese Industrial Economy
Late development and cultural causation
Ian Inkster

34 **China and the Long March to Global Trade**
The accession of China to the World Trade Organization
Edited by Alan S. Alexandroff, Sylvia Ostry and Rafael Gomez

35 **Capitalist Development and Economism in East Asia**
The rise of Hong Kong, Singapore, Taiwan, and South Korea
Kui-Wai Li

36 **Women and Work in Globalizing Asia**
Edited by Dong-Sook S. Gills and Nicola Piper

37 **Financial Markets and Policies in East Asia**
Gordon de Brouwer

38 **Developmentalism and Dependency in Southeast Asia**
The case of the automotive industry
Jason P. Abbott

39 **Law and Labour Market Regulation in East Asia**
Edited by Sean Cooney, Tim Lindsey, Richard Mitchell and Ying Zhu

40 **The Economy of the Philippines**
Elites, inequalities and economic restructuring
Peter Krinks

41 **China's Third Economic Transformation**
The rise of the private economy
Edited by Ross Garnaut and Ligang Song

42 **The Vietnamese Economy**
Awakening the dormant dragon
Edited by Binh Tran-Nam and Chi Do Pham

43 **Restructuring Korea Inc.**
Jang-Sup Shin & Ha-Joon Chang

44 **Development and Structural Change in the Asia-Pacific**
Globalising miracles or end of a model?
Edited by Martin Andersson and Christer Gunnarsson

45 **State Collaboration and Development Strategies in China**
The case of the China-Singapore Suzhou Industrial Park (1992–2002)
Alexius Pereira

46 **Capital and Knowledge in Asia**
Changing power relations
Edited by Heidi Dahles and Otto van den Muijzenberg

47 **Southeast Asian Paper Tigers?**
From miracle to debacle and beyond
Edited by Jomo K.S.

48 **Manufacturing Competitiveness in Asia**
How internationally competitive national firms and industries developed in East Asia
Edited by Jomo K.S.

49 **The Korean Economy at the Crossroads**
Edited by MoonJoong Tcha and Chung-Sok Suh

50 **Ethnic Business**
Chinese capitalism in Southeast Asia
Edited by Jomo K.S. and Brian C. Folk

51 **Exchange Rate Regimes in East Asia**
Edited by Gordon de Brouwer and Masahiro Kawai

52 **Financial Governance in East Asia**
Policy dialogue, surveillance and cooperation
Edited by Gordon de Brouwer and Yunjong Wang

53 **Designing Financial Systems in East Asia and Japan**
Edited by Joseph P. H. Fan, Masaharu Hanazaki and Juro Teranishi

54 **State Competence and Economic Growth in Japan**
Yoshiro Miwa

55 **Understanding Japanese Saving**
Does population aging matter?
Robert Dekle

56 **The Rise and Fall of the East Asian Growth System, 1951–2000**
International competitiveness and rapid economic growth
Xiaoming Huang

57 **Service Industries and Asia-Pacific Cities**
New development trajectories
Edited by P. W. Daniels, K. C. Ho and T. A. Hutton

58 **Unemployment in Asia**
Edited by John Benson and Ying Zhu

59 **Risk Management and Innovation in Japan, Britain and the USA**
Edited by Ruth Taplin

60 **Japan's Development Aid to China**
The long-running foreign policy of engagement
Tsukasa Takamine

61 **Chinese Capitalism and the Modernist Vision**
Satyananda J. Gabriel

62 **Japanese Telecommunications**
Edited by Ruth Taplin and Masako Wakui

63 **East Asia, Globalization and the New Economy**
F. Gerard Adams

64 **China as a World Factory**
Edited by Kevin Honglin Zhang

65 **China's State Owned Enterprise Reforms**
An industrial and CEO approach
Juan Antonio Fernandez and Leila Fernandez-Stembridge

66 **China and India**
A tale of two economies
Dilip K. Das

67 **Innovation and Business Partnering in Japan, Europe and the United States**
Edited by Ruth Taplin

68 **Asian Informal Workers**
Global risks local protection
Santosh Mehrotra and Mario Biggeri

69 **The Rise of the Corporate Economy in Southeast Asia**
Rajeswary Ampalavanar Brown

70 **The Singapore Economy**
An econometric perspective
Tilak Abeyshinge and Keen Meng Choy

71 **A Basket Currency for Asia**
Edited by Takatoshi Ito

72 **Private Enterprises and China's Economic Development**
Edited by Shuanglin Lin and Xiaodong Zhu

73 **The Korean Developmental State**
From dirigisme to neo-liberalism
Iain Pirie

74 **Accelerating Japan's Economic Growth**
Resolving Japan's growth controversy
Edited by F. Gerard Adams, Lawrence R. Klein, Yuzo Kumasaka and Akihiko Shinozaki

75 **China's Emergent Political Economy**
Capitalism in the dragon's lair
Edited by Christopher A. McNally

76 **The Political Economy of the SARS Epidemic**
The impact on human resources in East Asia
Grace O.M. Lee and Malcolm Warner

77 **India's Emerging Financial Market**
A flow of funds model
Tomoe Moore

78 **Outsourcing and Human Resource Management**
An international survey
Edited by Ruth Taplin

79 **Globalization, Labor Markets and Inequality in India**
Dipak Mazumdar and Sandip Sarkar

80 **Globalization and the Indian Economy**
Roadmap to a convertible rupee
Satyendra S. Nayak

81 **Economic Cooperation between Singapore and India**
An alliance in the making
Faizal Yahya

82 **The United States and the Malaysian Economy**
Shakila Yacob

The United States and the Malaysian Economy

Shakila Yacob

Routledge
Taylor & Francis Group
LONDON AND NEW YORK

First published 2008 by Routledge
2 Park Square, Milton Park, Abingdon, Oxon OX14 4RN

Simultaneously published in the USA and Canada
by Routledge
270 Madison Ave, New York, NY 10016

Routledge is an imprint of the Taylor & Francis Group, an informa business

Typeset in Times by
Keystroke, 28 High Street, Tettenhall, Wolverhampton
Printed and bound in Great Britain by
TJI Digital, Padstow, Cornwall

British Library Cataloguing in Publication Data
A catalogue record for this book is available from the British Library

Library of Congress Cataloging in Publication Data
Yacob, Shakila, 1962-
The United States and the Malaysian economy / Shakila Yacob.
p. cm.
Includes bibliographical references and index.
1. Malaysia—Foreign economic relations—United States—History.
2. United States—Foreign economic relations—Malaysia—History.
3. Investments, American—Malaysia. I. Title.
HF1594.6.Y33 2007
337.59507309'041—dc22
2007046652

ISBN 10: 0–415–43118–2 (hbk)
ISBN 10: 0–203–92721–4 (ebk)

ISBN 13: 978–0–415–43118–7 (hbk)
ISBN 13: 978–0–203–92721–2 (ebk)

Contents

List of Illustrations

Figures

Tables

Abbreviations

AIC	American International Company
ANM	Arkib Negara Malaysia
ATC	Ampang Tin Company
AVROS	Planters Association of the East Coast of Sumatra
BCL	Borneo Company Limited
BML	Borneo Motors Limited
BoE	Bank of England
BT	Board of Trade
CAB	Cabinet papers
CO	Colonial Office
C&C	Cycle & Carriage
EIC	East India Company
ESC	Eastern Smelting Company
FO	Foreign Office Files
FTZs	Free Trade Zones
GAJ	General Advisor Johore
GRC	General Rubber Company
HAPM	Hollandsch-Amerikaansche Plantage Maatschappij
HCO	High Commissioner's Office
HP	Horsepower
IA	Inchcape Archives
IPRC	International Plantation Rubber Company
IRRA	International Rubber Regulation Agreement
ITA	International Tin Agreement
ITC	International Tin Company
KLO	Kinta Land Office
KPS	Kumpulan Perangsang Selangor Berhad
KSF	Kedah Secretariat Files
MAP	Malayan–American Plantations Ltd
MCP	Malayan Communist Party
MSC	Multimedia Super Corridor
MRLA	Malayan Races Liberation Army
MSTL	Malay States Tin Ltd

NARA	US National Archives
NEP	New Economic Policy
NUSL	National University of Singapore Library
PRO	UK National Archives (Public Record Office)
PTCC	Pacific Tin Consolidated Corporation
RGA	Rubber Growers Association
RRI	Rubber Research Institute
RFC	Reconstruction Finance Corporation
RTEC	Rubber and Tin Exports Committee
SEDC	Selangor Economic Development Corporation
SSF	Selangor Secretariat Files
STC	Straits Trading Company
UGTC	Uniroyal Goodrich Tyre Company
UML	University of Malaya Library
USRPI	United States Rubber Plantations Incorporated
USRC	United States Rubber Company
YGC	Yukon Gold Company

Preface

This book is an extensive examination of the growth of US trade with, and foreign direct investment (FDI) in Malaya from 1870 to the country's independence in 1957. It identifies the competitive strategies of US multinational enterprises (MNEs), with a focus on case studies of three US companies operating in distinct sectors, and illustrates how their activities helped to shape economic development in Malaya. There is also due consideration given to the business transactions between foreign and local firms, with a particular focus on the role played by Chinese entrepreneurs.

Research in the area of FDI in Malaya has tended to be preoccupied by the impact of British-owned companies in the country. This work, with its focus on US MNEs in Malaya, therefore broadens the scope of international business history, US business history and Malayan historiography. It also serves as a platform for further research on comparisons between firms, industries and national economies, particularly in the three sectors examined. Placing emphasis on business–government relations, there is significant evaluation of the impact of colonial government policies on business development. Importantly, however, there is a shift away from the recent heavy critical analysis of the impact of the British government's (both metropolitan and colonial) policies on British firms, to the effect of those policies on the development of US firms. The discipline of business history is quite new to historians of South East Asia, in contrast, for example, to the United States, Europe and Japan, where there is extensive interest in the field. While this book will primarily be of interest to business historians studying the relationships between foreign businesses and local firms, it is hoped that this new and original research will encourage and enliven discussion of the rich and diverse business heritage in the region both by local and foreign scholars and will be of great significance to the wider US, European and Japanese audience where the history of business has long been celebrated.

Geographical Definitions

Prior to World War II, the term 'Malaya' in this study refers to the region comprising the territories of the Straits Settlements (Penang, Singapore and Malacca), Federated Malay States (Perak, Selangor, Negeri Sembilan and Pahang) and Unfederated Malay States (Perlis, Kedah, Kelantan, Terengganu and Johore). The term 'Malay Peninsula' (and briefly 'Peninsula') is used here to mean the Federated Malay States as well as the Unfederated Malay States. In a separate development, the territories of British North Borneo (abbreviated as North Borneo) and Sarawak became British colonies in 1946. In 1948, the Federation of Malaya (uniting Penang, Malacca, the Federated Malay States and Unfederated Malay States) was formed while Singapore remained a crown colony. In 1957, the Federation of Malaya gained independence from Britain.

Although North Borneo, Sarawak and Singapore were then distinct from the Federation of Malaya, for the purpose of clarity and consistency in understanding the development of US trade and FDI in colonial Malaya and post-colonial Malaysia, this study includes data from those areas because although these states were politically and administratively divided, economically they were unified. In 1963, the Federation of Malaysia was formed with the merger of the Federation of Malaya, Singapore (later expelled from the federation in 1965), Sabah (formerly North Borneo) and Sarawak.

Conventions

n.a.	not available (not published)
S$	Straits Settlements dollar
M$	Malayan dollar
US$	US dollar

Between 1906 and 1920, one Straits dollar was equivalent to Sterling 2s 4d (during the pre-decimal system). Hence, one pound sterling (or 240 pence) was equivalent to S$8.57. At this rate, one US dollar was equivalent to S$3.06 or one Straits dollar to US$0.33. This work refers to the above rates from 1906 to 1920.

Unless otherwise stated, all monetary figures are in nominal terms and most figures referred to in this work are in Straits dollars (from 1949 onwards Malayan dollars) or US dollars. US dollar amounts have been converted into Straits dollars at the contemporary average exchange rate for each year as shown in the table opposite.

The price of one US dollar US$ to one Straits dollar S$, 1906–1948 and one Malayan dollar M$, 1949–1957.

Year	*Rate*
1906–1920	S$3.06
1921	S$2.28
1922	S$1.97
1923	S$1.87
1924	S$1.95
1925–1928	S$1.78
1929–1930	S$1.79
1931	S$1.91
1932	S$2.48
1933	S$2.03
1934	S$1.69
1935	S$1.75
1936–1937	S$1.72
1938	S$1.76
1939	S$1.93
1940	S$2.13
1941	S$2.12
1942–1945	n.a.
1945–1948	S$2.13
1949	M$2.33
1950	M$3.05
1951	M$3.04
1952	M$3.07
1953	M$3.07
1954	M$3.06
1955–1957	M$3.07

Sources: Chiang Hai Ding, *A History of Straits Settlements Foreign Trade 1870–1915*, Singapore: National Museum Singapore, 1978, pp. 232–4; G.C. Allen and A.G. Donnithorne, *Western Enterprise in Indonesia and Malaya*, London: George Allen & Unwin, 1957, pp. 200–1; L.H. Officer, 'Exchange rate between the United States dollar and forty other countries, 1913–1999.' Economic History Services, EH.Net, 2002. www.eh.net/hmit/exchangerates/, accessed 3 February 2006.

Acknowledgements

My interest in business history began through email discussions with Geoffrey Jones while I was doing preliminary research on the history of US–Malaysian economic relations. I am deeply indebted to him for his continuous patience and guidance to someone who was very new to the field and trying desperately to grasp the various concepts of international business. His considerable knowledge of Malaysian history and his consistently perceptive and constructive comments has added considerably to the quality of this book. I appreciate the prompt replies and the good advice Mira Wilkins gave me when I consulted her on the available sources on US multinational enterprises in Malaysia. She said that I would have to do 'intense detective work' for these sources, and she was right! Records are available, but they are scattered through different libraries and archives in Malaysia, Singapore, the UK, US and Canada.

Thanks are due to the many people in these countries for their kind assistance in my research. I appreciate the valuable assistance of University Malaya's library personnel. The staff at the Arkib Negara Malaysia deserves special mention for their patience and understanding in providing materials and photo prints. This includes staff at the Rubber Research Institute and the Incorporated Society of Planters, Kuala Lumpur. Also, my thanks go to the staff at Ford Malaysia, especially Mike Pease (former managing director) and J. Barry Ashton (former business development manager) for sharing their insights and the resources available on both Ford Malaya and Ford Malaysia. I am also indebted to the staff at the National University of Singapore Library.

In the US, I had the kind assistance from staff at the following institutions: the Library of Congress, Washington DC; National Archives, College Park, Maryland; Hagley Museum and Library, Wilmington, Delaware; Historical Collections, Baker Library, Harvard Business School; and Lauinger Library, Georgetown University. I was very fortunate as the valuable assistance rendered to me by librarians from the US made it seem that there was no geographical distance between Malaysia and the US. A special thanks goes to Dennis Daily at the Rio Grande Historical Collections, New Mexico State University Library. In the UK, staff at the Public Records Office, Guildhall Library, and Bank of England, were very accommodating. In Canada, Sandra Notarianni, historical consultant, at Ford Canada, Oakville, Ontario, was particularly helpful.

I would like to thank my sponsor, the University of Malaya, for the financial support rendered throughout my research. I much appreciate the careful and thoughtful comments from colleagues and friends at the Department of History: Khoo Kay Kim, Ramlah Adam, Abdullah Zakaria, Adnan Haji Nawang and Sivachandralingam. To Siva, thank you for the generous loan of documents and books from your vast personal collection and also for your valuable insights on my work. I would like to thank Mrs Jagjit and Mary LeBlanc for lifting my spirits when I was down and showing me the way to persevere in my work. Thanks are also due to Peter Miskell and Lucy Newton for suggestions while reading the much earlier drafts of the work. To Teresa Lopes, Nicholas J. White and John Gullick for their comments while reading the various chapters of this book, I am grateful. My warmest thanks go to Greg Sibley who gave me constant encouragement and guidance throughout my research and writing of this book. Also, to Peter Sowden at Routledge for seeing the potential in my work.

My sincere thanks go to my aunt and cousins in High Wycombe and Reading, UK. To my friends in Washington DC and Virginia: Bridget Welsh, Pamela Sodhy and Mary Muller. Thank you for making my research stint there one of the most memorable periods of my life. The same goes to the family of Christine Fernandez in Scarborough, Toronto, Arva Rahemanji in Mechanicsburg, Pennsylvania, and Pon Jumat in Wilmington, Delaware. Also, I cannot forget all that Kak Timah and her family in Singapore did for me.

Finally, I reserve my deepest gratitude to both my families in Kuala Lumpur (Kamar, Ameer, Qistina, Quraisya, Qamaryna and Qasryna), and in Taiping (especially to my late mother, Shameen) for their prayers from a distance, unconditional love, support and endurance through the many months without me because of my endless travel and preoccupation with this book.

Shakila Yacob
University of Malaya
Kuala Lumpur, Malaysia
12 September 2007

1 Introduction

The United States, colonial rule and the Malayan economy

1.1 Issues

During its colonial rule of the country, Britain prized Malaya (now Malaysia) largely for its ready availability of natural resources, such as rubber and tin, but also for the country's regional location and cheap labour supply, which was then essential for these primary industries. An independent Malaysia, however, elected to diversify its economy, and has since gained global positions in the petrochemical, technology and manufacturing sectors. With the United States as its largest trading partner, in 2006 Malaysia ranked tenth in the US's own list of trading partners, making it the biggest in the South East Asian region, with bilateral trade totalling approximately US$44 billion. The US was ranked as Malaysia's largest foreign investor from 1997 to 2002 and, despite falling to third position in 2003, the US government's Bureau of Economic Analysis notes that foreign direct investment (FDI) increased by 42 per cent from US$7.1 billion in 2003 to US$10 billion in 2005.[1] This was despite a drop overall in inward FDI into Malaysia for the year.[2] In 2006, the US, along with the Netherlands, was Malaysia's second largest investor with investments worth US$2.21 billion, slightly lower than Japan.[3]

This work seeks to explore and chart the historical development of economic ties between Malaya and the US between 1870 and 1957. The tracing of economic ties prior to Malaysian independence in 1957 allows for in-depth investigation into what extent the role of the British colonial administration restricted or stimulated US–Malayan trade and FDI. Also intriguing is the close examination of the role of British businesses and to what extent they were complementing or competing with the US–Malayan trade and FDI in the country, and the role of local entrepreneurs in the promotion of US business interests. Together with the detailed analysis of three US inward investors – Yukon Gold Company, United States Rubber Company and Ford Motor Company – this work gives an assessment of the impact of US trade and investment on Malaya. In addition, there is careful evaluation of whether or not the relatively small amount of FDI in Malaya had a significant impact on the local economy. As it is crucial to an understanding of the economic situation in Malaya, due weight is also given to the strategic factors and the role of nationality in determining colonial trade and investment policies. An epilogue provides an account of the evolution of the economic relationship of the US with present-day Malaysia. The conversion from a colonial economy to a fully independent one in Malaysia highlights an intriguing contrast between the high level of US trade but the low level of FDI before independence, as opposed to both high-level trade and FDI after independence.

A brief survey of the historiography of US–Malaysia economic ties quickly reveals that while there is a preponderance of literature on the relationship between the colonial administrations with British businesses, little has been written on the relationship between the colonial administration (both in London and in Malaya) and foreign businesses. The literature is also sparse on US economic involvement in Malaya and this work is significant in that it is one of very few dedicated to identifying the scale and scope of US–Malaya economic relations within the context of British imperial rule. Despite the relative dearth of research in this field, a few notable works on the US–Malaysia relationship have contributed significantly towards giving this study a more comprehensive grounding. P. Sodhy's *The US–Malaysia Nexus: Themes in Superpower-Small State Relations* (1991) is useful in drawing attention to the political relationship between the US and Malaya, although it scarcely discusses the economic relationship between the two countries. In addition, there is no mention of how this political relationship impacted upon the growth of US trade and FDI in Malaya. An early work in this area, though arguably lacking in scholarly, empirical evidence regarding economic impact, is J.W. Gould's *The United States and Malaysia* (1969), which captures the socio-economic and political dimensions of the US–Malaya relationship in the 1960s.

M. Wilkins' highly respected work (1970, 1974) examine the evolution of US multinational enterprises (MNEs) overseas and the responses of the US and foreign governments to the development of these businesses over a significant period of time.[4] In contrast, this work focuses on a survey of US trade and FDI and detailed case studies of three US MNEs in colonial Malaya. Although this study concurs with Wilkins' suggestion that there existed both rivalry and cooperation between US and British business in the 1920s, it also argues that US businesses were more dependent on their British counterparts in Malaya. In addition, Wilkins' research on the experiences of foreign investors in the US and how the range of public policies affected foreign investments is particularly relevant on the subject of US policies toward foreign MNEs during the interwar years, as it provides a comparative perspective of how US protectionism and policies against foreign MNEs (especially British) contrasted with the liberal and open policies of the British colonial administration in Malaya.[5] However, this work goes further than presently available secondary sources such as Wilkins' (at least in level of detail), in its exploration of the nature and extent of the relationship between British and US businesses with local Chinese entrepreneurs.

This study also provides insight on US economic involvement in Malaya through its three case studies of US MNEs in three distinct areas of the Malayan economy: tin, through the study of Yukon Gold Company (YGC, later known as Pacific Tin Consolidated Corporation (PacTin)); rubber, with the focus on the

United States Rubber Company (USRC); and automobiles, through the analysis of the Ford Motor Company of Malaya (Ford Malaya). The discussion of the activities of the PacTin in the Malayan tin industry draws extensively upon Yip Yat Hoong's *The Development of the Tin Mining Industry of Malaya* (1969) and Wong Lin Ken's *The Malayan Tin Industry to 1914* (1965). The development of the rubber industry and its intricacies are sourced from numerous valuable works including J. H. Drabble's two volumes, *Rubber in Malaya 1876–1922: The Genesis of the Industry* (1973) and *Malayan Rubber: The Interwar Years* (1991), as well as P.T. Bauer's *The Rubber Industry: A Study in Competition and Monopoly* (1948) and Voon Phin Keong's *Western Rubber Planting Enterprise in South East Asia, 1876–1921* (1976). In addition G. D. Babcock's *History of the United States Rubber Company* (1966) enriches the discussion through its detailed account of the United States Rubber Company.

While most literature on the Malayan economy has typically focused on the strategic commodities of tin and rubber, this work adds a new dimension by also analysing the automobile sector. The research on Ford Malaya draws upon M. Wilkins and F. Hill's publication, *American Business Abroad: Ford on Six Continents* (1964), which provides an excellent backdrop to Ford's business developments and activities worldwide. C. Fyfe's *Wheels in Malaya: The Wearne Brothers and Their Company* (2002) also offers valuable insights into the development of the Malayan automobile sector while factoring in the role of British merchant firms in the Malayan economy.

Additional analysis focuses on the attitudes and policies of the British government in terms of three key concepts: monopoly, foreign ownership and colonial responsibility. What motivated the British administrators to embrace or oppose certain US investments in Malaya and to what extent were strategic factors the main consideration on the colonial administration policy governing economic relations with the US MNEs are two important questions which are addressed. Seeking answers to these questions also provide the basis for determining and understanding the core relationship between British governments and US businesses in Malaya. The interplay of roles and vested interests of the metropolitan authorities (the London-based government) and local colonial authorities with foreign firms is examined, as is the differing approaches of US and British governments towards business to determine whether the level of reciprocity was a factor in the forming of the colonial administration's policy towards US trade and FDI in Malaya.

Throughout this work a central argument is that the British presence, both government and business, helped facilitate US trade and FDI in Malaya, and that, despite remaining low, US FDI had a positive qualitative impact on the Malayan economy.

1.2 Concepts

Fundamental to this work, and to any discussion on FDI, is a clear understanding of the nature of MNEs. In an effort to define FDI and categorise MNEs, this work has drawn from the existing theories of the multinational and paradigms of international business. Particularly helpful in this respect have been J. H. Dunning's OLI paradigm and transaction costs theory and A. D. Chandler's historical model of the growth of managerial capitalism. Also important, although much less within the remit of this work, are theories of the entrepreneur.

An MNE can be defined as a firm which wholly controls operations or income-generating assets in two or more countries. Such cross-border investments can occur in the service, manufacturing or resource sectors and can either serve the market directly (market-oriented) or exploit sources of supply (supply-oriented). Investments by MNEs are known as foreign direct investment, or FDI, one of the modes available for serving foreign markets. The alternatives include exporting, licensing, franchising, cartels and alliances. FDI involves a cross-border investment with substantial managerial involvement and is conceptually different from portfolio investment, which is capital flow without managerial control. FDI may assume the form of a wholly owned venture, a joint venture or even a minority equity stake if there is management control.[6]

The OLI paradigm, developed by Dunning, provides a valuable framework for understanding the growth of multinational firms. Dunning called this the Eclectic Paradigm, and it combines the three common approaches of ownership advantages (O) or firm specific advantages, locational advantages (L) and internalisation advantages (I) to analyse why, where and how firms are motivated to undertake FDI.[7]

As first pointed out by S. Hymer, a firm needs some unique advantage to offset the costs of competing overseas. A firm's ownership advantages may include branding and product differentiation strategies, superior technology, management and marketing skills, access to finance, size of firm and access to raw markets and economies of scale. Hence, a firm chooses to set up a plant in a foreign country because it possesses some firm specific advantages over local companies in the host country.[8] Locational advantages include market size, natural resources, labour productivity, physical infrastructure, transport costs and trade barriers.[9] Hymer, as well as C. Kindleberger and R.E. Caves, suggests that government policies create market imperfections or asymmetries, something which can be seen in the three case studies discussed in this work.[10] Tariff jumping in order to overcome trade barriers, for example, is an important determinant for manufacturing FDI, and highly relevant for examining the rationale and the motivations of FDI for the case study of Ford Malaya. Tax policies, such as the tin-ore export tax, and restriction schemes (export quotas) imposed by the British authorities on the Malayan tin and rubber industries are considered through the examination of their impact on two US MNEs in resource-seeking industries.

Internalisation theory, which originates from R.H. Coase, emphasises assessing the favourability of transaction costs within the subsidiary and the industry over arm's length transactions.[11] In addition, this view examines the actual capability and feasibility of subsidiary production and marketing. O. E. Williamson emphasises that transaction costs arise from bounded rationality, opportunism and asset specificity.[12] Transaction costs theory has been applied to the realm of international business with great effect by P. Buckley and M. Casson and later by Jean-Francois Hennart.[13] Both Casson and Hennart, as well as other transaction costs theorists, stress the importance of internalisation rather than ownership and locational advantages in explaining multinational activities. However, internalisation theory has been criticised by Demsetz as a theory of market failure rather than a theory of firm success.[14] The 'I' factor helps explain the mode of entry of US MNEs and how these multinationals expand their operations in the Malayan market. While YGC and USRC began as a wholly owned subsidiary of the US parent firm, Ford Malaya initially preferred export as a mode of entry and later set up a wholly owned subsidiary.

Dunning proposes that a firm must have 'O' advantages in its home market that can be transferred abroad and at the same time the firm must be attracted by the 'L' characteristics of the foreign market. However, he also asserts that the 'O' and 'L' factors alone could warrant less intensive forms of entry such as exporting or licensing. FDI decisions should, therefore, be hinged on additional 'I' advantages that result in feasible transaction costs, operations and marketing in the proposed subsidiary. Dunning makes a systematic distinction between country (home and host), industry and firms' determinants of the OLI characteristics.[15] The Eclectic Paradigm provides a useful framework here for understanding the reasons for US FDI in Malaya. Nonetheless, discussions on the impact of non-economic variables such as the political, legal and cultural environment on the different industries (rubber, tin, automobile) in this work help facilitate a more comprehensive understanding of such FDI.

Chandler provides further insights into the growth of large US firms and argues that big business, managed by professional managers and emerging in late nineteenth century America, enabled these firms to gain competitive and first mover advantage in capital intensive industries where they could exploit economies of scale and scope.[16] Indeed, he attributes the success of US firms in this era to their first mover investment, their 'managerial capitalism' as well as their diverse, international product and service portfolios and their strides towards integration that resulted in higher economies of scale. In *Scale and Scope*, Chandler identifies managerial capitalism as consisting of planned organisational hierarchies and priority to a salaried, professional managerial class, and differing from the traditional personal capitalism where 'owners managed and managers owned'.[17] British enterprises at the time, Chandler suggests, were reluctant to think beyond short-term profitability, to employ professionals or to consolidate managerial structures, thus heralding the decline of traditional British industry.[18]

Business historians M. Wilkins and G. Jones, through their research on multinationals, have qualified Chandler's model, arguing that non-hierarchical and family-managed firms, such as business groups and 'free-standing companies', were also capable of building and sustaining competitive advantage in international markets. The term, 'free-standing company' or 'FSC', was coined by Wilkins to refer to a company incorporated with a small headquarters and without any prior business in the home country, but instead handles business activities exclusively in the host country.[19] Wilkins suggests that these transient FSCs were a typical form of foreign investment mainly found in Britain due to the powerful role of the City of London and its stock exchange in the capital market prior to World War 1.[20] Further research into FSCs by other business historians illustrates that such companies existed elsewhere around the world, in Europe and even in the US, particularly in rich capital markets, and were funded by shares sold to the public. In addition, these companies were sustainable over a longer period than originally assumed by Wilkins.[21] Jones, and to some extent Wilkins, has shown that non-hierarchical and family firms could be very effective in international business.[22] In his various works on British trading firms and merchants houses that formed business groups, bringing together several FSCs, Jones successfully illustrates that a number of family-owned and personally managed firms enjoyed entrepreneurial success in many parts of Asia, Latin America and Africa.[23] It may no longer be legitimate, then, to suggest a discernible difference in strategy between 'personal' and 'managerial' firms.[24] Certainly in this work YGC and Ford Malaya as family firms are shown to be able to sustain their business activities over a long period of time. Chandler's original thesis asserting managerial capitalism's superiority over family firms or personal capitalism empirically may no longer be applicable to the different models or paradigms of international businesses.[25]

The Chandlerian concepts of first mover advantages, economies of scale and scope, and managerial hierarchies are of particular relevance in analysing the competitive advantages of US firms in Malaya. By discussing the manufacturing and resource industries of tin and rubber in the developing economy of Malaya, this work opens up fresh considerations of Chandler's generalisations concerning the growth of large firms under different and changing cultural and socio-political conditions. Research here examines to what extent managerial capitalism was evident in the USRC, and whether the adoption of managerial capitalism provided the company with an added advantage over local competitors and this is in contrast to YGC and Ford Malaya, which remained family firms. Unlike the many British FSCs that came exclusively to carry out business activities, predominantly in the resource and service sectors, in colonial Malaya the three US firms discussed here had a vast domestic and international business empire with a network of subsidiaries worldwide.

A further area of theoretical discussion drawn from is that relating to entrepreneurship, as this work seeks to identify any, the pivotal roles played by entrepreneurs and the resultant effect on the firm and its international operations. There are a number of models of entrepreneurship with Knight, Kirzner, Schumpeter and Casson all providing useful definitions for this work.[26] These four schools of thought, while distinct, all emphasise the importance of entrepreneurship in MNEs. Knight views entrepreneurs as decision makers in times of uncertainty who reap economic rewards in return for their risk-taking. Striking a slightly different chord, Kirzner identifies an entrepreneur as being an 'opportunist', a person 'alert' to 'latent possibilities' and as being distinct from someone who has ownership.[27] Schumpeter similarly refers to the entrepreneur as an 'innovator', 'creator' of new markets and 'destroyer' of old through 'successful innovation'.[28] However, Schumpeter's and Kirzner's views differ with regard to the entrepreneur's motivation; the former being of the view that they are psychological and stem from ingenuity while the latter cites economic benefits. Finally, Casson adds a fourth dimension, referring to the entrepreneur as a manager of scarce resources in a dynamic world.[29] While Schumpeter and Kirzner stress that entrepreneurs are the driving force of change, Knight and Casson view them more as leaders who react to the changes around them. It is clear that decision-making, innovation, and the ability to seize opportunities and effectively manage resources are all important facets of entrepreneurism which in turn is essential to the growth and success of an MNE.

1.3 Colonial rule and the Malayan economy

It has now become widely accepted that imperialism facilitated the growth of international business in the nineteenth century through its internationalist outlook.[30] The introduction of international property law, closely associated with the spread of colonial rule, created a favourable legal environment for the growth of international business in many parts of Asia and Africa. Malaya came under British colonial rule in the late 1800s, and it is important to establish the nature of the colonial administration in order to understand the context in which US businesses operated. This facilitates an understanding of the power structures and policies that regulated US trade and investment and helps explain how these structures and policies restricted or promoted US FDI. Malaya was effectively ruled by two layers of imperial government – one metropolitan and the other local.

The Colonial Office was the main department of the central imperial government in Britain and had supreme authority to exercise full authority over foreign affairs in the colonial empire. Often known as the colonial secretary, the secretary of state for the colonies was head of the Colonial Office. In turn, he was supported by the permanent civil service headed by the parliamentary under-secretary. However, given that there were frequent changes to political appointments, the colonial secretary rarely had detailed knowledge of Malayan affairs.[31]

There were also trade and commercial associations in the metropole that played a role in influencing Malayan economic decision-making. In 1910, the Malayan Information Agency was formed, mainly to provide information on business opportunities and to handle issues pertaining to trade and investments between Britain and Malaya.[32] The Association of British Malaya was set up in 1920 while its predecessor, the Straits Settlements Association, had been formed in London in 1868. These associations were primarily concerned with safeguarding the interests of the Straits Settlements and the Malay States.[33] The Rubber Growers' Association, formed in 1907, wielded considerable power in the rubber industry, with members from Malaya, Sri Lanka, Indonesia, Burma, Nigeria and Ghana, controlling 1.75 million acres of plantation by the 1950s.[34] For Malayan-based mining interests, the Federated Malay States Chamber of Mines represented London-registered and Malayan mining firms.[35]

The British colonial administration took different forms during its presence in Malaya, starting with direct rule in the Straits Settlements. The Straits Settlements were formed in 1826[36] – a process which began with the British occupation of Penang (1786), Singapore (1819) and Malacca (1824).[37] In 1874, with agreement reached via the Pangkor Engagement between the governor of the Straits Settlements and the local sultan, British administration with 'indirect rule' was established in Perak. The same form of administration was established in three other Malay States – Selangor, Negeri Sembilan and Pahang – where a British resident was appointed to 'advise' the sultan on all matters except customs and religion.[38] In reality, the residential system, as detailed by J.M. Gullick, was a government in the name of the sultan of the state, whereby power was firmly held by the British.[39] By July 1896, the British had reinforced their position in Malaya with the formation of the Federated Malay States: Perak, Selangor, Negeri Sembilan and Pahang. Hence, the four residents were accountable to the resident general (a post created in 1895) based in Kuala Lumpur. The resident general in turn was responsible to the governor of the Straits Settlements.[40] With the formation of this Federation, the governor of the Straits Settlements also assumed the position of high commissioner for the Federated Malay States with the intention of unifying the two systems of administration. This high commissioner-cum-governor was the highest official in Malaya, responsible only to the Colonial Office in London.

British authority was extended over the north of the country in stages. So-called British advisors were appointed to the northern Malay states at different times – Kelantan in 1903, Kedah and Perlis in 1905. These states, along with Johore, which had signed a protection treaty with the British in 1885, became known as the Unfederated Malay States. On 11 March 1909, a treaty was signed between Britain and Thailand whereby the states of Perlis, Kedah, Kelantan and Terengganu were formally transferred to British control.[41] Not until 1910 was a British advisor appointed in Johore. A year before, in 1909, to further reinforce the administration of the Federation, a Federal Council was formed, which remained in place until 1941.

Following the Japanese occupation from February 1942 to August 1945, a Malayan Union was established, but this lasted just two years from 1946 to 1948.[42] It crumbled in the face of widespread protests by the Malays against the proposal for a liberalisation of citizenship for non-Malays and the loss of the Malay rulers' sovereignty.

In a separate development, British North Borneo (usually then referred to as North Borneo and now Sabah) and Sarawak became British colonies in 1946. North Borneo had been administered by the British North Borneo Company from 1881 to 1941 and Sarawak by a succession of members of the Brookes family, known as the 'White Rajahs', from 1841 to 1941. After World War II, a new position, governor general for South East Asia, was held by Malcolm MacDonald to oversee the administration of the Malayan Union, Singapore, Brunei, North Borneo and Sarawak. He continued his responsibilities despite being appointed to the new post of commissioner general for the United Kingdom in South East Asia based in Singapore in May 1948.[43]

The Federation of Malaya of 1948 replaced the controversial Malayan Union. The nine Malay States, as well as Penang and Malacca, continued under a central government while Singapore remained a crown colony.[44] This new federation was headed by a British high commissioner based in Kuala Lumpur who possessed wide legislative and administrative powers.[45] Modern Malayan politics, born against a backdrop of war and insurgency, saw the creation of a system of government that combined 'autocratic rule with the new democratic processes in a typically Malayan way'.[46] A state of emergency was declared on 18 June 1948 throughout the country after an insurgency led by the Malayan Communist Party, and about which Ramakrishna's (2001) and Stockwell's (1993) works are notable. The insurgency was seen as part of a Communist international agenda to spread communism in the region, and in the initial years the British government responded in a conventional manner by isolating the guerrilla forces from the general Malayan population. This costly and counterproductive strategy failed to emphasise the need to win the 'hearts and minds' of the general population, in particular the ethnic Chinese. A more successful strategy was that of assuring independence and to gradually allow the local multiracial administrative elites to participate in the political system.[47] As such, between 1948 and 1957, the British authorities took several steps to pave the way to independence, allowing for municipal elections in Penang (December 1951) and Kuala Lumpur (February 1952). In the federal elections of 1955, the Alliance Party, by then the leading nationalist movement, won the elections and shared power with British officials from the years 1955 until 1957. With the support of the British government, the independent Federation of Malaya was proclaimed on 31 August 1957.

An important dimension in the discussion of economic relations between the US and colonial Malaya is the examination of the policies of the metropolitan and local British administrators in their running of the Malayan economy. British policies were far from homogenous. There were conflicting interests and viewpoints between London and the colonial administrators on the ground. Tarling best sums up the relationship between the metropolitan and the local authorities as 'always one of by-play, if not tension'.[48] Prior to 1874, the Colonial Office adopted a policy of 'non-intervention' with regard to political and economic matters in the Straits Settlements and Malay States. This was grounded, to a degree, in the perceived lack of strategic importance of Malaya and was at odds with the local administrators' viewpoint,[49] as discussed by Mills and Ghazali.[50]

From 1874 to 1896, the handling of state affairs was in the hands of the residents, who enjoyed the highest executive authority in the states.[51] Major differences could be seen in the legislation and regulations of the four Malay States as these residents wielded wide influence in the investment policies of each state.

Early in the colonisation process, the British formed legal and administrative frameworks to create a favourable environment for the growth of international business. As proponents of laissez faire economic development, they placed emphasis on the establishment of institutions and creation of an environment that reduced the risks to FDI. This can be seen in Frank Swettenham's Perak Report of 1894: 'The Government cannot do the mining and the agriculture, but it can make it profitable for others to embark in such speculations by giving them every reasonable facility, and that we have tried to do.'[52] Drake argues that, 'the elevation of the government to the role of a leading agent of development seems to have been the result of an accidental interplay of attitudes, events, and personalities rather than a conscious policy imposed at the very beginning'. Despite the economic boom, Drake continues, 'officialdom still gave priority to state-building'.[53]

Although there was clear demarcation of power in theory with the formation of the Federation in 1896, the decision-making process was ambiguous in practice. Hence, it is difficult to determine the application of power vested in the hands of such officials as high commissioner and resident general, as there were times when decisions made by the high commissioner were overturned by the resident general and vice versa. The differences were accentuated by geopolitical divisions, with the high commissioner located in Singapore and the resident general located in the Federated Malay States in Kuala Lumpur. Clashes in personality often resulted in one of the two dominating. In addition, the residents often took crucial matters in their states into their own hands. S. Sundara Raja (2004), in his recent study of the relationships between British administrators and investors in the Federated Malay States, illustrates through various case studies how the balance of power between the Colonial Office and local administrators, and between the resident general in Kuala Lumpur and the high commissioner in Singapore was effectively determined by the personalities involved. He argues further that conflicts between British officials as well as between these officials and investors hindered investment flows into the Federated Malay States.[54]

The dependence of Whitehall upon British administrators in Malaya continued after the 1896 formation of the Federation. The Colonial Office continued to rely upon the information and suggestions from the high commissioner with regard to local affairs. This information was supplemented by occasional correspondence with the resident general. With the power of information in his hands, the high commissioner was able to influence the decisions made in London for, as Thio notes, although the Colonial Office 'laid down the broad lines of policy, it was not in full control of the process of expansion or consolidation, which depended partly on local developments and partly on the man on the spot'.[55] Again, the prevailing power broker was the man with the stronger personality.

In the late nineteenth century, 'the revenues of the expanding colonial state depended primarily on the exploitation of the Chinese mining and plantation proletariat'.[56] This situation was reversed when British capital in the early twentieth century was invested in rubber and the introduction of dredging technology. This revenue dependency extended to include US businesses and the massive surplus trade between Malaya and the US.[57] The Colonial Office did become more interventionist during the years of the World War I, especially on 'final decisions in questions with broad implications'. This is illustrated in the imposition of destination controls on tin and rubber by means of the London-based Rubber and Tin Exports Committee, to prevent strategic raw materials from reaching Germany and its allies.

The Colonial Office's laissez-faire policy also meant that there was minimal government assistance for business, including British business in Malaya. Drabble, in his study of the rubber industry, for instance, reiterates that the members of the metropolitan government, 'regarded the rubber industry as a whole as a prime asset in the imperial balance sheet, and were not inclined to intervene solely in the sectional interests of British companies'.[58] White reaches a similar conclusion in his analysis of government–business relationships during the decolonisation era, in which the broader agenda of the British government's economic interests, as dictated by London, took precedence over British firms' interests, and that business–government collusion on policy was not to be found.[59]

After World War II there was a gradual but perceptible shift from the pre-war 'hands off' policy towards a more interventionist approach which continued during the decolonisation era and was particularly apparent in the tin and rubber industries due to their importance in maintaining the dollar exchange.[60] White notes that there were also tensions between the colonial state and metropolitan interests over the question of 'whether to boost Malaya's hard currency contributions to the Sterling Area or to promote national economic development'.[61]

The monopolist tendencies of US MNEs had led the British colonial authorities, as well as local British businesses, to be suspicious of US business intentions since the beginning of the twentieth century. Fearing the loss of competition and control – mainly of strategic resources – this apprehension can be seen in the occasional restrictive policies towards US FDI in Malaya with attempts made to block large US firms from gaining control of strategic commodities. This was particularly transparent during World War I, when a number of US firms connected with the rubber industries sought to invest in Malaya. However, there is also evidence suggesting that, at least in certain cases, the British colonial authorities accommodated the interests of large US companies even if it meant the collapse of British firms and independent local entrepreneurs. For example, certain studies, such as those of P. Clegg and T. Shaw (2002), M. Moberg (1996) and others, have shown how British colonial authorities aided the Boston-based United Fruit Company at the turn of the twentieth century, which eventually came to control the banana industry in the Caribbean and Central America.[62]

1.4 Methodology

The growth of US MNE activities in Malaya can be traced to some extent in FDI data. However, there are limitations to this measure. As pointed out by Wilkins, Jones and others, there are conceptual problems when FDI is interchangeably used with multinational investment as 'figures on the size of, the level of, inward direct investment give only part of the story' as the more vital role of an MNE, lies in its ability to transfer organisational and technological capabilities across borders (an important focus in this work).[63] In addition, the definition of 'control' remains problematic and it is often difficult to distinguish between direct and portfolio investment: 'Measures of the flow of FDI may not include the reinvestment of earnings – a key means by which MNEs finance themselves – while measures of stock are quite often based on the historical value of an investment and are not updated at market prices'.[64]

Most of the US FDI data on Malaya and South East Asia for this work is drawn from the US Department of Commerce, with additional data from a wide range of sources including the US Treasury Department and US Tariff Commission, as well as the widely cited works by Helmut G. Callis on FDI in the region and Cleona Lewis on US FDI abroad. The US Department of Commerce defines direct investments as 'all American investments in those foreign corporations or enterprises which are controlled by a person or small group of persons (corporate or natural) domiciled in the United States, or in the management of which such person or group has an important voice. Equity and other security investments in foreign-controlled corporations and in the issues of foreign governments are classed as "portfolio" investments.' However, Callis in his study of foreign capital in South East Asia apart from using the terms 'portfolio' and 'direct' for the two different kinds of investments, introduced two new terms, 'rentier' and 'entrepreneur'. Rentier investments refer to investments made by investors while entrepreneur investments refer to those made by businessmen. Callis, however, does admit that his concept of entrepreneur investment 'is too easy a generalization'. He further notes that entrepreneur investment means 'foreign control of some sort and in some measure', where the foreign participants play an active role unlike the passive role of the rentier.[65] As Wilkins notes, estimates for US FDI the 1930s and 1940s are poor because of exchange rate problems, lack of uniformity in accounting on foreign properties, and other statistical inconsistencies.[66] These statistical differences can be seen in the different valuations of US inward FDI flows into South East Asia given by different US agencies at that time; in the case of the Philippines, for example, the US Department of Commerce, US Tariff Commission and Bureau of Insular Affairs gave different assessments on the size and level of FDI from the US.[67] Such factors were taken into consideration in this study in an attempt to provide as accurate as possible estimates of US FDI in Malaya and South East Asia in the period covered.

Trade figures relating to the Straits Settlements and also the Malay Peninsula are less robust than they may at first seem. Since all major ports were located in the Straits Settlements, these figures cannot be taken to represent the Malayan market as a whole, primarily because Singapore acted as a transhipping port catering not only for Malaya but also for Borneo, the Dutch East Indies, Thailand, Ceylon and Burma (although, some sources exclude re-export figures from Singapore's data). Even documents and figures from Ford Malaya, from the company's inception in 1926 until 1957, refer to these areas as a single market unit. Malayan trade figures, therefore, can be misleading in determining the levels of US trade in Malaya.

Another area of concern is that of imports that came from different source areas. From mid-1948 until the early 1950s, most US manufactured goods entered the Federation of Malaya via Hong Kong due to the imposition of exchange controls. It is unknown if these imports were officially recorded as Hong Kong imports or US imports. If these imports were recorded as Hong Kong imports, clearly US quantitative impact on the Malayan economy is larger than the official figures suggest. For example, in 1950, US imports via Hong Kong totalled approximately M$44 million (Malaysian dollars), while from January to June 1951 they amounted to M$37.9 million.[68] In the case of automobiles, it remains an issue whether imports from Ford England and General Motors UK were considered as imports from the UK or imports from the US.[69] A further example relating to the problems of confronting different source areas for automobiles are the imports from the GM assembly plant in Batavia (now Jakarta). These were considered imports from the US in British sources, whilst in US sources they were listed as imports from the Dutch East Indies.[70]

In the Malayan context, the British authorities, both at the metropolitan and at local levels, regarded Canada as a corridor for the US automobile manufacturers to evade duties imposed in the Empire market whereas the Canadians considered these factories as home manufacturers.[71] Although these trade figures may not reflect the true nature of Malayan automobile imports, the basic trends of automobile imports into Malaya are not obscured. This work is careful to take these issues into account when trying to determine accurate figures of US imports into Malaya and, in the case of the automobile sector, a distinction is made between the nationality of parent firm and nationality of production for figures relating to the US automobile imports.[72]

Conceptually, trade and FDI are wholly different, both in their determinants and in their consequences. Nevertheless, in practice, they are often linked. The relationship may be linear, with trade the first stage in a process of economic interaction, leading through a series of stages to a direct investment, or it may be complementary, with multinational firms active in the exporting and importing of goods and services. Of the three US MNEs selected for case studies, those from the tin and rubber industries were selected because of their importance not only to the Malayan economy but also to Britain and the US. Resource-seeking FDI is represented by YGC in the tin industry and USRC in the rubber industry, while the case of Ford Malaya is detailed as an example of market-seeking FDI. A number of issues are examined during the case studies, including what the formula was for their successful entry and whether there were ownership advantages over other foreign firms and, if so, how were these advantages used to enhance the company position in Malaya. By analysing the development of three MNEs in two different fields, it is possible to evaluate the diversity of expansion and to faithfully ascertain the existence of prevalent features of organisation.

The scope and limitation of this work is delineated by the dearth of sources on early Chinese businesses. It is not an exaggeration to state that the role of the pioneering Chinese businesses in British Malaya have been largely ignored, or at best only given parenthetical considerations, by Western academics writing on the subject of commerce during the nineteenth and twentieth century. Therefore, most of the data and information is gleaned from disparate sources such as contemporary newspapers, advertisements and sometimes archived materials. In addition, R.A. Brown's *Capital and Entrepreneurship in South-East Asia* (1994) proved to be an invaluable guide to conceptualising the comparison between

Western and Chinese entrepreneurship in the rubber and tin industry.[73] This work is able to reconstruct from the meagre available sources a clear picture of early Chinese businesses and their crucial role in mediating Western trade and business interests, and pays particular attention to their impact on the US presence in Malaya.

The span of this work, 1870–1957, covers a time of both significant US industrial expansion and dramatic growth in international business in Singapore and the wider region, and to the end of British colonial involvement in Malaya. Chapters 2 and 3 trace the evolution of British–US business relations in Malaya, focusing particularly on Singapore's prominence as a hub and the roles played by consuls and merchant firms. In addition there is an overview of trade and FDI in Malaya and the region. While Chapter 2 focuses on the period up to and including World War I, Chapter 3 divides into three distinct time periods: the interwar years, World War II, and post-World War II to independence. It examines the causes of the changing patterns in trade and, most importantly, explores the policies of both British colonial government and British businesses towards US trade and FDI in Malaya.

From the groundwork laid in Chapters 2 and 3, the next three chapters each provide a specific case study that examines in depth US FDI in Malaya. Each case shows when, how and why these firms invested in Malaya and their impact on the Malayan economy. Chapter 4 considers the growth and role of YGC, the one and only US entrant in the tin industry between World War I and independence. US investment in the tin industry and details the expansion of US FDI in Malaya from the early nineteenth century to Malaysian independence are also discussed. Chapter 5 considers US FDI in the rubber industry with a focus on a US-owned MNE, USRC, one of the major investors in rubber in Malaya, from its initial investments during the period covered. The focus of Chapter 6 is on US FDI in manufacturing through a case study on Ford Malaya, analysing Ford's strategies and performance within the Malayan automobile sector. To close, Chapter 7 draws together issues from the case studies and draws conclusions with regard to the relevance of this work within the literature on international business. An epilogue summarises the development of US trade and FDI in post-colonial Malaysia and details the evolution of the three specific case studies to the present.

2 US and Malaya connections, 1870–1918

This chapter traces the development of US trade and FDI in Malaya from 1870 to 1918, a period when trade and investment flows from the US became significant for the British colony. To put these developments in context however, it is necessary to give a brief outline of the historical antecedents, from when traders from North America first sought and found trading opportunities in South East Asia. The following section traces the development of trade until the late nineteenth century and is followed by an overview of US trade in Malaya between 1870 and 1918. Subsequently, there is an examination of the factors behind the rise of US trade in the years in the first decades of the twentieth century, in addition to a discussion of the issues concerning US FDI in Malaya, also up to the close of World War I.

Probably the first significant intent of the British Empire in the region was when Singapore came under British rule in 1819. Its free port status, established a legal framework, excellent harbour site and strategic geographical location at the southernmost tip of the Straits of Malacca, linking the east–west trade routes, drew international traders using it as a base to engage in both regional and international trade. Singapore became the centre for information on trade and investment opportunities for Straits produce, plantation developments, and mining and petroleum concessions in the Malayan Peninsula and throughout the region. International merchants, mainly though not exclusively British, quickly established offices in the trading outpost. Malay, Indian and many Chinese traders also settled and became intermediaries between the foreign merchant firms and local producers. By the 1870s, Singapore was showing spectacular growth.

During the mid-nineteenth century, US firms began to establish trade connections in Malaya with the help of the US Consul in Singapore. It became the centre of US trade and FDI in Malaya and provided a stepping-stone for investments into the British-controlled Malayan Peninsula, which by the early twentieth century included the Straits Settlements, Federated Malay States and Unfederated Malay States. In the years before the outbreak of World War I, US firms began to expand more aggressively abroad, seeking opportunities to acquire new sources of raw materials. US economic interests in Malaya began to centre on tin and rubber – which were the two vital commodities needed to supply US industries, particularly the automobile industry.

2.1 Historical antecedents

Examination of North American trade with South East Asia prior to 1870 reveals how early precedents influenced US perception of trade and business opportunities in the region, as well as the role played by successive US consuls in promoting US trade and FDI in Malaya. Early trade also impacted upon the nature of subsequent Anglo-US relations, concerning trade and FDI in the British colony, both at local and at metropolitan government level and also with local British businesses.

Some form of North American trade with Malaya goes back several centuries. By the end of the seventeenth century, traders from Britain's North American colony came across the Pacific Ocean in increasing numbers, either as pirates or as free traders, plying the India–China route and defying Britain's East India Company's trade monopoly. American interests in South East Asia grew when the American War of Independence (1775–1783) led to the closure of the British West Indian islands to traders from the newly independent United States. Thus US traders, who had earlier participated in the triangular trade between New England, the West Indies and the Gold Coast of Africa, began looking at the Far East for trading opportunities.[1] Trade with the Far East and South East Asia became buoyant and led to the enactment of a trade law in the US which gave preference to South East Asian goods. Interestingly, despite this preference, the US government rejected the idea of setting up a national monopoly in the Far East, such as the American East India Company proposed by John Wingrove in 1785.[2]

By the early nineteenth century, US traders had established direct trade with Malay ports, notably along the pepper coast of Sumatra and particularly Acheh, where they even began to replace British interests with the dominant share of the pepper trade between 1801 and 1815. The US traders' monopoly of the pepper trade in Acheh made Stamford Raffles (who was appointed the Governor of Sumatra in 1818) wary of US trade activities in the region. This can be seen in the treaty signed between Raffles and the Temenggung of Johore, which excluded the settlements of other foreign countries in Singapore, specifically mentioning interest from the US as a major rival.[3] In his attempt to attract traders to Singapore and away from the Dutch ports, Raffles introduced an entrepot system in Singapore and pursued a free trade policy, thereby opening new international trading opportunities.

However, the 1815 Convention, a treaty of commerce and navigation signed at the end of the Anglo-American War of 1812 which saw hostile confrontations between British and American ships in Malayan waters, effectively barred US traders from trading in Singapore by restricting US vessels entering certain ports in India and Penang.[4] Although Singapore was not covered by the 1815 Convention, as it was not founded until 1819, the British authorities in Singapore used this technicality to restrict US trade despite this being a violation of the free trade policy as it unfairly favoured the East India Company.

US traders desired to participate in the Singapore trade as it provided valuable opportunities with the Malay archipelago (Java, Sumatra, Celebes, Malay Peninsula), Siam, Cochin-China, China, New Guinea and Australia. By directing their trade to Riau in the Dutch East Indies, they could ship their cargoes to and from Singapore and evade the restrictions. As a result of this trade via Riau, the first US consul in the South East Asian region, Joseph B. Balestier, was appointed consul for Riau in 1833. In July 1836, he was appointed consul for Singapore.[5]

Realising the locational advantages of Singapore and the opportunities for lucrative trade with China by exchanging archipelago products for Chinese goods that were in demand in Europe, Balestier pressed for the abolition of the restrictions against US traders. Singapore was also considered a safe place for trading activities in the eastern islands as pirates and health risks were less of a concern. In fact compared with Batavia in Java, where US traders had a large coffee trade, it was considered a health haven.[6] In addition, trading in Singapore also meant not having to navigate the Malay islands where familiarity with local officials and local customs was necessary.

The merchant community in Singapore was equally dissatisfied with the exclusion of the US traders as they especially sought the large supplies of silver dollar coins brought by the US ships heading for the Dutch islands.[7] In fact it was largely due to the agitation of local merchants that brought about the intervention of the British government in India (which ruled the Straits Settlements from 1826 to 1867) and led to US ships finally being allowed to trade in Singapore without discrimination. In 1833, US commerce with South East Asia benefited when the East India Company lost its Chinese trade monopoly, resulting in free trade opportunities with China.[8] Essentially, the US government policy throughout the region remained one of non-intervention in local politics. Balestier, in a letter to Washington, stressed the importance of having regular US naval visits to protect and expand US trade in the region, including:

> the coast of Sumatra, the Straits of Malacca Singapore, the Gulf of Siam, the Coast of Cochin China, Lintin Manilla . . . Borneo and Java. In fact – all of the principal ports in or near this great equatorial basin.[9]

A subsequent US consul in Singapore, James Grey Jewell, similarly made the point when he urged the secretary of state, Hamilton Fish, to occasionally send US war vessels to Singapore as 'evidence of our power as a nation and greatness as a people, by creating respect for our merchants, our Consuls and our laws'.[10]

It is clear then that there was significant British–US rivalry for trade in the region before 1870. The capacity of US commerce to acquire a leading position in such a precious commodity as pepper had significantly alarmed the British authorities. This challenge to British hegemony and the response of introducing protectionist policies tended to characterise British–US relations in the region in subsequent years.

2.2 The Pacific pioneers

As the salaried representatives of the US government, US consuls played an important role in safeguarding American commerce in South East Asia by providing local information to US traders, and acting as middlemen between them and the British authorities. They also provided suggestions and ideas on how to advance US trade and investment in this region. These early US consuls, as Kirzner-style entrepreneurs, were quick to identify the opportunities in the South East Asian region, and were really pioneers of agricultural ventures of that time, such as sugar, rice and tobacco. These ventures, however, were generally unsuccessful because of lack of funds, the spread of tropical diseases and labour problems.

A number of the early and more enterprising consuls engaged themselves in trade and investment activities in Singapore and the Malay States. Joseph Balestier, for one, was the sole agent for US ships in the South East Asian region spanning two decades from the late 1830s. His activities included selling ships and goods, providing cargoes and arranging passages for the ships. The goods that were bought and sold by US traders reflected a general internationalisation of North American trade at that time. For example, the goods Balestier received from US ships included French wines, Manila cheroots, American bread, Dutch gin (genever), 200 bolts of superior sail cloth, champagnes and eau de cologne, which were sold to the merchants and citizens of Singapore through advertisements placed in the *Singapore Free Press*.[11]

The US presence was also evident in Malayan agriculture. Balestier was one of the founders of the first agricultural society, the Singapore Agricultural and Horticultural Society, in 1836 in Singapore. His pioneering efforts on a 220 acre sugar plantation produced 20–25 'pikuls' (unit of mass equivalent to 133⅓ pounds or 60.48 kilogrammes) of raw sugar per acre. He also invested in a steam engine for the manufacture of sugar and wanted his estate to serve as a model sugar estate. Balestier funded his venture through personal finances and through loans from Russell & Company of China, but it proved to be a losing venture as the later duty imposed by Britain on Singapore-grown sugar was higher than that of other British colonies.[12]

Attempts by Balestier to establish ties within the region with the support of the US government demonstrates that almost from the first trade with Singapore, US commerce was interested in expanding to the wider region. Balestier established a good rapport with the Sultan of Brunei and through an agreement which promoted trade relations between the two countries in 1850, received the rights to acquire property and conduct commerce in the sultanate. Thus, the US became only the second nation after Britain to successfully conclude a treaty with Brunei, although a consulate was only established in 1865.[13]

The US government then inadvertently became involved in James Brooke's plan for his personal annexation of Sarawak, when a US frigate, the USS *Constitution*, sailed into Brunei in 1845. Brooke used the presence of the US frigate, which was seeking an agreement for trade and coal mining at Labuan in return for protection, as an excuse for intervention in Sarawak. While on a visit to Singapore in 1859, Brooke worked with Balestier to obtain the first international recognition of his rule, but the British government did not acknowledge Brooke's power until it had extended its own protectorate over Sarawak in 1941.[14]

Table 2.1 US consular officers, 1833–1889

Name	*Period*
Joseph B. Balestier	1833–1852
T. Biddle	1856–1858
John P. O' Sullivan	1858–1864
Isaac Stone	1864–1870
James Grey Jewell	1870–1871
Adolphus G. Studer	1871–1889

Source: Adapted from P. Sodhy, 'United States Consuls in Singapore 1859–1880', *Journal of Malayan Branch of Royal Asiatic Society* 56, 1983, p. 14.

One US Consul also played a part in the founding of the North Borneo colony (now Sabah). Captain Claude Moses, the first US consul to Brunei, persuaded the Sultan of Brunei and the Temenggung to lease him large territorial concessions in North Borneo in August 1865.[15] Moses sold the leases to an American merchant, Joseph W. Torrey, in September 1865. Torrey, who set up the American Trading Company of Borneo, cleared land for sugar, rice and tobacco, and raised the American flag at Ellena on Kimanis Bay. In 1866, the company abandoned the settlement due to financial difficulties, labour unrest and the spread of disease among the settlers.[16] The leases were sold to British merchants, who formed the North Borneo Company, which ruled the area until 1942. In addition to Balestier, another US consul in Singapore, Major Adolphus Studer, launched a commercial venture, attempting to grow tobacco in Muar, Johore.[17] His venture, though on a large scale, was unsuccessful, and the Muar land concession later became a diplomatic issue between the US and British governments.[18]

The US consuls played an important part in advancing US trade and investments throughout the region however. James Grey Jewell (the US consul in Singapore from 1870 to 1871) saw the geographical advantages of Singapore as it being 'the halfway house between China and America and China and the continent of Europe', and 'the stopping place and refitting station for vessels of all nations bound either way'. His successor, A.G. Studer, was perceptive about the potential of the Malay Peninsula, stating that, 'the almost entirely undeveloped country round about the island is in many respects a mine of immense wealth'.[19] By also acting as intermediaries between US traders and both British and local traders, they helped establish links for future trade and investment opportunities in Malaya and the wider region.

2.3 US trade in Malaya, 1870–1918

The American Civil War (1861–1865) accelerated the transformation and expansion of an industrialised economy that was also facilitated by certain technological catalysts such as railroads and telegraphic communications. By the 1870s, the opening of the Suez Canal, the availability of telegraph services and the maturing of the domestic market in tandem with the inclusion of new states, were major factors in the increase of American trade. Singapore was already the hub of the world's communications network and, upon the completion of the laying of the Singapore–Madras submarine cable in 1870 was in direct communication with India, continental Europe, Britain and the US.[20] As such, an analysis of how Singapore provided a platform for expansion of US trade and investments in the Malayan Peninsula and the region helps put into context subsequent developments in US–Malayan trade and investments discussed later in this chapter. It will also be pertinent to then briefly review US trade with the Straits Settlements.

British intervention in the Malay Peninsula in 1874 provided increasing opportunities for the expansion of US trade and FDI in the Malay States. The presence of the British made the area more secure for traders, consequently strengthening the position of the Straits Settlements in foreign trade. Other factors promoting trade and FDI brought about by British control were an efficient and transparent legal system, an excellent transport system, laissez-faire economic policies and a cheap labour force.

Singapore's trade with the West tended to expand in phases, between 1871 to 1873 and 1897 to 1899, and again from 1911 to 1913. This trade growth coincided with, and was largely driven by, the growth of world trade as well as the development of other South East Asian countries and the Malay Peninsula. Singapore's increase in imports from Malaya, notably gambier and pepper, and tropical produce from Dutch East Indies, in turn became exports to the West. This was followed by an increase in the import and export of tin and in 1899, tin became Singapore's main export. Demand from the industrial West, primarily the US, for tin plate was boosted by two product innovations: petroleum barrels and canned foods.[21]

From 1871 to 1873, Britain was taking in two-thirds of Singapore's exports, but this fell to one-third between 1911 and 1913. This was mainly due to higher demands from continental Europe and the US for the region's products. In addition, Britain's role as an intermediary in East–West trade was superseded by a redirection of trade between Britain, continental Europe, the US and South East Asia. This redirection of trade was due to the establishment of the Straits Homeward Conference, a cartel controlling international shipping services to Britain and continental Europe through improved connections from Singapore, thus rivalling London's former position as an entrecote. Direct trade between Singapore and the US also increased due to the cheaper freight rates offered by the cartel and the tariff policies adopted between 1892 and 1912, encouraging imports of raw materials whilst curtailing imports of manufactured goods.[22]

Although Britain was still the leading European industrial economy, demand from continental Europe and the US for tin and rubber was also on the rise. Between 1897 and 1899 and from 1911 to 1913, Singapore's exports to continental Europe and the US increased significantly, with exports to the US expanding from 10.9 per cent and 12.1 per cent respectively, despite some fluctuation from year to year.[23]

In 1902, as detailed in Appendix A, tin at S$24.1 million (Straits dollars) became one of the most important exports from the Straits Settlements to the US, followed by Gambier, rattan, gutta percha and gutta inferior, black and white pepper, tapioca products and gum products.[24] By 1914, Malayan rubber exports exceeded those of Brazil and total world wild rubber exports and replaced tin as Malaya's most important export item. Rubber exports increased dramatically from 6,500 tons in 1910 to 47,000 tons and 112,000 tons in 1914 and 1918 respectively.[25] This phenomenal rise was due to the decline in wild rubber output, the expansion of the automobile industry in the US (from 187,000 in 1910 to 1,170,000 in 1918) and increased demand, mainly from the US, with the outbreak of World War I.[26] As such, the nature of British–US relations in the region began to move from an economic relationship into a political one when, with the outbreak of war, tin and rubber became strategic commodities.

As a major consumer of rubber since the 1900s, the US, absorbing 77 per cent of the world's rubber supply by 1917 became Malaya's major buyer, contributing enormously towards the early economic development of Malaya. Surpassing Britain as the largest importer of both tin (1870) and rubber (1915), the US economy became increasingly linked with the economy of Singapore as the main port of trade, and by extension the economy of Malaya where much of the tin and rubber was sourced. This 'high export dependence' on the US 'enabled Singapore to avoid the World War I contraction', thus joining 'the war time boom in the United States economy'.[27]

Imports from the US remained small, however, and recorded only a marginal increase in comparison with imports from Britain and continental Europe. Singapore imports from continental Europe rose from 3.7 per cent in 1871 to 5.1 per cent in 1911, whilst imports from the US rose a paltry 0.1 per cent in the same period. There was a three-fold increase in value for British imports despite the decline in percentage which reflected the enormous rise in tin and rubber imports from the Malay Peninsula from 1871 to 1873 (6.0 per cent) and 1911 to 1913 (17.5 per cent).[28]

Nevertheless, some imports from the US are notable. Import data from the US into Straits Settlements in 1902 show a variety of goods, with the highest figures

Table 2.2 Percentage of Singapore principal exports to Britain and US, 1870–1915

	Britain				*US*			
	Pepper	Gambier	Tin	Rubber	Pepper	Gambier	Tin	Rubber
1870	46.0	63.0	6.6	–	36.6	20.3	57.8	–
1875	48.4	51.6	37.2	–	23.2	10.3	41.6	–
1880	41.5	50.2	18.8	–	23.1	21.0	67.3	–
1885	54.8	47.8	63.7	–	4.9	18.2	23.2	–
1890	33.7	36.9	48.8	–	16.1	17.2	29.4	–
1895	26.8	34.4	37.3	–	23.9	21.5	26.5	–
1900	22.5	27.7	43.7	–	18.1	25.4	34.2	–
1905	13.6	16.4	52.0	87.3	30.2	35.0	25.1	2.5
1910	19.0	15.0	46.5	84.2	15.9	31.7	30.3	7.5
1915	31.0	34.7	20.0	15.0	19.1	24.6	55.7	70.1

Source: Adapted from Chiang Hai Ding, *Straits Settlements*, Appendix XII, pp. 196–202, 204–6.

being for silver dollars (S$445,000), lubricating oil (S$302,609), other petroleum products (S$123,982) and machinery (S$129,525) (see Appendix A).

As the main currency for trade, silver dollar coins were important for the Straits Settlements particularly so due to their relative scarcity and despite the US producing 36 million silver dollars for export between 1872 and 1878. This dependence on silver dollars for trade was somewhat alleviated in 1895 with the arrival of new British trade dollars in Singapore and the introduction of the Currency Note Ordinance of 1899 which introduced the gold standard and was declared legal tender in 1903. More importantly, Singapore was not dependent on supplies of 'foreign' dollars any longer. However, imports from the US continued until August 1904, when the silver dollars were demonetised.[29]

In addition to silver dollars, the US exported oil to the Straits Settlements. The petroleum imports consisted of several products, namely kerosene, lubricating oil, liquid fuel and motor spirit. Until the late nineteenth century the dominant oil company in the region was the Standard Oil Company, the largest US oil exporter. In 1885, Standard Oil met 100 per cent of the oil demand in the Straits Settlements. By 1890, however, that figure had fallen to only 54 per cent due to large supplies of cheaper Russian oil. In 1891, M. Samuel & Company of London secured a contract with the French firm, Rothschild, to buy their Russian oil, and in the following year started shipping through the Suez Canal to Asia, for which Singapore became the point of distribution.[30] By 1898, the market position of both Russian and US oil in the Straits Settlements was challenged by cheaper Sumatran supplies established by the Royal Dutch Petroleum Company. In 1900, Sumatran oil took over the market by providing more than half the imports, increasing to more than 80 per cent in 1902.

In 1903, the British oil company Shell, Royal Dutch and Rothschild formed the Asiatic Petroleum Company, a joint marketing company. Asiatic Petroleum focused on distribution and marketing in the East including Malaya, and provided stiff competition to Standard Oil and the Vacuum Oil Company that had earlier established a footing in the lubricating oil business in the region. Standard Oil was among the first to produce quality lubricants with its more perfected refining machinery. In 1907, Royal Dutch and Shell merged to form the Shell Group. Table 2.3 reflects the falling market share of the Standard Oil Company as the British and Dutch oil firms established their positions.

During the years 1900 to 1918, there was an increase of US trade where the US remained the major buyer of Malayan exports, and US imports from Malaya rose from an average of 1.5 per cent during the pre-World War I years to 6 per cent during World War I. Several factors led to this rise: first, the elimination of German competition; second, the improved services provided by merchant firms; third, the association of US firms with Chinese traders; and, finally, to a lesser extent, US firms' marketing strategies.

Continental Europe, mainly represented by Germany and to a lesser extent France, was Britain's main competitor in Malayan trade.[31] In fact, from the mid-nineteenth century, German investors had been particularly active in the Malayan economy.

Table 2.3 Straits Settlements percentage share of petroleum imports by country, 1886–1903

Year	*USA*	*Russia*	*Dutch East Indies*	*Dutch Borneo*	*Burma*	*Others*
1885	100.0	–	–	–	–	–
1890	53.7	46.3	–	–	–	–
1895	20.4	38.3	41.2	–	–	0.1
1900	9.3	11.8	67.2	7.0	4.8	
1905	33.3	–	56.2	n.a.	10.6	–
1910	30.1	–	67.2	n.a.	2.7	–
1915	13.2	–	86.8	n.a.	–	–

Note: Imports include kerosene, lubricating oil, motor spirit and liquid fuel.

Source: Report on the trade of Straits Settlements for the years 1890–1903; Chiang Hai Ding, *Straits Settlements*, Appendix XII, p. 209.

Despite some suggestion to the contrary by some scholars,[32] German interests, as was the case with American entrepreneurs, had no political interests in Malaya.[33] They were drawn mainly to the export–import business and the setting up of agencies for shipping lines. German manufacturers, like their British counterparts but unlike US business interests, sold their products through trade intermediaries. By the 1860s there were 15 German merchant firms in Singapore with one of the most prominent being Behn Meyer & Co. Ltd founded in 1840. By 1914, the firm had 11 branches in East Asia.[34]

Both German and US interests depended heavily on the locational attractions offered by the British presence in Malaya with German merchants' success in Singapore initially reliant on British shipping, finance, credit and insurance. By the late 1890s, the success of German businesses started to lead to keen competition with British interests. The strategies of these German firms included cost-competitiveness and diversification into shipping and insurance, just like their British merchant counterparts.

German firms also received the support of Chinese intermediaries because of their willingness to provide a system of long-term credit. Since the 1830s, European firms used Chinese traders as a medium of distributing and marketing their merchandise. Chinese traders had better knowledge of Asian market requirements and a closer connection with the consumer than their European competitors.[35] Their working costs were also lower, although a lack of capital was a problem faced by Chinese middlemen. Thus, European merchants had no alternative but to sell their goods on credit, ranging from a period of two to six months. Upon the expiration of the credit period, the Chinese traders would repay their debts in the form of Straits produce instead of money.[36]

Once German interests began extending credit to Chinese traders, British merchant firms were forced to adopt it as a means of competition.[37] British banks, for example the Chartered Bank in Taiping and Kuala Lumpur, began granting loans to petty traders and small contractors in 1888 and were very active in domestic banking.[38]

World War I effectively eliminated Germany's position in Malaya with the Alien Enemies Ordinance of 1914 officially terminating all German business in the country.[39] A significant portion of the German trade, as well as British and other continental European trade, was taken up by Japan, and to a lesser extent Canada and Australia.[40] The increasing demand for Japanese goods during World War I made Japan a serious competitor to Britain's trade with Malaya in the post-war years.

US trade with Malaya also threatened British interests as both import and export trade increased significantly, with US neutrality during most of the war bringing business opportunities. In addition, the US market was free from war-related interruption and shipping threats, and the Pacific route was conducive to imports from the North America. In the imports sector, the US was able to penetrate Britain's stronghold on several items of major importance such as automobiles, machinery, lubricants, electrical appliances and consumer goods.

With the disruption of European trade and increasing demands for new lines of trade, US business interests began to receive wider representation by British merchant firms. British merchant firms had played an important role in the growth of Britain's overseas commerce. In the early nineteenth century in Malaya, these firms included Guthrie (1821), Boustead & Co (1828), Paterson, Simons & Co (1828) and Mansfield (1866). By early 1900, several established agency houses began operating in Penang, including Boustead & Co, Gilfillan Wood & Co, McAlister & Co, and Sandilands Buttery. Initially, British merchant firms expanded both the import and the export sector of their business, acting as importers of European surplus manufactures under various brands and trademarks and exporters, mainly of Straits produce.

The British merchant firms began following diversification strategies to sustain their growth and survival in the early twentieth century. They illustrated Kirzner-style entrepreneurial qualities, as they were among the first to exploit the unlimited opportunities provided by their privileged access to the Malayan markets. By the middle of the nineteenth century, they were engaged in such diverse activities as shipping and insurance. The lack of infrastructure and local entrepreneurship in the developing regions (including Malaya) led them to invest in infrastructure, and later mines and plantations.

In the process of exploiting their ownership advantages, British firms changed and adapted as they began to venture into the foundation and development of the rubber plantation industry. They exploited their prior experience and expertise in marketing, financial knowledge, shipping and other services. The merchant firms became managing agents to mainly British-based free-standing plantation interests promoting the growth of the rubber industry. In 1906, Harrisons & Crossfield was managing six planting companies in four Malay states with capital worth more than S$2.4 million. This increased to S$22.2 million managing 28 companies in 1914. The same year saw Guthrie overseeing 17 free-standing companies worth S$9.9 million, while Thomas Barlow & Brothers was managing an investment of

S$7.9 million for 14 companies.[41] Other merchant firms in the lucrative rubber industry included Sime Darby & Co (1902) and Boustead Brothers (floated in 1905).

Over time, British merchant firms evolved from traditional consumer imports, such as cotton piece goods (chiefly from Lancashire), woollens, opium, cigarettes and liquor, to estate and mining supplies, machinery, and building materials. They also fulfilled orders from public authorities, including government departments controlling public utilities and municipalities.[42] The government purchasing departments always gave preference to British goods. Thus, there was a large volume of trade which was more or less reserved for British manufacturers and fulfilled by these merchant firms. A number of firms managed to secure lucrative government contracts with, for instance, Paterson, Simons & Co agents for the Johore and Sarawak governments, whilst Guthrie & Co was an agent for the government of British North Borneo.[43]

Earlier, British merchant firms had showed an interest in mining ventures during the tin boom of 1882 to 1884, acting mainly as promoters or managing agents of mining companies.[44] The failure of several tin mining ventures (as detailed in Chapter 4) resulted in a diminished interest in tin investments. US manufacturers in the late nineteenth century relied on an export strategy as the mode of entry into Malaya. The risks involved in exporting, and how British manufacturers relied upon the services of merchant firms in overseas trading, have been much discussed in the literature.[45] It was a similar experience for US firms in Malaya. US manufacturers, like their British counterparts, needed the sales and distribution facilities provided by the British merchant firms, which had had an efficient trade network in the region since the late 1890s. However, initially British merchant firms were mainly interested in representing British manufacturers, as British goods were very much in demand in Malaya. Thus, they had little motivation to be interested in representing US manufacturers and very few of them held American agencies.[46]

World War I brought significant changes to the activities of these merchant firms. With the limited availability and the declining competitiveness of British goods, they needed new trade opportunities and were aware of the importance of securing agencies from foreign manufacturers, including US and other European products which were in direct competition with goods made in Britain. Of particular importance was the automobile and automotive parts business.[47] These merchant firms began to hold agencies in the early twentieth century not only for British car companies but also for US, French and Italian car companies. In 1909, Paterson, Simons & Co was distributing Ford automobiles in Penang. In 1911, Wearne Brothers was appointed as a Ford dealer.[48] However, it needs to be noted that, at this point, reservations towards US automobiles were still prevalent among British merchant firms. Products from the US were also represented by German and Swedish merchant firms, as seen in the representation of Ford automobiles by Gadelius & Co in 1909.

Katz Brothers, a company of German origin and established 1901, had branches in Singapore and Penang and was among the earliest and largest importers of

US goods. This company dealt with all kinds of household goods from electrical items, cereals, disinfectant and soap, to baking powder.

Besides merchant firms, other forms of local intermediaries included Chinese traders as well as Indian, Arab and Japanese merchants. US manufacturers used Chinese firms to market their products, thus reducing the risks associated with exporting, while providing business opportunities to these firms. Chinese merchants were therefore a source of competition and US companies exploited the advantages provided by these entrepreneurs in advancing their goods. More importantly, they were the best links to the wider Chinese consumers and, to a lesser extent, the Malays in the Malayan market.

To have a clear understanding of the development of the business network in Malaya, it is useful to analyse the boycott against US goods by Chinese merchants in the Straits Settlements from 1905 to 1906. It reveals how the US firms adapted and reinvented their competitive strategies, including the impact of their goods in Malaya, and how US links with Chinese entrepreneurs became established. In addition, the boycott illustrates the significance of Chinese traders in the Straits economy.

In 1905, Chinese traders in Singapore and Penang joined forces with their counterparts in China and San Francisco who had initiated the boycott against US goods in retaliation for the anti-Chinese immigration law in the US.[49] This boycott permeated every level of the Chinese community in the Straits Settlements, with merchants going out of their way to assure consumers that their products were not made in the US. A long list of goods was boycotted in Penang and Singapore, ranging from kerosene oil to soaps and cigars which carried exotic Chinese names such as Tea Flower brand, White Flower musk soap and Golden Eagle brand cigars.[50] These latter items illustrate how US firms were shrewd to market their goods with localised names and labels of familiarity to the Asian market, especially among the Chinese.

A circular entitled 'American Boycott to Be Carried Out in Penang' stated that as of 13 September 1905, Chinese merchants had to adhere to an import ban on US goods, products and machinery into the Straits Settlements or Federated Malay States and not to deal with US products in any way, directly or indirectly. The penalty for violation was S$500 for the first offence, S$1,000 for the second offence and S$2,000 for the third offence.[51] Initially, David Wilbur, the US consul in Singapore, reported that the boycott was not serious, despite the fact that merchants from Perak and Selangor had joined the movement. However, on 14 November 1905, Wilbur reported to the US secretary of state that every firm dealing with US goods had reported that trade was at a standstill.[52] Anonymous threatening letters were circulated among the Chinese traders who dealt with goods from the US. For example, salesmen for British American Tobacco were warned to discontinue the sale of American products[53] and the Chinese Chamber of Commerce notified salesmen for the Standard Oil Company to do the same.

Wilbur finally requested British authorities to intervene and suppress the boycott, but, as British interests were unaffected, he found it difficult to obtain British cooperation in this matter.[54] In his report of 27 January 1906, Wilbur mentioned that American kerosene, flour, lard, tools, perfumery and provisions were all suffering under the boycott. The Chinese boycott against American flour, which paved the way for Australian flour to enter the Malayan market, had a lasting impact and led to greatly lower levels of American flour being imported into Malaya than would have been otherwise.

The Chinese boycott was, however, an isolated event and generally Chinese entrepreneurs did not hinder US trade. For the most part, links with Chinese traders gave US firms access to the Malayan market. US trade increased in Malaya despite difficult relations during the 1905 to 1906 boycott. From 1906 onwards good relations were resumed with Chinese merchants who were instrumental in introducing US goods in Malaya as Chapter 3 will discuss more fully.

In the Malayan market, price competitiveness was the most important factor. Quality goods with a high price were beyond the means of a large percentage of the Malayan population because Malayans had only relatively low purchasing power.[55] In Malaya, the consumer requirements of the population varied greatly, both among their different ethnic groups, and in relation to the requirements of the Europeans. While peoples with an Asian background formed more than 80 per cent of the total population, the Europeans formed less than 1 per cent, and others such as Eurasians, Armenians, etc made up a further 15 per cent (see Chapter 3 for more information). The multiracial Asian population required basic necessities such as cotton piece goods, tools and implements, lamps, bicycles and accessories, cigarettes and soap. The Europeans, meanwhile, in spite of forming a smaller percentage of Malayan consumers, had a wider range of demands, which included luxury goods such as fine clothing, cutlery, wines and alcohol, stationery, chinaware, drugs, specialised household fittings and motorcars. These luxury products were also in demand among certain groups of the population, but only the very wealthiest, mainly Eurasians, Chinese merchants, owners of mines and rubber estates and the Malay royalty and aristocrats.

British products, while exempted from tariffs and quotas, were known for their quality and enjoyed a prominent position in the market. At the same time, there were also high-quality goods available from continental European countries such as Germany. Thus, US firms were competing for a share in an already crowded market. Stiff competition for a small percentage of buyers led US firms to use marketing strategies such as branding and product differentiation to penetrate the Malayan market. However, US companies sought to fulfil both the demands of the majority of the Asian population as well as the wealthier group as illustrated by the nature of imports from the US detailed in Appendix A. US manufacturers made an effort to create a favourable image of American goods and services and realised the need to study the unfamiliar conditions which factored in the Asian markets. Decorative labels, for instance, carried greater weight than a written statement. Hence, tinned provisions were packed in containers with attractive and distinctive labels.

As early as 1902, there was awareness of the need to establish American distribution and supply chain firms to aid US manufacturers to market their goods in the area. The US consul continued to play a role, mainly providing information and suggestions on how to advance US trade in Malaya. The need for American intermediaries was advocated by O.F. Williams, the US consul in Singapore, who alerted the Department of State in 1902, citing the unfavourable trade balance due to the lack of US distributors. He emphasised the need for US manufacturers to have a local American intermediary rather than relying only on the medium of catalogue and circulars. He suggested that US manufacturers comply with recommendations regarding packing, shipping and style of goods to meet local tastes. He also cited the comparative advantages of British and German merchant firms which had their 'men on the ground' who knew the local market.[56]

An example of American tenacity in the marketing of their goods and services in Malaya is provided by the insurance company, The Equitable. Aside from the company running an advertisement in the *Perak Pioneer* on 1 September 1894, there were also several short articles about the company's manager for the East, J.T. Hamilton, concerning his seven-day tour of Perak which took him to Kinta, Tapah, Taiping and Batu Gajah. This suggests that great efforts were made to promote the company, not only in the bigger cities but also in the small tin mining towns in the area. Hamilton built an effective business and was proposed as a model for British insurance agents.[57]

Advertising was an important source of competitive advantage, and one means to break into the Malayan market and compete against long-established British manufacturers. One of the US firms' marketing strategies was, as discussed earlier, to exploit the extensive marketing networks offered by merchant firms, which were mainly, but not exclusively, British. Agency agreements made with these merchant firms include marketing services. For example, merchant firms holding American agencies of expensive high-grade articles such as fountain pens and propelling pencils made use of advertisements to penetrate the Malayan market.[58] The innovative use of advertisements could be seen mainly in the automobile advertisements of US cars in comparison with other foreign makes (primarily British) in the leading newspapers in Malaya beginning in the early twentieth century. While for the most part, these advertisements were placed by merchant firms, on occasion, US manufacturers also placed advertisements in the local newspapers (see Figure 2.1).

The establishment of US merchant firms such as Getz Brothers, Connell Brothers, and Dodge & Seymour increased the distribution and, subsequently, the promotion of American branded goods in the Malayan market during this period. Dodge & Seymour of New York held agencies for numerous US manufacturers, and, most notably, served as Ford's main distributor, working closely with Wearne Brothers in Malaya from 1911 to 1926. Getz Brothers of New York, established in 1871, had distributing agencies in Singapore, Penang, Kuala Lumpur, Bangkok, Manila, as well as Jakarta, and, as shown in Appendix B, dealt with many kinds of American products from various held agencies.

US firms, in their efforts to penetrate the Malayan market, also adapted their marketing strategies to the local market, and advertising and product differentiation strategies became a source of advantage for any firm competing in the Malayan markets. However, because of British predominance and the preference given to

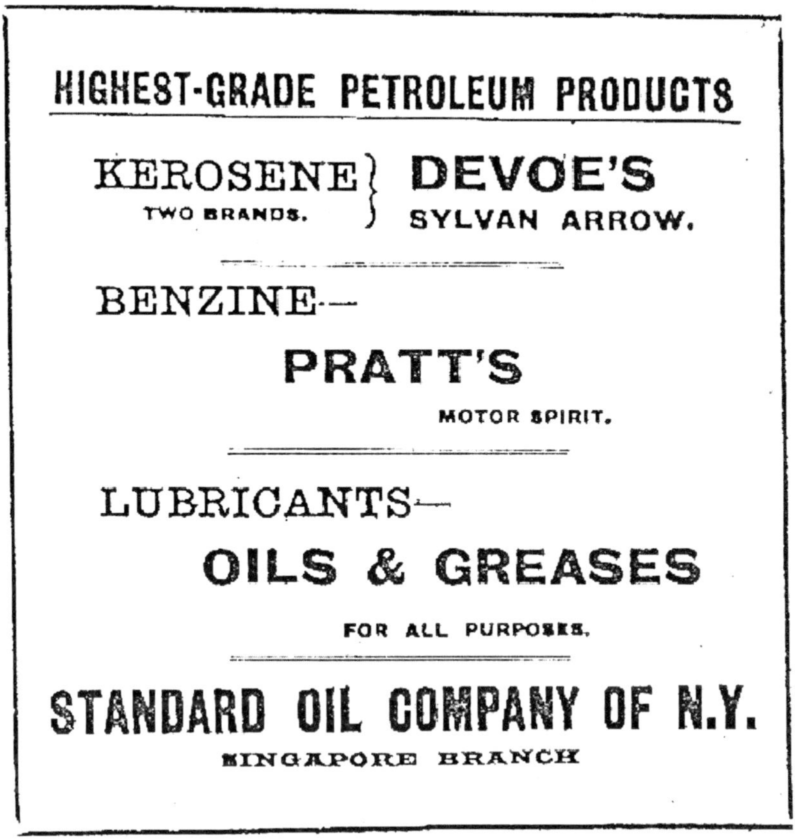

Figure 2.1 An advertisement by Standard Oil Company of New York (Singapore branch) promoting its petroleum products.

Source: *Straits Times*, 14 November 1916.

British business by government and firms alike, the marketing strategies adopted by the US firms captured only a small percentage of business for US goods in Malaya. It was only due to the disruption caused by World War I that US manufacturers were able to penetrate the Malayan market, and this set the stage for further developments in trade and FDI. US interests in rubber and tin would, in stark contrast to its other commercial interests, experience severe constraints due to the strategic importance of these natural resources to the British.

2.4 US FDI in Malaya, 1900–1918

The British government favoured an 'open' policy towards FDI. In South East Asia, Malaya ranked second after the Dutch East Indies in terms of FDI in 1914 despite being a much smaller market than the Dutch East Indies. However, as explained in more detail in Chapter 3, FDI flows grew rapidly in Malaya as well as the Dutch East Indies from World War I onwards with increased foreign activity mainly in the primary resource sector. This section discusses the development of US FDI in Malaya from 1900 to 1918 with American investments in the resource – petroleum, rubber and tin – and service sectors.

In the late nineteenth century, numerous British free-standing mining firms were floated in the UK and there were also several French and Australian ventures in the Malayan tin mining industry. However, as detailed in Chapter 4, and concurrent with the trend suggested by Wilkins on the fate of FSCs, most were generally short lived and unsuccessful. In the early twentieth century, foreign firms continued to show their interest in participating in the tin mining industry. The introduction of new mining techniques, the gravel pump and dredge, led to the dominance of FDI over Chinese entrepreneurs in the industry.

FDI in rubber remained significantly higher than tin with British FDI predominating. One Danish firm, United Plantations founded in 1906, also had considerable areas of land for rubber in the south of Perak.[59] Some Belgian, Japanese and other Dutch firms also had rubber plantations in the Federated Malay States. By World War I, Japanese firms had planted rubber on a large scale both in the Federated Malay States and in Johore.[60] However, despite the free flow of foreign investments into Malaya, there were periodic restrictions on FDI, including US FDI.

US consuls provided relevant business information to the Department of State, as evidenced by dispatches from the Singapore Consulate, and they followed Malayan economic trends closely. There were regular reports from 1887 to 1909 highlighting investment opportunities for US firms with regards to rubber plantation and agricultural development in the Federated Malay States and port activities in Singapore, Port Dickson and Port Swettenham.[61]

By the early twentieth century, US companies also began to actively seek opportunities for FDI in Malaya, notably in the area of the local natural resources of petroleum, tin and rubber. In these sectors, the large volume of US trade led to either supply or market-seeking investments in Malaya. This can be seen in the setting up of purchasing agencies, subsidiaries, branches and plants by major US MNEs in Singapore.

Table 2.4 Prospecting licences and mining leases held by foreign investors in the Malay States, 1907

Nationality	*Prospecting licences*	*Mining leases*
British	48	20
Dutch	16	4
German	6	–
Italian	4	–
Swiss	2	–
American	2	1
Total	78	25

Source: ANM, CO 273/343, No. 19223, Siam Annual Report 1907

In 1898, Standard Oil made market-oriented investments by establishing a distributing agency in Singapore, but British and Dutch oil firms challenged and overcame the US monopoly over oil in the region and, in 1911, Standard Oil was dissolved. Of the three successor companies, Standard Oil Company of New York (SOCONY), Standard Oil of New Jersey and Standard Oil of California, SOCONY was to play a predominant role in the region. The Singapore distributing agency later served SOCONY's Dutch East Indies subsidiary, the Nederlandsche Koloniale Petroleum Maatschappij, established in 1912.[62] This supply-seeking investment was achieved after several unsuccessful attempts in North Borneo and also the Dutch East Indies.[63] Another subsidiary distributing oil in the region was the Vacuum Oil Company. SOCONY remained active in the lubricating oil business, imported entirely from its US counterparts, in Malaya before World War I. This direct import ended when, in 1916, SOCONY set up a bulk oil installation at Bagan Luar near Province Wellesley.[64]

The Malayan mining industry also saw an attempt by US investors to break into the tin-smelting industry as early as 1900 when there were plans by the American engineer to set up a smelter in Telok Anson, Perak. A further serious effort to set up a tin-smelting operation was made in 1902 by the International Tin Company. However, as Chapter 4 shows, both attempts failed when the colonial government imposed duties on the export of ores. There was no attempt made to invest in tin mining during this period (1870 to 1918), although during World War I, the US Steel Corporation, the largest American purchaser of Malayan tin, set up a purchasing office in Singapore to buy directly from the smelters.[65]

The Malayan rubber industry attracted several US rubber firms to invest in Malaya. In 1905, the Malacca Rubber Company was established, and by 1911 it became one of the largest producers in Malaya.[66] Two further American rubber companies, the Pahang Rubber Company Ltd in Pahang and Tanjong Olak Rubber Plantation Company in Johore, were established in 1906 and 1907 respectively. There were no political or legal factors that blocked US rubber investments prior to Word War I and US firms enjoyed the same privileges afforded to British firms. According to a former administrator of the Mexican Crude Rubber Company, a large US firm that had been involved in rubber planting in Selangor since 1912, he had 'received from all the Federated Malay States government officials the most courteous treatment'. The administrator reiterated that the British authorities welcomed American investments if they were backed by responsible financiers. However, the restriction of land grants to 5000 acres to any individual or firm remained but large British investors were able to overcome this 'by floating as many separate companies as necessary'.[67]

During World War I, large US rubber firms attempted to integrate backwards into rubber plantations in Malaya. Shortages of natural rubber as well as failed investments nearer to home attracted these firms to Malaya to access adequate and cheaper sources of supply. Firestone appointed agents in 1916 to look for opportunities to invest in Malayan rubber in Perak. Another rubber giant, the United States Rubber Company (USRC), which had invested in Sumatra in 1910, began to evince an interest in buying existing rubber plantations in Malaya during the war. Goodyear also made an attempt to integrate backward into rubber plantation in Malaya. However, war-time protectionist measures imposed by the British government blocked these large US rubber manufacturing concerns from investing into the Malayan rubber industry.

Firestone and Goodyear instead set up purchasing offices in Singapore followed by BFGoodrich in 1918, while USRC had set up one by the beginning of World War I.[68] As suggested by Huff, these manufacturers purchased their rubber requirements from merchant firms rather than 'up-country buying'. They preferred the services of merchant firms rather than facing 'potentially high transactions costs of negotiation and contract' if they were to provide the services themselves.[69] Subsequently, some of these US rubber firms ventured into rubber manufacturing. Firestone, in 1918, set up a rubber refining and preparation mill including drying and storage facilities, saving freight costs on eliminated waste matter.[70] Like Firestone, USRC also ventured into rubber manufacturing as discussed in more detail in Chapter 5.

US investments were also seen in the insurance and banking sectors. In 1903, the International Banking Corporation (founded in 1902) had requested a share of the government account in the Straits Settlements. Their request, however, was rejected on the grounds that there were enough government banking accounts.[71] In the same year, a branch was established in Penang, Straits Settlements. In 1915 National City Bank acquired the International Banking Corporation and with it the branch in Malaya.[72]

One of the earliest US MNEs in Malaya was the Singer Sewing Machine Company, recognised as the first US MNE and the world's largest manufacturer of sewing machines.[73] Singer was established in Singapore in 1903, and later established branches in Kuala Lumpur, Selangor and Penang. The firm also employed local agents, mainly Chinese firms, to introduce hire purchase facilities, a marketing system pioneered by Singer that was later emulated by other US firms and insurance companies. Cycle & Carriage, a Chinese family firm formed in 1899, was one of Singer's first agents in Kuala Lumpur.[74]

2.5 US–Malayan economic relations, 1870–1918

This chapter traces the history of trade relations between the US and Malaya from the late 1800s until 1918. There was only marginal US investment interest in Malaya until the late nineteenth century, when growing US demand for tin and rubber led to a huge increase in Malayan exports to the US. However, direct imports from the US remained small in quantity, as there was little demand for US products apart from silver dollars and lubricating oils. In the case of petroleum, imports from the US were decimated by competition from British and Dutch firms, and the regional growth of crude oil production.

The low trade volume from the US meant that most US manufacturers were content to use the services of mainly British, but also Chinese and other merchant intermediaries, for their exports to Malaya. Representation by British intermediaries of US products grew during and post-World War I, particularly in automobiles, machinery and consumer goods and strengthened the complementary relationship which characterised the working association between US and British business.

US FDI in Malaya was resource-seeking rather than market-seeking (unlike US trade). During the period of time covered by this section, from the late nineteenth century until 1918, the US remained Malaya's largest export market while Malaya remained a small market for US imports. However, these trading links created opportunities for supply-led FDI and market-led FDI in Malaya. For oil, the high volume of trade led to market-seeking investments. In other natural resources, the large Malayan exports led to the establishment of supply-seeking and, later, market-oriented investments, especially in rubber. There were fewer incentives for US firms to engage in FDI beyond the fast-growing rubber plantation sector. Considering US and Malayan connections between 1870 and 1918, it can be asserted that, despite the liberal policies and the infrastructure provided by the British authorities in addition to support from British merchant firms, US imports and FDI into Malaya were almost negligible. However, as is discussed in the case studies, US FDI did have a dramatic impact on the host economy particularly in the areas of organisational skills, technological advancement and R&D.

3 Strengthening ties, 1919–1957

The decades from World War I until the outbreak of World War II saw radical changes in the international economy, including the spread of trade protectionism, the imposition of exchange controls, the collapse of capital mobility and the decline in commodity prices. As the US grew to be the world's largest industrial power entrenched behind the world's highest tariff barriers, the British remained committed to free trade, only introducing tariffs from 1919. Heavier tariffs were introduced from 1931, by which time staple industries such as textiles had been devastated by foreign imports.

During the interwar years in Malaya, there was a shift in government policy when the colonial authorities adopted protectionist import quotas, a 'Buy British' campaign and later, exchange controls. Malaya remained an important host economy for FDI, mainly in the resource sector. After World War II, Malaya, in spite of the damage to the economy brought about by both the Japanese occupation and the subsequent disruptive activities of the Communists during the Emergency, remained one of the world's major exporters of tin and rubber. The US continued to receive the largest share of Malayan exports, followed by Britain. Malaya's surpluses with the US boosted Britain's balance of payments, especially when the latter was hit by sterling crises in August 1947, September 1949 and November 1951. These economic downturns demonstrate the importance of Malaya to the imperial economy of Britain.

This chapter analyses the changing nature of US trade and FDI in Malaya, with respect to the challenges of economic boom and bust in Malaya (and elsewhere in the world) since the end of World War I, through World War II and the Emergency, until Malayan independence. The trade barriers imposed in Malaya by Britain are examined against the trade performance of its competitors: the Japanese, the continental Europeans and the Americans. The analysis takes into consideration the policies of both the metropolitan and the colonial authorities with regard to foreign imports (mainly from the US) into Malaya. Subsequently, the increase of US FDI in the world, South East Asia and Malaya specifically during this period is examined. The chapter ends with an overview of the impact of exchange controls on the flow of US imports into Malaya in the years leading up to the Pacific War and from post-World War II until Malaysian Independence.

3.1 US trade in Malaya, 1919–1942

Britain was the dominant power in the triangular relationship between the US, Britain and Malaya because, as the colonial power, it controlled the legal and administrative structures. In order to gain access to markets in Malaya, as well as elsewhere in the Empire, US firms needed to work with the British government and businesses. It is important to see the development of British and US trade in colonial Malaya within the wider context of the development of the relationship across the whole of the British Empire.

Until 1928, Britain was the most important trading partner for the British dominions of Australia, New Zealand and South Africa as well as the colonies of India and Malaya. However, the share of imports into these areas of the Empire from Britain declined from 44 per cent in 1913 to 35 per cent in 1928.[1] The US, much less debilitated economically by World War I than Britain, began to shift its trading activities from Western Europe to the Dominions, and broadly in these areas US exports grew while Britain's declined. Unlike Malaya, the Dominions had similar characteristics to a European or the US market, such as high per capita income and goods requirements. Thus, the percentage of US imports into Malaya was much lower than the Dominions (see Table 3.1).

After World War I, Britain secured a higher percentage of total exports to Malaya, albeit, on a much smaller scale than to the dominions (except Canada) and India. The low level of imports from Britain in relation to the dominions as well as India was largely due to Malaya's increased percentage of imported foodstuffs from neighbouring countries, as detailed later in this section. However, the growing specialisation and earning capacity of the Malayan commercial sector led to an

Table 3.1 Percentage share of UK and US imports into the dominions and Malaya, 1913 and 1928

Country	*Percentage of total imports (%)*			
	UK		US	
	1913	1928	1913	1928
Canada	21.0	15.0	64.0	69.0
Australia	52.0	40.0[a]	14.0	25.0[a]
New Zealand	55.0	47.0	10.0	18.0
South Africa	57.0	44.0	9.0	17.0
India	65.0	46.0	2.5	7.0
Malaya	11.5[b]	16.2	1.8[b]	3.2

Notes:

[a] Figures for year ended June 1929.

[b] Figures for SS only (although reflective of total imports into Malaya, it is important to note that the SS was also handling regional trade for areas such as Borneo, DEI, Thailand, Ceylon and Burma).

Sources: Adapted from PRO, CAB 58/149, 'Economic Advisory Council Reports, Proceedings and Memoranda of Committee on Empire Trade', (1930); Figures for Malaya: Mills, *British Rule in Eastern Asia*, pp. 130–1.

increase in demand for manufactured goods from Western countries, mainly Britain, continental Europe and the US.

In Malaya, in contrast to the dominions and India, there was competition from the Japanese. With the restriction into Malaya of German imports during World War I (see Chapter 2) there was a vacuum in the Malayan market, which came to be filled by imports from Japan and, to a lesser extent, the US. Japanese firms were most competitive in the retail trade, especially textiles, while Malaya's imports from the US almost doubled during the immediate years after World War I. In contrast, figures from 1913 and 1928 show a dip in imports from Britain declining from 42.0 per cent to 31.2 per cent respectively. Previously, US exports had been mainly in the areas of raw materials and foodstuffs, petroleum products, wood and timber, tobacco, wheat and wheat flour, but during the interwar years, and signifying a changing trend in US and Malaya trade, there was a notable rise in the export of manufactured items, mainly automobiles and accessories (including tyres), machinery and electrical apparatus.

During the mid-1920s the growth of Malaya's international trade was notable for several reasons. First, there was a lack of tariff barriers against British or indeed other foreign goods. In addition, there was a growing world demand for Malayan tin and rubber exports. Malaya's demand for imports also rose due to an increase in local development activities, particularly the government directed construction of public works, railways, hospitals, municipalities, ports and electrical power enterprise. There was also significant expansion during the 1920s of the agency system, whereby British merchant firms diversified into other business areas and with the establishment of palm oil estates.[2]

Foodstuffs, predominantly rice, were the main component of the Malayan import trade in 1920, but by 1940 manufactured goods accounted for a higher percentage of Malayan imports.[3] The increase in Malayan demand for manufactured goods was due to economic growth during the interwar years, which was only held in check during the Depression years from 1930 to 1933. There was also significant population growth, both in Malaya and in Singapore. As we have seen in Chapter 2, the expanding population in Malaya was of diverse origin although the majority had Asian roots (see Table 3.2). Such diversity was reflected in consumer demand, although apart from the Europeans, it was the Chinese who mainly lived in urban areas and who became the major buyers of manufactured goods. By 1938, ethnic Chinese had replaced Malays as the majority group.

The growth of manufactured imports reflects the lack of significant local manufacturing. The relatively small Malayan market provided few incentives for a manufacturing base, especially given the free trade regime before the 1930s.[4] Local ethnic Chinese entrepreneurs showed little interest in diversifying from trade and commerce and, unlike in India, the British agency houses were also reluctant to invest in manufacturing. Guthries, a British merchant firm, on several occasions contemplated manufacturing investments but was too cautious to act.[5] An exception to this norm was Harrisons & Crosfield's venture into rubber manufacturing in the late 1920s.[6] Despite the general reluctance of overseas investors to invest in Malaya, development in agricultural and mining industries did

Table 3.2 Malayan total population: 1928, 1931, 1936 and 1938[a]

Race	*1928*	*1931*	*1936*	*1938*
Malay	1,787,345	1,644,173	2,128,130	2,210,867
Chinese	1,374,832	1,709,392	1,829,137	2,220,224
Indians	628,418	624,000	642,198	743,555
Europeans	21,093	17,768	22,822	28,211
Eurasians	14,914	16,043	17,399	18,310
Others[b]	37,836	373,961	54,480	57,679
Total	3,864,438	4,385,337	4,694,166	5,278,846

Notes:

a Figures include data for Singapore.

b Others included Arabs, Armenians, Japanese, etc.

Sources: 1928 figures: Bliss, *Market for Machinery*, p. 5; 1931 figures: Directory of Malaya, 1932; 1936 figures: A. Hartland, *Economic and Commercial Conditions in Malaya*, London: HMSO, 1937; 1938 figures: R.B. Willmot, *Economic and Commercial Conditions in Malaya*, London: HMSO, 1939.

stimulate the growth of the primary processing, engineering and consumption goods industries.

Although Britain continued to be a substantial source, in quantitative terms for Malaya, the largest source of imports was from its neighbours. The Dutch East Indies was the largest supplier of Malaya's raw materials, especially petroleum products, coal, wood and timber. US imports were relatively insignificant, except for certain specialist products, although the US did supply one-third of Malaya's asphalt and bitumen and remained a major supplier of lubricating oil (see Table 3.3).

The US was also important for automobile and machinery imports to Malaya, although Britain remained the largest source of car and cycle imports despite a slight decline in its percentage of the market. Over the course of the 1920s the US share of automobile imports declined marginally, but it emerged as a substantial

Table 3.3 Malaya: percentage share of petroleum imports by country, 1927–1929 (annual averages)

Commodities	*UK*	*US*	*DEI*	*Sarawak*	*Quantity ('000 tons)*	*Imports (S$ million)*
Petroleum products:			Percentage			
Motor spirit	–	0.7	76.8	22.4	86,474	18.1
Liquid fuel	–	2.6	88.9	5.1	447,835	17.9
Kerosene	–	9.0	59.9	30.5	43,616	5.6
Lubricating	5.3	34.1	58.1	–	4,188,783	3.6

Note:

1. Figures include data for Singapore.

Source: Adapted from PRO, BT 70/32, 'Import Trade of British Malaya', Board of Trade Supply, 1929.

source of machinery imports. However, US steel imports collapsed due to fierce competition from continental Europe.[7]

The US also provided important supplies of refrigerators, tractors and agricultural machinery, wireless apparatus and electrical appliances and was the main supplier of high-tech cinema apparatus for sound projection, cinema theatre seats and insulating material for both sound and heat. Consumer goods from the US including cereals, canned fruits, electrical goods, typewriters, cars and parts were also able to penetrate the Malayan market. Still, total imports from the US never exceeded 4 per cent during the interwar years. In comparison, British imports fluctuated between 13 and 18 per cent annually from the years 1929 to 1939. Exports to Britain stayed within a range of 10 to 19 per cent between 1929 and 1934, but declined slightly in the late 1930s.[8]

During the interwar years, the US continued to be Malaya's major export market, with the percentage of US trade following the general economic conditions in Malaya. Malayan exports to the US peaked in 1929, declined during the Depression of the early 1930s, and improved again in the mid-1930s, with the percentage of exports to the US once again reaching a peak of over 40 per cent in 1936.[9]

Trade between the US and South East Asia shows a similar pattern to US and Malayan trade with high exports and low imports, but Malaya's exports to the US were unrivalled in the region, even by the Philippines, a US colony.[10] However, imports from Malaya as compared to total US world imports remained small, rising from just 1.5 per cent prior to World War I, to a peak of 6.2 per cent between 1926 and 1930. US exports to South East Asia in general were also low. Still, the consistently favourable trade balance for Malaya in relation to the US was not only a permanent feature of US–Malayan trade but also of US–South East Asia trade (see Table 3.4).

Table 3.4 Percentage share of US trade with South East Asia, 1910–1935 (five year averages)

Country	*1910–1914*		*1921–1925*		*1926–1930*		*1931–1935*	
	Imports	Exports	Imports	Exports	Imports	Exports	Imports	Exports
Philippines	1.1	1.0	2.3	1.2	2.8	1.5	5.2	2.3
Malaya	1.5	0.1	4.4	0.2	6.2	0.3	4.8	0.2
DEI	0.5	0.1	1.6	0.4	2.2	0.7	2.2	0.5
Indochina	a	a	a	a	a	a	a	a
Thailand	a	a	a	a	a	a	a	a
Burma	a	a	a	a	a	a	a	a
Total South East Asia	3.2	1.3	8.4	1.8	11.2	2.6	12.3	3.1

Note:
a Less than 0.1 per cent.

Source: Recalculated from Table 1, M.S. Farley, 'America's Stake in the Far East – 1: Trade', *Far Eastern Survey* 5, 1936, p. 168.

3.2 From open door to protectionism

The Depression of the 1930s and subsequent collapse of the international financial system led to a worldwide shift towards economic nationalism. Britain was forced to abandon the Gold Standard in September 1931, followed by the US in 1933. By the end of the 1930s, half the world's trade was restricted by tariffs.[11] Britain's abandonment of a policy of free trade reflected the scale of the problems faced by its export-dependent economy. As the world economy disintegrated into competing trade and currency blocs, the British found refuge in the Sterling Area, supported by an official policy of Imperial Preference.[12] While examining the impact of British government policies on the growth of international trade in Malaya, it is important to analyse the advantages enjoyed by British businesses over foreign competitors and to detail US firms' strategies to penetrate the Malayan market.

The British cotton industry experienced many difficulties in the 1920s due to the collapse of its overseas markets, largely a product of its own inefficiencies.[13] In 1929, the combination of falling purchasing power in the market and free trade led to a fall in sales of expensive British textiles in Malaya. Britain's exports of cotton piece goods fell from more than 50 per cent of the Malayan market in 1925 until 1929 to 25 per cent in 1932, declining further to 18 per cent in 1934. During the same period Japan's exports rose and remained stable at 20 per cent from 1925 until 1929 before rising to approximately 60 per cent in 1932 and 67 per cent in 1933.[14] During 1933 and the first half of 1934, many merchant firms, which traditionally had used Lancashire textiles, began to turn towards Japanese textiles.[15] In their effort to remain competitive in the import trade, price was the decisive factor for these merchant firms rather than the origin of the manufacturer.[16]

When negotiations for voluntary import restrictions through the Anglo-Japanese Conference in 1934 failed, the British government ordered her colonies (including Malaya) to protect the Lancashire textile industry by imposing quotas on all textile imports based on the 1927 to 1929 average. The secretary of state for the colonies, Philip Cunliffe-Lister, declared that the purpose of the quota system was to protect British manufacturers against Japanese competition in cotton and rayon piece goods and, at the same time, to restore Britain's dominant position in the region.[17]

The adoption of the system of quotas on textile imports brought complaints from the Straits Settlements Trade Commission (formed to enquire into the trade of the Colony in 1933 to 1934) and the Association of British Malaya. They forwarded a protest to the Colonial Office contending that cheaper Japanese goods, as compared to British goods priced according to European standards, were important for the poorer segments of Malaya's population. They further argued that the interests of British business in Malaya should be taken into consideration, and not only the protection of Lancashire manufacturers.[18] Despite strong objections raised in the colonial legislatures and although it contradicted the entrepot trade on which Penang and Singapore had been developed, the legislation was passed and became effective on 7 May 1934. The legislation imposed quotas on imports of textiles from China, Italy, Japan, the Netherlands and Dutch East Indies. By 1939, Japan's share declined to less than a third of Malayan imports of cotton goods. The import quotas imposed by the British authorities successfully checked Japanese competition in Malaya although the decline was also due in part to a local Chinese boycott of Japanese goods following the outbreak of the Sino-Japanese War (1937–1945).[19] The imposition of Imperial Preference on Japanese goods in the 1930s illustrates the conflicting interests of the Colonial Office and administrators on the spot in Malaya, with the former attempting to safeguard Britain's interests and the latter, local interests.

In addition to curbing Japanese imports, the British authorities also sought to hinder US imports, particularly automobiles, into Malaya. In the face of stiff competition from US as well as continental European models, government officials were encouraged to purchase automobiles made by British-owned firms in Britain. The general orders of the civil service specified that civil servants were entitled to a maximum loan of S$3,000 for such purchases.[20] In 1929, the new taxation policy based on horse power and introduced by the colonial authorities in the Federated Malay States did have an impact on the sales of American automobiles, including those from US subsidiaries in Britain and Canada, as generally they had higher horsepower. In 1932, Britain imposed a 25 per cent *ad valorem* duty on non-Empire-made cars (in comparison to 10 per cent for Empire-made cars) imported into Malaya as part of the policy of Imperial Preference established at Ottawa. This preferential treatment, however, had limited effect in increasing the market share of automobiles made by British-owned firms compared to American ones. As is detailed in the Ford case study in Chapter 6, US automobile manufacturers used their Canadian and British subsidiaries as an export platform to enjoy the same preferential treatment.

The preference for British businesses by British authorities was evident even before the shift towards trade protectionism in the 1930s. The colonial government intervened in the Malayan market with specific policies intended to promote British industries, such as the 'Buy British' campaigns in the 1920s and 1930s.[21] In addition, governmental departments and municipalities in Malaya gave preference to British goods, making their purchases through crown agents in London. Meanwhile, the Malayan plantation and mining companies placed orders for their equipment, machinery and material from British manufacturers through their head offices in London.[22] Between 1927 and 1929, the sale of British dredges to Malaya for example, amounted to S$8.57 million and at the same time generated a demand for spares at S$1.71 million per year thereafter.[23]

However, despite a preference for British businesses, there were occasions when the colonial authorities and British businesses chose to secure orders from US firms. In the spring of 1919, the Federated Malay States government placed an order for the purchase of 12 US-made locomotives, although locomotives made in Britain were available at a higher price and with a longer delivery date.[24] In a further example, a British firm, John Jackson Ltd, which in the late 1920s was granted an important contract for the dockyard of the Singapore Naval Base, purchased goods and dredging machines worth S$599,900 from the American

Bucyrus Company in preference to purchasing British-made machinery.[25] Clearly, British firms with their own economic interests were not always prepared to support the colonial government's policy of purchasing British-made goods when they were available. Thus, despite the shift towards trade protectionism, and the preference generally given to British interests, US firms did, on occasion, succeed in securing some contracts usually given to British firms.

During the interwar years, US manufacturers continued to use the services of local merchant firms in Malaya. These were predominantly British, but included Chinese and Indian traders, and US trade intermediaries played an increasing role. The US consul continued to provide vital information regarding trade opportunities for US manufacturers and with effective marketing by British merchant firms, Chinese businesses, and trade intermediaries in Malaya, more US products were able to enter the Malayan market. Similarly, local merchant firms there held US agencies in increasing numbers.

A comparison made in the listing of American agencies in the *Singapore and Malayan Directory* of 1932 and 1941 showed a 100 per cent increase, from 114 to 228, in the number of firms supplying goods. These goods ranged from canned food to boilers for the mining industries.[26] Due to their demand, British merchant firms were driven to represent US products and an increasing number of merchant firms were soon marketing them aggressively, particularly American automobiles. With its Ford agency established prior to World War I, Wearne Brothers was among the first merchant firms to hold an automobile agency. Apart from Wearne, the most successful firm in the business was the Borneo Company Ltd, holding, among others, a General Motors agency. (For a detailed discussion on the role of merchant firms in the Malayan automobile market, see Chapter 6.)[27] British merchant firms continued to provide distribution services for US manufacturers post-World War II, as examined in detail in Section 3.4.

It is also evident, that US manufacturers were increasingly being represented by Chinese trading firms. This is contrary to claims made by Huff who suggests that there was a lack of participation by local Asian (Chinese and Indian) firms in the agency system.[28] However, Cycle & Carriage, a Chinese family firm which was registered as a public listed company in Kuala Lumpur in 1926 and based in Singapore, held agencies for both British and US cars.[29] United Motor Works Ltd (UMW), registered as a public listed company in Singapore in 1927, began dealing with Ford Model-T spare parts in 1916 and this Chinese family firm only dealt with US goods.[30] (For a selective listing of other Chinese firms dealing with US consumer goods, see Table 3.5 and Appendix B.)

Similarly, there were increasing numbers of US trading intermediaries distributing US products in Malaya. Some set up branches in Singapore to handle the increase in trade around the region. By 1935, Getz Brothers & Co, Dodge & Seymour, Jacks & Company, Connell Brothers Company Ltd and Muller & Phipps were included among the US merchant firms, again as can be seen in Appendix B.

The US consul and vice consul in Singapore and Penang respectively continued to regularly file reports on trade and investment opportunities in Malaya with the

Department of State in Washington and play a role in the protection and promotion of US trade in Malaya. The protection rendered by the consul was mainly towards the tin and rubber exports to the US and it was the consul's main duty to 'investigate and report promptly on conditions in these two important industries liable to affect prices to the disadvantage of the American consuming public'.[31]

In addition, the US consul handled complaints from US manufacturers regarding infringement of their patent rights in Malaya, and in the 1920s and 1930s they contested cases of trade infringement. US manufacturers were wary of the Chinese and Japanese traders who were selling imitations of US-branded goods cheaply. Examples of these product infringement cases included branded pencils, gramophone needles and lingerie.[32] The consul's promotion of US trade is evident in its role as an intermediary in establishing business ties between Malaya and the US. Aware that their marketing needed to be tailored to Asian consumers, US manufacturers sought the direction of the consul[33] who was happy to give advice on market trends and tastes to these manufacturers.[34] By the 1930s, there were many trade enquiries filed with the US consulate general in Singapore, expressing interest in both trade and investment opportunities and in establishing agency agreements with ethnic Chinese and Indian merchant houses in Singapore and the Malay States. The US products marketed by these merchant houses ranged from brassieres to pencils, pens, typewriter ink, canned food, fruits and stick pretzels.[35]

From the data in Table 3.5 several deductions can be made. First, the list of agency agreements suggests that US firms sought and received help from the US consulate in Singapore for their efforts to establish agency agreements with local firms – mainly Chinese and to a lesser extent Indian. Second, despite the efforts to promote US trade, the estimated imports (taking several limitations into account, trade secrecy, the non-reporting of further business deals and the finalisation of agency agreements) from US firms, suggests there was only a very small market for US goods in Malaya. For example, the import figures for US products were from a low of S$193 to a high of only S$32,000. In addition, 'price competitiveness' remained an important factor in building businesses in the competitive Malayan market. Among reasons cited by local firms for business failure with US manufacturers was, for example, the expensive price in comparison with products from China.

American trade strategies – securing wider support from British merchant firms, Chinese and Indian firms, as well as US trade intermediaries and including the US consul's efforts to promote trade – failed to make a significant impact on the Malayan market. There was only a marginal rise in the percentage of imports from the US from the pre-World War I levels of 1.5 per cent to just less than 4 per cent during the interwar years. Overall, US imports to Malaya remained small.

Table 3.5 Agency agreements established by the US Consulate General in Singapore between US and local firms, 1937–June 1939

(a) Imports from US firms, 1937–1938

Local firms	*American firms*	*Imports (S$)*
Standard Machine Co, Singapore, SS	Regal Typewriter Co, NY	677
	Consolidated Sewing Machine Co, NY	1,936
	Wholesale Typewriter Co, NY	484
	International Typewriter Exchange, NY	3,520
	Moss Typewriter Co, NY	264
	Shitman Wald Company, NY	88
Heng Huat & Co, Singapore, SS	Witherbee Storage Battery Co, PA	1,408
	Balder Electric Co, MO	774
	S & M Lamp Co, CA	96
	Reliable Products Co, CA	1,302
	Champion Products Co, IL	241
Milady, Singapore, SS	Alexander & Co, NY	387
	French Sardine & Co, Inc, CA	5,632
	Liberty Gold Fruit Co, CA	5,280
	Adolph Hurst & Co, CA	352
	King Shirt Co, Inc, NY	968
Sim Ah Kow & Co, Singapore, SS	Hollywood Neckwear Co, CA	281
	American Commerce Co, CA	792
	Kramer Novelty Co, NY	704
	A.J. Flick & Co, CA	Unsatisfactory terms
	John Dunn & Sons, NY	Unsatisfactory terms
Nouveaux Co, Singapore, SS	Pioneer Rubber Co, Willard, Ohio	5,280
	Butler Brothers, CA	21,120
	Regal Musical Instrument Co, IL	1,760
M. Banerji & Co, Singapore, SS.	Park Drug Co, NY	5,280
	Mannington Mills Inc, NJ	440
	Silverman Brothers, R.I.	880
	Mohawk Carpet Mills Inc, NY	352
	The Astrup Co, Cleveland, OH	No business done
C. Motte & Co, Singapore, SS	Jeannette Glass Company, PA	5,280
	H.J. McGrath & Co, NY	1,760
	Universal Merchandise Co, NY	3,520
	Tropex Sales Co, NY	3,520
	American Chicle Co, NY	21,120
	American Chewing Products Corp, NJ	1,056
	United Packers, Chicago, IL	1,056
	Allen B. Wrisley Distributing Co, NY	880
Vijay Anandan, Singapore, SS	Roovers Brothers, NY	356
	Ketterlinus Lithographic Mf. Co, PA	1,760
		97,085

continued

Table 3.5 continued

(b) Imports from US firms for the year ended June 1939

Local firms	*American firms*	*Imports (S$)*
Monod & Company, Singapore, SS	Great Eastern Packing & Paper Stock Corp, NY	32,810
	Atlantic Brass & Copper Co, NY	
Hup Guan Chop, Singapore, SS	Weirton Steel Company, West Virginia	26,055
C.S. Soh, Singapore, SS	W.D. Blood & Co, Inc, NY	2,895
	Spane Argo, IL	528
Chin Ho & Co, Singapore, SS	William L. Barell, NY	2,823
C. Motte & Co, Singapore, SS	Trans-Ocean Export Company, NY	1,976
Sim Ah Kow & Co, Singapore, SS	Turner & Seymour Manufacturing Co, CONN	1,930
	Undine Twine Mills Co, CONN	308
Nouveax Co, Singapore, SS	Clemente Lopez & Co, NY	1,930
	Allied National Co, NY	1,930
	Ortis Export Co Inc, NY	965
Rahamin Penhaus, Singapore, SS	Arrco Playing Card Co, IL	530
United Agencies, Singapore, SS	Globe-Union Incorp, NY	386
	Chestermen Leeland Company, NY	193
Cosmopolitan Trading Co, Singapore, SS	Metropolitan Picture Frame Corp, IL	289
		75,601

(c) Reasons for business failures for the year ended June 1939

Eng Aun Tong, Singapore, SS	American prices far too expensive. Alternative is securing supplies from Shanghai.
United Agencies, Singapore, SS	Firm not able to handle hardware line.
Cosmopolitan Trading Co, Singapore, SS	Turbular Chromium furniture: No response; Managing partner contemplating trip to the US.
Mahwa Sporting Goods Co, Singapore, SS	Poor response, indenting through local American agents.
Lam Kheng & Co, Singapore, SS	Prices not competitive.

Source: Adapted from ANM, 'Annual Administrative Report', Singapore, Straits Settlements, 17 July 1939.

3.3 US FDI in Malaya, 1919–1957

FDI in Malaya grew rapidly after World War I and there were new entrants into tin mining (see Chapter 2). Although the British continued to dominate the rubber industry in Malaya, there were also Danish, Belgian, French and Japanese firms in the rubber industry. New entrants were also seen in other sectors. For example, the Japanese set up the first iron-ore mine in 1920 in Johore and soon dominated the iron industry, mainly in the Unfederated Malay States.[36] As well as the new entrants in Malayan industries, US FDI also expanded in Malaya between 1919 and the early 1940s. In the rubber industry, USRC successfully acquired its first plantation in Kedah in 1919. Between 1920 and 1928, USRC acquired seven plantations consisting of 31,000 acres (discussed in Chapter 5).[37] However, some US ventures were sold to British firms. In 1920, the Mexican Crude Rubber Company Inc of Detroit, Michigan, which began planting rubber in Selangor in 1912, sold out to a British rubber concern.[38] By 1922, the value of US rubber investments totalled S$12.07 million (US$6.1 million) with, significantly, 82 per cent coming from USRC alone.[39]

The period after World War I also saw the only US entrant into the Malayan tin mining industry, when the Yukon Gold Company successfully acquired mining leases in the states of Perak and Selangor. There were also a few instances when individual investments failed to come to fruition. In the 1920s, the New York Orient Mines prospected for iron ore in Malaya but failed to find suitable properties, unlike the Japanese, who were successful in the industry.[40]

In other instances, US firms used the tactic of investing in Malaya through Canadian subsidiaries in order to placate British reservations towards US investment. The most striking case was Ford Canada's establishment of Ford Malaya in 1926, which became the pioneer automobile manufacturer in Malaya when it set up the first assembly plant in the region. In 1927, General Motors also submitted an application to set up an assembly plant in Singapore. Oddly, however, General Motors failed to emulate Ford and make the application through its Canadian or recently acquired British subsidiary, and had its application rejected.

As well as increased activities in the resource and manufacturing sectors, expansion was also seen in the service sector. During this period, existing US MNEs also expanded their investments by setting up subsidiaries and some, mainly in the service sector, began to set up branches headquartered in Singapore, with distributors in the major cities in the Malay States. Singapore acted as the regional platform for these US subsidiaries for not only South East Asia but also, in some cases, the wider Asian region.

Apart from the establishment of purchasing offices by the four largest US rubber manufacturers in Malaya – USRC, Firestone, Goodyear and BFGoodrich – another US tyre manufacturer, the Fisk Tire & Rubber Co, set up a purchasing office in the 1920s.[41] These leading US rubber concerns added sales units to their organisations in Malaya, and the addition of local selling agents led to an increase in the US share of trade in rubber goods. For instance, in the 1922 *Singapore and Malayan Directory*, BFGoodrich Rubber Co (Singapore) Ltd was listed as a manufacturer of motorcar, cycle and solid tyres, mechanical and rubber goods, distributing its products in Malaya, Dutch East Indies, Thailand, Burma, Ceylon, Indochina and India. By 1929, the US was one of the major suppliers, with 28 per cent of total imports of rubber goods to Malaya.[42]

In addition to two US banks, Citibank and American Express, several US insurance firms and shipping lines set up their main offices in Singapore and expanded into major nearby cities including Kuala Lumpur, Penang, Ipoh and Seremban in the Malay States. By 1935, there was an American Foreign Insurance Association for fire, car and marine insurance representing several US insurance firms. American shipping lines also set up branches, mainly in Singapore, which included among others, the American & Oriental Line, the American Lloyd Agency Ltd, American President Lines Ltd and the Java-New York Line, while the American & Manchurian Line was located in Kuala Lumpur. In the entertainment industry, American films had also made an impact among Malayan audiences. By 1941 there were branches in Singapore of the American film distributors Metro Goldwyn Mayer, Universal Pictures and United Artist Corporation.

There were also divestments in the service sector. These included multinational banking, a sector in which US institutions had limited experience. The Asia Banking Corporation, which was launched in Singapore on 3 January 1921, closed down after just three years of operation. The corporation had been set up in China in February 1918 with several branches throughout China, Hong Kong and Manila and was notably formed by a powerful consolidation of American banks for the purpose of entering the field of Chinese banking.[43]

There was, then, increased US investment activity, mainly in the resource and service sectors, in Malaya during the 1920s, but it was followed by a period of stagnation, reflecting the general pattern of US FDI (see Table 3.6).[44] Total US FDI in Malaya remained small and did not exceed S$64.2 million (US$30 million) between 1923 and 1943.[45] Out of the total of US FDI worldwide, South East Asia experienced a slight increase from 2.2 to 2.9 per cent in 1930 and 1943 respectively. This increase was seen in resource-based investments: tin, rubber and mainly oil in the Dutch East Indies.[46] In contrast, as shown in Table 3.7, US FDI in most of the neighbouring regions saw a decline in percentage. This decrease is not surprising given the slower growth of world FDI in the 1930s and 1940s and also the mounting conflicts between host governments and resource-based MNEs in Latin America – for example, the nationalisation of foreign oil companies (including US-owned) in Mexico in 1938.[47] However, it should be noted that the percentages of US FDI in these regions were still significantly higher than in South East Asia. US FDI in the Western hemisphere had surpassed British FDI in Mexico, Cuba and parts of Central America since 1919, and in Canada since 1922.[48]

As shown by Table 3.8, in 1936, US FDI per capita in Malaya was much higher than in Thailand, Indochina or oil-rich Dutch East Indies. By 1943, it was even higher than in the Philippines. Unlike the FDI of other metropolitan powers, the French (in Indochina), the British (in Malaya) and the Dutch (in Dutch East Indies), the percentage of US FDI in the Philippines was relatively small. In Indochina, the

Table 3.6 US FDI in South East Asia, 1930–1943 (US$ million)

Country	*1930*	*1933*	*1936*	*1943*[a]
Malaya	27.00[b]	20.00[b]	23.70 23.75[c]	27.00 27.05[c]
DEI	66.00	68.00	70.00[d]	80.30
Thailand	[b]	[b]	3.30[e]	3.30
Philippines	81.00	92.00	92.00[f]	99.30
Indochina	[b]	[b]	3.30[g]	1.00
Burma	n.a.	n.a.	n.a.	2.80
Total South East Asia	174.00	180.00	216.5	240.75

Notes:

a The figures for 1943 presumably refer to US FDI prior to Japanese rule in Malaya which officially began in February 1942 with the occupation of Singapore.

b Figures include Thailand and Indochina

c As a Canadian FDI, Ford's investment was not included in the FDI figures, thus, the estimate above refers to the par value of shares issued by Ford Malaya (1936) at S$99,800 (US$58,000).

d The above estimate did not include US$100 million in oil investments.

e Figures include Indochina.

f US Tariff Commission estimates valued at US$163.5 million.

g Figures include Thailand.

Sources: Memorandum of Association of Ford Motor Company of Malaya, Limited; Director's Minutes, Ford Malaya, 1926–36; Callis, *Foreign Capital in South East Asia*, p. 32; *American Direct Investments in Foreign Countries*, US Department of Commerce, Washington, 1936; *Census of American-Owned Assets in Foreign Countries*, US Treasury Department, 1947; Philippines Trade Report No. 118, US Tariff Commission, 1937, pp. 189–90.

Table 3.7 Percentage share of US FDI by region, 1930 and 1943

Region	*1930*	*1943*
Canada	26.1	23.2
South America	20.8	21.2
West Indies	13.6	9.2
Central America and Mexico	11.8	7.8
Total South East Asia	2.2	2.9
Total World US FDI (US$ million)	7,841.0	7,365.0

Sources: 1930: *A New Estimate of US Investment Abroad*, US Department of Commerce, Washington, 1931; 1943: *Census of American-Owned Assets in Foreign Countries*, US Treasury Department, 1947.

metropolitan power held 97 per cent of the Western FDI and in both Malaya and Dutch East Indies the metropolitan powers had a 70 per cent share of the FDI, whilst in the Philippines, US direct investments accounted for only 50 per cent.[49]

Several factors accounted for the smaller percentage of US FDI in the Philippines.[50] First, the economic legacy of Spain, as the previous colonial power, was responsible for a substantial amount of FDI. In 1936, for example, 28 per cent

Table 3.8 US FDI per capita in South East Asia, 1936 and 1943 (US$ million)

US FDI per capita (approximate)	*1936*	*1943*
Malaya	5.04	5.19
	5.05[a]	5.20[a]
DEI	1.00	1.15
Thailand	0.22	0.18
Philippines	5.75	5.17
Indochina	0.14	0.04
Burma	n.a.	2.8
Total South East Asia	n.a.	0.16

Note:
[a] Ford FDI estimates.

Sources: FDI figures: As Table 3.10.
Population estimates for Malaya: 1936 figures; Hartland, *Economic and Commercial Conditions in Malaya*, 1943 refers to 1947 figure; M.V. del Tufo, *Malaya, a report on the 1947 census of population*, Malaya, 1949, p. 39. DEI: 1936 and 1943 refers to the 1937 population figure, Lauriston Sharp, 'Colonial Regimes in South East Asia', *Far Eastern Survey* 15, 1946, p. 437. Thailand: 1936 population refers to 1937 figure; 1943 refers to 1947 figure; Charles Hirschman, 'Population and Society in Twentieth Century South East Asia', *Journal of South East Asian Studies* 25, 1994, pp. 381–417. Philippines: 1936 population refers to 1935 figure; Sharp, 'Colonial Regimes', p. 437. 1943 refers to 1948 figure; Hirschman, 'Population and Society'. Indochina: 1936 and 1943 refers to 1938 population figure; Sharp, 'Colonial Regimes'. Burma: 1943 refers to 1941 figure; Hirschman, 'Population and Society'.

of FDI in the Philippines was Spanish, followed by 11 per cent British and 8 per cent Japanese. In addition, there was no special incentive offered to US businesses to invest in the Philippines. The land laws and labour policies introduced in 1902 to protect the interest of the local Filipinos had limited the range of agricultural activities by US companies.[51] This included rigid restriction of private and corporate land holdings to not more than 2,500 acres with an initial lease of 25 years.[52] There was also a ban on the importation of Chinese labour into the Philippines following the Chinese exclusion laws imposed in the US.[53] Both the US government and US enterprises undertook efforts to liberalise these restrictions, but they were rejected by the Philippine Legislature, mainly in an effort to discourage substantial investments that would reinforce the dependence of the Philippine economy on the US market.[54] In fact there was a particular disincentive as the Americans were subjected to double taxation: once at home in the US and again in the the Philippines. This created a competitive disadvantage for Americans against other nationals who were taxed only in the Philippines. Porter (1940) argues,

> As an entrepot to the Far East, the Philippines has been almost a complete failure; but again it is not clear whether this should be charged up against the Philippines. As an outlet for investment, it has been quite insignificant, due partly to handicaps emanating from tax bureaus in Washington and from the American-controlled government at Manila.[55]

Another significant reason for the low level of US FDI was that, just as the British authorities in Malaya, there was apprehension within the Philippine government about US big business. US rubber firms were allowed to invest within the limits stipulated in laws and policies. But due to their preoccupation with large-scale planting, they failed to develop a rubber industry in their own colonial backyard, unlike their British and Dutch counterparts. The laws limiting the size of land holdings led some US rubber firms to invest in neighbouring countries instead. Thus, in 1943, American agricultural investments were highest in the Dutch East Indies then followed by Malaya (see Table 3.9). Finally, the anticipated US withdrawal from its Philippine colony increased the risk of long-term investments. The continuous agitation for independence by the Filipinos and unstable political situation remained an entry barrier for US investment and a major deterrent towards US FDI inflows.

Most US investments in South East Asia took the form of direct investments rather than licensing or joint ventures, because of the shortage of local entrepreneurs with adequate knowledge to participate in such ventures as well as a lack of managerial expertise and skilled workers. A high level of skills was needed in resource and market-seeking FDI. Choosing FDI over export strategies also gave US MNEs the opportunity to exploit their competitive advantages and to ensure the fulfilment of local requirements and demands. In Malaya and elsewhere in the region, Americans were keener to set up subsidiaries due to the distance and time that it took to report to parent companies (see Table 3.9). Mostly due to the popularity of their respective brands, some US MNEs, such as Singer Sewing Machine Co, Remington Rand Inc, and Western Electric Co of Asia, did set up branches in Malaya, in order to gain increasing control over product distribution influenced by the prospect of potential growth. These MNEs set up branch offices in Malaya to serve not just the local markets, but also the broader regional South East Asian markets.

The data in Table 3.9 confirms that US FDI in Malaya was tilted towards resource-seeking at US$16.5 million rather than market-seeking at US$4.1 million investment, a reflection of the general trading pattern between the two countries. The US was a major export market for Malayan products, but this was not the situation in the other direction. Out of the total US FDI in Malaya in 1943, the largest portion was invested in agriculture (primarily rubber, a twofold increase from the US$6.1 million seen in 1922). This was followed by tin-mining, trading and manufacturing.

US FDI grew rapidly in Malaya in the 1920s and 1930s, and was second highest in the region after the Dutch East Indies between 1930 and 1937, as indicated by Table 3.10. In 1937, Malaya's FDI per capita was four times higher than in the Dutch East Indies and the Philippines, while in Thailand, Burma and Indochina, FDI was markedly lower still. Overall in South East Asia, British FDI predominated, both in its colonies, Malaya and Burma, and also in independent Thailand. In 1937, British FDI accounted for 90 per cent of total FDI in Burma, mainly in the natural resource sector.[56] In Thailand, 74 per cent of FDI in 1938 came from British interests, with principal investments in the tin and teak

Table 3.9 US FDI in South East Asia by industry and business type, 1943 (US$ million)

(a) US FDI by industry

	M'fact	Mining	Oil	Public Utility	Agri	Trade	Finance	Misc	Total
Malaya	1.3 1.4[a]	3.4	[b]	[b]	13.1	2.7	[b]	5.1	27.0
DEI	4.6	[b]	34.0	[b]	35.2	5.4	[b]	1.1	80.3
Thailand	[b]	Nil	–	–	–	0.8	–	1.7	3.3
Philippines	16.2	b	9.6	30.7	10.4	17.0	8.6	4.8	99.3
Indochina	Nil	Nil	–	–	[b]	Nil	–	0.1	1.0
Burma	[b]	Nil	[b]	Nil	Nil	0.6	Nil	1.8	2.8
Total SEA	22.1	3.4	43.6	30.7	58.7	25.9	8.6	12.8	210.8
Total Asia	67.2	3.4	86.7	39.9	58.7	38.4	6.5	93.8	489.6
Total World	2,153.2	625.2	1,392.6	1,227.3	502.5	653.9	74.4	156.5	7,365.0

(b) US FDI by business type

	Corp	Branch	Others	Total
Malaya	14.60	9.3	2.87	26.8
DEI	37.20	42.4	0.77	80.4
Thailand	[c]	0.9	2.39	3.3
Philippines	67.40	25.9	6.00	99.3
Indochina	0.09	0.9	Nil	1.0
Burma	Nil	1.0	1.80	2.8
Total South East Asia	119.3	80.40	13.83	213.5

Notes:

a Include estimates for Ford Malaya's investment.

b Include in total.

c Less than US$50,000.

Source: 1943: *Census of American-Owned Assets in Foreign Countries*, US Treasury Department, 1947.

Table 3.10 South East Asia: FDI and FDI per capita, 1914, 1930 and 1937 (US$ million)

(a) FDI, 1914–1937	*1914*	*1930*	*1937*
Malaya	150	447	372
DEI	675	1,600	1,411
Thailand	25	75	90
Philippines	100	300	315
Indochina	75	255	302
Burma	n.a.	210	225
Total	1,025	2,887	2,715
(b) FDI per capita[a]			*1937*
Malaya			79.1
DEI			20.2
Thailand			6.2
Philippines			19.7
Indochina			13.1
Burma[b]			14.2
Total South East Asia			152.5

Notes for Table 3.10 (b):

a As Table 3.8.

b Burma's 1937 population refers to 1939 figures.

Sources: Callis, 'Foreign Capital in South East Asia', pp. 23, 36, 56, 70, 85, 108; Lauriston, 'Colonial Regimes', p. 437.

industries.[57] Meanwhile in 1936, the US Department of Commerce reported the existence of eight US firms with a capital of US$3.3 million in Thailand and Indochina.[58]

In summary, although US FDI remained small in Malaya, it was still the major host economy within the region, where investment was often preferred by US firms over the US colony of the Philippines, and certainly to other European colonies or Thailand. British FDI, which was far greater than any other country in Malaya, was concentrated within the British Empire, while US firms tended to direct their investment to the Americas.

Malaya enjoyed the highest FDI per capita, as well as the most rapid per capita growth rate in the South East Asian region at 4.1 per cent, in the years 1900 to 1929.[59] Table 3.11 section (b) shows that by 1929 Malaya's GDP per capita was greater than that of Japan and was approximately one-third that of the UK and the US. Malaya's wealth derived from the rapid growth of the tin and rubber sectors and the related processing industries, and was also greatly aided by the development of Singapore as one of the world's major ports.[60] Although Malaya's development was somewhat lopsided, with a high ratio of exports (almost entirely tin and rubber) to GDP, as high as 38 per cent in 1920, it was the most developed country in the region despite its relatively small land mass and population.[61] In conclusion, the British presence and Malaya's high growth rate were important

Table 3.11 South East Asia, Japan and metropolitan countries: GDP, 1870–1938 (1990 international dollars)[a]

(a) Growth of per capita GDP, average annual per cent		*1870–1900*	*1900–1929*
Malaya		n.a.	4.1
DEI[b]		0.4	1.7
Thailand		0.4	0.2
Philippines		–	1.4
Burma		–	0.8
Japan		1.4	1.7
UK		1.1	0.4
US		1.8	1.5
Netherlands		1.0	1.5
France		1.4	1.6
(b) GDP per capita[c]	*1870*	*1900*	*1929*
Malaya	n.a.	588	1,871
DEI[d]	611	659	1,078
Thailand	603	675	708
Philippines	n.a.	797	1,200
Burma	n.a.	605	753
Japan	650	980	1,614
UK	3,342	4,605	5,188
US	2,483	4,207	6,568
Netherlands	2,648	3,545	5,533
France	1,870	2,844	4,515

Notes:

a International dollars refer to a hypothetical currency that is used as a means of translating and comparing costs from one country to the other using the US dollar as a common reference point. A purchasing power parity exchange rate is used to convert local currency into international dollars equivalent to the purchasing power of the US dollar.

b 1870–1900 per capita growth refers to 1880–1900.

c Figures are three-year averages centred around the year shown except 1870 for the UK, the US, the Netherlands, and France, which are averages for 1870 and 1871.

d The 1870 figure refers to 1880.

Source: Huff, 'Monetization and financial development', p. 326.

factors that helped to attract some US FDI in Malaya, even though the region as a whole did not appeal to many US multinational investors.

During the Pacific War, Japanese occupation put an end to all US FDI in Malaya. In the post-World War II years, the political and economic risks that came with the Emergency of 1948 to 1960, the imposition of exchange controls and the winds of Independence inhibited US FDI flows into Malaya and the region. As seen elsewhere, exchange controls discouraged new FDI as the repatriation of dividends and profits were restricted. Similarly, in Malaya, the US dollar shortage led the colonial authorities to resist the establishment of American manufacturing investment unless a US dollar earning capacity could be shown.[62] The same rule applied to US investments in the UK.[63] The repatriation of profits from US investments was restricted by the Federation government.[64] World FDI recovered from the 1950s onwards, with US FDI accounting for 85 per cent of all new FDI flows. Most of it, however, went to the developed economies.[65] Malaya remained a marginal recipient of US FDI during the post-World War II years to Independence.

3.4 US trade during World War II and beyond

The outbreak of World War II in Europe in 1939 did not have any immediate impact on the Malayan economy. The patterns of trade between the US and Malaya did differ from those prevailing before World War II, although Malaya still benefited from the large volume of rubber and tin exports. The war seriously affected British industry and British war debts increased the need for US dollars. As the US was a major consumer of Malayan exports, Malaya played an important role in sustaining Britain's dollar earnings.

Trade between the US and Malaya steadily improved as shipping facilities in the US were unaffected by the war (when the US was yet to be attacked by Japan at Pearl Harbour) and US shipping was transferred from the Atlantic to the Pacific. As the war in Europe intensified, American sales increased as Malaya turned to US sources due to inadequate British and European sources of supply. However, the opportunity to develop trade on a wider scale was limited by the imposition of exchange controls in Malaya in mid-September 1939. Malaya was part of the Sterling Area – an economic block originated in the 1930s and made up of most of the British Empire (except Canada and British Honduras).[66] The Sterling Area discriminated against trade with 'hard currency' countries, mainly the US, in an effort to preserve dollars.[67]

Yet US imports did rise in 1940 to approximately S$33.2 million (US$15.6 million) from just S$19.3 million (US$10 million) in 1939.[68] The reasons were several. First, although strict interpretations were placed on 'essential' import products and import permits were required to purchase goods from countries not on a sterling basis, these restrictions were relaxed in the areas of foodstuff and machinery. Consequently, the US became the major supplier of both, as foodstuff and machinery were not available for export by countries in the Sterling Area.[69] Second, the US took over the main imports that had previously come from Germany and Japan, when trade with these now enemy countries was prohibited. The restriction on trade with Germany and Japan led to a rise in chemical and textile imports from the US. In spite of the handicap of a sharply appreciated US dollar against the Straits dollar which was tied to the pound sterling, demand for US products increased in many areas (besides the chemical and textile imports), including building materials, mine and estate supplies such as dredging equipment, hardware, paper and paper products, and foodstuff.[70]

Trade with the US continued to be favourable in terms of sizable dollar balances to Malaya due in large part to extensive US imports of rubber and tin. These commodities amounted to 80 per cent of total Malayan exports in 1940, 52 per cent of which went to the US. In 1939, these same commodities had made up a slightly lower share of total Malaysian exports at 71 per cent.[71]

The Japanese occupation from February 1942 to September 1945, however, halted all trade and investment activities in Malaya (for details refer to the three specific case studies discussed in Chapters 4, 5 and 6). Post-World War II Britain and its colonies required all kinds of goods for rehabilitation, but British industry was largely exhausted by its war effort and from the war damage. Hence, Britain was unable to provide sufficient goods for its own requirements let alone produce enough surpluses for export. This significantly changed the character of US imports into Malaya. Unable to purchase these goods from Britain, US exports into Malaya of cement, iron and steel, machinery items, cotton, grains and flour increased markedly. Machinery imports rose from 10 per cent (S$1.7 million) of the total value of machinery imports into Malaya in 1939 to 25 per cent (S$10.8 million) in 1948. Total Malayan imports of manufactured articles from the US rose substantially from less than 6 per cent in 1939 to more than 21 per cent in 1948. Over the same time period, US sales of cotton yarn and manufactures to Malaya jumped from 1 per cent of total Malayan imports in that category to 46 per cent.[72]

A shortage of rice supplies made wheat and wheat flour the largest single item in Malaya's import trade which accounted for approximately 19 per cent of total imports in 1948 and 27 per cent in the first half of 1949. Although considerable progress was made in expanding its rice production, Malaya remained in rice-deficit and dependent chiefly upon Burma, Thailand and Indochina for supplies. Post-war shortfalls of rice exports from these countries had necessitated increased purchases of wheat and wheat flour from the US, but from 1948, wheat and wheat flour were obtained from sterling sources.[73] Hence, purchases from the US dropped dramatically to US$0.5 million in 1948 as compared to US$ 5.6 million in 1947.[74]

By the late 1940s, Malaya experienced foreign trade deficits because of the expansion of imports. In 1949, trade suffered a deficit three times larger than the deficit of 1948. As shown in Table 3.12, Malayan trade with the US suffered a deficit in the post-World War II years in contrast to the surplus enjoyed in the

Table 3.12 Foreign trade in Malaya, 1937–1949 (S$ thousands for 1937–39, 1947, M$ thousands for 1948, 1949)

Year	*Imports*	*Exports*	*Balance*
Annual Averages, 1937–1939	615,714	734,306	+118,592
1947	1,367,453	1,294,878	–72,575
1948	1,785,758	1,724,162	–61,596
1949 (Jan–June)	936,626	790,181	–146,445

Note: Figures include data from Singapore.

Sources: 'Malayan Basic Industries Respond to American Demand during 1940', *Foreign Commerce Weekly*, 19 April 1941; 'An Economic Review of Malaya, 1945–1949', London: Central Office of Information, 1950, p. 221; 'Economic Review of Malaya, 1948', Lot File Malaya, Box 14, US Department of Commerce, RG59, General Records of the Department of State Consular Correspondence, NARA, College Park, Maryland, USA.

pre-war years, which were exceeded only by imports from the UK and the Dutch East Indies. However, exports to the US fell significantly in 1949, declining further in 1950.[75]

There were other factors that led to the drop in US imports in 1949. These included tighter controls on US imports when Britain was able to start meeting demands from Malaya and neighbouring regions.[76] A ban was also imposed by the Federated Malay States and Singapore governments on the issuance of permits for imports of textiles from all hard currency sources in June 1948. This ban discriminated against US textiles.[77] Furthermore, during the same year as the ban on permits for imports of textiles, another ban was imposed by the Singapore and Federated Malay States colonial governments on the importation of automobiles of over 20 horsepower from the US. This was aimed to thwart the great demand for US automobiles (including British-made Fords) as compared to other British models during this period.[78]

British authorities restricted direct importation of US goods not only to conserve dollars but also to protect British industries in the home country. The question of the importation of US refrigerators provides a good example. Beginning in July 1949, these refrigerators had to be imported via Hong Kong for payment in sterling so as to save dollars. However, due to a technical mistake, licences were issued for direct importation of refrigerators (mainly of Kelvinator and Frigidaire brands) from the US. This led to a complaint by the Britain's trade commissioner in Malaya. He stated that this would affect British manufacturers of refrigerators as they would now have to compete with US refrigerator manufacturers. The commissioner felt that such direct access to the Malayan market would cause local firms to import from the US manufacturers in the US and, consequently, damage development of production capacity in Britain.[79]

By 1950, US imports declined to pre-World War II levels. Exchange controls imposed after World War II discriminated against direct imports from the US and were an important factor in reducing the total value and volume of imports. The controls initially had minimum impact as imports from the US were permitted by the British authorities in Malaya to be brought in via Hong Kong, a move taken by the authorities in response to demands made by local importers to purchase US goods.[80] This reprieve, however, was short lived, with the imposition of tighter exchange control against hard currency imports and the devaluation of the pound in September 1949.[81]

With the devaluation of the British pound, US goods suddenly became much more expensive in terms of the Malayan dollar, and in the open market in Hong Kong, US dollars also sold at a premium, making it very expensive to import US goods via Hong Kong. A good example to illustrate this is the decline in the sales of US typewriters from 80 per cent of the Malayan market in 1948 to 60 per cent and 50 per cent in 1949 and 1950 respectively.[82] Despite their increased prices, certain US goods, including luxury goods, continued to be in demand and brought into Malaya via Hong Kong.[83] Merchant firms brought US goods into Malaya via Hong Kong when permits for direct importation from the US were denied to them.

Henry Waugh & Co, a merchant firm with headquarters in Singapore and branches in major cities throughout Malaya, represented large US firms as well as British and German firms, and was the sole agent for US manufacturers of strategic and near strategic goods such as industrial engines, mining machinery and pharmaceuticals. There was an increased demand for such goods in the early 1950s. When not securing the import permits for these goods from Malaya, the firm brought in US goods via Hong Kong. In spite of a 4.5 per cent duty on goods imported via Hong Kong, such imports continued due to a high demand for certain US products.[84] However, any increase in US imports into Malaya during this period was marginal.

US manufacturers were also able to penetrate the trade barriers by working in cooperation with British merchant firms. In addition to large British merchant firms including Boustead, Borneo Co Ltd and Sime Darby in the 1940s and 1950s, there were other smaller-sized British merchant firms holding distributorships for US manufacturers. These included John Dickinson & Co Ltd, and Harper Gilfillan & Co. British merchant firms began to move from representing US automobiles to other US products, including foodstuff, consumer goods, and strategic and near strategic goods. The need for merchant firms to secure competitive products from US manufacturers and the need for those manufacturers to secure the services of agents to distribute and market their products, shows that the relationship between US and British businesses was at times more complementary than competitive.

In the 1950s, British merchant firms took several steps to secure distributorships from American manufacturers. Borneo Co Ltd stressed the need to look out for new products from the US and sometimes sent agents there to secure new lines of business or to seek new suppliers.[85] Letters were also sent to US firms seeking opportunities for franchises, highlighting the company's ability to do a 'first class competent marketing job.'[86] Borneo Co Ltd admitted that its business was 'heavily orientated' towards the US, holding franchises for, among others, Campbell Soups, Sheaffer, General Electric Refrigerators and Yale.[87]

The significant rise of US imports from Malaya, in part facilitated by the intermediary role provided by British merchant firms, during the early post-World War II years, was important for Malaya's recovery. The US remained Malaya's major buyer of tin and rubber, giving support to Malaya's export industries and boosting Malaya's dollar earnings.[88]

In 1950, the US remained Malaya's main consumer of rubber, purchasing 30 per cent of Malaya's rubber exports. However, by 1952, the US fell second to Britain with rubber purchases of 26 per cent compared to Britain's 30 per cent. The fall in US rubber purchases was due to increased production of synthetic rubber and increased purchases from the Dutch East Indies. Despite the fall in rubber purchases, trade with the US, mainly in tin and rubber, contributed towards the sterling dollar pool. From 1948 to 1950 Malaya contributed US$650 million to the Sterling Area's reserves.[89] For Britain, Malaya was the 'greatest material prize in South East Asia'.[90] In 1955, the Federation alone contributed M$670 million (US$218 million) to the Sterling Area dollar pool.[91]

While US imports remained limited in Malaya due to the small and competitive Malayan market, to a certain extent the chances of greater US participation in Malayan trade were partly impeded by the British government's efforts to restrict trade within the Empire and the Sterling Area. The official policy of the Sterling Area and the preference shown towards British-owned businesses in Britain demonstrated the metropolitan government's attitude: the strategic interests of the metropole took priority over Malaya's.

3.5 US–Malayan economic relations, 1919–1957

During World War II and immediately afterwards until 1957, the US continued to be Malaya's largest export market and remained one of Malaya's biggest consumer of tin and rubber. US imports from Malaya continued to have an impact on Malaya's dollar earnings. However, despite the large Malayan exports to the US, imports from the US remained small.

Several factors accounted for the low US imports in the region. First was the low purchasing power of the population despite a relatively growing population base. Thus, US firms preferred to target sales in the developed economies of Canada and Europe, where the purchasing power of the population was far greater. Second, the Americans were late-comers on the scene and had to compete in an already crowded South East Asian market. In most South East Asian countries, the predominance of trade with the metropole was evident – with the British in Malaya and Burma as well as in independent Thailand, the Dutch in the Dutch East Indies, and the French in Indochina. Finally, notwithstanding the free trade practices supported by the British and Dutch, the French pursued prohibitionist policies in Indochina where preference was often given to metropolitan trade.

As discussed in Chapter 2, US firms depended upon British merchant firms and Chinese entrepreneurs to expand their trade in Malaya, and US competitive success was seen in a range of consumer products such as lubricating oil, machinery, electrical apparatuses and automobiles. From the interwar years until Independence, the relationship between the British merchant firms, Chinese entrepreneurs and US firms in Malaya was mutually supportive.

Generally, US FDI that did come to the region did so because it was attracted to South East Asia's natural resources, system of governance, political climate and infrastructure. In addition the British presence and Malaya's high growth rate attracted US FDI, although such US investment remained small. Although the US remained one of the major buyers of Malayan tin and rubber, the capital invested in both industries was relatively small compared to investments made by British firms. Malaya lacked sufficiently large quantities of accessible mineral resources (except for tin-ores) that could attract US MNEs with their financial resources and technological superiority, to invest on as large a scale as they had done in Canada, Mexico and South America. As outlined in Chapter 2, the oil industry in Borneo and the Dutch East Indies was already controlled by British and Dutch interests and therefore limited US FDI in oil in the region. In addition, there were periodic restrictions on US interests in Malaya. Despite US FDI in the South East Asian region being minimal, a number of US MNEs did enter into the Malayan market, while others elected to invest in neighbouring countries in the region.

4 Mining

Yukon Gold Company to Pacific Tin

The Yukon Gold Company (YGC) first invested in Malaya just after World War I and was the sole US entrant in the Malayan tin mining industry. YGC was owned by the Guggenheim Brothers, who were actively involved in the development of mining properties worldwide and controlled 75 to 80 per cent of the world's production of silver, copper and lead by 1915.[1] Because of its ownership by the Guggenheims, YGC benefited from managerial, technological and financial advantages, elements that are key to a successful high-capital intensive venture. The financial advantages made it possible for YGC to undertake innovative ventures in Malaya, and use their extensive experience in the gold fields of the Yukon and California to replicate these earlier successful mining projects. Tin and rubber formed the two main pillars of the Malayan economy and thus YGC, which in 1939 became the Pacific Tin Consolidated Corporation (PacTin), makes for an informative and revealing case study.

First, however, it is pertinent to briefly outline the history of the tin industry in Malaya and examine the evolution of Western penetration into a business sector that was dominated by local Chinese firms, before tracing the growth of US FDI in the sector. There is also discussion of the extent of British government control over US FDI flows and the efforts of US MNEs to invest in the Malayan tin mining industry. An overview of the relationship between business and government in Malaya is provided, in order to shed light on the effect of regulation in the industry.

4.1 The Malayan tin industry before World War I

In the late nineteenth century, Malaya became the world's largest producer of tin, producing about one-third of the world's total supply by 1883.[2] From 1895 to 1914, tin became the leading revenue for the Malayan administrators. Chinese miners, who aggressively advanced the economic value of tin mining, had replaced the Malays who had earlier monopolised the industry.[3] Between 1874 and 1896, Chinese miners were the main producers of tin in Malaya.

In the late nineteenth century, with the growth of the tin plate industry and the diminishing output of tin from Cornish sources in England and then Australian mines, tin prices rose significantly.[4] During this time, British authorities in Malaya offered special concessions in the form of advantageous leases and reduction of tin duties in an attempt to encourage Western firms to participate in the Malayan tin-mining industry. Although 35 companies were registered in Britain to mine tin in Malaya between 1882 and 1897, most failed in their ventures. Their unrealistically ambitious schemes, the high costs of employing European staff, the difficulty in employing Chinese labourers as compared to the relative ease with which Chinese mine owners were able to do so,[5] the use of expensive European machinery and, most importantly, the failure to adapt to local mining conditions, all contributed to the failure of these British companies.[6]

There were also two Australian firms that mined tin in Perak in 1883: the Sandhurst Company and the Melbourne Tin Mining Company. Both soon closed after ten and eleven years respectively.[7] In 1897, only four Western firms remained active. These were the Gopeng Mining Company and the Societe des Etains de Kinta in Perak, the Malay States Tin Mining Company in Selangor and the Pahang Corporation Ltd in Pahang.[8]

In 1892 Cornish mining interests floated the Gopeng Mining Company in London.[9] Using American equipment, Douglas Osborne and G. Pike of Gopeng introduced a new technique called hydraulic mining, which was already in use in California gold mines.[10] This technique was perfected over time, providing the springboard for Western penetration into tin mining industry in Malaya. By 1905, there were nine hydraulic mines, with only one being Chinese-owned, in the Federated Malay States.[11] This marked the successful beginnings of FDI in the Malayan tin mining industry.

Like tin mining, the Malayan tin smelting industry was dominated by ethnic Chinese in the late nineteenth century. However, unlike the tin mining industry, in which it took a long time for Western MNEs to make inroads and not until 1920 to really challenge local Chinese domination, the tin smelting industry was penetrated as early as 1896. Again, in contrast to the tin mining industry where it took a number of Western firms to make a significant impact, it was only one locally registered firm, the Straits Trading Company (STC), with European expatriates (mainly British) as shareholders that initially challenged local Chinese dominance in the tin smelting industry.[12] STC had access to European banks, and initially borrowed from the Chartered Bank of India, Australia and China where it was able to secure funds at lower interest rates than Chinese ore buyers.[13] The firm made concerted efforts to secure the purchase of tin-ore from several tin-producing states and due to its cash rich position it soon became one of the major buyers of Malayan tin.

At times, STC's efforts were facilitated by the support of local British authorities and the company was thus able to gain a competitive edge over rival Chinese smelters. This support came principally in the form of concessions given by the Selangor and Sungei Ujong authorities in April and November 1886, respectively. The firm was initially given exclusive rights to export tin-ore for three years by both states and in Selangor this concession was extended for another two years. However, in Perak the British authorities, concerned at a possible monopoly of tin-ore export by STC and anticipating strong opposition from Chinese smelters, did not provide any concessions to the firm. A further competitive advantage provided by the colonial authorities to STC over its Chinese rivals, even in Perak, was the lower duties levied against the firm.[14]

One Chinese smelter established in Penang in 1898 that did offer some competition to STC in the tin smelting industry, the Eastern Smelting Co Ltd, was bought in July 1911 by British interests and to secure financial access was floated in London as a free-standing firm.[15] By then, STC had a major lead over its rivals, both Eastern Smelting and the small Chinese smelters. By 1911, STC smelted approximately 70 per cent of the Federated Malay States total tin exports compared to 50 per cent in 1901. The Chinese smelters' share in the years 1910 to 1914 averaged 15 per cent while the remaining 15 per cent was in the hands of Eastern Smelting.[16]

Despite ostensibly supporting competition, the British allowed STC greater control by taking steps to check Chinese dominance in the tin smelting industry. In contrast, local British authorities resisted attempts by US business interests to invest in the tin smelting industry as detailed below.

4.2 Business, government and tin

At the turn of the twentieth century, both the local British authorities and the metropolitan government were guarding all sectors of the Malayan tin industry against foreign ownership, but mainly from the US. The preference given to British smelters was also evident when US firms attempted to participate in the Malayan tin smelting industry. In 1900, an American engineer announced plans for the erection of a smelter at Telok Anson using petroleum refuse from Sumatra as fuel. With S$1 million he estimated production of 50 tons of refined tin per day. Telok Anson was chosen because of its location, at the time being the gateway to the Kinta tin mining district in Perak and only 160 miles from the oilfields in Langkat, Sumatra. Petroleum refuse was chosen over coal as this meant increased output at lower cost.[17]

The proposed scheme at Telok Anson is one example of American efforts to provide competition to STC. Aside from a local newspaper report, nothing substantial was heard of this scheme again.[18] Another serious attempt to compete with STC was made in 1902 by the International Tin Company (ITC), a US corporation registered in the state of New Jersey on 19 November 1902 with a capitalisation of US$1 million and with shareholders from the mining and smelting business in the US and worldwide. These shareholders included key players from the Standard Oil Company and the Amalgamated Copper Company namely, C.D. Burrage, Albert C. Burrage and Henry H. Rogers.[19]

Other American trusts involved in ITC were the United States Steel Corporation, the largest US producer of tin plates, and its subsidiary, the American Tin Plate Company. The main objective of ITC was to purchase from Malaya 70 per cent Malayan production of tin-ore and to smelt it in the US.[20] The ore, shipped as return freight from Malaya to the US on Standard Oil steamers, would provide a ready supply of tin to these US tinplate manufacturers, allowing Standard Oil to obtain better tin plate rates from them. Standard Oil's main products were packed in tin cans, and the demand for kerosene in the region meant the company was among the largest users of tin cans.[21] ITC invested S$100,000 in the Federated Malay States and Straits Settlements through large purchases of land, office buildings and equipment. They also spent S$250,000 erecting a smelter in Bayonne, New Jersey.[22] The construction of this smelter was sponsored by the US Steel Corporation.[23]

However, ITC failed to carry out its plan when, on 1 June 1903, the Federated Malay States legislature passed a law imposing a prohibitive tax of 33 per cent on ores exported to countries outside the Straits Settlements.[24] An equivalent rebate would be given on all ore smelted in the Straits.[25] The protest filed by the US government with the metropolitan government in early 1904 failed to bring any results.[26]

The 1903 legislation, advocated by both Frank Swettenham, high commissioner of the Federated Malay States, and William Treacher, resident general, was clearly designed to retain control of the Malayan tin industry. As the US was the largest buyer of Straits smelted tin, had ITC been able to go ahead to procure 70 per cent of Malaya's tin-ore, American interests would have consequently obtained control of the entire industry in Malaya and thus been able to control the price of tin.[27] The establishment of smelting works in the US would presumably have lead to a protective duty against smelted tin, meaning that in the future only tin-ore could be exported to the US.[28] The British authorities, perhaps feeling it was part of their colonial responsibility in Malaya, deemed it important to maintain value-added activities such as smelting rather than just becoming a primary commodity exporter.

The US companies' attempt to take control of tin consumption was in the end badly misjudged. First, the export duty acted as a major deterrent. In addition, attempts to control one of the largest smelting works, STC, failed as shares of the company were widely distributed and firmly held by various European shareholders.[29] STC received widespread support from the 'expatriate European mercantile capital' in Singapore because of its substantial profits. In Singapore nearly all the 'local' business leaders were listed as its shareholders in the Share Register list of 1901–1906.[30]

The failed attempts did not deter ITC, which instead offered the alternative of a merger with STC in May 1907. This meant that ITC was willing to invest in the Malayan tin smelting industry, diverting from its original plan to smelt tin in the US.[31] This merger plan also failed, when the Federated Malay States government passed legislation that empowered it to refuse to allow a company to purchase ore with the intention of securing monopolistic control of the metal.[32] According to the resident general at the time:

> The precedent established by Lord Curzon in refusing to allow the Standard Oil Company to exploit Burma may very properly be followed in this case, and the principle recognised that British territory and British industries are not to be absorbed by American capitalists.[33]

This raises important questions concerning monopoly and competition. The British repeatedly hindered attempts by US big business to smelt tin in Malaya. As discussed in Chapter 1, the US government was also opposed to trusts as shown in 1911, when it ordered Standard Oil to be dissolved into several companies. The exclusion of Standard Oil from Burma in 1902 by the British government in India was aimed at preventing monopoly and not as a target against a non-British concern per se. As with oil, issues of national security had also become involved because of the strategic value of tin.[34] The precedent set by the colonial authorities in India was followed in Malaya and the imposition of the prohibitive export tax excluded the establishment of US big business, including the United States Steel Corporation and Standard Oil in Malaya. Concerted British efforts to impede US investment in the tin smelting industry helped Britain retain control of the industry in Malaya before World War I.

Repeated British attempts to impede US investments in the tin smelting industry helped retain British control of the industry in Malaya. US businesses tried to access Malaya's tin-ores through the ITC scheme to purchase tin-ore and then smelt it in the US, which would have offered a token amount of smelting in the host country. However, the scheme was blocked by the colonial authorities, which were suspicious of the intentions of large US firms with long-term interests in the Malayan smelting industry. The colonial authorities' main objective was to retain British control of such a strategic commodity as tin.

Prior to World War I, the L. Vogelstein Co of New York failed to win approval for its application to erect tin smelting works in Singapore, leading to a debate in Malaya on the British 'open door policy' and the entry of US business into the colony. A US subsidiary of a German enterprise active in non-ferrous metal prior to World War I, this firm started dealing in tin as early as 1905, acting as sole agent for the United States Smelting, Refining and Mining Co and was ranked among the six major US copper exporters.[35] The Colonial Office proposed to limit foreign ownership of the tin industry, especially during wartime, but the local British authorities and the governor of the Straits Settlements suggested that if Americans were not allowed to erect smelting works in Singapore, they would do so instead in Java and China. If that happened, the British would not only lose the revenue from these smelting works but also control of their output during wartime. Furthermore, according to the governor:

> Once restrictions begin it will go on increasing and I feel convinced that attempts to reserve the British Empire exclusively for British subjects will mean in the long run the loss of our foreign trade and the ruin of the Empire.[36]

The debate about L. Vogelstein Co's application to enter into the Malayan tin smelting industry was brought to a close when the firm was prohibited from doing business in Malaya after the outbreak of World War I because of its German origins.

Another firm to retain its interest in the tin smelting industry during World War I was the American Smelting and Refining Co. The firm set up a tin refinery at Perth Amboy, New Jersey between 1915 and 1916, while a subsidiary of the National Lead Co, the Williams, Harvey & Co of the United States, set up a smelter and refinery at Jamaica Bay, New York.[37] Both these smelters processed Bolivian concentrates and took advantage of the shipping difficulties in sending Bolivian ores to British smelters during World War I. Low-grade Bolivian ores were easier to smelt when mixed with alluvial ores. However, the prohibitive tariff introduced by the British in Nigeria in 1915, by then another source of alluvial ores, added to higher coal and labour costs and led to the closure of the two American smelters in 1929. Despite the problems encountered by these two smelters in the US, interest in purchasing Malayan ores continued. In the early 1920s, there was an enquiry from the Buckman Corporation of Florida to the US consul in Singapore regarding the feasibility of importing tin-ore, as the company had a client with an intention to set up a smelter in Jacksonville, Florida.[38]

World War II saw a shift of smelting operations from Europe and South East Asia to the US. The Texas City Smelter, a US government enterprise, began to gain importance because of the German occupation in Europe gaining control of Dutch and Belgian smelters at Arnhem and Hoboken, and the Japanese occupation in South East Asia controlling the Malayan and Indonesian smelters. From 1945 until 1946, the Texas City Smelter smelted more than 40 per cent of the world's tin output and smelters in Singapore and Penang briefly lost their position as the world's leading producers of tin metal. In 1948, after the rehabilitation of its tin industry, Malaya regained its position as the world's biggest producer of tin. Firms from the US, however, continued their attempt to break into the British tin smelting monopoly in Malaya and there were complaints from both sides: 'the US wanted a larger share while the British companies resented the American competition'.[39] By 1957, the Texas City Smelter was closed due to the same high operating costs experienced by earlier American smelters, including prohibitive tariffs on sources of alluvial ores, and higher coal and labour costs.[40]

In addition to tin smelting, some US firms were attracted to the business of shipping tin-ore. W.R. Grace & Co, owner of the International Tin Mining Co which was actively involved in producing Bolivian tungsten and to a lesser extent tin, ran a steamship service between the Far East and the Pacific Coast of the US. The company had set up a London agent, Grace Brothers & Co Ltd, to ship tin to the US from Singapore at the end of World War I. However, its application for an export permit was refused. This decision was not specifically targeted against an American firm, but generally towards new entrants, partly to protect the British firms involved in the export of tin from the Straits Settlements.[41]

Thus, it is reasonable to assert that US FDI in the Malayan tin smelting industry was restricted by British administrators. Like the contemporary US government, the British authorities were suspicious of trusts and big business interests. The local British administrators and the metropolitan government preferred to keep the tin industry under British control, both because the commodity was so important to the Malayan economy as a large part of the government revenue came in the form of mining licences, royalties and export duties, and because it helped preserve the country's independent tin smelting capacity. Without government restrictions,

US firms would undoubtedly have invested further in the Malayan tin smelting industry and the shipping of tin-ore. Obstacles such as the tin-ore export tax imposed by the British authorities to protect the tin smelting industry may also have deterred potential US FDI in tin mining. In addition, the British control over the tin smelting industry in Malaya prevented efforts by US MNEs to integrate forwards from tin mining into tin smelting.

Consequently, while the tin smelting industry attracted serious investment attempts by a number of US firms, the tin mining industry managed to attract only a single US entrant, PacTin. This firm was, however, successful in its endeavours and its success, like that of other Western firms in Malaya, was due to the introduction of superior technology, and in PacTin's case, dredging technology in particular.

At the end of the nineteenth century, resources both in the Cornish mines in England and the mines in Australia were becoming scarce, while the world demand for tin was increasing. Some of the early mining firms in Malaya were from these areas of the world, but there was also the successful French mining venture, Societe des Etains de Kinta. Malaya was perhaps an obvious choice for mining companies to venture due to its rich natural deposits, but the tin deposits in Malaya were mainly alluvial rather than the lode deposits found in Cornish mines. Consequently, the technology of the Cornish mining companies was not particularly compatible with Malayan conditions, except in Pahang where lode deposits were found and where in 1897 the Pahang Corporation Ltd began to successfully mine.[42] Certain Australian, and later American, entrepreneurs familiar with gold mining were able to successfully transfer the technologies of gold mining to tin mining because of the similar occurrence in alluvial deposits.[43]

It is not possible, however, to evaluate the American innovations independent of those of other Western firms as every Western firm contributed in its own way to the technological knowledge and skills in the Malayan tin mining industry. This is effectively summed up by Allen and Donnithorne who suggest that French, Australian and US firms all contributed innovations in mining and that certainly 'Cornwall did not provide all the pioneers nor all the new techniques'.[44]

One piece of dredging technology known as the 'bucket elevator', originally developed in New Zealand in the 1880s to recover gold, would later have a significant impact on the tin mining industry.[45] The technology was transported to the gold and tin mines of Australia and finally underwent important transformation in the gold fields of the Yukon and California where dredging techniques were perfected. The first tin bucket dredge used to mine tin in South East Asia was brought into Penang by an Australian company, Tongkah Harbour Tin Dredging Company, in 1907 to work at a concession granted by the Thai government at Tongkah Harbour, Phuket.[46] It was also to become one of the principal tin mining methods in Malaya.[47] In 1912, the bucket dredge was introduced in Perak by the Americans (though sources are not clear who exactly did so) through a London firm, the Malayan Tin Dredging Company. The new technology allowed the recovery of tin at a lower cost with one estimation suggesting that a dredge with 12 foot buckets was the equivalent to 2000 labourers, thereby not only reducing production costs but also solving labour shortage problems.[48] As such mining technology shifted from labour-intensive techniques to capital intensive techniques, Western firms gained an added advantage over local enterprises which were mainly represented by small-scale local Chinese miners. The high costs of the dredges created barriers to entry into the industry, thus radically shifting the balance of power from local Chinese to Western firms.

The onset of World War I greatly disrupted shipping lines and so delayed the full exploitation of dredging. There was, however, still an increase in the use of dredges during this period. In 1913, Western mines produced 25 per cent of total Malayan output, although dredging contributed only 1 per cent of the output. By 1917, these figures had risen to 30 per cent and 38 per cent respectively.[49] By the 1920s, Malaya's full mining potential had been realised.[50] In 1920, there were 20 dredges operating, and by 1928, dredging made up 30 per cent of all tin mined in Malaya, compared to 45 per cent by gravel pumping, 6 per cent by open cast, 6 per cent by underground, and 2 per cent by dulang (the working of surface tin deposits by panning) (see Table 4.1). By 1937, dredging produced 48.1 per cent of the total Malayan tin output.

Tin dredging equipment probably became the most important item of machinery imported into Malaya. In 1928, dredging equipment accounted for 55 per cent of total machinery imports, and in 1929 it accounted for 44 per cent, with the US ranked third after Britain and Netherlands in supplying this machinery to Malaya.[51] The increasing predominance of dredging technology and involvement of Western mining companies led to drastically reduced levels of participation by Chinese mining concerns in the Malayan tin mining industry. However, technical limitations associated with dredging meant that these local firms did retain a share of total Malayan tin output. In 1930, Chinese mining production accounted for only 37 per cent of total Malayan output, compared to 72 per cent in 1915, whilst Western production rose from 28 per cent in 1915 to 63 per cent in 1930.[52] For a brief description on mining methods, see Appendix C.

The diffusion of this new mining technology equally led to an increase in FDI in the Malayan tin mining industry. Between 1920 and 1927, FDI in the Malayan

Table 4.1 Mining method: total percentage of Federated Malay States output

Method	*1928*	*1937*
Dredging	30.24	48.14
Gravel pump	45.05	38.22
Hydraulicing	8.39	4.32
Open cast mining	6.45	4.02
Lode mining	5.57	3.82
Dulang washing	1.82	1.33
Alluvial washing	0.42	0.05
Combined methods	2.04	–
Other	–	0.09

Source: Adapted from Fermor, *Mining Industry of Malaya*, pp. 112–13.

tin mining industry more than doubled, rising from approximately S$45.5 million in 1920 to S$103 million in 1927. Of this increase, S$57 million or 85 per cent were British investments. In 1923, the US Department of Commerce reported the value of S$9.35 million in US tin investments in Malaya.[53] Such figures clearly illustrate British predominance over US FDI in tin mining in Malaya. Though the US was the main consumer of Malayan tin, US MNEs did not play a considerable role in the production of Malaya's tin. YGC was one US concern that did invest in Malaya's tin mining industry and made its mark with the new mining technology.

4.3 Tin and American entrepreneurship

By 1916 Guggenheim Exploration Co had turned over its entire holdings to the Yukon–Alaska Trust.[54] The trustees, mainly officials and directors of YGC, including the Guggenheims, were its main creditors and major stockholders, who had wide discretionary powers in matters involving its properties, borrowing and lending money, investing in trust funds, acquisitions and development of new sources of profit. By the outbreak of World War I, the Guggenheims had come to dominate the silver, copper and lead mining industries,[55] and by 1929, Guggenheim enterprises had both market-oriented investments in Europe and supply-seeking investments in Latin America, Africa, Malaya and Canada.[56]

In 1906, YGC was operating gold mines in the Klondike, the Yukon Territory and California. However, due to losses incurred at its Yukon mines in 1917 and 1918, YGC began to explore the possibilities of tin mining overseas. The company needed to find further mining opportunities to employ its specific physical assets of expensive dredges and power plants, which were released after their gold operations in the US expired. A mission was sent to the Federated Malay States to explore the viability of producing tin in Malaya. In addition to advanced machinery, YGC also had staff with considerable mining experience in the Klondike and California fields. These assets would come to provide the company with a distinct advantage over its competitors in Malaya and is a useful example of Casson's model of entrepreneurship. Aware of the uncertainty in using the gold dredges in a wholly different environment in the Malayan tin mines, decision-makers at YGC nevertheless deemed the risk worthwhile to make an investment.

The management of the Guggenheims placed emphasis on the need to seek and acquire new properties to replace exhausted properties, using current earnings to defray the cost. This was achieved through YGC's policy of recruiting engineers to find potential properties throughout the world. In January 1919, a year after Malayan tin potential was brought to the Guggenheim brothers' attention, a prospecting party headed by engineers Charles H. Munro and Professor John F. Newsom was sent to Malaya, followed by Colonel O.B. Perry, consulting engineer and general manager of YGC.

Colonel Perry was impressed with the promise he saw in Malaya's tin mining industry. Newsom and Munro, in the meantime, sought out prospecting licences and mining leases for YGC. Their activities were concentrated in the main tin producing states of Perak and Selangor, filing several applications for prospecting licences at the Kinta Land Office, Perak, and at the Land Office in Kuala Lumpur, Selangor from 1919 to 1921.[57] If the prospects were deemed suitable, they would then file applications for mining leases.[58] YGC carried out extensive research to ensure the viability of its investment. Two special reports were prepared by Perry and Munro, with the former dealing with all the properties leased, and the latter pertaining to the newly acquired alluvial tin properties in the Malay States. Munro's report also included a comprehensive review of the situation of the mining industry in Malaya.[59]

At the beginning of the twentieth century, colonial mining legislations had been established in Malaya with a series of enactments giving official control to the local authorities over tin mining in all stages. Thus at that time, local authorities controlled all mining lands in the Federated Malay States. One of the most important factors influencing official decisions on the granting of mining licences was the amount of capital a firm could raise.[60] The standard mining lease was generally granted for 21 years.[61] A prospecting licence was issued for six months at a fee of S$25, with the right to choose to mine the whole area at a premium of S$10 per acre. If certain requirements were met, the lease could be renewed when it expired. The colonial authorities encouraged large mining operations, provided they did not interfere with government development policy or indigenous and local interests. However, there were inconsistencies in approving mining leases, and they frequently took a long time to be processed and approved. It should be noted that decisions as to whether applications were successful or not were made by the colonial authorities at several different levels, and depended very much on the discretion of the official in charge.[62] Although applications for British concessions were generally dealt with and approved promptly, there were instances when their applications were delayed, refused or forfeited for a variety of reasons. For example, there were cases, as detailed in Chapter 1, when indigenous interests took priority over British mining investments.[63] Applications for mining leases were also refused when they were deemed to be speculative ventures.[64] There were also instances when environmental protection took precedence over approval for British FDI.[65]

Like some British applications, most foreign applications took several months to process and were occasionally refused on the grounds already mentioned. In the early 1920s, YGC experienced similar delays in their applications.

> When asked if it was difficult for an American company to invest in Malaya, Charles Earl, a director of Yukon Gold, replied that it took two to three years for the company to get established. The company sent out several engineers, and, with the assistance of native engineers, they finally gathered up this territory, the tin bearing areas, and then they went through a long siege with the government officials to get the necessary licenses and permits and concessions in exchange for agreements on their part concerning supervision, limitation of production when required, rate of development, the disposal of the product to local smelters and various other things. They had to make these agreements in order to get permission to mine the ground.[66]

These delays, however, did not deter the entrepreneurial efforts of PacTin engineers, who persisted with their applications to invest in Malayan tin mines. They had to overcome several further challenges before they were able to make the Malayan tin mining endeavour profitable.

The initial difficulty encountered by the company was in securing options large enough to justify the use of large-scale dredging operations. As dredging operations were capital intensive, there was a need to secure large tracts of mining land to cover costs. The company had acquired extensive tin land in Perak and Selangor in the Federated Malay States and set up dredges and power stations.[67] Dredging was successfully carried out, as YGC had the added advantages of advanced, highly specialised knowledge as well as extensive experience with dredging technology in the gold fields of the US. However, it proved to be very difficult to consolidate other tracts of land in the tin areas of Perak and Selangor as the British had been granting private leases in individual blocks with different expiry dates. There were times when applications had to be made to convert agricultural titles into mining titles and to relocate local squatters.[68]

Ampang, for example, one of the main centres of Chinese mining, had been mined since the nineteenth century and several blocks of land were either owned or leased out to different Chinese individuals. By the end of 1922, YGC had successfully consolidated several of the Chinese-owned mines into a 3300 acre mine known as the *Fah Kee Kongsi*, which in English translates as the 'Starry Flag Company'.[69] Munro and Newsom, as the representatives of YGC, managed to secure mining leases for some large tracts of land, although, as noted above, this was achieved with difficulty and through long months of correspondence with the various local authorities.

There was also the issue of environmental protection, for which British administrators drew up special conditions by which YGC was required to abide. In December 1920, YGC agreed to adhere to the special conditions set by the collector of land revenue, Batu Gajah, Kinta. The company undertook to preserve the channel of Sungei Kranji, and agreed to level off the land to suit future building purposes within six months upon the cessation of dredging operations or the expiration of the lease. YGC also agreed to execute a bond of S$25,000 for the 'due performance of these conditions'.[70]

By 1920, options were secured in Kinta District on properties near Tronoh and Kampar and in Kuala Lumpur on properties near Ampang and Salak, leading to the formation of two subsidiaries, YGC Kampar, Perak, and YGC, Ampang, Selangor. The area in Ampang was slightly larger than that in Kampar. The total area size finally selected after the acreage was drilled was less than half of what was initially prospected, demonstrating the considerable amount of work that had to be put in before the final acres were selected (see Table 4.2).

The acquisitions at Ampang and Kampar were high risk, as in both areas the high-grade tin-ore was embedded in tenacious clay with extremely irregular limestone bedrock beneath. The first dredge failed to deal with the clay problems and even after several attempts at improving the mining methods, the clay retained a considerable percentage of valuable ore. However, this problem would

Table 4.2 Acquisitions in Kinta and Kuala Lumpur, 1920

District	*Acres Drilled*	*Acres Selected*	*Yardage*	*Metallic Tin (lbs)*[a]
Kinta (Tronoh & Kampar)	3,079	1,052	67,247,000	40,715,000
Kuala Lumpur (Ampang & Salak)	2,734	1,130	58,880,000	34,400,000
Total	5,813	2,182	126,127,000	75,115,000

Note:
a Estimates.

Source: Special Report YGC, 1920.

eventually be resolved through dredging technology breakthroughs and YGC's persistence was finally paid off when extensive modifications to the dredges bore fruit. YGC's risk-taking activities, innovative ideas and improvements to the dredging technology had a significant impact on the Malayan tin industry as other mining firms came to realise that dredging technology could be used to dredge tin-ore embedded in extremely difficult conditions.

YGC went through many trials in adapting dredging technology to Malayan tin mines. The company's modification of existing technology and use of the latest tin mining techniques impacted on the Malayan tin mining industry, as these modifications and techniques were often adopted by its competitors.

Acquiring its first property near Tronoh, Perak, in 1919, YGC put its first dredge into operation in October 1921. This installation included an electrically driven dredge, a steam turbine generating plant, a machine shop and a supplemental plant. Hydroelectric power plant equipment from the Klondike was readily available, but there was a need to modify it for Malayan conditions.[71] Power was readily available and inexpensive so the company was able to operate its dredges at a low cost.

At the same time, an experimental department was set up, mainly to improve methods of recovering tin and to increase dredging capacity. The department in Malaya was made up of a group of men with significant mining experience, transferred from every department of the Alaskan operations. By December 1922, this research department had spent S$100,000 on a new experimental plant on YGC's holdings in Kuala Lumpur, with the intention of designing improved dredging equipment. Two dredges brought in for use at Kampar and Kuala Lumpur from the Alaskan operations were used in the experiments.[72]

YGC experienced continuous delays in its mining operation due to the difficulty of treating the tin-bearing clay. Numerous changes made to the dredge incurred considerable loss of time and resources. However, the experimental work brought major improvements to the recovery of tin and to operating profit. The newly designed dredge, equipped with a clay extractor, puddler and log washer, was among the first to be introduced in Malaya.[73] By 1923, two electrically operated dredges were completed, each equipped with a new tin concentrating system in which classifiers and jigs were used instead of the old Malayan table type. This system had much greater capacity and flexibility than the table system, as there was minimal wastage of tin.[74] YGC's technological innovation allowed for increased dredging capacity, good recovery of tin and, most importantly, the lowering of production costs.[75] By 1927, YGC had dismantled and shipped four dredges to its Malayan mining operations – three from the Yukon and one from California.

The ownership advantages that YGC enjoyed included knowledge embedded in plant and machining technology, experienced employees and management as well as crucial technical skills. The lack of skilled workers in Malaya did not deter YGC as highly skilled personnel within its affiliates were brought to Malaya. At the same time, YGC did not train indigenous or local workers in either the managerial or technical areas. However, it can be asserted that YGC investments led to beginnings of a modern technology-based FDI flow from a developed to a developing country.

YGC's success in surmounting the problems when adapting to the Malayan tin mining industry was largely due to the company's access to financial resources, a key ownership advantage also enjoyed by other Western MNEs in the Malayan tin mining industry. In 1920, the Yukon–Alaska Trust had allocated S$2.18 million to the development of the Malayan tin and Mayo silver-lead projects.[76] By November 1921, YGC had spent S$2.7 million, which had increased to S$4.9 million by December 1921.[77] This initial expenditure included the acquisition of properties, installation of dredges, and other equipment needed prior to the operation and production process. Apart from the Yukon–Alaska Trust, funds also came from the income of other YGC mining operations.

In addition, the board of directors agreed to release S$1.74 million for further expenditure for its Malayan Tin Project, and to be met by both the resources of YGC and the Yukon–Alaska Trust. YGC was not only able to secure large areas of tin, but was also able to deliver technological breakthroughs because of the new sources of financing available to the company. This extensive programme of expansion into new fields was made possible because of the good rapport between the YGC and the Yukon–Alaska Trust.[78]

Despite access to considerable resources, YGC still faced financial difficulties, as sizable funds were required to complete the acquisition of properties and the installation of additional dredges and power plants in order to successfully carry out its ventures in Perak and Selangor. Unexpected difficulties arose, such as the suitability of the dredging equipment, and time was needed to adapt the dredging equipment to Malayan conditions. Thus, in their initial stages profitability eluded these ventures. The Guggenheims offered important financial support by agreeing to assume responsibility for whatever sums might be required by the company to complete its programme as then outlined. On 15 January 1924, an agreement was undertaken between the Guggenheims, YGC and the Yukon–Alaska Trust to provide a guarantee that would enable the company to borrow S$2.92 million over two years on favourable terms. With readily available financial resources, YGC was finally able to realise profits from its Malayan tin ventures in 1924, within five years of its initial operations.[79]

YGC was also able to secure additional funds by employing a scheme known as the tribute system for the small areas it owned containing good tin deposits. Under this system, tin mining areas were leased to local Chinese miners who were the minority shareholders by the main shareholders, the mine owners. Capital and equipment was supplied and under a royalty arrangement, an agreed percentage of profits went to the mine owners and the balance to the Chinese miners.[80] Mine owners, such as YGC, adopted this system for several reasons. The small areas leased to the Chinese operators were isolated from dredging areas and the tin concentrates were often too shallow to be dredged. Income from tributors, despite enormous fluctuations (dependent upon the total output mined and fluctuating tin prices), proved the scheme's viability. The first rewards were reaped by YGC in 1926 (see Table 4.3).

Able to draw on the substantial financial resources YGC continuously modified, reinvented and maintained the dredges brought in from the Yukon and California to better suit Malayan conditions and reduce production costs. It was essential to transfer technologies through adaptation from one environment to another.

YGC provided technological leadership through the diffusion of the latest innovations in dredging technology to other dredging operations in Malaya. The flourishing tin mining industry in Malaya attracted California gold mining entrepreneurs. One such company was the Yuba Construction Company, later to be succeeded by the Yuba Manufacturing Company. Yuba designed and built YGC's dredges in California and then shipped them in pieces to worldwide markets including Malaya, the Philippines, Bolivia, Columbia, China and Russia. Dredges were then assembled on site. In Malaya, the dredges provided by the firm were distributed by one of the most renowned British merchant firms, Sime Darby & Co Ltd.

In 1920, another US firm, the Bucyrus Company (founded in 1893 as the Bucyrus Steam Shovel and Dredge Co of Wisconsin), made agency agreements

Table 4.3 YGC's income from tributes, 1926–1934

Year	*Net profit (S$)*
1926	107,743
1927	116,895
1928	n.a.
1929	79,067
1930	163,131
1931	85,399
1932	34,005
1933	51,801
1934	114,987

Source: Annual Reports YGC, 1926–34

with McAlister & Co Ltd, a wholly owned subsidiary of a locally registered European engineering firm, United Engineers Limited, to distribute its dredges and other excavating machinery.[81] At that time, the use of dredges was gaining momentum in the Malayan tin mining industry. Like Yuba dredges, those of Bucyrus had worked the California gold mines. Both examples, as highlighted in the advertisement in Figure 4.1, illustrate the role of British merchant firms and local firms in promoting US trade and FDI into Malaya.

Newton Cleaveland, then the chief operating officer of Yuba Manufacturing, sent out dredging engineers to investigate opportunities to provide the technology to other companies in order to upgrade the standards of the tin mining industry as a whole. This illustrates the indirect role played by YGC in providing assistance to other tin mining companies.[82] A further example of technology transfer was the cooperation extended to Anglo-Oriental (Malaya) Ltd, a subsidiary of Anglo-Oriental Mining Corporation (later to become known as the London Tin Corporation). This corporation was established in 1925 by John Howeson, a London financier. Howeson had links to British capital and international connections with Bolivian entrepreneur Simon Patino as well as to the Yuba Manufacturing Co in California.[83] In 1930, two new dredges were supplied to Anglo-Oriental Malaya, by then the largest British tin mining concern in Malaya, along with technical management from engineers associated with Yuba. Norman Cleaveland, son of Newton Cleaveland, happened to be one of the engineers who participated in the erection and initial operation of the two dredges. One of these American dredges was the first dredge in Malaya to reach a digging depth of 100 feet below pond level.[84]

Another American, W.M. Warren, was made managing director of Anglo-Oriental (Malaya) Ltd in 1930 and was later elected chairman. Upon retirement from Anglo-Oriental, he became the managing director of the London Tin Corporation in London. Besides Americans, Gerald H. Hutton, a New Zealander who emigrated to California to participate in the gold dredging industry, was also sent to Malaya. Hutton was then appointed as general manager at the Ipoh headquarters of Anglo-Oriental Malaya.[85]

YGC was then willing and able to provide opportunities for other US firms to become established in Malaya. The company was also prepared to provide technical and managerial support for existing mining firms, as in the example of Anglo-Oriental Malaya when American managerial and technical expertise played a part in its development. This shows the qualitative impact of YGC in providing a base and launching pad for other interested US firms, which impacted upon the progress of the Malayan tin mining industry.

As we have seen, YGC suffered significant losses in the early years of its ventures in Malaya after World War 1. In 1923, those losses had not abated and the company reported deficits amounting to S$44,498, largely due to high operating costs. When dredging operations in the Yukon and California ceased in 1923, YGC's holdings in Malaya were among its most important, aside from the Nevada lode mines and Mayo silver-lead properties. In August 1923, a subsidiary, the Ampang Tin Company Limited (ATC), was formed in Malaya by YGC with

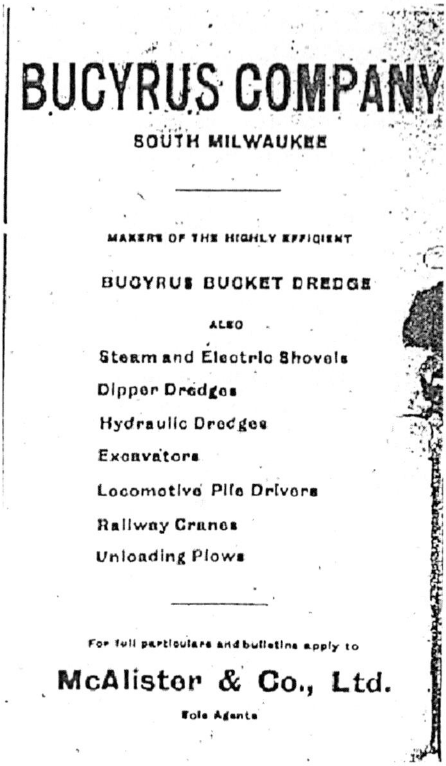

Figure 4.1 Advertisements placed by a British merchant firm and a local firm on American dredges.

Sources: Yuba Manufacturing Company, *Straits Times Annual*, 1941; Bucyrus Company, *Straits Times*, 9 February 1920.

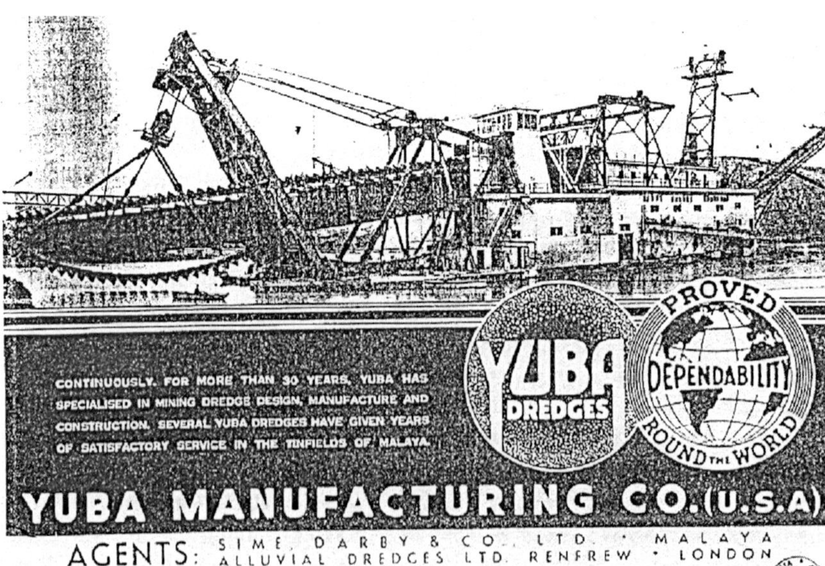

YGC holding 90 per cent equity. ATC took over the entire acreage of the Ampang–Salak project, which at the time was approximately 3900 acres.[86]

As YGC got over its initial problems of the suitability of dredging equipment, the company's Malayan operations gradually became profitable. YGC's tin was sent for smelting at the Eastern Smelting Company in Penang.[87] By 1924, YGC had started running at a profit, which increased substantially the following year. By the end of 1925, two dredges were operating in Kampar and Ulu Klang, loans that had been taken were fully paid and expansion programmes were funded out of the earnings from its operations. This was largely due to the steady price of tin, as well as the high volume production of high-quality material, despite numerous engineering problems. Two additional dredges were completed in 1926 and early the following year were in use in Kampar and Ampang. Both of these dredges belonged to ATC, which was also operating an open-cast mine utilising excess power from its central power plant at Ampang. When all four dredges were in use in 1927, the firm drew its highest profits to date (see Table 4.4) and this did not include profits made from the open-cast mining by ATC of S$91,269. In the same year, YGC held 88.2 per cent interest of ATC.[88]

As tin-ore is a non-renewable resource, depletion must be offset by further improvement in production methods or through the acquisition of new mining sites. YGC attempted to undertake both advancements, and though successful in introducing new production methods, after actively seeking new properties in 1927, and despite examinations and investigations, no new sites were found to be suitable.

YGC continued to look for new properties in Malaya when its subsidiaries Elkoro Mines and Keno Hill Ltd were near exhaustion. There was stiff competition in Malaya at this time owing to high tin prices and abundant capital, and not until right at the end of the 1920s was YGC able to find enough tin dredging properties warranting acquisition to fulfil its needs. To facilitate acquisitions, YGC formed a new company known as Malay States Tin Ltd, which was financed partly by

Table 4.4 YGC's Malayan performance, 1923–1927 (S$)

Year	*Operating Income*	*Non-Operating Income*[a]	*Operating Costs*[b]	*Operating Profit*[c]
1923	509,024.07	Nil	553,523.47	–44,499.40
1924	1,770,859.20	Nil	1,154,808.10	616,051.10
1925	1,926,116.90	Nil	943,973.16	982,143.74
1926	1,427,773.30	107,743.07	895,254.07	640,262.30
1927	2,784,731.50	106,895.03	1,422,804.60	1,468,821.90

Notes:

a Income from leases or tributes.

b Operating costs includes duty, freight, smelting and royalty charges.

c Operating profit did not take into account YGC's general expenses, taxes, depreciation and depletion as YGC's consolidated account includes YGC's subsidiaries in the US.

Source: Annual Reports YGC, 1923–27.

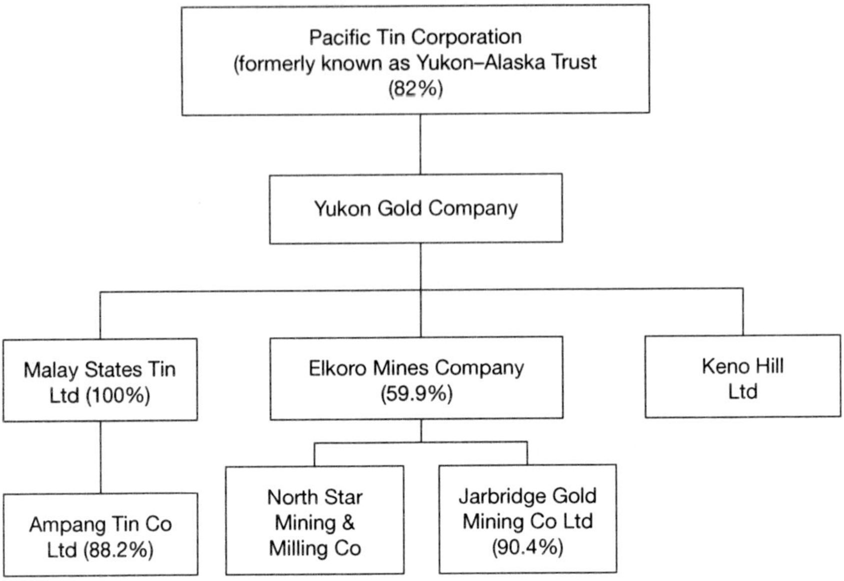

Figure 4.2 Percentage share of Pacific Tin's subsidiaries in Malaya and US, 1931.

Source: Annual Reports YGC, 1930–31.

ATC funds and partly by loans from YGC (see Figure 4.2). This company was incorporated under the laws of the Federated Malay States in May 1930 with capital of S$3,000,000. Malay States Tin purchased properties in Kinta Bharu in Perak and in Gombak near Kuala Lumpur. By 1932, its Malayan ventures remained an important undertaking for YGC, despite the Elkoro Mines closing down due to exhaustion of sites, and the Keno Hill lead and silver property meeting the same fate shortly thereafter. YGC now therefore relied heavily upon the prospect of tin, and the company's efforts to expand tin mining operations in Malaya paid off. By 1933, their operation was entirely confined to tin production in Malaya, with the consequence that the future of tin was now of paramount importance to YGC.

In February 1931, in an attempt to regulate prices of tin, the governments of Bolivia, Nigeria, Malaya and the Dutch East Indies, the four major tin producing countries representing 87 per cent of the world's tin production, formed the International Tin Committee and agreed to impose a compulsory production restriction. Under the International Tin Restriction Scheme, each of these governments would limit both production and export of tin according to its allocation of the quota. The basis of the control was the levels of output in 1929, and the total output for each country was as follows: Malaya 37.9 per cent, the Dutch East Indies 20.6 per cent, Bolivia 23.6 per cent and Nigeria 5.3 per cent. During the early months of 1931, all operators were allowed to produce 75 per cent of their rated capacity.[89]

Restriction not only limited new investments but also led to the merger of existing, mainly British, mining companies. The structure of the tin mining industry thus changed from the independent groups of the 1920s to large London-based holdings in the 1930s promoted by the restrictions imposed by the International Tin Committee in an effort to stabilise tin prices. A useful example to illustrate this shift towards merging tin mining concerns is that of the London Tin Corporation and its subsidiary Anglo-Oriental's acquisition of Malayan tin companies. By the end of 1928, Anglo-Oriental controlled 50 tin mining companies in Malaya, Nigeria and Bolivia with a market value of approximately S$90 million.[90] During the 1930s, this group absorbed many of the Australian mining firms in Thailand including Tongkah Harbour Dredging Co in 1934.[91]

By 1937, three groups – the London Tin Corporation, General Tin Investment Ltd and the British Tin Investment Co – owned 43 per cent of Malayan output. These three large holding companies with interlocking directorates controlled 17 per cent of the world's output. London Tin, for example, controlled one-fifth of the Malayan, half of the Nigerian, one-third of the Burmese, and one-tenth of the Thai tin production.[92] These holding companies were associated with Consolidated Tin Smelters, Straits Trading Co and Billiton Joint Mining Co, the three smelting companies comprising 62 per cent of the world's smelting capacity prior to World War II.[93] In 1937, more than half of the world's tin output was controlled by either government or cartels, with the rest under the control of a large number of small mining firms (see Table 4.5).

YGC abided by the tin control scheme.[94] For YGC, the restriction curtailed further mining investments, but the company was successful in finding solutions to limit the effects of restriction. They included, among others, allowing its recently

Table 4.5 Government and cartel control of tin mining, 1937

Country	*Control*	*Extent of Control*	*Total World Output (%)*
DEI	Government Joint venture[a]	All	19
China	Government	All	5
Congo	Government	All	4
Malaya	3 Cartels	43%	17
Bolivia	Cartel	50%	3
Nigeria	Cartel	50%	4
Thailand	Cartel	10%	4
Burma	Cartel	33%	4
Total			60

Note:

[a] In the 1930s, a joint venture between private company (N.V. Billiton) interests and the Dutch government controlled the DEI tin industry.

Sources: Adapted from, PRO, BT 64/2162, 'International Cartels – Tin Control', 5 January 1945; Hennart, 'The Tin Industry', pp. 232–33.

acquired properties to remain unequipped until 1935, thereby reducing the amount of tin produced to 75 per cent and, most importantly, curtailing the operations of the dredges. These steps were taken to conserve ore reserves until prices rose. The company had already adopted other cost-cutting measures in 1930 and 1931, including the retrenchment of personnel while maintaining the nucleus of the organisation.[95]

From 1929 to 1936, YGC's profits fluctuated according to tin prices and the heavy curtailment of production imposed by the restriction scheme (see Table 4.6). In June 1932, the governments involved in the tin restriction scheme implemented further drastic restrictions. As a result of these measures, tin production was brought below consumption levels. Thus, world tin stocks began to decline, and by the end of December 1932, the price of tin rose to US 22 cents per pound. Because of extremely low tin prices and heavily curtailed production (at an average of 30 per cent capacity) and the working of low-grade deposits, YGC made reduced profits in 1932. The recovery of tin prices in 1933 allowed YGC to sell its tin at an average of US 37.2 cents per pound as compared to US 20.8 cents per pound in 1932.[96] This led to an increase in profits in 1933.[97] Overall, despite reduced output which meant an increase in unit costs of production, YGC was able to maintain the profitability of its Malayan ventures, reflecting the managerial efficiency of the organisation.

There was further recovery in tin prices in 1934 and the world's output of tin had increased to 108,000 tons from 85,000 tons in 1933 and would increase further to 138,000 tons in 1935, largely due to the increasing demand for tin for the canning and automobile industries. These developments were reflected in YGC's higher annual profits.

By May 1938, with YGC's activities confined to tin mining in the Federated Malay States, the firm changed its name to the Yukon-Pacific Mining Company. However, this was not to last and on 21 November 1939, Yukon-Pacific acquired all the assets of the Pacific Tin Corporation, which was then dissolved, and took the new name of Pacific Tin Consolidated Corporation (PacTin). The business of the corporation remained entirely in tin mining in the Malay states. The company, now trading as PacTin, continued to operate on a restricted production schedule

Table 4.6 YGC's profits, 1929–1936

Year	*Profit (S$)*
1929	1,976,682
1930	690,694
1931	71,995
1932	153,130
1933	576,785
1934	1,200,000
1935	794,704
1936	1,440,000

Sources: YGC Annual Reports 1929–36

after the International Tin Restriction Scheme was extended for another five years, until the end of 1941.[98]

The challenges encountered and surmounted during the restriction years provided experience for PacTin which would prove useful during the Japanese occupation of Malaya. The rehabilitation period after World War II and the later years spanning the Emergency saw PacTin playing a significant role in the reconstruction of the Malayan economy, with the company able to recognise the strategic importance of tin and be fully prepared to capitalise on it.

4.4 Pacific Tin: World War II and the post-war years, 1942–1957

With the Japanese occupation of the Federated Malay States in 1942, the mines of PacTin and its subsidiaries came under their control and had to be evacuated. Previously, dredging operations had only been allowed at the company during daylight hours and by 18 December 1941, two dredges were closed down followed by two further closures at the end of December. The dredges were sunk in accordance with the Malayan government's order to render them useless to the Japanese. Net profit from mining declined between 1940 and 1941, due, first, to the higher costs of labour and mining supplies and, second, to the increase in export duty from 2.5 per cent to 5 per cent because of taxes imposed by the British government to support the war. In 1942, for the first time since its operation in Malaya, the corporation experienced losses amounting to S$52,636.

Mining operations remained suspended throughout the Japanese occupation years of 1942 to 1945, but after the war PacTin and its subsidiaries promptly filed claims for war losses with the metropolitan government and with the US Department of State.[99] Due to the cessation of mining operations, personnel adjustments had necessarily been made in Malaya in addition to the retention of only key personnel at the headquarters in New York. Cost reduction measures included salary and administrative cuts. This was in keeping with the corporation's decision to conserve cash resources for rehabilitation purposes.

PacTin had two power stations: one of which had been completely dismantled by the Japanese while several generators from the second power station were deliberately damaged by staff during evacuation. The Japanese did manage, however, to refloat and operate three of the corporation's dredges, but in the process damaged the machinery because of the shortage of lubricants and spare parts.[100] Consequently, much of the machinery of these dredges was either worn out or damaged beyond repair. In addition, the Japanese removed equipment from some of the dredges which later had to be replaced by PacTin. Further damage occurred from the looting of corrugated iron house coverings, electrical equipment, tools and fittings. The warehouses, with stocks of dredge repair parts and mining supplies, as well as staff houses and other buildings had also been looted. Despite PacTin employees burning the records of the Malayan office, the Japanese kept detailed records, which survived the war, of production and inventories of PacTin's properties. The damage brought about during the Japanese occupation was met with the corporation's determination to overcome the setbacks as soon as possible. This was evident from the immediate efforts taken to ensure the smooth running of the corporation's mining activities as soon as the occupation ended.[101]

The Federated Malay States were reoccupied by British military forces in September 1946 after two weeks of political vacuum. The metropolitan government appointed a small committee of experienced engineers from the tin mining industry, including PacTin's resident manager, Arthur D. Hughes, to inspect and report on the condition of the Malayan tin mines.[102] In fact, prior to the Japanese withdrawal, the British Ministry of Supply had devised plans for rehabilitation by securing funds for compensation to mining firms in Malaya. This was intended to revive both the Malayan and the British economies. Similarly, the US government, realising the importance of tin to US industry and the country as a whole being a major consumer, wanted to rehabilitate the Malayan mines as quickly as possible. Several American experts were sent to investigate the mining, smelting and stock situation in the Far East, including Malaya, Thailand, the Dutch East Indies and Japan. These experts checked on the availability of tin stocks for exports and the materials and equipment needed to restore mining operations. As the tin mines in Malaya were in urgent need of transportation, the US delivered the trucks needed to continue mining operations.[103]

The activities of PacTin contributed to the revival of the Malayan tin industry and, at the same time, the corporation was able to benefit from British policies. In fact, PacTin had a further advantage as it was not as dependent as the British mining firms upon the British government for dollars or the need for new equipment and parts. This was mainly due to the fact that it had sustained less damage during the war.[104] It proved possible to repair and put back into operation all five of the damaged and sunken dredges. Unlike other, mainly British, mining firms, PacTin's installation also survived the civilian looting during the brief communist uprising that occurred during the political vacuum at the end of the war and which was a foretaste of what was to happen and become known as the 'Emergency'. Because of the swift response of its managerial staff to salvage mining operations in Malaya, PacTin was quickly able to reoccupy its mines and as such prevented further damage by the civilian looting. PacTin's resident manager, Arthur D. Hughes, devoted his efforts to getting the corporation's largest dredge back into production, replacing vital parts worn out by the Japanese or looted by the civilians. He also played an instrumental role in providing basic necessities such as food and clothes for undernourished workers so that they could return to work.[105] Important, too, was the role played by F.W. Gurr, PacTin's chief accountant and a former prisoner of war. Upon release from prison, he was accompanied by a US army officer to Kuala Lumpur, despite rulings forbidding POWs to travel in the country. Gurr was also able to enlist the support of two Russian POWs, V. Schamraeff and P.R. Sokolov, both former employees of the company. They formed the supervisory staff while Gurr rallied former clerical staff and workers to work.[106]

In 1941, because of the Japanese army occupation of Malaya, all PacTin's Malayan assets had been written off. Talks were held in 1945 between the Malayan

Chamber of Mines (an organisation in London representing the Malayan tin mining industry including PacTin) and the British government regarding compensation for war losses. In 1946, the British Ministry of Supply purchased all Malayan tin production at a fixed price of US 53.9 cents per pound of tin until 30 June and about US 66.2 cents per pound thereafter.[107] The British and Malayan governments offered loans to mine owners in exchange for the monopolisation of rates. The loans were intended to finance the cost of repairing war damage and were to be offset against any compensation for war losses.[108]

Also in 1946, the British administrators in Malaya approved loans totalling S$1.83 million (£213,000) to PacTin and its subsidiaries. Several PacTin staff returned immediately to rehabilitate the property and equipment. By 1 March 1946, the least damaged dredges had resumed operation and three dredges had been rehabilitated to service all the properties recovered by PacTin. The ore reserves of the corporation's mining properties were insufficient to justify the revival of the two other damaged dredges. However, efforts were made to acquire additional mining properties, and it was determined that if successful, the dredges would be recovered. To achieve these objectives, PacTin hired Norman Cleaveland, an experienced dredge worker who, as mentioned above, was the son of Newton Cleaveland one of the pioneers of the US dredging company Yuba Manufacturing.[109]

Norman Cleaveland accepted an offer from PacTin to undertake a prospecting campaign in an effort to expand the company's ore reserves in Malaya. Cleaveland played a major role in resurrecting the corporation's operations in Malaya and, in 1948, he was appointed manager. Three years later he became the president of PacTin, opting to remain at the corporations' Malaya headquarters in Ampang rather than its headquarters in New York. Cleaveland's experience and technical expertise helped improve the financial position of PacTin and he later played a vital role during the Emergency by initiating an order of arms and munitions from the US government which allowed both his and the British mines to continue production.[110]

PacTin had put back into service its mining operations two years in advance of other British mining firms. The British firms were not able to resume operations until 1948 when mining equipment, fuel and regular power supplies became available. However, inflation caused a tripling in the cost of production compared to pre-war levels. PacTin's quick rehabilitation aided a quick rejuvenation of the Malayan tin industry and the Malayan economy overall.

During 1947, the British Ministry of Supply continued to purchase the entire Malayan tin production, leading to a rise in the price of tin from US 66.2 cents per pound in January to US 89.6 cents per pound at the end of the year. PacTin's tin production continued to be restricted, however, and the operation of dredges was curtailed.[111] During wartime controls, US consumers bought tin from the Reconstruction Finance Corporation (RFC) that in turn bought tin from the British Ministry of Supply, the sole buyer of Malayan tin. RFC strictly controlled the consumption of tin in the US. By 1949, Malaya's tin production reached 55,000 tons per year, but RFC was slow to purchase the tin, which caused an accumulation of stocks.

In September 1949 came the sterling devaluation and the British government was obliged to dispose of 20,000 tons of tin from its stockpiles. The US Congress failed to act however, which meant that this tin reserve the British had intended to sell to the US entered the market as soon as market restrictions were lifted in November 1949. Almost immediately, speculative activities caused tin prices to plunge, and producers again sought the revival of the pre-war tin control schemes.[112] This led to the first International Tin Agreement (ITA), which was finally adopted at the International Tin Study Group (established in 1947 to survey the world supply and demand of tin) meeting in March 1950 on a vote of 12 to 1, despite US government opposition.[113] The fall of tin prices was temporarily alleviated when the communist armies of North Korea invaded South Korea in June 1950. In fact there was a short boom in tin prices, due to the reactivation of the US stockpile programme being maintained mainly for strategic reserves.[114] A US government tin mission, which visited Malaya in November 1951, resulted in the setting up of a Malayan Tin Bureau in Washington. In 1952, the British prime minister, Winston Churchill, and US president, Harry Truman, entered a barter agreement to exchange US steel for Malayan tin and Canadian aluminium. However, the US government, following its earlier opposition, refused to adopt the 1953 International Tin Agreement (fully operational in 1956 with the formation of the International Tin Council), despite realising the need to stabilise tin prices to aid producing countries, including Malaya, in the fight against communism.

Washington's continued determination to stay outside the agreements, in spite of attempts by British and Malayan authorities to persuade the US as the largest consumer of tin to join the ITA, greatly frustrated not only British businesses and government, but also the only US tin company in Malaya, PacTin, well into the 1960s. Cleaveland, with the support of British dredgers in Perak, also urged the US to join the ITA.[115]

The communist revolt of the late 1940s and what was to become known as the Emergency had a significant impact on Malayan mining activities, including those of Pacific Tin. The Malayan Communist Party, which had fought side by side with the British against the Japanese occupation, in 1948 began a rebellion in Malaya against its British colonial rulers. In the same year the Federation of Malaya was established in place of the Malayan Union. The MCP organised a guerrilla force, the Malayan Races Liberation Army (MRLA), and re-established its rural support network known as Min Yuen. During World War II, a proportion of the urban population, mostly Chinese, had moved out of the cities and towns to effectively become squatters in suburban or rural areas to avoid the harsh Japanese regime. Most of these 'jungle-fringe squatters' were vulnerable to the Min Yuen demands for food, supplies, cash and information. A government census in 1948 revealed that there were over 20,000 Chinese living on PacTin's Ampang properties.

Post-war preparations for resuming mining operations suggested the need for large-scale removal of squatters to enable the corporation to resume the use of dredges and open-cast mines.[116] PacTin initiated its own action to remove squatters because of the preoccupation of British law-enforcing agencies with persistent

MRLA guerrilla activities. In any case, the instigation of a proper legal eviction of squatters would have involved a long bureaucratic process. PacTin's then manager, Norman Cleaveland, was instrumental in overcoming squatter problems at his company's Ampang property. He came up with the novel idea of population control, protecting and isolating the Chinese squatters vulnerable to intimidation from the guerrillas, and intended to serve both the welfare of the corporation and the squatters themselves. Through his long experience in dealing with Chinese labourers at the corporation's mines, Cleveland was able to effectively deal with the Chinese squatters, including those who were communist sympathisers.

However, Cleaveland did encounter difficulties, such as in Ampang in early 1948, when the corporation's dredge could not proceed to dig because of the presence of 50 squatter homes. He took it upon himself to allocate lots of unused mining lands to the squatters on a 'first come, first served' basis, promising to help them with the Temporary Occupation Licence (TOL) application as the land in question was state land and PacTin's title covered mining rights only.[117] By March, the dredge was ready to start digging, and Cleaveland was 'pleased at having set precedence for dealing with numerous other squatter settlements on our Ampang property and the same 4,000 homes which would eventually need to be moved'.[118]

By time the Briggs Plan was announced in April 1950 by the director of operations, General Sir Harold Briggs, advocating a plan to undermine the Min Yuen whereby squatters were moved to heavily policed areas outfitted with lighting and barbed wire fences, Cleaveland had already implemented population control at PacTin's Ampang mines.[119] Ampang, just six miles from the political and business centre of Kuala Lumpur, was given top priority, as it was the prime source of information, recruits, money and supplies for the Min Yuen. Cleaveland's example was also taken by other miners and planters who stated that his success was due to guidance given by Colonel H.S. Lee, a prominent Malaysian Chinese Association leader and miner who was later appointed Malaya's first minister of finance and conferred the highest honour of Tun. Cleaveland was also assisted by two other Chinese friends, a businessmen called Lee Nam, who was later killed by the communists in the early days of Emergency, and his son Lee Kok Chee.[120] The second phase of the Briggs plan, which included the provision of new quarters and security, was deemed the responsibility of individual companies.

At Ampang, PacTin cooperated with several local Chinese miners in the building of nine fortified police posts, which were put under the supervision of PacTin's security officer, Guy Golden.[121] Efforts were intensified when General Sir Gerald Templer replaced both Henry Gurney as the high commissioner and Briggs as the director of operations in the Federation of Malaya in February 1952.[122] Templer used the term 'New Villages' for the new settlements and included in his plans the provision of adequate medical, educational and social facilities for the general welfare of the squatters.[123]

After PacTin began to encounter problems with armed communist insurgents, the corporation requested help from the British authorities and sought permission to bring in arms and munitions from Australia. As soon as the Emergency was declared, PacTin, with several other mining companies in Malaya, sent a combined order for arms and ammunition through Anglo-Oriental Malaya Ltd, using its Australian affiliates in Sydney. The Malayan government, due to the dire shortage of firearms for law enforcement, gave its approval, whereupon the order and safety of mining companies' personnel and properties was put under the mining companies' own control. However, the Australian government refused to permit delivery of the order so the munitions were not provided.[124]

When this effort failed, Cleaveland sought, with more success, consulate aid to obtain arms and ammunition from the US. He wrote to the consulate stating the company's need for these goods to protect its mines and properties because the arms supplied by the British government were inadequate and outdated. In addition, he pointed out that by June 1948, PacTin's 19 European and four American staff in Kuala Lumpur, all of whom had previous military training, had been sworn in as 'special' police officers.

According to Cleveland, it would be prudent to withdraw his staff until the police and military had the situation under control or adequate arms were available to them to provide at least some protection. However, such action would end the production of tin and thus fulfil one of the objectives of the insurgents. In addition, the locals in exposed areas would need to seek the protection of the insurgents, which in turn, would strengthen the communist's position. Finally, Cleaveland suggested that:

> As the only American tin mining company in Malaya, pride alone would deter withdrawal until other companies took similar action. America is the principal consumer of tin which is an essential to industry.[125]

Despite the constant threat of attack, the corporation refused to withdraw its staff because doing so would have halted tin production. Early during the Emergency, the struggle against the communists seemed bleak and numerous acts of violence occurred on the PacTin's properties despite the protection provided by the corporation's security forces. Most of the corporation's Asian labourers and their families were subject to intimidation, extortion and, in some cases, violence by the insurgents. The supervisory staff frequently came under communist gunfire. Although the corporation's installations were not damaged, operations were frequently interrupted by curfew and military actions.

Within a few weeks of the outbreak of violence in 1948, PacTin had flown arms across the Pacific by chartered planes, not only with the intent to protect its own personnel and installations, but also to assist other mines and rubber estates. A force of some 150 full-time armed guards was organised, and all of the corporation's supervisory staff served as auxiliary police. Armoured cars were obtained and for the next few years it was routine for the shifts to be escorted to and from the dredges thrice a day with armoured cars and armed guards.

As mentioned in the report to stockholders for the second quarter of 1960, the staff and property of the corporation were deeply involved in the 12-year struggle, which finally resulted in defeat for the communists. The outlook for tin production in Malaya in the 1950s was more promising than that of the next three largest tin producing countries after Malaya – Indonesia, Bolivia and the Congo – where political upheavals had caused a decline in the production even without further tin export restrictions. Malaya, therefore, assumed a greater role in supplying the world's tin needs although, in 1954, PacTin was only producing 3.5 per cent and 3.3 per cent of the European and Malayan output respectively, and was ranked only fifth behind British tin mining agencies. However, despite consolidation efforts among British firms, PacTin remained independent. Table 4.7 illustrates that the three main agencies, all British – Anglo-Oriental, Neill & Bell and Osborne & Chappel – produced more than 800,000 lbs or 75 per cent of the output of the European firms, 65 per cent of Malaya's output.

In December 1957, a sudden increase in tin from Russia to the European markets led to restrictions by the International Tin Committee on exports of tin from Malaya and the other five tin producing countries included in the International Tin Agreement. For PacTin, despite export quota limitations, the company acquired a new property (see Appendix D) at Batang Berjuntai, Selangor.[126] The acquisition of this property was not entirely smooth. British reservations towards US FDI were still prevalent, as was noted by Cleaveland, who suggested that although the official British position remained 'Welcome Americans', he was always given the 'run-around'. On the other hand, he argued that the British were given easy access to new land for tin mining.[127]

In the meantime, Cleaveland continued with his efforts to nurture links with indigenous politicians. He made acquaintance with Dato' Nik Ahmad Kamil, then menteri besar or chief minister of Kelantan, who later became the ambassador to the US and UN. Realising that he would be on the same flight to the US with Dato' Nik who was on the State Department's programme of leadership grants, he went

Table 4.7 Percentage tin output of Malayan mining agencies, 1954

Name	*No of firms*	*No of dredges*	*Lbs*	*%*
Anglo-Oriental (M)	19	40	39,456,800	32.2
Neill & Bell	9	24	26,126,800	21.3
Osborne & Chappel	19	10	15,329,500	12.5
Borneo Co	4	2	7,464,800	6.1
Austral-Malay Tin	2	4	2,932,600	2.4
Guthrie & Co	1	1	2,532,700	2.1
Harper, Gilfillan & Co	4	n.a.	1,199,700	1.0
General Mining & Agency Co	4	n.a.	n.a.	13.2
Gremitt, Reid & Co	2	n.a.	n.a.	
Others	12	n.a.	n.a.	
Total European	76	108	111,172,200	90.8
PTCC	2	4	3,983,206	3.3

Note: Total Malayan output for the year 1954 was 122,490,000 lbs.

Sources: Adapted from Puthucheary, *Ownership and Control*, p. 85; Annual Report PacTin, 1954.

out of his way to make arrangements for a stopover in Hawaii and took Dato' Nik on a tour with his friends there. Overall, the management of PacTin welcomed Malayan independence as the corporation thought that the country was being 'well run' and with 'good men' in control.[128]

PacTin made significant impact not only in the tin mining industry, but also on Malayan socio-economic conditions, through the company's technological innovation and managerial skills. The corporation played an important role in initiating the rehabilitation of the Malayan tin mining industry immediately after World War II, and in the process it introduced plans that suggested ways of combating the communist insurgents during the Emergency. Success on both counts was only achievable through close cooperation between the state and the multinational corporation. Unlike its British contemporaries, PacTin welcomed decolonisation and was not afraid to face the challenges of political change. The firm worked closely with indigenous politicians and businessmen and maintained social contacts with these leading Malayans, a vital element in ensuring the growth and survival of US firms during the post-war decolonisation era.

4.5 US enterprise in tin: a summary

As we have seen, there was considerable cooperation as well as competition that led, at times, to mutual support and, at others, to quite intense rivalry grounded in strategic interests between the British and US governments as well as British, American and local firms involved in the Malayan tin mining industry, from the early nineteenth century until Malaysian Independence. The mutual support took a political turn and intensified when tin became a strategic commodity during the two world wars and intensified again during the Emergency years, as detailed in Chapters 2 and 3 respectively.

For PacTin, it was the exhaustion of its gold mines in the Yukon, Alaska and California that brought it to Malaya to face the challenges of adapting to a wholly new environment. This case study shows that the corporation was largely successful in overcoming these challenges, and highlights the importance of technological advantages in resource-oriented FDI, how a firm's organisational and entrepreneurial efforts in R&D can spread innovations across borders, and in the case of PacTin, from the US to Malaya.

PacTin surmounted bureaucratic delays in its Malayan tin ventures through the entrepreneurial efforts of individual promoters and the ready access to financial resources. The specific advantages enjoyed by the company, including knowledge, technology and financial resources, are broadly consistent with Dunning's OLI framework and underline why PacTin was successful in the Malayan tin mining industry.

Despite the initial reservations presented by the British government, PacTin's operations in Malaya highlight US firms' compliance with British policies and procedures in tin mining activities in Malaya. The British and US governments cooperated in re-building the Malayan economy after Word War II and there was mutual support between both governments and businesses, particularly in their efforts to protect the Malayan tin mining industry during the Emergency period. Though PacTin's contribution to the output of Malayan tin was relatively low, the evidence strongly suggests that the corporation had a significant impact on the progress of the Malayan tin mining industry, primarily in the areas of technology and managerial skills and the diffusion of its R&D activities among other mining firms undoubtedly increased production.

The technological expertise did, however, remain with the Western firms, as local miners, primarily local Chinese, lacked funds to invest in the capital intensive dredging technology. Nevertheless, PacTin was prepared to give support to Chinese miners through the tributary system, which enabled some miners to use conventional methods to work sections of PacTin mines unfit for dredging.

The transformation of YGC from a gold mining firm into tin mining and other minerals ensured the continued existence of the US firm. The profits gained from the tin mining activities in Malaya ensured the continual survival of the firm into its transformation as Pacific Tin Consolidated Corporation, or PacTin. During the Emergency, PacTin portrayed its corporate social responsibility when it lent support to the British government's fight against the communists. The US MNE quickly rehabilitated its mining activities and thus boosted the Malayan economy and provided local employment opportunities. PacTin, through its effective management in the post-World War II years, went through rapid rehabilitation and its decision to continue production during the Emergency years set a precedent for other mining firms.

5 Plantation

United States Rubber Company

The United States Rubber Company (USRC) began as a consolidation of nine footwear manufacturers in 1892 and expanded into tyre production in 1905. Prior to World War I, the firm emerged as one of the four largest US rubber manufacturers, along with Goodyear, Firestone and Goodrich and together they formed the 'big four' in the tyre production business. USRC soon became the pioneer and largest investor to integrate backwards into rubber plantations among these big four, which marked the company's transformation into a true multinational company. Although not the first, USRC was the largest US MNE in the Malayan rubber growing industry. Similarly, USRC's Sumatran investment was one of the largest US-owned rubber plantations in the world in the early twentieth century.

This chapter examines USRC's attempt to integrate backwards into plantation development in Malaya. In addition, some consideration is given to the firm's earlier investments in the Dutch East Indies as USRC's Sumatran investments were extensive and this factor would ultimately affect the development of the Malayan plantations. Like the Yukon Gold Company, by World War I USRC was already a well-established manufacturer in the US. It had developed managerial and technical competencies that made it easier for the company to sustain its overseas investments, including those in Malaya. It is also important to consider the locational advantages of Malaya for USRC. Entry barriers imposed by the British government initially limited not only USRC interests, but also other US investments in the Malayan rubber industry. Like tin, rubber was an important source of dollar earnings for Malaya and Britain and similar issues of competition and cooperation transpired in both sectors from the end of World War I until 1957. Through analysis of such issues it is possible to make a thorough assessment of the impact made by USRC on the Malayan rubber industry.

5.1 USRC: the origins

In the early twentieth century, USRC adopted a policy of meeting its own crude rubber needs by acquiring extensive concessions in northern Brazil, then the world's largest rubber exporter. However, this cross-border investment failed in 1903 due to labour problems, leaf blight disease and high government taxes. USRC instead worked to secure crude rubber supplies for its manufacturing purposes by establishing purchasing offices. This was achieved by the formation of its subsidiary, the General Rubber Company (GRC), in 1904. GRC set up purchasing offices in the rubber markets of Para and Manaos in Brazil and also in the British cities of London and Liverpool, giving the company 'advantages as to prices and guarantee as to supply', which was not enjoyed by any other consumer in the world.[1] Edgar B. Davis was the key figure behind USRC's initial investment in rubber plantations in South East Asia and was one of the few American entrepreneurs who wanted to vertically integrate rubber plantations with manufacturing.[2]

Because of the ample supply of wild rubber, Davis failed in his attempts in 1907 and again in 1908 to convince cautious officers at USRC to pursue plantation development. However, when inadequate and volatile supply meant that wild rubber producers could not fulfil the rubber manufacturers' demands, USRC decided to venture to South East Asia and secure a reliable source of rubber for itself in an effort to avoid the speculative activities that caused violent fluctuations in rubber prices. It was at this crucial time of fluctuating rubber prices that USRC decided to reduce transactions costs by accepting Davis's proposal to grow its own rubber.

In December 1909, the USRC board of directors appointed Edgar B. Davis as vice president in charge of plantation and allocated S$4.6 million for initial expenses to acquire rubber plantations in South East Asia. The rubber industry entered a phenomenal boom period between 1909 and 1910, with the growing demand for rubber in the US largely due to the tripling of automobiles sales, from 65,000 in 1908 to 187,000 in 1910. However, rubber prices tended to fluctuate dramatically. By 1909, the price for rubber per pound rose rapidly to S$2.50 and touched a record high of S$5.50 in 1910.[3]

Meanwhile, several British and Dutch firms had already been established in Britain and the Netherlands to operate rubber plantations in Ceylon (now Sri Lanka), Sumatra, Java, Borneo and the Malay Peninsula, before the American foray into plantation development. This, however, did not deter Davis, who was driven by the success of the British and Dutch planters. He was determined to ensure that US companies, too, had a share in the lucrative rubber industry. He hired both British and Dutch rubber experts. William J. Gallagher, the former director of agriculture for the Federated Malay States, was enlisted for his expertise in rubber cultivation and Huibreght Ketner, a veteran Dutch tobacco planter with 22 years' experience, was put in charge of operations. As a latecomer to the rubber industry, the hiring of both British and Dutch experts gave USRC the much needed expertise to be competitive in the industry. In the meantime, for managerial organisation, USRC provided a young Harvard graduate, John W. Bicknell.

Davis looked for the location with the greatest and most suitable potential for his needs. He purchased 88,000 acres of an old tobacco plantation in Sumatra in 1910 for S$2.14 million and sold the tobacco crop for S$0.92 million. Consequently, it cost USRC only S$1.2 million to get into the rubber plantation business and USRC soon began to profit from Davis's enterprise.[4] Already the first US rubber plantation owner in the world, by 1912 USRC became the largest.

Simultaneously, USRC became the world's largest single manufacturer and distributor of tyres, supplying 25 per cent of America's consumption.[5]

USRC's preferred strategy was to acquire established firms, which had the advantages of cleared land, a working organisation and an existing labour force that would become the nucleus of the firm's new plantations. By the beginning of the World War I, GRC had purchasing offices in Singapore, the Straits Settlements and in Colombo, Ceylon.[6] USRC's initial success was largely down to the vision of Edgar B. Davis, who portrayed the qualities of a Kirzner entrepreneur. His entrepreneurial alertness towards the rubber planting opportunities had successfully set a foundation for USRC's rubber enterprise in South East Asia.

5.2 Business, government and rubber

By the outbreak of the World War I, US business and government leaders began to see the strategic significance of rubber to the US economy. Rubber played a dominant role in the automobile industry and there was concern that US industry as a whole was dependent upon overseas supply. These fears seemed justified when the British placed an embargo on rubber as a strategic commodity, to keep it from falling into the possession of Germany and its allies. From September 1914, the destinations of rubber exports from the Federated Malay States and Straits Settlements were progressively restricted. By October, rubber could only be delivered to British ports and by November, the export of rubber from Britain to all destinations was banned. The control over the export of rubber from Britain and its possessions was assigned to the Rubber Exports Committee set up in London in January 1915 (from March 1915, this Committee also controlled tin exports and was known as the Rubber and Tin Exports Committee). The Committee exercised strict surveillance and was able to control both primary exports to and re-exports from consuming countries.[7]

This embargo seriously affected both the US and British rubber manufacturers, as well as consumers. A series of discussions ensued between the British government and US rubber MNEs leading to the 'Rubber Agreement' whereby the rubber companies, including USRC, agreed to pay cash bonds as surety against disposing of their raw rubber and manufactured articles directly or indirectly to enemy countries.[8] Two weeks after the US entered World War I in April 1917, Britain relaxed its restrictions on rubber shipment to US rubber factories and USRC received British approval to fulfil its rubber needs for the first time since August 1914. By the end of the war, ample supplies of rubber were reaching US factories.[9]

However, the difficulties encountered during World War I, including the British embargo on rubber exports, the dislocation in European shipping and trade, and the wartime cessation of the European rubber markets, led US rubber manufacturers in their search for new sources of rubber to set up purchasing offices in Singapore. Instances of US rubber manufacturers buying and growing rubber in South East Asia is a clear example of backwards integration and is exemplified by attempts made to establish rubber plantations in Malaya at the time.

In contrast to the small US rubber firms that came to Malaya in the 1900s, as detailed in Chapter 2, during the war years of 1916 and 1917 large US rubber firms began to show interest in Malaya. In August 1916, the Firestone Rubber Company attempted to purchase 25,000 acres of state land in Lower Perak to start a rubber plantation in the Federated Malay States.[10] In September 1916, USRC sent two representatives, Edgar B. Davis and Stuart Hotchkiss, through its subsidiary GRC, to meet the high commissioner of the Federated Malay States.[11] They wanted to ascertain the government's stand on their wish to acquire rubber plantations.

US rubber MNEs' attempts to make inroads into the Malayan rubber industry sparked a major debate among various commercial and official British interests. Among those who were opposed included the British planters of the Central Perak Planters' Association, and the Rubber Growers Association Council (RGA). The most vocal opponent of US investment, the RGA was a large concern representing the interests of British rubber producers. Apart from the Rubber and Tin Exports Committee, the Commercial Department of the Board of Trade was also drawn into the debate.

Several factors led British commercial interests, the RGA mainly but not exclusively, as well as government interests, to protest against allowing large US rubber firms to invest in Malaya. First, the ban imposed by the British Treasury as a wartime measure restricted British rubber firms from further investments in Malaya although there was no restriction upon the alienation of land in the Federated Malay States to persons of non-British nationality. Hence, US entry would disadvantage British planters that had hitherto been instrumental in building the economic success of the Malayan rubber industry. Second, there was the inherent fear of the threat posed by US big business. Being the largest consumers of rubber with rising future demands, it was feared that because of their strong financial resources and capacity for economies of scale and scope, US firms would quickly take over an industry that was a British innovation.

The significance of historical antecedents should not be underestimated (as argued in more detail in Chapters 2 and 4) and is apparent in the protests made by the RGA when it cited the attempts made by Americans to usurp British tin smelting interests in Malaya. The Board of Trade reiterated that 'it is most desirable both on economic and military grounds that the rubber growing industry in the British Empire should be kept under British control as far as possible'.[12] In addition it was feared that the entry of US firms would compound the existing problems in the labour market of the rubber industry. The Rubber and Tin Exports Committee highlighted labour issues, stating that the US entry might entice British assistants from present employers with the promise of higher salaries.[13] According to Lord Balfour of Burleigh, then chairman of the Committee, 'labour snatching' incidents in Sumatra revealed the tendency of US corporations to take unfair advantage of their rivals, which in the case of Malaya meant the British.[14]

Intriguingly, British rubber interests, however, did not receive the full support of the British administrators in Malaya and the chief secretary of the Federated Malay States, Sir Ernest L. Brockman, upheld the laissez-faire policy of allowing foreign investment 'irrespective of nationality'.[15] Although the high commissioner, Sir Arthur Young, perceived this as a case of producers versus consumers of rubber, the RGA viewed the participation of US rubber firms in Malaya clearly as a case of British interests versus those of the US. There was, for example, no agitation against investments by the Dunlop Rubber Company, the largest British rubber manufacturer and a large rubber consumer, which had integrated backwards into rubber plantation in Malaya on a large scale in 1910 even before the war and the rubber embargo.

As detailed in Chapter 4 in relation to the tin industry, the British authorities were suspicious of monopoly or 'trusts' and speculative activities from either British or other foreign firms were not tolerated. However, in the case of rubber, the question of monopoly did not arise as, according to the Federated Malay States authorities, there were 'ample means to check any attempt by an American rubber manufacturer in creating a rubber monopoly'. The local colonial government believed it had the capacity to 'neutralise monopolies' and for these administrators it was more important to promote competition and efficiency in the Malayan rubber industry.[16] Chief Secretary Brockman, for instance, praised the excellent methods employed by the Americans on their plantations in Sumatra and considered it 'a great loss to British Malaya that they should have taken up land in Sumatra and not in this country'.[17]

There was, of course, also the question of revenue. Like tin, rubber was a leading revenue earner for the Malayan administrators, derived largely in the form of land rents and sales as well as railway receipts. Unlike tin, however, rubber export duty was of lesser significance to the government income which made tin revenue was generally higher than that from rubber.[18] For example, between 1920 and 1938 (excepting 1932), tin revenue contributed 10 to 24 per cent to the total revenue in comparison with 1 to 11 per cent for rubber. Significantly though, rubber brought in higher export income for the Malayan administrators.[19]

The debate about large US firms' entry into the Malayan rubber industry was brought to a close with the Colonial Office's decision to restrict foreign investments. In considering the importance of rubber as a raw material and the control of it as an important 'imperial asset', the Colonial Office sided with British rubber interests and supported the Board of Trade's argument for protective measures rather than the impartial treatment of foreign investment favoured by local British administrators.[20] These differing approaches advocated by the Colonial Office and the British administrators in Malaya illustrate the tension between the metropolitan and the state colonial interests. While the metropolitan's aim was to protect its interests during the war, the local administrators were more concerned with the advancement of the Malayan rubber industry and the Malayan economy, even if it meant allowing non-British business interests to compete on an equal footing.

In January 1917, the Colonial Office, with the agreement of the Rubber and Tin Exports Committee, instructed the Federated Malay States government to prohibit the alienation of land for rubber exceeding 50 acres to non-British subjects pending further instructions.[21] This brought about the passage of the Rubber Lands

(Restriction) Enactment effective from 25 July 1917 in the Federated Malay States with 'No alienations over 50 acres were permissible except to British nationals, subjects of the Malay rulers, corporations registered in the United Kingdom, Dominions or locally in Malaya, and persons resident in the Peninsula for at least seven years and intending to so continue'.[22] Similar legislation followed in the Straits Settlements and Unfederated Malay States. The restriction also applied to sales of existing rubber land and transactions were only allowed between people of the same nationality and the transfer of funds for investment purposes was also prohibited.[23]

Although Drabble argues that such protective legislation arose from British fears of not only US but also Japanese firms extending their holdings in Malaya, it is clear that the reservations about Japanese interests were minimal compared with the perceived threat of US investment given its monopolist tendencies.[24] By 1918, the total area of the Japanese rubber plantations in the Malay Peninsula was 112,000 acres (100,000 acres were in Johore) and this constituted only 8.6 per cent of total rubber acreage of 1,307,022 in the Malay Peninsula in 1918.[25] USRC's investment in Sumatra alone, however, notwithstanding potential investments from Goodyear and Firestone, were already close to 90,000 acres and the company was in a strong position to make significant inroads into Malaya. Nevertheless, the legislation drew protests from Japanese rubber interests in Malaya. The Japanese Planters' Association urged the Japanese ambassador in London to protest against the restriction suggesting that 'this constitutes a very extreme instance of repression by the British government of the honest enterprise of Japanese in that region, and of obstruction to their legitimate development'.[26] Meanwhile the Japanese consul in Singapore took the case to the high commissioner of the Malay States.[27]

US rubber manufacturers had little choice but to accept this unfavourable provision as they had no holdings in Malaya at that time. The General Rubber Company withdrew its application without protest. Due to the restriction, US firms again turned to Sumatra where new entrants' established estates and existing firms expanded their acreage. The second US venture in Sumatra was the 12,000 acre plantation in Deli by Hawaiian Sumatra Plantations Ltd in 1916. In the same year, Goodyear leased 20,000 acres of the Dolok Merangir Estates in Sumatra and Firestone began seeking opportunities for a US-controlled supply of rubber that was independent of British and Dutch domination, urging the US government to look into the legal barriers that restricted large-scale rubber planting in the Philippines (see Chapter 3 for more details).

The Rubber Lands (Restriction) Enactment, however, lasted for less than two years and was repealed on 3 September 1919. Although the act was imposed as a wartime measure and was not specifically targeted against US investors, its impact was to drive possible US investment away. US MNEs, except for USRC, which had invested in Sumatra in 1910, tended to shift their attention to the neighbouring Dutch East Indies when they were blocked in Malaya. While USRC came to invest in the Malayan rubber industry when the above act was repealed, Goodyear and Firestone remained outside the Malayan rubber investment scene.

The onset of World War I in Europe heightened fears about the supply of crude rubber among US rubber manufacturers. Several attempts were made by American organisations and rubber manufacturers for cooperative purchasing and plantation investments. The American International Company (AIC), founded in 1915 by F.A. Vanderlip, president of the National City Bank of New York, suggested a consolidation of US tyre companies to develop rubber plantations and to work in close cooperation with USRC.[28] After the war, AIC's efforts to consolidate US rubber-producing companies failed, with these rubber manufacturers preferring an independent course of action.[29]

An attempt was also made for consolidating cooperation among British and US rubber producing and rubber manufacturing firms. This is evidenced in Edgar B. Davis's proposal in May 1914 when he sought the support of USRC's directors for the establishment of an international rubber organisation, the so-called 'International Plantation Rubber Company' (IPRC). Although then unsuccessful, after World War I Davis tried again, even resigning in January 1919 from the USRC board in order to pursue the establishment of IPRC.[30] He lobbied for support from US financial interests and the RGA, who Davis informed that the formation of IPRC would achieve nine objectives to help solve problems in the rubber industry, including,

> an international market for securities, the joint formulation of policies affecting output and surplus stocks, a scattering of risks from diseases and pests, winds, floods, deterioration of trees, etc., the reduction of costs through economies of large-scale management, the centralized administration of labour, benefits to manufacturers and planters through large-scale production of a uniform product under new processes as developed, an organized campaign for the extensions of rubber's present uses, and stimulation of new uses, the maintenance of efficient research and statistical departments to secure accurate knowledge of progress in all phases of the industry and a stabilizing influence in the industry.[31]

According to Davis, the proposal for the organisation of IPRC represented 15 years' research on the industry by him and his two co-workers, Walter B. Mahony and David M. Figart. He also highlighted the economic benefits of 'contemporary amalgamations' and the lessons that had been learned from the US experience. According to Davis, £150 million had been invested in the industry and a further £50 million (IPRC would be registered in Britain with an authorised capital of £50 million) would be ample to stabilise it.[32]

While Davis was working to set up the IPRC, the rubber industry in Malaya was hit by post-war recession from a combination of over-production caused by good yields and increased acreage, and a fall in demand for the commodity. The 1920–1921 depression led to lower rubber prices, impacting on the US automobile and tyre industries, and leaving many British rubber firms on the verge of bankruptcy. Fears of a US takeover of the rubber plantations led the RGA to revive its 1918 scheme for voluntary restriction during these two years.

In 1921, the British government demonstrated its own concern over the struggling rubber industry by forming a committee chaired by Sir James Stevenson and with significant RGA representation, with the remit to find ways of protecting the rubber industry. By August 1922, the price of rubber had dropped to S$0.31 cents a pound[33] and, despite the RGA's support of restricted production, the committee was prepared to listen to Davis's IPRC proposal on three occasions in September, including two meetings at the Council Chamber of the RGA in London, and once at the Hague.[34] The RGA unanimously resolved in their meeting of 22 September 1922 that they were unable to proceed further with the IPRC proposal until the British government's decision regarding the restriction scheme was known.[35] Davis's proposal stressing the benefits of large-scale production as practised in the US failed to impress the British planters, who refused to surrender direct control of their estates to a board of directors which, they claimed, included significant US representation.[36] The British planters did not agree with the internationalisation of the industry, and, as seen in the Rubber Lands Enactment debate, suspicion of US businesses remained pervasive.

As such, there were a range of approaches and solutions advocated by US and British interested parties in an attempt to reinvigorate the rubber industry. Davis preferred the creation of a large company, of both British and US interests, to control the supply and demand of rubber in the world market. His proposed plan was not adopted because of several weaknesses, including only obtaining the support of a few US financial interests, the perception that the grand scale of the scheme might have been difficult to manage, and the difficulty of reconciling the differing interests of producers and consumers. While Davis's plan showed a preference for big business and, ultimately, the creation of a monopoly, the RGA preferred the formation of a cartel. However, when Anglo-Dutch negotiations for the formation of an international cartel failed in August 1922, the British government proceeded to restrict rubber production through the Stevenson Scheme.

The Stevenson Scheme, which ran for six years, was introduced on 1 November 1922 in an effort to stabilise the price of rubber by curtailing production.[37] While British rubber producers accounted for 70 per cent of total world production, US firms consumed 70 per cent. Thus, when the British government initiated the Stevenson Scheme, the US government and one of the 'big four' rubber firms, Firestone, opposed the plan. The Rubber Association of America, in a memorandum to the Department of State, highlighted the dangers posed to the US rubber manufacturing industry by the restrictions and condemned the scheme as 'economically unsound and absolutely unnecessary'.[38] The British administrators were accused of using the Stevenson Scheme to limit US investment in the rubber industry during the slump period.[39] Perceiving that the US companies were attempting to buy bankrupt British rubber companies, the British hit back and accused US firms of trying to take over the rubber industry. The chairman of the Amalgamated Rubber Estates wrote to the British Prime Minister, Lloyd George, with the accusation that there was a plot to 'Americanise' the industry.[40]

The British government also saw the Stevenson Scheme as a convenient strategic tool to repay war debts to the US. As indicated by Winston Churchill, secretary of state for the colonies, increased prices for rubber would support the international position of sterling against the US dollar.[41] Meanwhile, the introduction of the Stevenson Scheme divided US rubber firms with USRC, Goodrich and Goodyear supporting its introduction and Firestone firmly opposed.[42] Stuart Hotchkiss, vice president USRPI, stressed that criticism of the scheme was due to a lack of understanding of the real cost of producing rubber. In his letter to the RGA secretary, he stated that GRC and USRPI concurred with other large rubber manufacturers in the US on the merits of the proposed restriction plan.[43] Most US rubber manufacturers preferred higher prices but ready supply rather than low prices but inadequate supply.[44]

Firestone owner Harvey S. Firestone, an economic nationalist and opponent of the Stevenson Scheme, argued that US rubber manufacturers should open rubber estates in countries free of Dutch and British control. He felt it was necessary to resist the restriction plans of the British government, which he estimated would cost US rubber users S$187 million in 1923.[45] He continued his efforts with the support of Henry Ford for a US-controlled supply of rubber and urged the US government to look into the possibilities of developing rubber plantations on an extensive scale.[46] Firestone conducted an investigation on the viability of planting rubber in Mindanao in the Philippines, but did not invest when it again failed to overcome legal barriers.[47]

Between 1923 and 1926, there were wild swings in the price of crude rubber largely caused by the adoption of the Stevenson Scheme. Initially, increased consumption by the US in the aftermath of the slump due to increased auto sales and good business conditions led to the rise of US crude rubber imports from 692 million pounds in 1923, to 735 million pounds in 1924, and 888 million pounds in 1925.[48] However, by 1925 rubber prices began to fluctuate, and in 1926 they dropped significantly. In 1928, when Prime Minister Stanley Baldwin announced the removal of the Stevenson Scheme effective from 1 November 1928, the New York price of crude rubber fell further to US20 cents (S$0.35 cents) per pound.[49] As such, the Stevenson Scheme largely failed its objective to stabilise rubber prices.

Several factors worked against the success of the Stevenson Scheme. A real challenge came from the Dutch East Indies, which was outside of the scheme, and where there was a significant increase in production as the local government encouraged smallholders to plant rubber. In 1923, out of 137,000 tons of rubber exported from the Dutch East Indies, 55,000 tons came from smallholders. In 1925, exports from these smallholders rose to 85,000 tons reaching a peak of 99,000 tons in 1927.[50] A further factor working against the scheme was the smuggling activities in Malaya which contributed to a fall in the price of rubber. In addition, the greater use of reclaimed rubber in the US, from one-fifth of rubber requirements in 1922 to one-half in 1928, undermined the scheme's ability to stabilise rubber prices.[51]

The US government also intervened on behalf of US interests after Firestone won the support of Secretary of Commerce Herbert Hoover. Hoover instituted a number of measures to protect the interests of US businesses against British control of rubber. These included restricting the consumption of rubber goods, not allowing US bankers to grant credits to foreign commodity control, encouraging home production and consumption of rubber substitutes (to reduce imports by conservation and by substitution of reclaimed rubber), supporting production in countries void of monopolist tendencies, legalising pooled purchases to remove competition within US businesses and searching for alternative areas for rubber plantation development.[52]

In March 1923, the US government conducted a congressional investigation and allocated US$593,000 for a joint investigation by the Departments of Agriculture and Commerce to find areas suitable for US investment.[53] Prior to the congressional investigation, all of the US-owned rubber plantations were located in the Dutch East Indies and Malaya. These plantations had a total of approximately 150,000 acres in 1920, of which less than 47,000 acres were in production, or only 1.07 per cent of a grand total of 4.29 million acres under cultivation in South East Asia.[54] Of the total 150,000 acres, the plantations of USRC constituted the great majority at 117,000 acres. Goodyear had 20,000 acres whilst the Continental Rubber Company and The Manhattan Rubber Manufacturing Company had 2,000 acres in Sumatra and Java, respectively.[55]

By 1928, the holdings of US companies, notably USRC and Goodyear, had increased in South East Asia. Goodyear's holdings grew to 62,500 acres when it added a second plantation of 40,000 acres in Sumatra and a 2500-acre plantation in the Philippines.[56] USRC remained the largest of the US investors, commanding 58 per cent of the rubber area owned by all US companies and contributing 72 per cent of the production.[57] It should be noted that from 1925 to 1928, British rubber firms also expanded their investments in South East Asia. A temporary price boom from 1925 to 1926 not only 'strengthened their financial positions in the short term, it also transformed the climate for further investment'.[58] From the mid-1920s onwards, an additional 400,000 acres were added to the Malayan rubber acreage and 59 new sterling companies, 36 in 1925 alone, were floated.[59]

Having been driven there by British restrictions in Malaya, US rubber investment was largest in the Dutch East Indies, followed by Malaya and then the Philippines. There was no US investment in Thailand where, unlike Malaya, the Dutch East Indies or the Philippines, there was hardly any Western enterprise. In rubber, there was no Western investment in Thailand as rubber cultivation there had a late start, only beginning in 1920, due to the misconception that land conditions there were unsuitable. Consequently, in Thailand the rubber industry was dominated by local smallholders. In 1926 to 1927, rubber formed only 2.2 per cent of Thailand's exports, increasing to almost 20 per cent in 1937 to 1938.[60] For Firestone and Ford, the limited opportunities in the Philippines and Malaya and their desire to invest outside British- and Dutch-controlled territories led them to invest in Liberia and Brazil respectively. In 1926, Firestone went to Liberia while Ford went to Brazil in 1927.[61]

Although the production of US-owned estates increased to an estimated 47.1 million pounds, or 4.47 per cent of US consumption, in 1928, it was still relatively insignificant and did not guarantee the independence of a US rubber supply. The preoccupation with economies of scale and scope, as seen in Firestone's 988,000-acre investment in Liberia, Ford's 3.7 million-acre investment in Brazil and USRC's 90,000-acre investment in Sumatra, kept US rubber enterprises from appreciating the potential of rubber planting in the Philippines, and US rubber firms failed to develop a rubber industry in what was then a US colony. Meanwhile, British and Dutch rubber planting companies in Malaya and Sumatra were successfully operating on a much smaller scale. Most of these companies owned between 2000 and 10,000 acres of land. Voon Phin Keong argues that the 'financial performance of these companies showed no meaningful correlation between the amount of profit and size of plantation'.[62]

Wilkins argues that US tyre manufacturers integrated backwards into buying and growing rubber in South East Asia to avoid the European rubber markets and because they expected higher prices post-World War I.[63] However, in the case of USRC, although the firm wished 'to secure at least partial immunity from market fluctuations', its directors were less concerned about the possible increase of costs.[64] The decision-makers at USRC were aware of the problem of over production and low prices in the industry, but decided to go ahead and acquire new plantations after World War I. It is probably the case, as with other US tyre firms, that USRC's goal was to achieve steady supplies irrespective of costs in the belief also that the economies of scale would stabilise in the course of time.

The same attitude can be discerned from Goodyear's activities. French, in his study of Goodyear, claims that despite declining prices and over capacity, 'long-term investment decisions' were driven by 'short-term fluctuations and the fear of restriction schemes rather than from clear cost considerations'.[65] US rubber manufacturers' efforts to control their own supplies were overly ambitious, and spurred mostly by an 'emotive' decision to control supply rather than rational economic considerations. The decision to control supply was made not in response to the actual situation on the ground because at the time there were low prices and overcapacity but an instinctive desire to circumvent the imposition of unfavourable policies which were deemed as anti-American.

The fragility of US rubber manufacturers' investment in rubber became apparent with the collapse of rubber prices in 1929. That year, Firestone limited its investments in Liberia and USRC bore the financial burden of its once profitable plantations. In retrospect, British fears of the US threat to the Malayan rubber industry appeared unjustified, although in later years the US interests – despite their small rubber investments – did make headway into R&D over the British and Dutch rubber movers.

5.3 USRC: from World War I to post-World War II

By May 1913, USRC had planted 32,500 acres in Sumatra with 3.9 million trees.[66] In 1914, the first rubber shipment from Sumatra arrived in the US, a year earlier than expected. Under the leadership of Huibreight Keitner, 14,200 acres were planted in 1915, a record which was said to be unbroken for ten years. At this time,

USRC's Sumatran venture employed 14,000 Chinese and Javanese labourers with a staff of 90 Europeans and Americans.[67] By 1915, USRC had invested S$27.5 million in its Sumatran rubber venture and with record plantings, rubber shipments to the US increased substantially between the years 1916 to 1918.

In 1917, a subsidiary of GRC, United States Rubber Plantation Incorporated (USRPI), was formed in New York State with a capitalisation of US$10 million preferred stock and US$20 million common stock, and took over the management of the plantations and the operating subsidiaries.[68] USRC was satisfied with its investment, stating that the cost of production in South East Asia, mainly because of the cheap labour, was one-third of the cost in Brazil.[69] By 1919, the company owned approximately 93,000 acres, of which 44,227 acres had been cleared and planted with more than 5 million rubber trees.[70] This was on a much larger scale than the Dunlop Rubber Company in Malaya, the largest European rubber plantation owner, which in the same year had a total planted area of 39,000 acres.[71]

With the end of World War I, USRC began an expansion programme to double the productive capacity of its tyre plants in the US by 1920. As part of this plan, the firm decided to obtain a much larger percentage of its rubber requirements from its own plantations, culminating in a need to expand its operations. USRC chose to invest in Malaya when the Rubber Lands (Restriction) Enactment, which had restricted USRC's entrance into Malaya during World War I, was repealed on 3 September 1919. However, the timing was also partly due to the diminishing advantages of labour, duties and taxation in Sumatra since 1910 when compared to Malaya.[72] For USRC, it was deemed that 'there would be an element of safety' if the firm was to invest in Malaya.[73]

Consequently, in 1919, USRC approached the local governments of Johore, Pahang, Perak and Kedah for land concessions of 50,000 acres. In Pahang, the firm spent S$140,000 on a survey of potential rubber plantation sites. This greenfield investment plan was, however, abandoned when USRC decided to acquire existing rubber plantations in the Malay states. In the same year, USRC acquired 13,000 acres in the northern state of Kedah for rubber plantations. By 1923, its Malayan properties consisted of 22,000 acres, with 10,000 acres planted and 1500 acres in production.[74] In July 1925, 6300 acres, known as the Harvard Estates, were purchased in Kedah, Malaya. USRPI ran these estates under a subsidiary known as the Malayan–American Plantations Ltd, which had been incorporated in the Federated Malay States in 1920. Table 5.1 details the acreage managed by Malayan–American Plantations while Figure 5.1 shows the various locations in Malaya.

USRC's Malayan acquisitions and the cost of their development were financed from the income of plantations in Sumatra where the firm had some of the largest rubber plantations in the world. USRC also owned 22,226 acres in the Malay states, of which 10,311 acres were planted with 1500 acres of rubber producing plantations. With over 110,000 acres under its control, the firm was able to supply 20 per cent of its rubber needs from its own plantations in 1922.[75]

By 1926, USRC, through its subsidiaries, owned more than 104,000 acres in Sumatra and 30,000 acres in Malaya, representing an investment of S$52.9 million,

Table 5.1 Malayan–American Plantations Ltd, 1925

	Total Area (acres)	*Cultivated Rubber (acres)*
	Kedah	
Scarboro Estate (Sungei Patani)	5,055	4,137
Maryland Estate (Kulim)	989	825
Dublin Estate (Kulim)	9,839	9,640
Harvard Estate (Sungei Patani)	6,300	1,200
Total Area – Kedah	22,183	15,802
	Johore	
Wessyngton Estate (Rengam)	3,096	3,045
Linden Estate (Johore Bahru)	2,312	1,470
Total Area – Johore	5,408	4,515
	Selangor	
Bristol Estate (Kuang)	2,099	1,915
Total Area – Malaya	29,690	22,232

Source: *Malayan Tin and Rubber Journal*, 15 (1926).

compared to a total of 124,000 acres and an investment of S$44.5 million in 1925. The parent company had invested S$32 million, with the balance of S$20.8 million coming from earnings from the plantation subsidiary companies. The total investment by the end of 1927 was nearly S$59 million, which was the equivalent of S$678 per planted acre.[76]

In the late 1920s USRC's plantation venture was more profitable than the parent company and these profits kept the parent company afloat. In 1926 and 1927, USRPI declared dividends of S$10.7 million and S$7.1 million respectively to the parent company. A total of S$14.2 million was transferred from USRPI profits in 1927, sufficient to finance the parent's company's operations until December 1928 through short-term bank loans.[77] The financial statement of USRC in 1927 proved the profitability of this venture, when profits from the plantation were able to eliminate a deficit of several million dollars and turn a loss on the total yearly business of the company into a substantial profit.

Throughout the period of the Stevenson Scheme, USRPI was able to cushion the effects of violent fluctuations in the prices of crude rubber on the company by having its own rubber plantations. Its ability to guarantee a steady supply of rubber provided it with a sense of security and self-sufficiency. However, USRC's backward integration did not guarantee reduced transaction costs, as not only did this vastly increased management costs but the percentage of USRC's supply met by its own plantations also remained marginal, providing only 25 per cent of its total requirement by 1925. On the other hand, USRC's plantation arm, USRPI, was able to record significant profits on its transactions with the parent company. In the

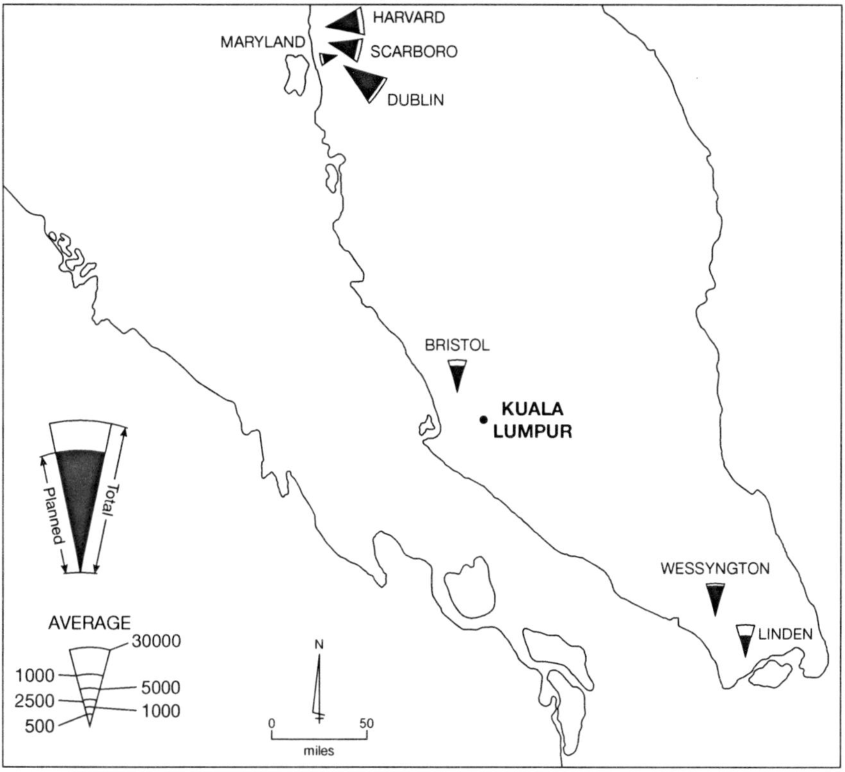

Figure 5.1 Location and acreage of Malayan–American Plantations Ltd in Malaya.

Source: Adapted from Voon Phin Keong, *American Rubber Planting Enterprise*, pp. 22–3.

final analysis, the total aggregate of crude rubber produced from US-owned properties formed a small and insignificant percentage of the total tonnage consumed by the US rubber industry. The total production of US-owned rubber plantations in 1927 was 35.5 million pounds, equivalent to only 2.6 per cent of total world production and 4.3 per cent of US consumption.[78]

With the worldwide depression from 1929 to 1933, rubber prices plummeted. US automobile production fell by about 74 per cent between 1929 and 1932.[79] Simultaneously, sales of original equipment tyres dropped from 21 million to 6 million, and replacement tyre sales declined from 47 million to 33 million.[80] As a consequence, rubber prices fell from an average of S$0.19 cents per pound in 1930 to S$0.10 cents in 1931, S$0.07 cents in 1932 and S$0.10 cents in 1933.[81] During the Depression the supply of natural rubber exceeded world consumption and from 1930 until mid-1933 the price of rubber fell below the cost of production. While in 1933 the average annual wholesale price of rubber in New York rose to almost US$0.06 a pound, the production costs on the plantations were variously estimated at US$0.08 to US$0.12 a pound.[82]

Thus, in an effort to regulate rubber exports and to maintain the price of rubber the International Rubber Regulation Agreement (IRRA) was introduced in 1934.[83] This five-year restriction plan was signed in London on 28 April 1934 by representatives of the countries producing about 98 per cent of the world supply: Britain, the Dutch East Indies, India, Burma, French Indochina, North Borneo (now known as Sabah), Sarawak and Siam (now Thailand). The scheme allocated quotas to each country based on average exports for the years 1929–1932 and planting of new areas were restricted.

USRC's reaction to the introduction of the IRRA was highly acrimonious. On 6 January 1934, Lucius D. Tompkins, a member of the firm's executive committee, attacked the inclusion of USRC's Malayan and Sumatran plantations in the restriction of IRRA, citing that they would be subjected to higher costs for crude rubber than the plantations of their competitor, Firestone, which, being in Liberia, was outside the restriction.[84] Goodyear also filed a complaint with the State Department when requests made for exemptions were rejected.[85]

To escape the restrictions imposed by IRRA, US rubber concerns took similar steps as they had done in response to the Stevenson Scheme. Some extended their holdings outside the restriction while a number of new US interests likewise sought to enter the rubber field in areas not under IRRA control. For example, Goodyear acquired experimental plantations in Panama in 1935 and Costa Rica in 1936 and Firestone expanded its holdings in Liberia in the mid-to-late 1930s. Goodrich attempted to vertically integrate when it explored the possibilities of buying rubber plantations in Malaya in 1934, but decided against locking up its much-needed capital in a long-term investment.[86] Investment decisions were clearly influenced by the restriction schemes and not cost considerations. USRC clearly suffered the disadvantage of having to abide by the restrictions. The impact on the firm can be seen in the reduction of USRPI's rubber shipments from nearly 51 million pounds in 1934 to 40 million in 1935, and likewise its profits from S$2.9 million to S$1.7 million.[87]

Gradually the US was recovering from the worst of the Depression. The sale of motor vehicles, a good barometer of the health of the economy, in three years more than doubled from 1,890,000 in 1933 to 4,461,000 in 1936. US tyre shipments rose from nearly 40 million in 1932 to 52 million in 1936 as did rubber imports into the US from 427,000 tons to 496,000 tons for the same period.[88] The increase in demand for rubber raised the New York price from the 1935 average of US12.4 cents a pound to the 1936 average of US16.4 cents and reached US27.2 cents a pound in March 1937.[89]

The higher prices for rubber enabled USRPI to show a net profit of S$3.3 million for 1936. In 1937, the increased export quotas set by the International Rubber Regulation Committee allowed a 39 per cent increase in pounds of rubber shipped by the firm's plantations. With increased shipments and higher prices throughout most of the year, USRPI's net profits increased to S$7.9 million. Despite these increases in profits in the latter part of the decade, because of the depressed price of rubber in the early 1930s, USRPI was unable to follow its 25-year replanting schedule. To cushion the consequences of fluctuations in the price of rubber, USRC executives set aside a reserve of S$2.3 million in 1935 and S$1.2 million in 1936.[90]

In the five years from 1937 to 1941 preceding the Japanese occupation, the plantations in Sumatra and Malaya produced 20 per cent of USRC's crude rubber requirements.[91] Significant progress was made in increasing yields and production increased from 37.4 million pounds in 1938 to 57 million pounds in 1941, the last year USRC received crude rubber shipments from its plantations prior to the war. Average yields per acre also increased, (see Table 5.2) from 652 pounds per acre in 1937 to a record high of 741 pounds per acre in 1940, a new record.

In December 1941, the Japanese invaded northern Malaya leading Malayan–American Plantations (MAP) to abandon its headquarters in Penang. During the Japanese occupation, more than 21,000 acres of the company's plantations were destroyed. Of the S$5.1 million in funds held by MAP in Singapore, S$4 million was transferred to London by January 1942. Under the Revenue Act of 1942, USRC's investments in rubber plantation subsidiaries and other foreign investments were written off as foreign war losses. The total write off for 1941 and 1942 was S$42.6 million, of which S$20.2 million was for MAP and S$21.3 million for its Sumatra subsidiaries.[92]

The seizure of the USRPI estates in Malaya and Sumatra by the Japanese meant the loss of some of the world's largest rubber plantations. Although by 1941 USRPI had 104,000 acres in Sumatra and 31,000 acres in Malaya, the amount or crude rubber shipped in that year managed to serve only 15 per cent of USRC's requirement. The lack of crude rubber supply led USRC to devote its effort to producing synthetic rubber, and the firm played a significant role in meeting the wartime requirement for rubber products.

The Japanese invasion caused tremendous damage to USRPI plantations due to neglect as well as attempts to plant substitute food crops. Damage was also caused by the Chinese communists when they looted plantation properties immediately after the Japanese left in August 1945.[93] By 17 November 1945, according to John W. Bicknell, the managing director of the plantations of USRPI, one out of five and a half trees on USRC plantations in Malaya and Sumatra were destroyed. This meant a loss of 1.8 million trees out of 10 million trees on the plantation during the Japanese invasion. The pre-war planted area was 102,000 acres.[94] As early as

Table 5.2 USRPI: production and average yield per acre in Sumatra and Malaya, 1937–1941

Year	*Acreage Owned*	*Acres Tapped*	*Production (in lbs)*	*Average Yield Per Acre (lbs)*	*Total Employees*
1937	135,000	89,075	58,072,000	652	17,059
1938	132,000	57,530	37,428,000	653	13,160
1939	132,000	77,700	53,501,000	689	n.a
1940	132,000	87,903	65,157,000	741	n.a.
1941	131,000	n.a.	57,000,000	n.a.	n.a.

Source: Annual Reports USRC, 1937–1941

March 1946, USRPI took action to enquire about the status of MAP land titles in Malaya.[95] Later in the year a survey party reported on the condition of the plantation properties and submitted plans and cost estimates for rehabilitation and the cost of future production. At this time, there were tapping activities on some Malayan plantations including the MAP estates and by the end of 1946, USRC had repossessed and resumed operations on these.[96] The net recovery value was S$11.6 million of the S$20.2 million loss written off in 1942.

USRC was among the first US rubber producers to return to its Malayan plantations and the firm proposed a S$7.5 million programme for rehabilitation. By the end of 1946, S$1.3 million had spent producing 12 million pounds of rubber, one half of the pre-war annual output, and employment was brought back up to pre-war levels. Included in the programme of rehabilitation of the plantations was the hiring of local staff, although the firm resisted setting a precedent of high wages for labourers. Still, during the period of rehabilitation, and later through the Emergency years, it is probably fair to say that USRC did cater to the welfare of its labourers, as it had done before the war, through such measures as providing adequate healthcare and recreational avenues. USRC's quick restitution of its plantations certainly contributed towards the speed of recovery of the Malayan rubber industry and, by extension, the Malayan economy.

Because of the speed of the rehabilitation programme, the plantations in Malaya and Sumatra were quickly able to produce significant quantities of rubber. By 1952, Malayan and Sumatran output combined was 50 million pounds, fully 20 per cent more rubber than in 1951. This was achieved despite continued harassment by the Communists of the estate management and labourers of USRPI as they pressed ahead with the replanting programme. By the end of 1952, the replanting was completed, with 84,000 acres planted with rubber at the estates in Malaya and Sumatra. Of this, 76,000 acres were already producing rubber.[97] In 1955 plantations in Malaya and Sumatra produced 49 million pounds of rubber, a 4 per cent increase from 1954. Profits in 1955 were higher due to increased production and improved rubber prices.[98] Post-war replanting continued through the 1950s and at the end of 1958 amounted to 9500 acres in Sumatra and 11,000 acres in Malaya. The higher figure for Malaya reflected the stable environment provided by the Malayan government – notwithstanding the Emergency – compared with the volatile political situation under President Soekarno in Indonesia.

After getting its own plantation operations up and running again, USRC then started purchasing raw latex from other rubber plantations and local rubber producers for processing at its plant in order to increase the rubber supply to its parent firm. In 1951 alone, USRC bought 8 million pounds of raw latex for processing.[99] In this way, USRC's position as both rubber manufacturer and producer with access to external markets meant that it was able to assist other rubber producers in Malaya. There was also important transferral of technology, organisational and entrepreneurial skills by USRC, which had a significant developmental impact on the Malayan rubber industry.

5.4 Rubber and American entrepreneurship

Comparisons were often made between the methods employed by the British, the Americans and the Dutch to maximise production, including scientific activities such as bud grafting, the use of statistical and research bureaus, estate management and labour control. In a short period of time, as the British rubber community had feared, the Americans were able to surpass their nearest competitors by a wide margin with their quality investments in rubber, though not in total production output. Their results proved the managerial competencies of the USRC and the importance of having a long-term strategic outlook in rubber investments. This would not have been achieved without the recruitment of experienced British and Dutch rubber experts. Both J. Grantham and Coombs Barclay, from the Malayan Agricultural Department, joined USRPI in Sumatra. Grantham later pioneered bud grafting and manuring experiments and in the early 1920s his advice was sought to reduce the soil deterioration in Malaya.[100] Similar to many British firms in Malaya, USRC's policy was to bring in personnel from the home country for its rubber operations in Malaya. US personnel, engineers, chemists and foresters were also brought in from USRC's research department in New York. They worked with the experienced British and Dutch scientists.[101] Similarly, Dunlop adopted the policy of hiring Dutch rubber experts, such as Dr P.J.S. Cramer, formerly director of agriculture at Bogor, Java, who joined the company in 1928 and the following year carried out large-scale budding programmes.[102]

Apart from hiring rubber experts and bringing skilled personnel from the US, USRC's long-term outlook can be seen in the capital costs incurred in their rubber investments in Sumatra and Malaya. The variations in capital costs between rubber producers show the comparative advantages enjoyed by different countries. Table 5.3 compares the capital costs and cost per acre among various nationalities in their South East Asian rubber ventures. In 1923, Britain, the largest investor in South East Asia, owned two-thirds of the rubber plantations with a capital cost of S$944 million, but the cost per acre was S$503.90. This figure was close to the average of all nations, excluding the US, at S$496.28. US cost per acre stood 39 per cent above that of Japan, and 64 per cent above the lowest, France and Belgium.

The variations in capital costs between rubber producers reflect their short- or long-term strategies in rubber investments. Rubber producers with comparatively low capital costs can be considered as 'penny wise and pound foolish' as Schwinges noted at the time

> they start wasting money by saving in the very first step of operations – clearing the jungle. After cutting and burning they leave the stumps to rot in the ground, because their removal is rather expensive. But to leave them is often more expensive because they rot and spread contagious diseases among the growing rubber trees, destroying sometimes acres and acres of planted rubber.[103]

Table 5.3 Rubber plantations: differences in capital costs and average cost per acre by various nationalities in South East Asia, 1923[a]

Country	*Acres (S$'000)*	*Capital Costs (S$'000)*	*Average Cost Per Acre (S$'000)*
Britain	1, 874	944	503.90
Netherlands	535	243	454.39
Japan	125	79	628.32
France and Belgium	134	56	418.66
China	52	26	503.46
Denmark	40	21	514.25
Others	37	9	550.00
United States[b]	87	60	686.51
Total	2, 884	1,438	532.44

Notes:

a Capital costs or 'one-off costs' refers to costs for acquiring, developing, or installing fixed assets of the firm.

b The Americans were mainly represented by USRC, one of the largest rubber investors in South East Asia.

Source: Adapted from Schwinges, 'America's Greatest Stake in Rubber, *The Outlook*, p. 157.

In the early 1920s, due to the depressed rubber prices and the effect of the Stevenson Scheme, some Malayan estates (with the exception of large rubber firms which were financially secure enough to see out the period of financial turmoil) adopted a tight fiscal policy and did not take adequate measures to protect, sustain and maintain their rubber estates. There was a need to raise estate costs to boost efficiency in the long term but this was not carried out due to cost-savings activities that unfortunately brought long-term consequences on production output and profitability.[104] In addition, some rubber producers sought to save on the construction cost of labour lines resulting in poor and more expensive labour due to a larger turnover.

The Americans incurred the highest capital cost per acre because being late-arrivals they had the advantage of learning from the mistakes of earlier planters and, thus, were able to carefully examine the costs and benefits of a long-term rubber investment. Since its early beginnings, Edgar B. Davis, the managing director from 1911 to 1918, ran the plantations 'on high efficiency, including scientific care of men and of trees, and a working organization of both coordination and cooperation' and Hollandsch-Amerikaansche Plantage Maatschappij (Holland American Plantation Company – HAPM) became 'the first concern that spent real money on research'.[105] Efforts were taken to guarantee the best conditions and highest efficiency in every branch of the operation to ensure the overall smooth running of the estate from initial clearing to the shipping of the finished product (plantation to commercialisation). Labourers were given clean and comfortable living quarters. Progressive personnel practices not only retained skilled and loyal workers but also increased productivity and workers efficiency. For USRC, the costs were subordinated to the emphasis given to these factors and its labour policies and procedures reflected the company's progressive personnel practices. USRC's long-term outlook led to increased output per acre throughout the years (see Table 5.2). A study of the Dublin Estate in Kedah illustrates this multinational's organisational and managerial skills and its developmental impact on the rubber industry in Malaya.

Model plantation: the Dublin Estate

In June 1923, USRPI based in Penang in the Straits Settlements, acquired a grant of undeveloped land in the Unfederated Malay States from the Kedah government. Proceedings had been initiated nearly a year previously in July 1922.[106] The price of land in the state of Kedah at the time of acquisition was S$20 per acre. The Kedah concession comprised a tract of approximately ten thousand acres on the Muda River in Central Kedah and was known as the Dublin Estate. The effective management practices of HAPM in Sumatra were applied to the Dublin Estate, which became a model plantation in Malaya. This new estate was considered a valuable addition to USRC's holdings in Peninsular Malaya (see Figures 5.1 and 5.2).

The internal operations of the Dublin Estate, the largest single unit of rubber estate for MAP as well as for the state of Kedah, makes for interesting evaluation on several levels including the extent of Anglo-American cooperation, the extent of R&D as well as the style of management of an estate under the MAP organisation. As has been noted, MAP played an important role in transforming the rubber industry in Malaya through application of modern technology in botanical research, mechanisation and the shipping of rubber in liquid form. In evaluating the managerial competencies of this company there is a need to first outline the organisational methods employed by USRC's largest single rubber plantation, HAPM in Sumatra. There was constant communication between HAPM and MAP, (including the exchange of rubber samples)[107] and the organisational methods and research findings of the former were then applied not only to latter's rubber estates in Malaya, but also diffused to the Malayan rubber community as a whole.

This greenfield investment was one of the largest reclamation projects ever attempted in Malaya. The reclamation took five years to complete and 12 to 15 years (in the early 1930s) for the entire 10,000 acres to be at full production. Seven thousand acres were cleared within four months and following the company's expansion programme this new acreage was quickly planted with rubber. The highly economical clearing process was implemented with the intention of saving everything for possible future use in the plantation's development.[108]

The Malayan rubber industry's experience of labour shortages and high turnover rates made recruiting and retaining workers very costly. In the mid-1920s, MAP provided housing, pension plans, a bonus system, medical and recreational facilities for its employees. These paternalistic practices, designed to improve worker well-being and enhance employee commitment while reducing costly turnover rates, known as welfare capitalism, or corporate welfarism, were not exclusive to MAP as British rubber firms in Malaya also implemented such practices. These paternalistic policies had their origins in the welfare capitalist systems developed in nineteenth-century Western Europe. The major difference, however, was that in Europe there was a tendency for the state (i.e. the government) to provide welfare benefits, while in contrast in the US, large firms used welfare capitalism to prevent the development of a welfare state and minimise government intervention.[109]

The mainstream view among labour historians suggests that the welfare capitalism introduced in the US in the late nineteenth century reached its peak in the 1920s and began to decline during the Depression in the 1930s.[110] The rise of big business in the US required a new approach to labour relations and led to a combination of scientific management and corporate welfarism. In order to increase productivity and quality at a reduced cost, the focus was not only on new technology, but also worker competency. This systematised welfare programme was employed by progressive employers such as USRC, Firestone, Goodyear, United States Steel and Ford in the US and provided economic and non-economic benefits to employees in an effort to deter unionism and secure company loyalty.[111] Thus, employers provided voluntary provisions of housing, healthcare, pension and profit-sharing plans, hoping to create a loyal, productive and dependable workforce. In the decades preceding the Depression, there were advocates of some state intervention in the economy, which did bring major changes to the welfare system. However, Jacoby provides evidence on the endurance of welfare capitalism among US firms despite the financial constraints imposed by the Depression. He asserts that some employers maintained their paternalistic practices well into the twentieth century, albeit with a modified approach.[112]

For USRC, even after World War II, these practices continued at its subsidiaries in the two largest plantation colonies in Asia: the Dutch East Indies (which was the largest plantation colony in the world) and Malaya. MAP followed the initiatives of its parent firm, USRC, but for a different motivation and specifically because of the location-specific differences. Similar to the practices in Europe, in Malaya, the state intervened to provide cheap land and labour to promote the growth of the rubber industry. With state patronage and protection, the motive for welfare capitalism in Malaya cannot be correctly defined as simply anti-union. MAP's strategy was not to forestall unionisation, as trade unions were only legally allowed to be formed in Malaya after World War II, but to gain competitive advantage in the rubber industry.[113]

MAP made concerted efforts to carefully recruit experienced and well-qualified staff in an attempt to avoid costly mistakes. These early efforts included the recruitment of such staff as factory engineers, mycologists, soil analysts, foresters, genetic botanists, planters and accountants from the US. Meanwhile the supervisory personnel comprised of different nationalities and the company also recruited experienced European managers to try to ensure the success of its rubber enterprise. Previously, USRC had clearly stated its intention to the British administrators in Malaya, to selectively hire British planters in British colonies and protectorates, when the company first came to invest in Malaya during World War I.[114] The Dublin Estate, for example, employed four Irish managers to supervise estate labourers and 2600 Chinese and Tamil labourers.[115] As competition for labour was keen, MAP plantation managers needed to gain a reputation for fair and tolerant treatment in order to keep loyal labourers. There was also a need to establish healthy living conditions as pursued by MAP at the Dublin Estate in Kedah.

After the success of USRPI's good planning at HAPM Sumatra was correctly applied, the Dublin estate proved to be an ideal model for a rubber plantation.[116] The European manager lived in a spacious bungalow built on a hilltop and, as on most estates, both managers and assistants were provided with free housing, medical attention and, in the case of managers, a car for transportation. The Dublin Estate was divided into four sections where each assistant occupied an attractively built home placed at the highest point in his respective section, with these bungalows supplied with every modern utility. A small department store supplied day-to-day requirements. There was also a brick plant with two large kilns and a saw mill for future building requirements.[117]

Special effort was made for the comfort and well-being of labourers, and the Dublin Estate was equipped with up-to-date labourer housing built on well-drained and ventilated sites placed throughout the estate to minimise travel time. J.T. Clarke, a medical officer for Malaysian–American Plantations at Dublin, argued that workers' housing sanitation may incur extra expenditure, but cleanliness would be repaid in the form of increased worker's efficiency.[118] In addition to a profit-sharing and bonus system, USRPI also adopted a pension plan for both managers and labourers who had served the company for more than 25 years.[119] Various different kinds of remuneration system were also adopted by British rubber firms, such as Guthries and Harrisons & Crosfield, for the same reasons: to attract and retain skilled employees.[120]

By the mid-1920s, in accordance with British law, ample hospital facilities were provided by MAP.[121] The Dublin Estate secured approval from the Kedah state government to set up and maintain its own hospital, which was designed after the most modern facilities in the Sumatra plantations.[122] The hospital at Dublin Estate was erected at a cost of S$100,000. MAP also built its own hospital at the Harvard and Scarborough estates in Kedah at a cost of S$55,000 each. In Dublin, a fully equipped hospital with highly trained nurses was built near the headquarters bungalow. This, according to Stuart Hotchkiss, then president of USRPI, was in the business interests of the company, because it maintained the highest degree of efficiency in its labour force.[123] As a result, production greatly increased.

Although these paternalistic practices were not exclusive to the US rubber manufacturer, none of the other large rubber producers implemented these policies as early and on such an extravagant scale as USRC. While similar practices were employed by British rubber manufacturer Dunlop at its Ladang Geddes estates where there were well-organised Tamil 'villages', which claimed to be 'a paradise for Tamils', and similar but distinct facilities for Chinese labourers, Dunlop only began to implement these practices on a grand scale in the late 1920s and early 1930s. USRC, however, implemented this policy as soon as it entered into rubber plantations in 1910 in Sumatra and in 1919 in Malaya. The Danish firm, United

Plantations, founded in 1906, also practised welfare capitalism, but it was not until the late 1920s that the company was able to display good living standards not only to satisfy government officials who regularly made routine checks, but also to attract free labourers who were in a position to choose the best options offered by estate employers.[124]

Corporate welfarism, as implemented by USRC, ensured workers' loyalty and support, which in turn promoted the growth of the rubber industry and provided an example of good labour relations in estate management. However, similar to the practices of British rubber firms in Malaya, top managerial positions were held by expatriates, either recruited locally or from their home countries (they were mostly British in Malaya, or Dutch in the Dutch East Indies).[125] There was never any effort to give management training to either the indigenous population or the immigrant labourers, which left them at a distinct disadvantage. Like other British rubber firms, only clerical staff were recruited from the Indian immigrants as well as a very few Chinese.

USRC's primary purpose, and the chief concern of its management, was to produce superior grades of rubber that could not be obtained on the open market. Initially HAPM worked with both the Rubber Growers Association (RGA) and the Planters Association of the East Coast of Sumatra (AVROS) research stations, but later set up its own research department headed by the well-experienced rubber expert James Grantham.[126] This research station attracted world-class researchers of various nationalities including British and Dutch scientists and agriculturalists. Its laboratories contributed to knowledge on budding, tapping, manuring, prevention and cure of rubber plant diseases, and other important problems affecting the industry. The limited number of experts compared to the large number of rubber firms led to the need for sharing the expertise of scientists, most importantly, geneticists and mycologists. This included the research findings of the research stations.[127] The research results and findings were disseminated among plantation owners. For example, HAPM research staff made contributions to scientific publications. These contributions and the willingness of the Americans to share their knowledge were noted by the British in the *RGA Bulletin*:

> The contributions to the Archief and other scientific publications by members of the H.A.P.M. are read by all interested in the well-being of the industry, and the broad-minded view of the administration in giving free access to their laboratories and records is an example which might be followed by many other organisations.[128]

In fact, the British rubber manufacturer Dunlop sent R.B. Carey, the head of its research activities, to HAPM and AVROS to find out about the latest budding activities established there.[129] Stoler concluded that US influence in the estate economy was strong, as it was in the post-World War I period when people such as the 'King of Kisaran' (the contemporary term of reference – not address – for the American manager of URSC's Asahan estate) 'exercised disproportionate influence on policy decisions in the planters association of AVROS'.[130]

As a latecomer on the scene, USRC owning less than two per cent of the world's rubber plantations, adopted a progressive policy to catch up with the British- and Dutch-pioneered rubber industry, emphasising the financing of quality research work by British and Dutch rubber experts.

The late 1910s marked a watershed in the rubber industry when emphasis on research led to new practices and modern cultivation of rubber. These changes in estate practices began with HAPM tapping methods, use of fertilisers, and bud grafting programmes. HAPM investigation into tapping methods showed that alternate monthly tapping on half of the circumference was beneficial to the life of the rubber tree and increased productivity. This alternate tapping method would become standard practice on the Sumatran plantations after 1922 and in the mid-1920s there was a shift from daily tapping to alternate tapping in Malaya.[131]

In 1919, Grantham carried out a large-scale experiment on the use of fertilisers to raise production at HAPM. The manuring experiments proved that regular application of nitrogenous fertilisers (sulphate ammonia) could increase the annual yield per acre by 100 per cent (from about 350 pounds to 675 pounds). Thus, in 1923, USRC began the practice of annual fertilisation of the whole plantation. There was also wide adoption of this practice by planters on the east coast of Sumatra, and there followed a large increase in US imports of sulfate ammonia, with a 75 per cent increase in 1925 alone.[132]

HAPM also pioneered the bud-grafting methods supervised by US botanist Dr Carl LaRue in 1917. By 1921, the first yield was realised from the budding experimentation and it marked the beginning of high-yield rubber trees of 900 pounds per acre. In 1922, large-scale plantings were carried out employing the budding system and the total area of bud-grafted trees on estates controlled by the USPRI was about 10,000 acres. By 1924, the use of selected seedlings brought even higher yields of 1000 pounds per acre.[133] This was a courageous initiative, for there were potential high risks involved with the yielding power of budding and the effect on the root system not previously determined. However, planting was done alternately between budding and selecting seeds so as to be able to rely upon the yield of selected seeds if the budding trees failed.[134]

Grantham, director of research at USRPI, in his presentation at the Paris Rubber Conference in 1924 entitled, 'The Development of Methods of Obtaining Areas of Increased Productivity', stated that the total area planted with budding and selected seedlings in Malaya and Sumatra was 29,000 acres. In his paper, he outlined the development of the methods used in both Sumatra and Malaya to develop new areas of Hevea Brasiliensis, of inherently higher yielding capacity than ordinary plantations. According to him, the largest application of the new methods had been carried out by USRPI, mainly as a result of its own research work.[135] USRC had a lead in R&D in the early 1920s. USRC's research station at HAPM released information on seed selection, bud grafting and the cloning of higher yield rubber trees in the early 1920s while RRI released the information only in the late 1920s.

Aside from the US estates, the only other area of budded rubber in the Federated Malaya States was the Prang Besar estate established in April 1921. This 1000 acre-estate, granted by the Selangor authorities through the War Service Land Grants Scheme, was owned by Major H. Gough. Gough disclaimed any scientific training but he learned of the method through visits to Sumatra and was motivated by the progress made by MAP at Kedah.[136] His Prang Besar estate was bought by Harrisons & Crosfield in 1925.[137] These bud-grafting techniques were then diffused among its subsidiaries in Malaya.[138] Meanwhile, by 1927, USRC had planted 30,000 acres of budded stock.[139] In contrast, Guthrie did not establish its own research station until 1934 and only then started to make advances in bud-grafting and selective breeding.[140]

There was a gradual increase in USRC's yield per acre from 1922 to 1927. The firm's yield per acre for 1926 was 441 pounds, slightly more than the 1927 average yield per acre in the Federated Malay States of 420 pounds, while the average yield per acre throughout South East Asia was less than 350 pounds.[141]

By the late 1920s, genetic selection and bud grafting successfully developed strains of trees capable of yielding superior results. The trees could produce approximately 1000 pounds (dry rubber content) per acre – cutting down the cost of production enormously. By 1957, the yield per acre was increased to 2000 pounds per acre. This was achieved by genetic selection and grafting, applying plant hormones and feeding the trees with traces of metallic salts.[142]

US R&D did indeed increase and revolutionise rubber production and simultaneously decreased production costs. Innovations were widely disseminated to other rubber firms in the Dutch East Indies and Malaya. USRC diffused the bud grafting techniques not only within its subsidiary plantations in Malaya but also to other rubber firms within the industry via its research station at HAPM. Increasingly, large British rubber firms began to invest in R&D in the mid-1920s and early 1930s.

However, while USRC's findings were able to promote the widespread use of new tapping methods and fertilisers to increase rubber production among planters in the Dutch East Indies and Malaya, the use of high-yield trees and selected seeds (because of the high risks and costs involved) were mainly adopted by large rubber firms with financial capabilities, such as Dunlop, Harrisons & Crosfield, and Guthrie. These new technologies were not adopted by local competitors, rubber smallholders and small Western firms until after World War II.[143]

Overall, despite its small percentage of rubber investment compared to British interests as a whole, USRC was able to have a significant impact on the industry, as seen through the efforts of the firm in R&D. Besides ownership advantages, the ability to exploit locational factors enabled USRC to be a leader in rubber research. With the dissemination of research findings by USRC, most rubber firms adopted better growing practices bringing higher yields per acre. In addition, large British rubber firms were motivated to engage in R&D, adopting and further improving these new technologies.

USRC, through R&D, had promoted the growth of the rubber industry in both the host (Malaya) and home (US) economies. Despite being late entrants and owning only a small percentage of the rubber estates in Malaya, USRC, through the work of the British and Dutch rubber experts the company recruited, was able to innovate the industry with their aggressive pursuit of R&D.

One of the most important contributions made by USRC at its research centre at HAPM was the handling and shipping of latex from the tree to the rubber manufacturers in the US. The shipping of latex in liquid form was essential for manufacturers, as liquid latex retained certain important chemical properties. As early as 1913, liquid rubber was shipped in 5 gallon kerosene cans; in 1920 it was shipped in 50 gallons of steel drums; later the fore and aft peak tanks of cargo steamers were used for this purpose. USRC used 1000-gallon containers, filled on the plantation and sent to the harbour by rail. The next step was to induce steamers to clean their ballast and oil tanks and fill them with latex for the trip home. Initially, shipping companies were reluctant to do so; however, there was soon competition for this business and several lines began to equip their vessels for this kind of cargo.[144] Inadvertently, USRC had initiated and facilitated the latex shipping business, proving that plantation economies were able to provide linkages with other areas of services.

Being both a rubber manufacturer and a rubber producer, USRC had the advantage of creating new inventions to supplement the needs of both consumers and producers. One company employee for example, Ernest Hopkinson, the person in charge of development and the patent department, was credited with the commercialisation of latex. Liquid latex was turned into a solid mass by what was known as the Hopkinson spraying process. This process converted latex into a dry spongy mass, making it easier to handle. USRC had nine spraying plants with a capacity of about 17,000 tons of dry rubber annually. An unconfirmed report stated that in 1923 USRC contracted to buy all the latex output of a company with estates near Kuala Lumpur. USRC erected a factory at Port Swettenham to treat part of the latex by the Hopkinson process.[145] By 1925, USRC shipped approximately 250,000 gallons monthly from Belawan, Sumatra and Port Swettenham, Federated Malay States. These ports were equipped with storage tanks and there were four steamship lines which were equipped to carry latex cargoes.[146] See Figure 5.2 for the location of USRC's latex station, latex shipping stations and spray plants in the mid-1920s in Sumatra and Malaya.

The manufacture of the special latex-treated web cord used in the manufacture of its cord tyres was perhaps the most important among many patents owned by the company.[147] In its advertisements and news releases for 1923, this invention was claimed to increase tyre mileage by 30 per cent and the improvement of tyre construction was made possible by the dependable supply of latex from USRC's plantations.[148]

USRC's R&D activities had both successes and failures. At times, the new inventions failed to produce the expected economic improvements due to lack of coordination between USRC's manufacturing and plantation units. Despite the publicity given to USRC's sprayed rubber patent, granted in 1922, it was found that the disadvantages outweighed the advantages. The retained organic non-rubber ingredients caused product failures in tyres, sundries and insulated wires. Sprayed rubber also carried a premium price over ribbed smoked sheet and pale crepe.

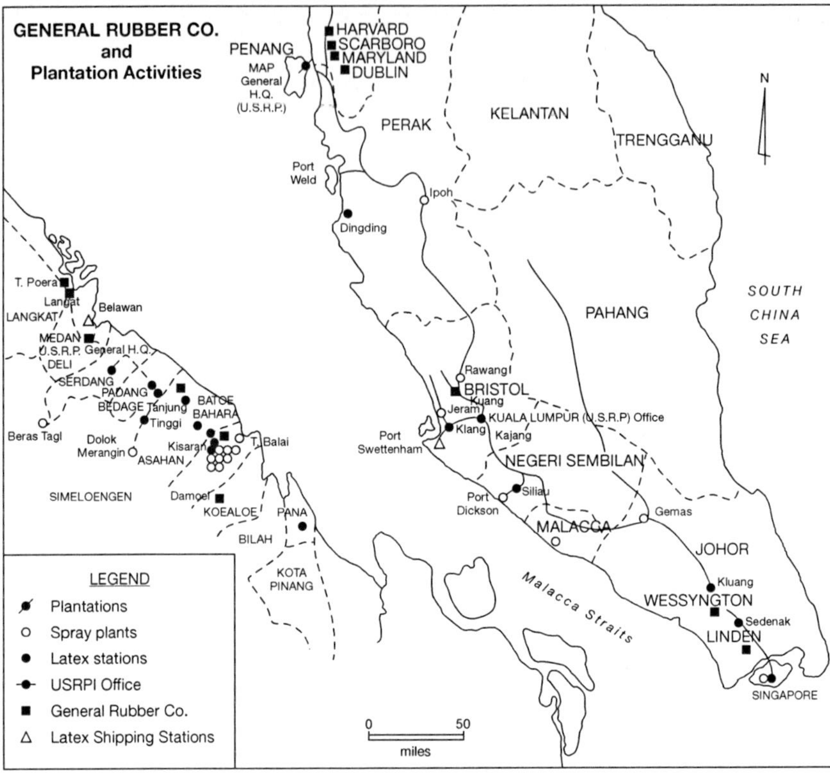

Figure 5.2 USRC's properties in Sumatra and Malaya in the 1920s.

Source: Adapted from Babcock, *History of the United States Rubber*, p. 186.

In 1925, all of the 20 million pounds of rubber from USRC's plantation came to the US in the form of sprayed rubber.

Although USRC's plants in the US began to revert to rubber produced by conventional methods, spraying plants on the plantations continued to produce sprayed rubber. The rush into large-scale production and the failure to coordinate the production of the factories and the output of the plantations led to heavy inventories. When rubber prices fell in 1928, USRC experienced severe losses on stockpiled crude rubber. Production of sprayed rubber was at first curtailed and eventually discontinued with the onset of World War II.[149]

USRC played an important role in assisting the Rubber Reserve Company, which was set up on 25 June 1940 by the US federal government under the Reconstruction Finance Corporation, to accumulate a strategic stockpile of natural rubber to meet war demands. USRC, in its attempt to limit the use of natural rubber, had also enhanced its facilities for production of reclaimed rubber. USRC also worked with the US government to produce synthetic rubber.

The Defense Plant Corporation, a subsidiary of the Reconstruction Finance Corporation, made agreements with the 'big four' to construct and operate synthetic rubber plants. However, it was USRC which played the most important role in the production and management of the government's synthetic rubber facilities. A synthetic rubber division was set up in July 1942 and production began in September 1942. Its first pilot plant at Naugatuck, in the US state of Connecticut, proved to be a valuable aid to the US government's synthetic rubber programme.[150] Even during the war years the company placed continuous emphasis on R&D, leading to the development of many new rubber products useful in both war and peacetime.[151] A large percentage of the synthetic rubber production went to the manufacture of tyres for both military and civilian uses, mechanical rubber goods, footwear, drug sundries and other products.

Often there was competition within the firm between the production of natural rubber in the host country and the production of synthetic rubber in laboratories in the home country.[152] USRC continued its dedication to R&D (mainly in synthetic rubber) during World War II and through its research programme, contributed to quality improvement, cost reduction, increased output per labourer, and registered many notable advances in synthetic rubber technology. In 1945 the company pioneered the development and production of the tyre tube made of butyl synthetic rubber, which had higher tear resistance and air retention ability compared to tyres made with natural rubber.[153]

In 1945, the US became the world's largest producer of synthetic rubber, with USRC playing a major role in its development. By 1950, synthetic rubber held 42 per cent of the US market.[154] USRC's venture into synthetic rubber, designed to aid its manufacturing activities, had threatened the future of Malayan natural rubber and the Malayan economy. However, despite USRC's progress in synthetic rubber production, its plantations in Malaya were maintained and, as discussed above, efforts were made to revive its plantations after World War II. Notwithstanding the phenomenal growth of synthetic rubber, the demand for natural rubber continued, mostly because synthetic rubber could not replace natural rubber in all applications.

Overall, USRC's investments in rubber in Malaya provided a qualitative impact on the industry. Although there were downsides to USRC's investment in Malaya, on balance, it can be asserted that the positive impact outweighed the negative influence on the Malayan economy.

5.5 US enterprise in rubber: a summary

US rubber MNEs, in their attempts to reduce risk, had originally invested in geographically nearer countries in their early stages of growth. However, as these investments failed, and rubber supply and price swings became increasingly erratic, they became attracted to South East Asia in the early twentieth century. US investments in rubber plantations were primarily in the Dutch-ruled Dutch East Indies rather than British-ruled Malaya or US-ruled Philippines because of the various restrictions imposed in those countries.

Although the British government did favour a laissez-faire approach towards FDI in general, there was a degree of political interference and regulation at certain times in the rubber industry, just as there was with tin although with a lesser degree of success. This interference came from British administrators in both Malaya and London and was largely dictated by issues relating to the competing interests of producers and manufacturers. US firms benefited from low rubber prices while British exporters from high prices. However, political intrusions by the British government and the reservations that British rubber interests had towards large US rubber investors were dictated by fears of foreign dependency and monopoly power. In addition, because rubber was a strategic commodity and considered as an imperial asset, issues of national security were also of concern.

The rubber industry attracted three of the four largest US rubber firms to invest in rubber plantations in Malaya although they met with varying degrees of success. USRC remained the predominant US investor in the Malayan rubber industry. Goodyear invested in Sumatra and the Philippines whilst Firestone went to Liberia. Goodrich showed interests in Malaya on several occasions, but, unlike the US rubber firms, clearly made the right decision in not adopting a long-term plantation investment that would ultimately not be effective strategy. USRC remained subjected to erratic costs and supply swings because its plantations provided only a small percentage of its rubber requirements. Clearly, for rubber manufacturers such as USRC, rubber production remained marginal to its performance as a rubber manufacturer.

The history of USRC in Malaya began with the relentless pursuit of rubber investments by the US rubber entrepreneur, Edgar B. Davis. Once successfully entrenched in Malaya, USRC reaped the benefits of locational advantages of the British presence. Drawing on the experience of British and Dutch experts, they made important advancements in R&D. In the early 1920s, USRC had a comparative lead in R&D against the British rubber pioneers who dominated the rubber industry in Malaya. USRC had been a latecomer to the industry. However, through its ample financial access and resources, it was able to reap economies of scale and scope.

USRC's position as a rubber producer (host country) and rubber manufacturer (home country) gave it an added advantage in R&D as it enabled the firm to integrate the needs of both the production and the manufacturing divisions. Through the transfer of scientific research and knowledge, plantation technologies and managerial and organisational skills, USRC bequeathed on the Malayan rubber industry a legacy of pre-existing economic assets. The recurring theme here, as in the tin industry, was the use of technological innovation. Ultimately USRC's investments in the Malayan rubber industry contributed, alongside the British and other Western plantation firms, to the development of the modern Malayan economy.

6 Taking the high road

Ford Malaya

Of the three largest automobile manufacturers in the US – Ford, General Motors and Chrysler – only Ford elected to invest in Malaya. Notably, too, none of the British automobile MNEs invested in Malaya despite being early movers into the Malayan market.[1] The establishment of a Ford subsidiary in Malaya can be seen in the wider context of the company's policy which, after World War I, saw the adoption of a greater international approach to its automobile business, and its worldwide operations become highly integrated. Although Ford England was set up in 1911, it had been preceded by Ford Canada in 1904, and the Canadian company, in addition to establishing Ford Malaya in 1926, set up affiliates in South Africa, Australia, India and New Zealand to handle the British Empire markets.

This chapter analyses Ford's strategies in Malaya from the early twentieth century until Malaysian Independence in 1957 within the framework of the Malayan automobile sector. While initially detailing the trends in, and development of, the Malayan automobile sector, this chapter examines the country-specific as well as firm-specific advantages that enabled Ford to establish its position in Malaya. There is also, importantly, an evaluation of the British role and impact of colonial policies on the development of US automobile MNEs in Malaya. This is followed by an assessment of Ford's strategies and its performance in Malaya from 1911 to 1925, prior to the formation of Ford Malaya, as well as after its formation, from 1926 to 1957. Finally, there is an exploration of Ford's competitive strategies and how the company's worldwide operations led to its growth in Malaya.

6.1 Malaya as a host economy for automobile MNEs

When Ford first became interested in investing in Malaya in the first decades of the twentieth century, the country was seen as an attractive host economy for automobile MNEs for several reasons. These included the British presence, a strong government, growing population density, Malaya's strategic location, a well-developed transport network, the existence of merchant firms and ethnic Chinese entrepreneurs, and an expanding regional market.

Automobiles appeared in Singapore as early as 1896. In 1903, the Singapore authority drafted an Automobile Enactment, regulating the registration of cars and issuance of licence plates. That same year saw the establishment of the Federated Malay States Automobile Club and in 1907, the Singapore Automobile Club. A year earlier, in 1906, the Straits Settlements Blue Books[2] for the first time began to use the term 'cars' in place of 'wheeled carriages on springs'. Automobile sales in Malaya began on a small scale in these early years but steadily grew before the outbreak of World War I. Predominantly British makes including Talbot, Arrol-Johnston, Humber, Argyll, Swift, Adam-Hewitt, Albion, Siddeley, Rover and Orlean, there was some competition from cars from the US, Italy, France and Germany. In 1909, the Ford Model N (the predecessor of the Model T), appeared in Malaya, the first Ford automobile to appear in the country.

During World War I, because of the difficulty in obtaining supplies of British makes in Malaya due to production difficulties in the British motor industry, there were increased demands for US automobiles. Moreover, US cars offered a cheaper alternative to British cars. In addition to British makes, the 1920s saw other European makes appear on the Malayan market. High-priced British cars such as Vauxhall, Wolseley and Crossley competed with makes such as Daimler and Benz. At the lower end of the market, the British Austin and Morris saw competition from the Italian Fiat, Alfa Romeo and Bianchi, the French Citroen and Peugeot, as well as the German Opel.[3] In addition, by 1921 a large stock of American makes, including the Hudson, Cleveland, Reo and Studebaker, was available in Singapore and Penang.[4] Ford's Model T and Model TT (a one-ton truck) as well as General Motors' products such as Pontiac and Chevrolet were also widely distributed in Malaya by the mid-1920s.

Automobile manufacturers had excellent prospects in Singapore and the Malay States because of the good network of roads that had been built, mainly to support the tin and rubber exports economy. In 1911, there were 800 miles in the Straits Settlements of which 100 miles of road were in Singapore and 3439 miles in the Federated Malay States. By the 1920s, it was possible to drive from Singapore to Bangkok, with the Malayan north–south highway being completed in 1922 and by September 1923, the Johore causeway linked Singapore to the Malay States. By 1930, there were 4735 miles of road serving the Federated Malay States, Malacca, Province Wellesley, Johore and Kedah. These highway developments provided excellent motoring facilities and lead to a large increase in the number of registered vehicles in Malaya as a whole, with a 400 per cent increase from 1910 to 1915, a 1000 per cent increase from 1910 to 1925 and a 1600 per cent increase from 1910 to 1930.

British engineering, building and construction activities allowed US manufacturers to take advantage of the investment opportunities available in Malaya, as was noted by the then US vice consul in Penang. Although opportunities abounded for the sale of American road-building equipment, as argued in Chapter 3, because of the British colonial presence and closer links to British businesses, there existed a natural bias towards British-made machinery and materials.

As we have seen, Malaya's economic prosperity derived from being one of the world's major producers of tin in the late nineteenth century and rubber in the early twentieth century. There was a direct correlation between the prices of rubber and tin to the percentage of automobile sales. This meant in consumer terms the increase in sales of both US automobiles and US tyres in Malaya.

There were three potential sources of demand for automobiles: owners of rubber plantations and tin mines (private ventures), salaried executives, and shareholders (those who received dividends from the good performance of the tin and rubber companies during boom periods). These were mainly European and Chinese buyers who formed the main users of automobiles in Malaya; few Malays, except royalty, owned cars. However, in contrast to the majority car buying, largely urban-based Chinese, who outnumbered Malays by 1938, the European percentage of the local population was very small.

In terms of market size, despite Malaya being a relatively small market, there was high purchasing power among Malayans compared with their South East Asian neighbours. By 1930, Malaya's total car registration reached approximately 165,000 with a car to person ratio of 1:93 in the Straits Settlements (figures for Federated Malay States and Unfederated Malay States are unavailable), in contrast to the Dutch East Indies where 85,000 cars were registered at a ratio of 1:584.[5] The Straits Settlements' level of ownership was much higher than in Japan where every 1136th person owned a car.[6] Besides regionally high rates of car ownership, mainly in the Straits Settlements, Singapore provided Malaya with a strategic networking position as the avenue for automobile MNEs to tap into the regional market. Hence, in terms of market size, as detailed later, automobile MNEs were often attracted to Malaya for increased access to the regional market.

Increasing purchasing power and stiff competition made automobile advertisements a constant feature in local newspapers in the early twentieth century. By the 1920s, automobile advertisements were placed regularly by long-established agents such as Borneo Company Ltd, Wearne Brothers, Cycle & Carriage, and Guthrie & Co extolling the features of all kinds of different makes and including Ford, Daimler, Chevrolet, Morris and Austin. Newspapers provided an excellent medium to reach potential consumers. There were papers in the three main languages spoken in Malaya – English, Chinese, and Malay. Among the widely circulated English-language newspapers where automobile advertisements could be found were the *Straits Times*, *Malay Mail*, *Singapore Free Press*, *Malaya Tribune*, *Penang Straits Echo*, *Penang Gazette* and *Times of Malaya*. The Chinese newspapers, such as the *China Press*, *Sin Chew Jit Poh* and *Chung Shing Jit Pao*, also provided advertising opportunities. Another important medium was publications on the tin and rubber industries, used to reach potential customers in both industries. The *Malayan Tin and Rubber Journal*, *The Times of Malaya* and *Planters & Miners Gazette*, for instance, carried motor car advertisements. There was also a widely distributed motor journal, *Motors in Malaya*, that became an avenue for these advertisements.

At the initial stage of penetrating the Malayan market, automobile manufacturers had to choose between exporting or making FDI. The need to invest in showroom and service facilities discouraged forward integration into distribution, while local assembly also incurred extra costs, making the final product much more expensive than imported vehicles. Both forward integration into distribution and local assembly required high sales volume. Thus, the ready availability of distribution facilities and the market access (for the Malayan and regional markets) provided by merchant firms led automobile manufacturers to favour exporting automobiles over FDI.

By the early twentieth century, merchant firms began to diversify into automobile distribution, providing services for foreign automobile MNEs. By 1928, there were 16 merchant firms representing ten automobile manufacturers distributing 58 different automobiles and trucks in Singapore.[7] Table 6.1 identifies the three largest merchant firms – Wearne Brothers, Borneo Company Ltd and Cycle & Carriage – that represented both British and US makes in Malaya. This shows US automobile manufacturers' reliance on (mainly British) merchant firms.

However, most leading automobile manufacturers from Britain, continental Europe, as well as the US did rely on merchant firms, which held various agencies to distribute their automobiles. The Borneo Company diversified into automobile distribution in the early 1900s and was among the pioneers in Malaya.[8] In 1905, the Borneo Company held the Foden steam wagons agency, adding two further agencies, the Humber and Sizaire-Naudin, by 1909.[9] Car agencies were at that time secondary to its other trading activities.[10] By 1925, the Borneo Company diversified further into motor distribution and set up Borneo Motors Ltd, which became one of the largest overseas distributors for its Austin, Chrysler and General Motors franchises. In 1938, the group had thirteen distributing centres in Thailand, Malaya and North Borneo.[11] There were other merchant firms involved in automobile distribution, including Guthrie, which acquired agencies for Swift, Phoenix and Daimler from 1905 to 1908. In the late 1920s, Guthrie expanded further by adding the Buick, Renault and the Rudge-Whitworth (motorcycles) agencies.[12]

Initially, in the early 1900s, when car agencies were secondary to their main business interests, and the low trading volumes presumably discouraged

Table 6.1 Top three merchant firms and various agency agreements held in Malaya, 1928

Merchant Firms	*Subsidiaries*	*Passenger Cars*	*Commercial*
Wearne Brothers	Universal Cars	Ford	Fordson tractors
	Lyons Motors Federated Motors	Hillman, Buick, Durant Dodge, Vauxhall	Rugby, Reo
	Malayan Motors	Morris, Humber, Hillman	Morris, Dennys
BCL	Borneo Motors	Austin, Riley, Plymouth, Chrysler	Bedford
	Borneo Chevrolet	Buick, Cadillac, Chevrolet, Chrysler	Chevrolet
C&C	Straits Motor Garage Eastern Auto Oriental Motors	Hudson, Essex, Renault Oldsmobile Pontiac, Oakland	Willys, Renault

Sources: 'Automotive Chart', 1929; *Malay Mail*, 3 December 1926.

investments into distribution, merchant firms made arrangements with other motor firms (mainly Chinese automobile distributors) to use their showrooms for display purposes. The Borneo Company and Guthrie used the Straits Motor Garage showrooms to display their automobiles.[13] Other merchant firms operated in a similar manner; Syme and Company displayed their automobiles at the Singapore Motor Car Company, another Chinese distributor.[14] For some time none of the merchant firms in Malaya dealt solely with an individual automobile manufacturer. Separate companies were formed, however, when automobile manufacturers insisted on individual distribution or when sales volume increased. In 1949, when Austin objected to its vehicles being distributed with General Motors' products within the Borneo Company, a separate company, the Orchard Motor Company, was formed solely to handle the distribution of General Motors' products including Chevrolet cars and trucks.[15] Wearne Brothers, which held the franchises of several, mainly British, motor manufacturers, also set up a separate company exclusively for Ford products due to the rapid growth of its Ford business.[16]

While merchant firms provided secretarial services and were sometimes producers in the rubber and tin industries (as detailed in Chapters 2 and 3), in the case of automobiles, they acted largely as distributors. This role was vital for the automobile sector in Malaya because the survival of the automobile sector depended on its distribution and networking facilities. The capital intensive nature of these merchant firms' business through the need to invest in showroom and repair facilities, and keep stocks at hand, placed them at constant risk of incurring huge losses if they lost contracts from automobile manufacturers once a market was established. However, these merchant firms were invaluable partners because they not only provided sales and distribution services but also the services of maintenance and repair, as is evident in the relationship between Ford and its main dealer, Wearne Brothers.

In Malaya, apart from merchant firms, the ethnic Chinese also played an important role in the automobile business. As early as 1914, Chinese firms were distributing both British and US makes and placing automobile advertisements in the local newspapers (see Figure 6.1), with one leading example being Cycle & Carriage. Among the first motor distributorships acquired by Cycle & Carriage in the early twentieth century were smaller ones from US companies, such as Willys-Overland, Chandler, Hudson and from British the producers BSA, and Singer. Later, the company also distributed the French de Dion Bouton and German Opel. Cycle & Carriage, just as other companies were doing at the time, set up branches in major cities throughout Malaya including Ipoh in 1906, Penang in 1914 and Singapore in 1916. By 1926 the company was also dealing with General Motors' products such as Oldsmobile, Pontiac and Oakland.[17]

Chinese firms were also actively involved in the distribution of spare parts and accessories, an important component of the automobile services sector.[18] United Motor Works, for instance, held agency agreements with US car, tyre and spare parts manufacturers, establishing a strong position in the automobile and spare parts sector in Malaya. In 1920, the company was appointed General Motors' first exclusive distributors for Malaya and Thailand.[19] By 1951, United Motor Works had branches and warehouses in Malacca, Kuala Lumpur, Ipoh, Penang and Bangkok as well as 200 automotive parts dealers in all these areas supplying over 30 bus companies and truck fleet owners, car dealers, garages, government and municipality departments and airline companies.[20]

The importance of the merchant firms in motor distribution in Malay cannot be undervalued. Ethnic Chinese entrepreneurs, with their close connections with ethnic Chinese, the major buyers of automobile products, further enhanced the market with their excellent distribution and repair services. For US automobile MNEs, including Ford and General Motors, the services provided by the British merchant firms and Chinese firms demonstrated the importance of such cooperation in the expansion of their automobile business. This cooperation limited the need for US automobile manufacturers to invest in market-seeking FDI. However, as trading volumes increased in the market, US manufacturers, unlike their British counterparts, sought to integrate forwards into distribution and to establish local production.

6.2 Business, government and automobiles

While a measure of Anglo-US cooperation was evident in the relationship between manufacturers and merchants, on a political level, Anglo-US relations were defined more by a spirit of competition or rivalry. British administrators actively restricted the advancement of US automobile MNEs in Malaya in order to protect British business interests.

Prior to World War I, the US had become one of the major suppliers in the Malayan automobile market, followed by the UK, France and Italy. As can be seen from Table 6.2, the US gained majority market share during World War I, reaching a peak of 83 per cent in 1916.[21] It is also clear that the US remained Malaya's major supplier of automobiles including spare parts and accessories, from 1925 to 1929. Automobiles manufactured by Ford Canada accounted for the Canadian share of total Malayan automobile imports (see Table 6.2). However, as discussed in Chapter 3, Malayan trade figures, including those of the automobile sector, can be misleading in determining the levels of US trade in Malaya because of the different source areas.

As such, firms located in Canada, including Ford Canada, generally considered themselves as home-based and distinct from the US companies from which they derived, but the British authorities (at both the metropolitan and local levels) regarded Canada as a convenient corridor for the US automobile manufacturers to evade duties imposed in the empire market. Similar issues arose when the British subsidiaries, Ford England and General Motors UK were set up as export platforms to supply the Empire markets. Further to illustrate the sometimes unstable nature of accurately defining source, automobile manufacturers often used Singapore as an export platform to reach the regional market. Consequently, imports into Malaya included areas such as Borneo, the Dutch East Indies, Thailand, Ceylon and Burma. Since 1911, Ford Canada (in 1926 Ford Malaya) has referred to these

Table 6.2 Imports of automobiles, spare parts and accessories into Malaya, 1913–1929

(a) Imports of automobiles into Malaya by country of origin, 1913–1921 (in S$)

Country	*1913*	*1916*	*1917*	*1918*	*1920*	*1921*
UK	907,558	251,646	266,154	57,627	2,409, 259	1,470,985
US	1,281,460	1,844,976	2,287,210	1,024,489	11,662,882	2,869,606
Canada	n.a	n.a.	499,220	245,882	1,001,735	488,953
Italy	11,000	96,200	18,000	n.a.	560,400	297,625
France	14,096	13,800	n.a.	n.a.	120,200	359,352
Others	n.a.	n.a.	n.a.	n.a.	n.a.	n.a.
Total	2,214,114	2,206,622	3,070,584	1,327,998	15,754,476	5,486,521

(b) Imports of automobiles into Malaya by country of origin, 1925–1929 (in units)

Country	*1925*	*1926*	*1927*	*1928*	*1929*
UK	2,064	2,621	2,495	1,759	2,207
US	5,570	4,705	2,100	2,233	2,708
Canada	n.a.	2,618	2,411	1,183	1,412
Italy	527	667	253	316	831
France	200	453	491	100	138
Others	635	199	303	139	113
Total	8,996	11,263	8,053	5,730	7,409

(c) Imports of spare parts and accessories into Malaya by country of origin, 1925–1929 (in S$)

Country	*1925*	*1926*	*1927*	*1928*	*1929*
UK	536,551	801,929	719,574	626,166	731,394
US	1,388,847	1,786,252	1,349,040	1,560,803	1,605,124
Italy	8,870	26,862	45,963	51,978	
France	8,081	12,755	11,836	11,746	[a]134,138
Germany	21,294	62,337	27,314	32,446	
Others	33,692	119,927	439,065	268,628	192,838
Total	1,997,335	2, 810,062	2, 592,792	2, 551,767	2, 663,494

Notes:

1. Panel (a) Total direct imports from country of origin. Total imports do not include figures for other areas that are unavailable.
2. Panel (b) and (c) Total imports include re-exports from the Straits Settlements (mainly Singapore) to other areas in the region.
3. Panel (c) [a] Figure represents total imports from Italy, France and Germany.

Sources: Panel (a) Irvine, 'Automotive Markets', p. 73.
Panel (b) and (c) A.W. Childs, 'Marketing of Parts and Accessories in British Malaya – Part 1, *Commerce Reports*, December 1930, p. 550.

areas as a single market unit. It is therefore important to consider these factors when trying to determine accurate figures of US automobile imports into Malaya. A distinction is made between the nationality of parent firm and nationality of production for figures relating to the US automobile imports into Malaya.[22] Although these trade figures may not reflect the true nature of Malayan automobile imports, the basic trends of automobile imports into Malaya should not be obscured. Exports from US-owned firms (regardless of where they were manufactured) obviously retained a strong hold on the Malayan market.

After World War I, the metropolitan government launched a campaign to assist British automobile manufacturers to strengthen the economy and to relieve the 'grave unemployment' in Britain.[23] The secretary of state for the colonies, Winston Churchill, was concerned with the ascendancy of automobiles made by US-owned firms (including those from Canadian and British subsidiaries), particularly passenger cars and light lorries. Ford automobiles manufactured in Canada entered Singapore under the Imperial Preference Act of 1917 with a 15 per cent duty advantage (similarly enjoyed by British-made automobiles) over continental European imports. Concerned with the ascendancy of US automobiles in the Malayan market, the British authorities in Malaya were directed by the metropolitan government to introduce measures to assist British manufacturers, who had overrated the superiority of their products and had been surprised at the inability of 'reliable and well-finished English cars in competition with the cheaper, inferior, product of American manufacture' to secure a larger market share.[24] This ascendancy of US automobile manufacturers was noted at the time by J.H. Robson, a member of the Federal Council of Malaya, in his 1923 publication, *Illustrated Guide to the Federated Malay States*:

> Ford cars are in the majority. Hupmobiles, Overlands, Dodges, Buicks, Chevrolets and other American cars are very much in evidence. The more expensive English and Continental cars are not in such general use, although a certain number of Wolseleys, Austins, Napiers, A.C's and so forth are still to be seen.[25]

The local authorities were directed to give preference to automobiles made by British-owned firms in Britain when placing orders, as, according to the colonial government, the 'home producer has the first and producers in other dominions the second claim' to the Empire market.[26] This underlines the argument stated in Chapter 1, that when there was any conflict of interest between Britain, the dominions and the Colonial Empire, metropolitan interests reigned supreme. Colonial officers were encouraged to purchase automobiles made by British-owned firms and efforts were made to persuade private users to purchase British cars in preference to US automobiles, particularly 'Ford' and 'Dodge' makes of Canadian and British origin which held a large share in the colonies during the 1920s.[27]

By the late 1920s, the Federated Malay States authorities had introduced loans at a nominal interest rate for officers to buy the automobiles to use while on duty. Monthly repayment could be made via salary deductions. The British government then urged the crown agents for the colonies to propose specially designed colonial models 'to take the place of the American cars'. The crown agents were successful in proposing the 8 horsepower (HP) Rover two-seater and the 16/20 HP 'Cubbit' 5-seater colonial model, as possible substitutes for Ford and other low-priced US cars. They also had the added advantage of lower petrol consumption.

Ford had also been enjoying high demand for its one-ton lorry as there was no comparable vehicle of British or continental manufacture prior to World War I, and its very low price created a barrier to potential competitors entering the market. After the war, a British manufacturer, Cubitt Engineering Company, designed the Cubitt light lorry which was recommended by the crown agents as the best substitute for Ford one tonners and Ford 6½ cwt vans.[28] However, a statement released by the Public Works Department in 1921 continued to underline the ascendancy of vehicles of US and Canadian origin in the Federated Malay States and Straits Settlements (see Table 6.3).

As discussed previously, British administrators made decisions that limited the expansion of FDI in Malaya despite their emphasis on competition and the promotion of revenue-generating investments. In 1927, a decision was made (with a slim majority of eleven to nine) by the municipal commissioners of Singapore to reject the application of General Motors to set up a central assembly plant in Katong, Singapore, to serve neighbouring regions. The reason given was that a motor assembly plant employing 400 men would spoil Katong, a seaside suburb, which should be preserved for at least another 25 years. However, the site proposed by General Motors was, at the time of its application, an abandoned godown, or storehouse, of the Pacific Trading Company within the specified industrial area. There were other factories in the vicinity, including pineapple processing plants, rubber plants and sawmills. Furthermore, a new power plant had recently been completed in the area to serve local industrial needs, and General Motors would have made a good customer for the plant. In addition to the added competition to British automobiles, there was also concern that General Motors' readiness to pay high wages would set a standard for increased wages among all classes of employees involved in the automobile sector. General Motors elected instead to establish a plant in Batavia (Jakarta) despite the taxes imposed by the Dutch East Indies government. The company's failure to use its Canadian or British affiliates to avoid British restrictions led directly to its proposal being rejected in Malaya.

On the one hand, Ford lagged behind its rival because of the erratic leadership of Henry Ford, his lack of organisational innovation and late adoption of product differentiation. Strong competition and the superior products offered by General Motors, as well as Alfred P. Sloan's large-scale organisational innovation at the company which resulted in the adoption of an M-form structure, made General Motors the US market leader and transformed the automobile industry.[29] On the other hand, by using subsidiaries to get around nationality restrictions, it appears that Ford understood the international economy much better than General Motors.

In 1929, the colonial authorities in the Federated Malay States imposed a new taxation policy based on horsepower rather than the size of the automobile, as had

Table 6.3 Taxation policies in Federated Malay States, 1929

Horsepower	*Per month (S$)*	*Per year (S$)*
10	2	24
16	3	36
20	5	60
25	7	84
Over 25	10	120

Source: NARA, Records of the Department of State relating to the Internal Affairs of British Asia 1910–1929, US Consulate General, Singapore, Monthly Report 1929.

been the case in previous legislation. The new taxes were based on the same taxation policies put into effect in the UK (but not implemented in the dominions) at a much earlier date (1 January 1921).[30] Because of cheap fuel and low taxation in the US and Canada, as compared to the UK, US cars and those built in Canada were of 20, 25 and 30 HP and of five-seater capacity. While US automobile manufacturers had to bear the added annual cost due to the imposition of the HP-based tax, UK automobile manufacturers, Austin and Morris, and also other continental European manufacturers which produced smaller cars with lower HP, mainly 8 and 10, offered reduced running costs as well as tax advantages. The fact that US-owned firms made cars with higher HP meant that US makes were at a disadvantage both in higher taxes and in higher operating costs.[31] As such the adoption of tax based on HP for a Ford Model A amounted to S$84.00 compared to S$24 for Austin cars (see Table 6.3). This was an increase of S$58.00 from the old tax rate of S$36. If these cars were used for hire, which was quite popular in the Federated Malay States, an additional tax was imposed. The US companies most affected were Ford and General Motors.[32] The new taxes were responsible for an increase in the sale of automobiles made by British-owned firms as well as their two strongest competitors, Fiat and Citroen.

In Sarawak a tariff preference was also imposed in favour of British cars. A rebate of 50 per cent was refunded to the manufacturer if proven that the automobiles and accessories were made by British-owned firms in Britain.[33] Yet, the decline in American automobile sales was not as severe as it might have been, as the Straits Settlements (which had the highest automobile imports annually) had different motor tax legislation, with the discrepancy in tax on an automobile from a US-owned firm versus a British-owned firm amounting to only S$18 per year.[34] The British administrators placed emphasis on the purchase of the automobiles made by British-owned firms in Britain in an attempt to protect British trade balances in Malaya. The policy was, to a degree, successful. The municipal commissioners of Singapore, for instance, only purchased trucks from British-owned firms such as Dennis and Thornycroft.[35] Thus, in an attempt to protect British trade balances in Malaya, the local authorities imposed protectionist policies and introduced cheaper British makes. Despite these obstacles, US automobile firms did have an impact on the Malayan automobile sector as can be seen in the example of Ford.

6.3 Ford Canada: strategies in Malaya

The establishment of Ford affiliates in the British Empire, including Malaya, was initially achieved by Ford Canada and it is pertinent to give a brief outline of the company's history. An examination of the strategies implemented by Ford Canada to break into the Malayan market follows, and an evaluation of Ford's performance in Malaya from 1909 until 1926.

Ford Motor Company of Canada Ltd (Ford Canada) was incorporated on 7 August 1904 with a capital of US$125,000 after agreement was reached between Gordon M. McGregor, Henry Ford and Ford's stockholders in Detroit.[36] McGregor, based in Ontario, proposed setting up a company to manufacture the Model A in Canada in order to reduce the tariff burden incurred by importing parts, which compared favourably to the 35 per cent duty rate imposed on ready-built car. Ford Canada, for a fee, would receive all the patents, plans, drawings and specifications, including 'proper mechanical construction', needed for assembly of Ford automobiles provided by Henry Ford and the American Ford Motor Company. In return, The Ford Motor Company of Michigan received paid-up shares of US$63,750 (51 per cent of the capital).[37]

Ford Canada received exclusive rights to manufacture and sell its automobiles in Canada and became an export platform to capture the British Empire markets, not only to evade Empire market duties but also to achieve economies of scale. The company secured distributorship rights for British colonies, possessions and dependencies. However, in the interwar years, Ford Canada took direct control of activities in these areas by setting up subsidiaries in South Africa (1923), Australia (1925), India (1926), Malaya (1926) and, finally, New Zealand (1936).[38] Ford Canada went on to make Ford Malaya an export platform for the non-British Empire markets of the Dutch East Indies and Thailand in the South East Asian region. Ford Malaya's marketing strategies included agency agreements with merchant firms and ethnic Chinese entrepreneurs.

US automobile MNEs generally favoured exporting to, as opposed to investing in, Malaya primarily due to the presence of large numbers of foreign merchant firms in the country. As distributors these merchant firms, along with local Chinese entrepreneurs, provided excellent marketing opportunities. In order to break into the market, Ford Canada contracted with an American trading intermediary, which in turned made agency agreements with foreign merchant firms and local Chinese entrepreneurs.

Beginning in 1911, Dodge & Seymour, a US trading intermediary run by the two Dodge brothers, V.A. Dodge and Henry T. Dodge, based in New York, started handling the sales of Canadian Ford models in India, Sri Lanka, Thailand, Burma, the Dutch East Indies, Borneo, Malaya and as far away as Aden. The Dodge brothers approached Wearne Brothers, an Australian merchant firm, with a contract to sell 12 Ford cars in the state of Perak.[39] Other parts of the country were covered by Gadelius & Company and Paterson, Simons Company Ltd of Penang.[40] Aside from representing other US makes such as Reo, Studebaker and Oldsmobile, the Swedish merchant firm, Gadelius, was the first sole Ford agent.[41]

Later, upon Wearne Brothers request, the Dodge brothers offered the company the sole agency for Singapore and Malaya with a contract of 60 cars a year.[42] Wearne Brothers promptly placed a large advertisement in *Straits Times* on 4 November 1911, stating their appointment as the sole agent for Ford cars in the Straits Settlements and the Malay States beginning 1 October 1911 (Figure 6.1). Wearne Brothers' acquisition of the Ford agency coincided with the boom in tin and rubber prices leading to an increased demand for Ford automobiles.

Customer service was of primary importance to the Dodge brothers who insisted that their British agents employ 'American marketing methods' to win over customers.[43] According to the Dodge brothers, Wearne Brothers became one of their most-prized agencies, while for Wearne Brothers, the Ford agency gave impetus to its automobile sales.[44] The agreement provided Ford with the avenue it needed to break into the Malaya market. As one of the pioneers in the automobile business with a large stake in the motor trade, Wearne Brothers was able to fully concentrate on automobile trade and services, providing Ford with excellent

Figure 6.1 Wearne's announcement as sole agent for Ford, 1911.

Source: *Straits Times*, 4 November 1911.

distribution facilities. This was in contrast in the early twentieth century to firms such as the Borneo Company and Guthrie, where the car agency was secondary to their main business concern.

Wearne Brothers's success as a Ford distributor was evident when, at their annual meeting in 1926, the company proposed establishing a separate company for Ford products because of the brand's popularity and rapid growth in sales. This suggestion led to the formation of Universal Cars Ltd. Another subsidiary, Malayan Motors, became a limited company and both these subsidiaries handled aspects of the organisation including sales, employment and service facilities. This restructuring exercise allowed Wearne Brothers, as the parent company, to promote the sales of Ford automobiles as an entirely automotive financial concern, providing hire purchase and lending facilities with reasonable rates of interest.[45]

In March 1924, Dodge & Seymour established a Singapore office. In addition to serving Singapore and the Malay States, the company exported to the regional market both inside the British Empire in places such as Borneo, Burma, Sri Lanka, Aden and India and outside in Thailand and some Dutch colonies.[46]

Dodge & Seymour's export summary for the 16-year period of 1911 to 1926 demonstrated the high purchasing power in Malaya. Singapore commanded an average of 20 per cent export (or 21.2 per cent including Penang and Port Swettenham) despite the relatively lower density population, compared with 25 per cent in the Dutch East Indies. Sales data also reveals that tin and rubber price cycles directly affected automobile demand in Malaya. The rubber and tin price boom led to record export sales during World War I, up 55 per cent in 1916 and 49 per cent in 1917, higher than any other area, India included. Conversely, sales were low for the Depression years in the early 1920s.[47]

To further tap into the Malayan sales potential, Ford Canada established agency agreements with local Chinese entrepreneurs because of their networking with major buyers, usually also ethnic Chinese, who were capable of providing efficient distribution and repair services. One such agreement, struck as early as 1916, was that of Ford US with United Motor Works. Ford Canada mainly used these local entrepreneurs' expertise to promote Ford spare parts and accessories, while other small Chinese dealers played a role in Ford's distribution. Over time, Ford Canada and its main dealer, Wearne Brothers, increasingly appointed such dealers in major cities throughout Malaya, as evidenced by the advertisements frequently placed in major local newspapers.

For Ford, the British presence and the distribution services provided by locally based firms led the company to adopt an export strategy as its mode of entry into the Malayan market. Despite the good performance of Dodge & Seymour, Ford Canada, in 1926, decided to take direct control of its activities in Malaya. The head of Ford Canada, Wallace R. Campbell, sent his export manager, Roy Stanley Milliken, to effect the takeover. Dodge & Seymour was accommodating over the loss of the Ford agency because their business portfolios were diverse and not restricted to automobile distribution. Consequently, there was a smooth transition and Ford Canada took on their employees, including 250 Ford dealers and service stations throughout Singapore and the Malay States.[48] This transition from exporting through agents (1909–1926) to assembling activities at the local plant and, after 1926, selling subsidiaries, was adopted in response to the increased sales volume in the Malayan and regional markets. In addition, there was a desire also to protect the intangible assets associated with product development, branding and advertising.[49] Elsewhere in Europe, including Britain, Ford's mode of entry was almost similar.[50] Following the general pattern of other US manufacturing firms seeking to sell in foreign markets, Ford would initially export, and then employ agents before moving into distribution and finally investing in production. However, it is important to note that, unlike those in developed economies such as Canada, Britain or Australia, Ford was not manufacturing in developing markets such as Singapore but just operating an assembly plant.

6.4 Ford Malaya: origins and performance, 1926–1957

An examination of the origins of Ford Malaya and its affiliation with its parent company, Ford Canada, reveals a close parent–subsidiary relations with cordial ties. This is followed by an analysis on the performance of Ford Malaya from 1926 to 1957. It is useful to divide an analysis of the performance of Ford Malaya into the period prior to the Pacific War (1928–1941) and the post-World War II years (1946–1957). Despite the war providing an obvious time marker, there was also a significant shift in the Ford models imported, the declining share of Ford automobile sales in Malaya and, most importantly, the transfer of majority stake from Ford Canada to Ford US by 1948.

The Ford Motor Company of Malaya Ltd was incorporated on 9 November 1926 as a private limited company. This included distribution of 500 capital shares at S$100 (US$56) each with Ford Canada holding 498 shares and the director in Malaya, Roy Stanley Milliken, and the alternate director, Clement Everitt, receiving one share each. The Chartered Bank of India, Australia and China was appointed bankers of the company.[51] Like Dodge & Seymour had done for Ford products, Ford Malaya emphasised regional distribution. The company's announcement in the *Straits Times* stated that the formation of Ford Malaya was mainly to supervise the supply and distribution of Ford products including Lincoln automobiles and Fordson tractors in Malaya, Burma, the Dutch East Indies and Thailand (see Figure 6.2). Ford maintained its dealers, including its major distributor, Wearne Brothers, to conduct retail sales and direct services for owners.[52]

Despite being a latecomer, Ford became a pioneer in 1926 in the Malayan automobile sector after the company founded its first assembly plant in the Southeast Asian region, the only automotive assembly in Malaya, in a two-storey shop house in Singapore. In 1929, the plant moved into bigger premises: a warehouse located along Prince Edward Road near Singapore harbour where semi-knocked down units were assembled.[53] At the time Ford also extended its local representation in Malaya.

Figure 6.2 Advertisement announcing the formation of Ford Motor Company of Malaya Limited.

Source: *Straits Times*, 20 November 1926.

In December 1926, two new directors, H.A. Denne and Basil Stevenson, were elected to the board of Ford Malaya and Roy Stanley Milliken was elected chairman. Denne, who had formerly handled Ford's business in India through a subsidiary named Russa Engineering, was first offered a position in Singapore to launch the Malayan venture at a meeting in London with Ford Canada's head, Wallace R. Campbell. On 30 December, Denne became the first managing director of Ford Malaya and he was assisted by Basil Stevenson who is based in Australia.[54] His appointment set the pattern for Ford Malaya whereby experienced Ford personnel were solicited to hold managerial positions in the company.

At the time of its incorporation, Ford Malaya brought its executive personnel from Ford's headquarters and factory in Canada, the company's intention being 'to bring resources and facilities of the Ford organisation closer to the owners in the east'.[55] Denne started with a staff of six men based in Singapore, where operations began with wheel fitting and touch-up jobs on Model Ts as the launch pad for distribution to the Malay States and the Dutch East Indies.

Denne actively promoted Ford distributorships among the Dutch and British merchant firms by sometimes highlighting potential Chinese competition.[56] He was keen to leverage on the marketing experience presented by these foreign merchant firms and their connections with local Chinese entrepreneurs to distribute automobiles in Malaya. Ford Malaya was responsible for marketing all Ford automobiles as well as supplying parts and accessories as a source of revenue and to complement this vehicle marketing. As detailed earlier, the ready availability of parts contributed to the popularity of Ford models in Malaya.

The performance of Ford in Malaya was similar to the other affiliate companies during the period up to the outbreak of World War II. Failure of Ford's multinational strategies began to appear in the late 1920s when Ford's performance in both Britain and the US was on the decline. In 1913, Ford's market share in Britain was 24 per cent, declining marginally to 22 per cent in 1921. But, by 1929, it had dropped to a mere 4 per cent. Ford's managerial failures put it at a disadvantage as this setback placed British automobile producers, mainly Austin and Morris, in a default position to secure a commanding market share. While Ford was able to rebuild its share of the market in the UK to 18 per cent by 1938, it never regained the dominance it enjoyed at the end of World War I. Although its huge Dagenham factory, which opened in 1932, helped Ford regain market share by producing automobiles designed specifically for the British market, the plant's production ratio was not commensurate to the market share and was poorly located.[57] By 1929, Ford had also lost its leadership position in the US with just 31.3 per cent of the market compared to General Motors' 32.3 per cent.[58]

Ford Malaya's performance mirrored that of its parent, Ford Canada, which reported huge losses ranging from US$1 million to US$5 million in the years 1931 to 1933. Ford US was reported have suffered losses of US$1.4 million annually from 1927 to 1937.[59] In its first year of operations (1926–1927), Ford Malaya incurred losses not only because of depreciation in its fixed asset investments such as assembly machinery and real estate, but also because of the drop in the total aggregate value of vehicle imports into Malaya from S$21 million (US$11.8 million) in September 1926 to S$13million (US$7.3 million) in 1927.[60] In 1928, however, Ford Malaya earned a profit and paid a dividend of S$150 (US$84).

The new Model A, successor to the Model T, introduced in the US in late 1927, proved to be a great success. By 1929, Ford Canada had sold 85,135 units to Ford South Africa, India, Australia and other countries, including Malaya.[61] Ford sales in Malaya rose from 2036 units in 1927 to record highs of 4658 in 1928 and 4392 in 1929. In 1931, the outstanding shares of the company owned by Ford Canada increased from 500 to 998, but Ford Malaya reported a loss in that year with further losses in 1932. These corresponded with lower units shipped from Ford Canada: 1128 units in 1931 and 313 units in 1932 compared with 2251 units in 1930.[62] Imports of vehicles into Malaya fell drastically by 55 per cent in 1931 with a further drop in 1932.[63]

Several factors led to the import decline in the early 1930s. These included a worldwide depression, a slump in rubber and tin prices and the flooding of the market with used cars, which was made worse by retrenchments. However, Ford Malaya was able to provide dividends in its early years and then ride out the depression, faring comparatively well against its counterparts, Borneo Motors Ltd and Cycle & Carriage. The latter two companies had also been incorporated in Singapore in 1926.[64] From profits made in 1933, Ford Malaya was able to declare a dividend of S$50 (US$25). This reversion to increase in sales was, among other reasons, due to the rise in tin and rubber prices and also a growth in sales of the Ford Model Y. In 1933, within the five Ford Canada subsidiaries, Ford Malaya imported 419 units of Model Y, lower than Ford India's 444 units but higher than Ford Australia's 401, Ford New Zealand's 298 and Ford South Africa's 232 units. In 1934, Ford Malaya's import of the Model Y was highest among the five affiliates at 585 units.[65]

Similar to the challenges faced by Ford England, Ford Malaya began to face stiff competition from its mainly British competitors which, in the mid-1930s, were able to capture a significant percentage of the Malayan automobile market. Ford began introducing new models in the Malayan market, several of which were displayed during the British Trade Fair held in Singapore in May 1936, with the Ford V8 (10 and 8 HP models) among the most popular. At the same time, the Lincoln Zephyr was introduced with 10 HP and a V12 engine.[66] Ford advertisements continued to dominate over Wearne Brothers representation of other makes of British or US cars, and the Fords 'retained their pre-eminent place in the firm's sales figures'.[67] Throughout 1935 to 1940, sales increased for Ford Malaya as commodity prices improved. Yet Ford failed to regain its dominant position in the Malayan automobile market post-World War I. Morris in 1936, for instance, captured 25 per cent of the automobile market in Malaya.[68]

In 1938, there was again an overall decline in vehicle imports due to lower tin and rubber exports and this was reflected in Ford's performance. However, as indicated in Figure 6.3, Ford captured a significant share of the Malayan market in 1939, reaching a peak of almost 80 per cent due to the war disruption that had led to the dwindling supply of British and continental European automobiles. Although Canada declared war on Germany in September 1939, this had little effect on overall production unlike in Europe.[69] Hence, market demand was fulfilled by Ford Canada, which continued to export automobiles which were shipped in a completely knocked-down condition for assembly in Malaya.

In the years leading up to the outbreak of the Pacific War, an average of 50 per cent of Canadian total sales (reaching a record of 61.95 per cent in 1942) were

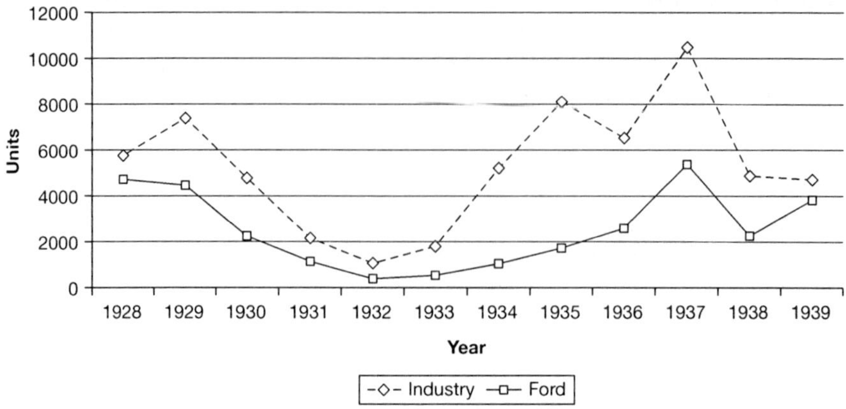

Figure 6.3 Total automobile sales in Malaya vs Ford Malaya (in units), 1928–1939.

Notes:

a Ford Malaya figures for 1928–1939 refer to Malaya, Singapore, Sarawak and North Borneo as Ford Malaya managed these markets as a single market area.

b Industry figures for 1928–1937 refer to Malaya and Singapore only. These figures (except for 1937) include imports of second-hand vehicles.

c Industry figures for 1938–1939 refer to Malaya, Singapore, North Borneo and Sarawak.

Sources: Industry: Reports from Motor Traders Association of Malaysia.[70] Ford Malaya: General Accounting and Financial Analysis, Overseas Division, Ford Motor Company of Canada Ltd., Oakville, Ontario; PRO: BT59/24, 'Motor Industry: Discussions with UK Trade Organisations', 1938.

shipped to the company's subsidiaries in South Africa, Australia, New Zealand, India as well as Malaya. Thus, Ford Canada relied on its export sales as much as, and sometimes even more than, its domestic sales. The average percentage of sales to subsidiary companies shipped to Malaya between 1926 and 1941 was approximately 12 per cent. The annual figure ranged from a low of 4 per cent in 1933 to a high of 26 per cent in 1927 and 23 per cent in 1941.[71] In 1941, to meet the demand for vehicles, Ford Malaya moved its operations to its new assembly plant in Bukit Timah, Singapore and in October of the same year, the company began body assembly for the first time in its history. The Pacific war broke out just two months later.[72]

General Yamashita, the Japanese military commander, summoned the British general, Percival, to the Ford Motor Co premises in Bukit Timah for a formal surrender, which was made in the boardroom of Ford Malaya on 15 February 1942.[73] The Japanese occupied Ford's plant and assembled Toyoda and Nissan trucks there during the war. They also interned several Ford Malaya employees during the occupation who, upon their release, reported the bad state of the plant after travelling to the assembly plant in Singapore. However, a US State Department official later reported the good condition of Ford's assembly plant.[74]

Immediately after the Japanese occupation, there was a huge shortage of vehicles, which impeded the early reconstruction of Malaya. Delivery of new cars into the country was delayed by strikes in the US and Canada, shipping difficulties and exchange controls. During these difficult times, Ford England largely filled the vacuum. In late 1945, a shipment for Malaya of British vehicles contained 74 Ford cars, in addition to four Standard sedans, 40 Bedford three-ton trucks, five truck chassis and 40 Norton motorcycles. In January 1946, Wearne Brothers received a consignment of 45 cars, mainly Fords, Morrises and Standards, whilst Borneo Motors received ten Austins.[75]

By June 1946, further shipments of vehicles had arrived. Vehicle purchasing priority was given to rubber estate owners to expedite the rejuvenation of the rubber industry. In an endeavour to facilitate delivery of more cars in the same year, the controller of foreign exchange in Malaya granted an 'increased measure of US currency for the import of American cars'.[76] There was a sharp increase in the total number of automobiles imported into Malaya in the late 1940s after the Federation of Malaya government lifted control on automobile sales in October 1947.[77]

Merchant firms also took the initiative and helped revive the industry after the war by actively promoting automobile sales. In a rare move, Wearne Brothers formed a trading partnership with its old rival Borneo Motors, holding a 60 per cent share of the joint venture known as Wearne Brothers–Borneo Motors Service (Malaya) Ltd. They acquired premises and properties, undertook repairs to military vehicles and, with the assistance of the Colonial Office, secured the importation of both passenger and commercial vehicles. However, the two merchant firms had ended the partnership and gone their separate ways by 1 April 1946.[78] By the mid-1950s, as shown in Table 6.4, Wearne Brothers was by far the top distributor of passenger cars in Malaya, easily outstripping its closest competitor, the Borneo Company Ltd. Wearne Brothers and its subsidiaries (often operated by local Chinese entrepreneurs) held a large number of rival agencies. Indeed, local Chinese firms such as Cycle & Carriage, as seen in Table 6.4, were increasingly commanding a greater share of the Malayan automobile market, holding agency rights from British and continental European firms. George Lee, for example, held a diverse range of agencies from the Italian Fiat, the British Alvis and Armstrong to the American Packard and Nash.

In addition to Wearne Brothers and other local agents, Ford Malaya also continued to use British merchant firms such as Sime Darby, which was appointed Ford's agent (in 1951) to market Fordson Major tractors (produced at Dagenham, London) throughout Malaya and Singapore.[79] Ford also used British merchant firms to distribute its vehicles including in North Borneo, Harrisons & Crosfield, while its agent in Thailand was Anglo-Thai Motors Ltd (a subsidiary of Anglo-Thai Corporation).[80]

Similar to the resource-seeking industries of tin and rubber, American companies also took swift action to re-establish the automobile industry in Malaya. By January 1946, the manager of Ford Malaya, C.J.R. Michels, had returned to the country and was attached to a government unit to assist in the recovery activities for the automobile industry. Yet more than a year later, Ford Malaya was still not able to start civilian production, as the British Military Administration, established at the end of World War II, had turned the plant into a base workshop. It was finally

Table 6.4 Percentage sales held by Wearne Brothers, BCL and others, 1953–1955

(a) Approximate percentage of motor vehicles sold in Malaya

	Full Year 1953 %	*Full Year 1954* %	*Nine Months 1955* %
Passenger Cars			
Wearne	58	68	52
BCL Group	31	20	20
Others	11	12	28
Total	100	100	100
Commercial Vehicles			
Wearne	41	39	33
BCL Group	47	44	45
Others	12	17	22
Total	100	100	100

(b) Agencies held by Wearne Brothers and its competitors, 1955

Wearne Bros Ltd Group a) Universal Cars Ltd b) Malayan Motors Ltd c) Progress Motors Ltd	Nuffield, Ford, Bootes, Rolls-Royce, Dennis, Albion, Leyland, Dodge, Buick, Daimler, De Soto, Hillman, Singer, Sunbeam, Holden and Renault
C&C	Jaguar, Singer, Hudson, Plymouth, Mercedes, Dennis and Fargo
Eastern Autos Ltd	Citroen, Aston-Martin
George Lee Ltd	Fiat, Alvis, Armstrong, Packard and Nash
Singapore Motors Ltd	Pontiac and Opel
Champion Motors Ltd	Rover, Volkswagen and Studebaker

Source: GHL, MS 271371, BCL Report on the Finances of Borneo Motors Ltd, of Singapore and its subsidiaries with related correspondence 1955–56. F.B. Proctor, Peat, Marwick, Mitchell & Co, 5 December 1955.

released back to the company in April 1947.[81] By December of the same year, Ford Malaya had resumed operations and the assembly plant in Singapore was reopened, although there were only 68 employees and unit sales for the year was only 44 compared to 4700 in 1941. In 1948, despite a state of emergency being declared by the colonial government because of a communist guerrilla insurrection, sales improved and Ford Malaya was able to expand sales with Ford cars being used extensively as scout cars.[82]

However, from 1949 to 1950 sales dropped due to several factors. First, as detailed in Chapter 3, the ban on the import of cars with 20 HP or more from hard currency areas (including Canada), which Singapore and the Federation of Malaya governments imposed in an effort to save dollar exchange, began to have an impact.[83] This was in contrast to the earlier 1946 policy that had positively encouraged US automobiles to be imported into Malaya. In addition, the situation worsened when the sterling devaluation of September 1949 led to the devaluation of the Canadian dollar against the US dollar. This increased the price of American automobiles of Canadian origin, making them much more expensive than cars from Europe[84] (predominantly automobiles from British manufacturers). European cars had an added advantage in that they could be purchased in sterling while the scarcity of dollars in Malaya made it difficult to purchase American cars.

From 1949 onwards, Ford Canada's total sales to subsidiaries declined markedly from a pre-war average of between 40 and 45 per cent to 11.5 per cent. Similarly, Ford Malaya reflected the performance of its headquarters Ford Canada. By 1950, Ford Canada lost its first place in dominion production and between 1950 and 1952 exports accounted for only 16 per cent of Ford Canada's output. Reasons for the decline were the same as could be seen in Malaya with the effects of exchange controls and the proliferation of small European automobiles providing stiff competition for Ford's automobiles.[85]

In 1951, despite the demand caused by the Korean War, Ford Malaya only captured 15 per cent of the annual total industry sales, which peaked at 18,500 units (see Figure 6.4). The ban on Ford Canada's products (except spare parts) continued throughout the year.[86] The aftermath of the Korean War was a depression between 1952 and 1953 in the automobile industry, which correlated with reduced rubber and tin prices. Hence, the lower sales figures in 1953 for total automobiles sold, including cars, trucks and tractors, at just 1644 units.

In 1954, sales figures increased, due mainly to the improvement in rubber prices and the introduction of two new models, the Anglia and Prefect. The figures

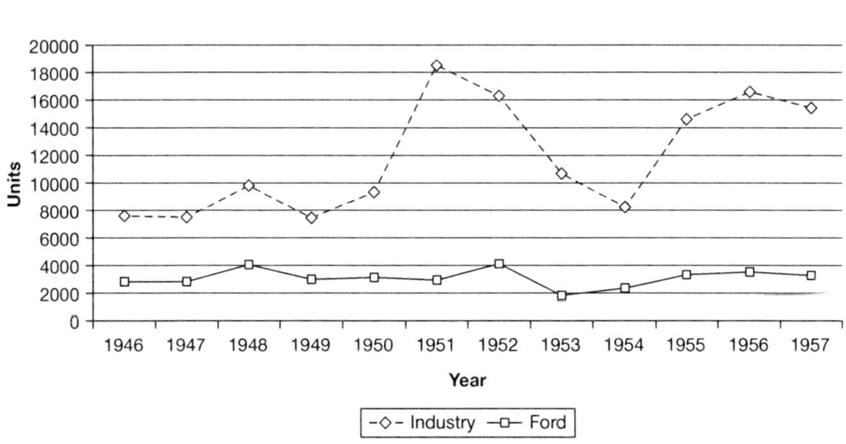

Figure 6.4 Total automobile sales in Malaya, Singapore, Sabah and Sarawak vs Ford Malaya, 1946–1957.

Notes and sources: As Figure 6.3.

Table 6.5 Malayan car imports by country, 1951–1957 (in units)

Country	*1951*	*1952*	*1953*	*1954*	*1955*	*1956*	*1957*
Britain[a]	5,374	12,467	11,261	7,285	5,767	9,083	9,086
West Germany	–	59	14	15	75	645	1,785
Italy	332	995	187	212	239	2,187	1,918
France	10	51	24	3	–	176	674
Australia[b]	–	–	–	–	–	2	105
US	45	1,530	1,714	189	268	678	587

Notes:

[a] Figures include Ford England automobiles.

[b] Holden was the popular Australian make.

Source: Adapted from *Far Eastern Economic Review* 9, 1960, pp. 455–7.

steadily improved over the following two years, and in 1957 the company introduced three new models: the Mark II Consul, Zephyr and Zodiac. Net profit rose in tandem with sales increasing from M$1.22 million in 1954 to 2.02 million in 1957.[87]

Notwithstanding the increase in number of units sold, Ford's overall percentage of the Malayan market share declined, which coincided in the 1950s with changing trends in consumer demand. The trend in Europe for small and medium cars quickly caught on in the Malayan automobile market with, apart from the predominant British 'mini' Morris, Austin and Hillman, a shift in demand for other makes, such as the German Volkswagen, Italian Fiat and Alfa Romeo, and the French Renault and Peugeot. Britain commanded a large share of the Malayan market and import values rose from M$1.7 million in 1951 to M$3.43 million in 1957.[88] These figures included imports from Ford England and General Motors' Australian subsidiary, General Motors-Holden Ltd.[89]

Imports from West Germany and Italy saw a significant increase in trade (see Table 6.5). The Malayan consumers were spoilt for choice, becoming more price-conscious and selective, but Ford failed to compete in the small car market. The depreciation value was higher for large US cars than small European cars, which, 'in addition to being produced cheaper', were able to be purchased in sterling.[90] The decline in sales of large US cars was further exacerbated when the Federated Malay States and Singapore governments, in an effort to save dollars, imposed a maximum price limit on US cars of S$9,500 in 1952.[91]

6.5 Competitive strategies

From its inception, Ford Malaya, through its competitive strategies, was able to capture and retain a significant share of the Malayan market until the onset of the Pacific War (except for a short decline in the 1930s). The same strategies allowed Ford to check its post-World War II decline, when, because of restrictions, product sourcing was switched from Ford Canada to Ford England. Ford Malaya's growth can be attributed to ownership advantages derived from Ford's national and international operations and enabling them to use common governance in the areas of organisational skills, product sourcing and production technology.

Ford Canada and Ford England became export platforms for Ford automobiles to evade duties imposed in the Empire markets. By using these export platforms, American automobile manufacturers were also able to escape the imposition of a 33.5 per cent *ad valorem* tax on the landed costs of imported cars, the so-called 'McKenna duty' introduced in 1915, intended to eliminate foreign competition in the British domestic market. For these reasons Ford was able to compete on an equal footing with British-owned automobile manufacturers. Ford Canada and Ford England are good examples of how US manufacturing MNEs exploited locational advantage to compete worldwide. Both these Ford affiliates played a role in ensuring the success of Ford Malaya, contributing managerial and technological expertise at different times.

As Chapters 2 and 3 have demonstrated, US business viewed Malaya as a useful regional export platform. For market-seeking FDI, this factor was of great importance. Ford Canada went on to make Ford Malaya an export platform for the non-British Empire in South East Asia, capturing the markets of the Dutch East Indies and Thailand. Export sales were much higher than domestic sales at significant periods of time, indicating the importance of these foreign markets.

The same desire to establish a regional export platform in Malaya can be seen in General Motors' (albeit failed) plan to build a plant in Singapore. While General Motors' plant in Java was used to serve the Dutch East Indies, Straits Settlements, Indochina, Borneo, Malay States and Thailand, the company's regional administrative office for the Far East, which controlled its Java, India and Japan plants, was located in Singapore due to its 'rather unique geographical situation, its exceptionally fine transportation facilities for the movement of the members of the regional staff to and from various plants, and also because of its dominating position in the commercial activity of the East'.[92]

Ford Malaya, since its early beginnings, had received significant input from its worldwide affiliates. Its first mover advantages, as the first automobile assembly plant, provided it with an opportunity to tap into the regional market. Ford initially used multiple sourcing from its worldwide operations, mainly in Canada and Britain, in its attempt to evade duties and to provide the latest Ford models to Malaya and the regional market.

During the interwar years, Ford Canada was the main source of imports of Ford cars for Malaya.[93] However, the post-war period saw changes in sourcing imports as wartime and exchange controls imposed in 1939 continued after World War II, as did an emphasis to source materials first from sterling countries. Ford products sourced from Ford England since the early 1930s, reached a pre-war peak in 1937, and post-World War II the number of units shipped started to increase again (see Table 6.6). As in other empire markets, particularly Australia, after the devaluation in September 1949, Ford England being located in a soft currency area became an important source of supply for the Malayan market.[94] British Ford models such as the Prefect, Anglia and the Temp truck were particularly popular in the Malayan market.[95]

Table 6.6 Units shipped from Ford England, 1936–1949

Year		*Malaya*	
	Passenger	*Commercial*	*Total*
1936	893	21	914
1937	2,399	20	2,419
1938	n.a.	n.a.	
1939	1,405	13	1,418
1940	935	9	944
1941	690	Nil	672
	No records (1942–1945)		
1946	1,534	455	1,910
1947	1,255	141	1,396
1948	1,817	93	1,910
1949	1,912	92	2,004

Notes:
1. Figures include data for Singapore.
2. Passenger cars refer to Ford Anglia, Prefect and Lincoln only.

Source: Overseas Shipments, Sales Division, Ford Motor Company Canada Ltd.

It is clear that Ford was able to evade certain taxes and controls by capitalising on its worldwide operations, saving costs across borders in an effort to remain competitive.

At the time of its incorporation, Ford Malaya employed its executive personnel from the Canadian headquarters and factory and the subsidiary maintained a direct link to its parent company. Dearborn officials in the US were seldom consulted on matters relating to either Malaya or other Canadian affiliates. As we have seen, this close relationship was maintained between the parent and subsidiary when personnel from Ford Canada held important positions in Ford Malaya and its worldwide affiliates.

The Malayan executives (represented by Canadian personnel) exercised a degree of independence due to the physical distance from the parent company. However, areas such as vehicle prices, dividends declared, purchase of property and remuneration required consultation with Ford Canada. As a result of both the distance and the need for consultation, country managers commuted frequently to Canada to report and to discuss future policies.[94] Ford Canada and its affiliates – Ford Malaya, Ford India, Ford South Africa, Ford New Zealand and Ford Australia – regularly rotated managers for their shared expertise, drawing on their experiences in setting up business at foreign localities. In fact, there were instances of Ford Canada's managers being sent to Ford England. At Ford Malaya, well qualified and experienced country managers were appointed to launch Ford products both in Malaya and in South East Asia as a whole. The managing director from 1947 to 1951, Gordon Withell, had been an employee of Ford Canada since

1935. However, he was also monitoring Ford's subsidiary activities in South East Asia and South Asia.[97] Despite Ford Canada losing the leading role as a major exporter in 1950, the Canadian headquarters continued to participate in the management of Ford Malaya. As such, from time to time the remuneration of the managing directors of Ford Malaya was determined by the vice president (overseas operations) of Ford Canada.[98]

This system of management meant that there was little development of local expertise in Malaya. Most Chinese auto firms were family-run concerns, such as Cycle & Carriage and United Motor Works. Only middle- or lower-rank employees came from the local population. In contrast, Ford affiliates in Australia, New Zealand and England had greater autonomy and by the interwar years locals held managerial positions.[99] Ford England, for example, witnessed the appointment of a British MD and by 1948 'had an all-English management'.[100]

Ford, however, was very much involved in training local staff for specific non-management positions in Malaya. Several technical staff were brought in to supervise the training and education programme of dealers, mechanics and other personnel. Hence, Malayan dealers and mechanics benefited from the technical expertise provided by Ford's specialised training.

Apart from making agency agreements with merchant firms and Chinese traders, Ford's marketing approach included an emphasis on spare parts and accessories in keeping with providing excellent auto services, unlike other car manufacturers. All Ford dealers and service stations throughout the territories offered these services. In addition to undertaking this part of the marketing process for all Ford automobiles, Ford Malaya took responsibility for supplying parts and accessories to complement its vehicle marketing and as a source of revenue. The sale of certain makes depended on the availability of spare parts and accessories, so this was an effective means of promoting Ford sales. Ready availability of parts contributed to the popularity of Ford models in Malaya. The British adviser in Kelantan remarked on this, stating it was difficult to get replacement parts for British makes and 'in my opinion this is one of the factors which have made the Ford and Dodge so popular'.[101]

Facilities for repair also gave US cars an advantage and in the 1920s Ford was able to capitalise on fuel savings, where mileage per gallon was much more favourable than that for British models.[102] In a letter to the then secretary of state for the colonies, Winston Churchill, the British representative in the Unfederated Malay States also stressed the availability of facilities for purchase and repair and the lower petrol consumption of US cars.[103] Ford's sole agents (mainly Wearne Brothers and Chinese firms) continued to place emphasis on the marketing of spare parts and accessories and the provision of service facilities during the interwar and post-World War II years. Though not as frequently as Wearne Brothers as its main distributor, Ford also used advertisements as a marketing tool in Malaya, using local newspapers mainly to introduce or to announce the demonstration of new models in the Malayan market.

Ford Malaya gradually appointed local dealers to market its products in a strategy to expand its network and cover a wider sales area and bigger base of consumers in the peninsula. These dealers were often local Chinese but, in 1950, the appointment of a Malay dealer in Kelantan, M. Jaffar Ltd, also began to appear in its advertisements.[104] By the early 1950s and as Ford stated in its advertisements in major newspapers, its dealers were now available in the major cities throughout Malaya, including North Borneo, and in Sarawak, Thailand and Indonesia. In 1956, Ford Malaya carried out a programme to strengthen its dealer network in the Federated Malay States. It appointed five new dealers in Kuantan, Kuala Terengganu, Taiping, Alor Star and Johore Bahru, all previously administered by Wearne Brothers. The same year saw the transfer of Ford India's marketing services to Ford Malaya, making it responsible for sales in the territories of India, Pakistan, Ceylon, Burma, Nepal and Goa.[105]

The method of mass production and technological innovation synonymous with 'Fordism' was pioneered at Ford Motors and successfully produced the Model T. Fordism also involved a management style that simultaneously boosted mass production through 'welfare capitalism' and led to drastically reduced production costs.[106] This gave Ford a considerable price advantage vis-à-vis other automobile manufacturers including those that were British owned. As observed by one journalist, British automobiles in the mid-1920s could not compete with US automobiles when it came to 'power for price', hence the considerably larger number of US cars to be seen on Malayan roads.[107] British makes were markedly more expensive than those of their rivals, Ford and Dodge.[108] Fordism soon became a source of competitive advantage for the company, reflecting its position as the world's leading producer of automobiles.

Price competitiveness proved an important factor in both the South East Asian and the Far East Asian markets. In the 1920s, cars selling under S$2800 captured 80 per cent of the Malayan market, more so if there was a good spare-parts service support. The latter was appreciated by both foreign and local users.[109] Ford had a distinct price advantage in the mid-1920s providing the cheapest models for passenger and commercial automobiles in Malaya.[110]

The period from 1920 until 1929 saw a reduction in the prices of British Morris and Austin models due to the adoption of efficient mass production techniques and also a consolidation within the British motor industry. Despite these reductions, however, British costs and prices remained higher than those of US makes worldwide. US cars were still 30 per cent cheaper than British ones in 1938.[111] Whilst some of the price difference may be accounted for by HP duties, the price differential is still significant. The same could be said of US affiliates in Britain. Though much more productive than their local competitors, these US overseas subsidiaries were not as cost effective as their parent companies in the US or Canada.[112]

As detailed in this chapter, Ford Malaya's production technology continued to evolve throughout its history, with the gradual transfer of skills and expertise from both Ford Canada and Ford England to the Malayan plant. Beginning with wheel-fitting and touch-up jobs of Model-Ts in Singapore to assembling automobile units imported in semi-knocked down conditions, the Malayan subsidiary steadily expanded its capacity. By 1941, due to increased demand of these assembled vehicles both in Malaya and in the region, Ford Malaya began operating in a newly built assembly plant at Bukit Timah, Singapore, the only automotive assembly plant in Malaya. By October 1941, Ford Malaya had begun body assembly, but the onset of the Pacific War halted production.

Following the reopening of Ford's plant in 1947, Ford Malaya immediately began assembling, and the vehicles were well-received locally. In 1951, the Canadian Ford Custom was assembled, followed, in 1954, by the more popular British model, the Ford Anglia. In early 1956, Ford Malaya purchased jigs from the Dagenham plant for the assembly of the Mark II Consul cars, introduced in the same year, along with two other new models, Zephyr and Zodiac.[113]

6.6 US enterprise in automobiles: a summary

By offering wider opportunities for worldwide sources of input, Ford was able to enhance its operational flexibility in Malaya. There was significant integration within its affiliates, leading to reduced transaction costs. In addition, Ford's ability to achieve economies of scale led to its success, for a period, in a price-conscious market in Malaya. In the case of Ford Malaya, aside from exploiting the ownership-specific factors of organisational skills and superior production technology, the significance of location-specific factors also needs to be recognised.

Location-specific factors include Ford's ability to evade tariff barriers by using Ford Canada and Ford England as export platforms to penetrate the Empire market. Ford Malaya was a classic example of the importance of a firm's strategies relative to government policy and which turned market unfamiliarity into a competitive advantage. This gave Ford the competitive edge, for a time, over continental European imports.

The automobile industry in Malaya represents a fascinating case of Anglo-US competition as well as cooperation. Competition can be seen in the implementation of certain British policies, including the imposition of preferential duties, taxation based on HP rating, and the introduction of government loans meant specifically for the purchase of British makes. Cooperation occurred mainly at the marketing and distributorship level between Ford and British merchant firms. Ford also worked with merchant firms, relying upon the distribution facilities provided by one of the best agencies in Malaya, Wearne Brothers This cooperation continued even after Ford established its own distribution unit.

Managerial failure in the 1930s and again in the 1950s led Ford to lose market share in Malaya although latterly this decline was compounded by exchange controls imposed by the British government after World War II. To avoid the adverse effects of exchange controls Ford sourced its products from Ford England. While this allowed Ford to hold its leading position in the Malayan market, its overall percentage of the market declined, as Ford was successfully challenged, mainly in the small car market, by its European competitors.

Ford provided business opportunities by appointing dealers and establishing service stations throughout Singapore and the Malay States. In addition, Ford developed a complementary relationship with local enterprises by giving franchising opportunities to local Chinese and, to a limited extent, Malays. The automobile trade in Malaya generated substantial government revenue through petrol taxes as well as licence and registration fees. Ford's sizeable share in the Malayan automobile market meant that Ford also contributed towards this revenue.

Although it did not establish R&D units in Malaya as seen in the resource-seeking FDI, there was a gradual transfer of production technology to Malaya, from semi-knocked down units to complete knocked down units in the interwar years, to the assembling of various Ford's products from Ford Canada and Ford England post-World War II. Ford's assembly plant and its dealer network throughout Malaya also provided employment opportunities for local workers, at both middle and low-level income levels. Unlike in the resource-seeking industries where expatriate technical staff generally did not provide any training to the locals, several technical staff brought in from Ford Canada supervised training and education programmes for dealers, mechanics and other personnel. This was not the case at the managerial level however, with Ford's practice of staffing its affiliates with home officers effectively denying the local labour force the opportunity to improve its managerial skills. Hence, only low-level skills were imparted to the local personnel force. Still, it can be asserted, that Ford's extended presence in Malaya had a significant impact on the Malayan economy.

7 Conclusion

Counting the cost

7.1 Restatement

This work, while exploring the relationship between the US and the Malaysian economy between 1870 and 1957 addresses two main issues. The first considers the reasons behind the generally low levels of trade and US FDI in Malaya during the period, asking whether the colonial administration restricted or stimulated, and British business competed with or complemented, the development of US trade and FDI in the country. The second core issue in this book is an examination of the impact of US FDI on the Malayan economy supported by three case studies of US MNEs in the tin, rubber and automobile industries. This analysis provides insights on colonial trade and investment policies and US economic involvement in colonial Malaya.

7.2 Dimensions of US–Malayan trade and FDI relations

During the nineteenth century, US exports to Malaya were mainly silver dollars and, towards the end of the century, petroleum products. Later, starting in World War I, there followed an increased demand for US automobiles, machinery and other consumer goods. However, the US continued to purchase more from Malaya than it sold, and US imports into the country remained almost negligible from the 1870s until 1957. Since the late nineteenth century, the US had been one of Malaya's major trading partners because of the large Malayan tin and rubber exports to the US. As a result, economically at least, there was a degree of mutual dependence between the US and Malaya with, for example, the US able to obtain cheap tin and rubber while in return Malaya enjoyed a steady demand for its natural resources. US imports, although still negligible, gradually increased during World War I when there was virtually no German competition and only limited supply of British products, but fell during the interwar years. After World War II imports from the US increased marginally due to the demands of economic rehabilitation after the Japanese occupation, with cotton textiles and machinery being the main imports. In the 1950s, exchange controls reinstituted by the colonial administration made US goods more expensive and thus, imports again fell.

In contrast to the highly protectionist policies of the US, the British colonial government pursued free trade policies within a broad framework in Malaya until the 1930s. Official government policy only partially accounts for the low level of US imports. Even the Imperial Preference system or exchange controls, which were implemented in the 1930s, could have only been marginally responsible for the reduction. Low levels of US imports in Malaya and elsewhere in the region were more due to the limited market for US manufactured goods, given that the economies in the area were still developing. This was also true for Malaya, despite the fact that per capita incomes were high compared to those in other developing economies in the region. In addition, US imports had to compete with British and continental European goods, which were already well-established in the local market. US companies were able, however, to take full advantage of the marketing channels provided by the British, ethnic Chinese and other trade intermediaries, but they still failed to make a significant impact on the Malayan market despite the market intelligence provided by US consuls and some attempts to adapt products to local market conditions.

Compared to the present-day, US FDI in Malaya for the period covered appears quite marginal, although it was significantly higher than in the neighbouring South East Asian countries. This was mainly facilitated by the British presence which provided the valorising factor of a stable regulatory framework and the active business participation. As such, the US was a major trading partner but only a minor direct investor in Malaya due to the highly competitive nature of the small Malayan market, the geographical distance and the presence of British incumbents.

The case studies examined in this work support Wilkins' previous assertions made in her surveys on US FDI concerning 'nearby' influences and resource availability. In short, that most US FDI went to regions geographically close to the US and to developed, rather than developing, economies. As such, substantial US FDI in resources went to neighbouring regions in the Americas with USRC in 1903 acquiring extensive concessions in northern Brazil, then the world's largest rubber exporter, and YGC investing in gold mining in the Yukon Territory in Canada. US FDI in manufacturing went to developed market economies, particularly Canada and Britain, the latter being one of the world's most industrialised economies. Ford, for example, invested in both countries.

The investments of US firms in Malaya and South East Asia were always marginal to their main concerns, though they were prepared to venture into the region if there seemed to be profitable opportunities, as in the case of US rubber investments. The dislocation of trade in Europe, the British rubber embargo, and fluctuating rubber prices caused by World War I, as well as the British restriction schemes between 1922 and 1928 and again in 1934, led major US rubber MNEs to initially establish their own purchasing organisations in Singapore, and for some to integrate backwards into rubber plantations. The vertical integration model assumes that reductions in transaction costs are achieved by investing across borders. However, this research shows that backward integration by USRC into rubber plantations was not an effective strategy. This was true either in relation to cost savings or stability of supplies for, as it turned out, these plantations never came close to satisfying USRC's requirement for rubber or reduced their dependence on the international market. In contrast to USRC's backward integration, there was no incentive for Pacific Tin to integrate forwards into smelting due to restrictions on tin-ore exports and the predominant smelting concerns in Malaya. Ford chose to internalise its distribution because of growing market demands and increasing monitoring costs in distant markets such as Malaya and the South East Asian region.

The existence of powerful British incumbents, mainly merchant firms, which had first mover advantages, also contributed to the low level of US FDI in Malaya. They had the advantage of superior networking with internal and external markets through the support of local entrepreneurs and other British free standing companies and foreign merchants. The British merchant traders who came to Malaya evolved, over time, into direct investors. The Americans were dependent upon the services of these merchant firms as well as on US trading intermediaries, with the latter primarily focused on trade. However, it was British merchant firms that excelled at both trade and FDI, beginning in the late nineteenth century and evidenced by the evolution of merchant firms into diversified business groups driven by managerial and enterprising competencies. Merchant firms such as Wearne Brothers, Borneo Company, Harrisons & Crosfield, Guthrie and Sime Darby, with their knowledge of the South East Asian region, played an important role in the modern Malayan economy.

While on the one hand, the existence of these British incumbents limited the growth of US FDI, on the other these mainly merchant firms, through the provision of services to a number of US MNEs, also enabled US FDI in Malaya. Pacific Tin, despite its independence from merchant firms, drew on the secretarial services of Osborne & Chappel in its initial dealings with the local authorities in Malaya. Ford Malaya drew on the support of Wearne Brothers, one of the largest automobile distributors in Malaya, to distribute its automobiles. Even though some US firms, such as USRC and Dunlop, remained independent of merchant firms, the evidence suggests that business links were generally not dictated by nationality, but categorised by sector. Overall, the relationships between US firms and British firms were more complementary than competitive.

British rule in the Straits Settlements and the intervention in the Malay States from the 1870s were important prerequisites for flourishing international trade and FDI in the region. When US firms invested in Malaya, they were motivated by the many advantages provided by the British presence in Malaya including strong government, good legal framework, free trade policies, their common use of English and a well-developed infrastructure. US firms exploited Malaya's potential as a regional export platform. Singapore was the springboard for investments into the Malay states and the surrounding South East Asian region. For some US MNEs, Singapore became a platform for South Asian as well as Far East markets.

In an era when international business could operate worldwide almost without restriction, the Malayan market was open to investors from all countries. Aside from British predominance in FDI, continental European and Japanese foreign direct investments also preceded US interests. German firms invested in services, mainly merchant and shipping firms, the French in tin and rubber, the Belgians in rubber, and the Danes in palm oil. Likewise, Japanese FDI was also present in the resource-oriented areas of iron-ore and rubber as well as in shipping. Despite the sometimes restrictive policies of the British and the challenging 'nearby' factors, with so many apparent advantages it is interesting that the number of US MNEs directly investing in Malaya remained relatively low.

7.3 Impact of colonial decision-making

As the colonial power in Malaya, the British government, represented by both the metropolitan Colonial Office and the British administrators in the Straits Settlements, Federated Malay States and Unfederated Malay States, played an important role in both enhancing and limiting business opportunities for American investors. As Drabble, White and other recent historians have argued, the British colonial government never sought to protect British-owned firms as a matter of policy. While politically these colonial authorities were trying to satisfy the locals and morally they saw themselves as paternalistic guardians of the colonies, strategically they were very much servants of the British Empire, for as a colonial government it was bound to make decisions that maintained the security of its empire. This position adopted by British colonial administrators goes a long way to explain why the administration generally opposed monopoly and was suspicious of large corporations and as such was apprehensive of US firms' intentions, fearing they could damage Malaya's, and in turn, Britain's economic standing. Similar anti-monopoly views were held by the US government of the time, although the US generally took more aggressive steps against large firms by introducing anti-trust regulations. This opposition suspicion of big business is made apparent in the three case studies of US MNEs in the tin, rubber and automobile industries.

US entrepreneurs used several strategies to invest in Malaya and the surrounding region. When US firms failed in their initial attempts to establish large firms under their control because of restrictions, as seen in the example of the International Tin Company in the tin-smelting industry, they offered the alternative of an Anglo-American merger, with a prime example being the International Plantation Rubber Company. US investments were sometimes blocked not only in Malaya, but also in the US colony of the Philippines because of their monopolistic ambitions and tendencies. In Malaya, small-sized US rubber firms could enter freely in the 1900s, but the large, competitive US rubber concerns that tried to invest after World War I were blocked due to the British authorities fear of US MNEs gaining too greater control of the industry. Pacific Tin, the only US entrant in the Malayan tin industry, did not face any restriction because it did not pose any threat as its limited output was sold to a locally registered smelting concern, the Straits Trading Company. General Motor's grand plans to build an assembly plant in Singapore were seen as too ambitious by the local authorities and potentially exerting too much influence and were ultimately blocked.

Another strategy employed by US firms to enter into the Malayan market was to make business arrangements with (mainly British) merchant firms. Ford entered Malaya through agency agreements with these merchant firms as well as ethnic

Chinese entrepreneurs to distribute their automobiles and spare parts. Ford then invested in an assembly plant in Singapore in the mid-1920s. Unlike Ford, General Motors failed to use its Canadian or British affiliate to enter the Malayan market. This was one reason why its application to build a plant was denied and represents one of the missed opportunities by US firms to invest in Malaya.

It seems clear, then, that US firms were free to invest in Malaya as long as they did not pose a threat to other business interests, particularly British business interests, while some US firms were blocked if it was perceived that their presence could lead to monopoly or foreign dependence. In general, when considering the relationships of British government and businesses with US firms, the positive effects of the British presence in Malaya far outweighed the negative effects of restrictive British policies aimed at US companies.

7.4 US competitive strategies

The few US MNEs that successfully invested in Malaya did so largely because of their managerial skills, technological superiority and competitive ability to adapt and innovate. Aside from these inherent advantages, most importantly, the three US MNEs that are the subject of case studies in this work fully exploited the locational advantages of Malaya. In fact, over time, investments in Malaya became vital in supporting the continued existence of the firms, including their parent firms back home. In the mid-1920s, USRC's plantations subsidiary (including Sumatra) was more profitable than its parent company, while in the 1930s, YGC was kept afloat by its profitable tin venture in Malaya. Overall, US MNEs evolved with the times, surviving various economic cycles of boom and bust and political upheavals, including the two world wars and the Emergency.

In addition, the US investors realised the strategic importance to their businesses of developing and maintaining links with local Chinese entrepreneurs in Malaya. For foreign firms, these Chinese trading companies were vital intermediaries between local and colonial as well as foreign economies. They also served as agents for local communities, buying primary produce at the main ports and the interior, and sometimes even financed local productions through cash advances or goods on credit. In return, the primary produce might be exchanged for textiles, kerosene or other various foreign goods. It was important to gain access to the ethnic Chinese community as they represented a major proportion of Malayan consumers of foreign goods, automobiles included. The Chinese entrepreneurs' ability to use local networks, and sometimes regional networks, meant that foreign firms had much to gain from working closely with these intermediaries. Even though the US firms were late-arrivals in Malaya, they recognised the opportunities provided by these Chinese intermediaries and quickly appointed them as dealers and distributors, much to their advantage.

US firms continued to take relevant steps to ensure the growth and expansion of their firms in Malaya during the decolonisation era, and some firms took steps to nurture links with indigenous politicians post-World War II. For example, Norman Cleaveland, then manager of the Pacific Tin, admitted that the consultation and advice he received from his old friend, Tun H.S. Lee (the Malayan Chinese business and political leader and first finance minister) was crucial in his success of reviving his firm's mining operations in the Ampang area. US firms responded to the post-colonisation threat of Communist insurgency, helping to ensure it was defeated, and thereby maintaining a pro-Western leaning of an independent Malaya and safeguarding their investments in the country.

While there is no evidence to suggest that Malayan–American Plantations or Ford Malaya nurtured links with indigenous politicians or businessmen, the fact that these firms were keen to expedite their rehabilitation operations suggests that they were not as fearful of political change as their British counterparts, who perhaps had more to worry about if the outburst of nationalistic feelings led to action against the former colonial rulers. Evidently, existing US firms in Malaya had no intention to pull out their investments despite the drastic political changes that came with the Emergency and the Independence movement. However, it is important to note that there were no new US entrants into the Malayan market during the decolonisation era, and even though this was also partly due to the imposition of exchange controls when world FDI had substantially recovered from World War II from 1950s onwards, US FDI still tended to be directed towards developed economies.

Due to its limited number of case studies, this work cannot provide a basis for testing models of entrepreneurship. However, it is possible to discern different aspects of entrepreneurship within the different studies. Drawing from the Kirzner and Casson entrepreneurial models, this research has shown how entrepreneurs played a role in establishing and promoting US firms and, in the process, transferred technologies and organisational skills to Malayan industries. Edgar B. Davis is a prime example of a Kirznerian entrepreneur, having taken the opportunity to invest in rubber in Sumatra and Malaya in the early twentieth century. Davis's endeavour laid the foundations for the largest American rubber company in Sumatra, popularly known as the 'Mecca of the rubber growing world'. Casson's model of entrepreneurship is well illustrated by YGC's investment in the Malayan tin mining industry. The driving force behind YGC's investment into tin mining in Malaya did not come from the company's managers themselves, but was mainly due to the exhaustion of gold reserves in its US mines. Given the changing environment in which they now found themselves, YGC's managers were forced to make the decision to invest their resources elsewhere. They were also aware of the risks and uncertainty in transferring gold dredges to the altogether different industry of tin mining and in a different environment. YGC's technological innovations allowed it to successfully adapt the gold dredges to Malayan tin conditions. With this technological superiority YGC, and other Western firms which had earlier failed in their competition against Chinese miners in the use of conventional tin-mining methods, gained dominance in the Malayan tin mining industry.

Such entrepreneurial skills, as demonstrated by YGC's technological adaptations, were undoubtedly vital to the success of many US firms in Malaya. YGC managers exemplified entrepreneurial skills within the US MNEs in Malaya, as they were willing to take substantial risks, as seen in the resource-seeking FDI. This kind of entrepreneurialism was not without substantial risks, typified by US firms' FDI in Malayan natural resources with the uncertainties involved in the exploration process, time constraints of mine construction, finding suitable technology and price fluctuations.

Unlike the many British free standing companies active in the mining and resource sectors, all three US MNEs focused on in this work had performed in a sophisticated domestic market and all had worldwide operations. With this prior experience came access to information, technology and managerial expertise. They also had financial resources. These ownership advantages assisted the three firms in overcoming location-specific challenges in Malaya, such as bureaucratic delays, technological suitability and lack of local skilled workers. There was a need to adapt and re-invent to create competitive advantages. Pacific Tin adapted tin technology originating in New Zealand and Australia to the unique alluvial tin deposits of Malaya. USRC exploited the pioneering efforts of British and Dutch rubber firms. Similarly, Ford's mass production techniques and cost-competitiveness gave the manufacturer a comparative advantage over other early movers in the Malayan automobile market. Such advantages also gave US MNEs the flexibility to move to other markets when they faced restrictions in Malaya.

7.5 Significance of US FDI on the Malayan economy

US MNEs did not make large contributions to Malaya's industrial capital formation although they did initially make capital investments in Malaya due to the capital intensive nature of their ventures. For example, Pacific Tin spent US$2.15 million within two years of its initial investments in Malaya. Expansion was generally financed by profits being ploughed back into the Malayan subsidiary. This is significant, as these companies' qualitative impact is not measured so much in the balance of payments but in the areas of organisational skills, technology and R&D transfer.

Innovative employment opportunities and labour management policies were also implemented. The employment practices adopted at its rubber plantation in Sumatra were also followed in USRC's Malayan operations. Although USRC was not the only company to engage in such corporate welfarism, none of the other large rubber producers implemented such policies as early and on such an extravagant scale. The much improved employment packages attracted workers from the limited labour market, tending to drive up labour costs and thus became a particular disadvantage to local rubber firms and smallholders, mainly Chinese and Malays, who could not always offer such attractive conditions.

US MNEs, including the three that are the subject of case studies in this work, staffed their affiliates with expatriates, which was generally the case with other foreign firms in Malaya and probably due to the lack of local managerial expertise. However, there was also reticence to train locals to be managers that continued even into the decolonisation era. As a result, only low-level skills were imparted to the local labour force. Forward and backward linkages by US MNEs did provide business opportunities to both local and foreign firms, thereby benefiting the Malayan economy. Pacific Tin sold its tin output to the Straits Trading Company and supported ethnic Chinese miners as well as adopting their traditional tributary system to work its low-capacity mines, which were not suitable for dredging technology. While USRC produced rubber mainly for the home market, it bought rubber latex from local suppliers, and set up a latex station, spray plants and latex shipping stations, providing not only job opportunities but also business for shipping lines. Ford also provided business opportunities by appointing dealers and establishing service stations throughout Singapore and the Malay States. The automobile company promoted a complementary relationship with local enterprises when it gave agency opportunities to ethnic Chinese and, to a lesser extent, Malays.

A more significant transfer of skills and specialised knowledge was seen in the areas of technology and R&D, whereby competitors were stimulated or compelled to adopt improved methods introduced by US firms. For the extractive sector, unlike manufacturing, the Pacific Tin and USRC established R&D units within the host economy and freely transferred knowledge and technical know-how to the Malayan tin and rubber industries. As a result, they brought knowledge as part of the FDI flows from a developed to a developing country. Ford, as a manufacturing concern, established R&D units within the home country, although the company did gradually bring in assembly machinery from its affiliates in Canada and England for the assembly of different Ford models in Malaya. There is no evidence to suggest that these US firms attempted to achieve monopoly control with their technological advantage against either Western rivals or local entrepreneurs. Yet, the superior technology did marginalize local producers, such as local Chinese miners, and at times destroyed the local competition. As noted by Wong Lin Ken and Yip Yat Hoong, local miners, unlike Western firms which could draw on funds from their home countries, were restricted not by lack of entrepreneurial skills but by their inability to secure funds.

This work also supports Drabble's view that the 1920s Stevenson Scheme undermined the drive for further innovation in the rubber sector. Only in the late 1920s and early 1930s, as seen in the activities of Harrisons & Crosfield and Guthrie, did British firms begin to reinvest in R&D and acquire relevant information and techniques from the USRC and Dutch research in Sumatra. Only large British rubber firms were willing to sink large funds into R&D, while the smaller British rubber firms, just like their local counterparts, apart from the lack of financial resources, were generally more interested in short-term gains and lacked confidence in these new technologies which the far-sighted US firms had introduced.

Pacific Tin, USRC and Ford all resumed operations as soon as circumstances permitted after World War II, ahead of their rival British firms, providing local job opportunities and expediting the rehabilitation process. During the Emergency (1948–1960), efforts were made to continue production despite the Communist insurgency. Pacific Tin's manager implemented a novel method of squatter control on the company's properties that served both the welfare of the corporation and the squatters themselves, and, most significantly, hindered the spread of communism in Malaya. Ford provided armoured vehicles greatly needed by the British government and the owners of tin mines and rubber plantations.

The overall significance of US MNEs in the Malayan economy was undoubtedly limited. Yet, all three US MNEs – Yukon Gold, United States Rubber and Ford Malaya – had a qualitative impact in terms of introducing technological innovations, R&D and managerial skills, not only contributing to the overall performance of the industries they were involved in, but also laying a concrete foundation for the modern Malayan economy. By building on relations with government and other Western and local enterprises, they contributed towards the qualitative development of the tin, rubber and automobile industry in Malaya through its positioning as a major exporter.

This work, with its analysis of the growth of US trade with and FDI in Malaya, sheds light on the role of government and foreign MNEs in shaping the development of international business in developing economies. It identifies the competitive strategies of US MNEs and illustrates how their activities helped to shape economic development in the host country. It is surely time now for a scholarly re-assessment of the policies of the New Economic Policy during the 1970s and 1980s, encompassing the problematic relationships with foreign-owned companies in many sectors and despite foreign firms being given extremely favourable terms to open plants in the export processing zones. In addition, this work provides a basis for future study of the impact of regime change on FDI flows and trade patterns. Although the focus has been on US MNEs in Malaya, many aspects of a colonial administration's policies towards MNEs have also been analysed. An exploration of the response of US firms to Malaysian independence would undoubtedly yield insights hitherto overlooked. How did this event affect investment decisions? Did US firms look upon Malaysia less favourably or more favourably than other countries for investment? If the latter was the case, this would in turn suggest that the impact of colonialism on investment and trade flows may have been largely positive, a view which the research in this work essentially supports.

8 Epilogue

The future looks bright

This epilogue brings to date the developments of US trade and FDI within the changing competitive context in post-colonial Malaysia. The first section briefly discusses the economic developments through five decades starting from the 1960s. Section two traces to the present day the three MNEs that are the subject of case studies in this work. This is followed by a brief account of the reasons why Ford Malaya, in contrast to Pacific Tin and USRC, chose to remain in the country. External influences and internal factors together played a role in the divestment of US FDI in post-colonial Malaysia. The slowing demand of the US industries for rubber had a significant impact on how, what were once, strategic commodities became valued. Synthetic rubber overtook natural rubber as the dominant material for tyre production. In the case of tin mining, Pacific Tin chose to diversify into mica and plastics production, thus reflecting the increasing consumer (as opposed to industrial) demand for household products and electrical appliances.The post-Independence period also saw a shift in Malaya's status within the global tin and rubber market. Malaya was no longer a colony where it was conveniently subservient to the economic needs of the colonial masters. The localisation factor (referring to the efforts of newly independent countries to increase local self-determination and participation in the economy as well as national identity) entered into the equation, in some cases sooner than must have been anticipated. The localisation factor for Malaysia came in the form of the New Economic Policy (NEP) in 1970, where a timetable was specifically set and the agenda of pursuing the creation of a bumiputera capitalist class explicitly formulated. Since then, the reversal of the colonial past has assumed an accelerated propensity through acquisition of shares with the objective of securing a controlling stake in large firms and corporations which were mainly owned by foreigners.

8.1 US–Malaysia economic relations after independence, 1957–2007

In order to gain competitive advantage, the newly independent administration continued with the open economy promoted by the British colonial government. The economic roadmap outlined by the post-colonial government underscored Malaysia's locational attractions, making her a popular trade and FDI destination not only for some US MNEs, but also for investors from the UK, Canada, Australia, West Germany, Japan, the Netherlands, Taiwan, India and others. To counterbalance the protectionist stance of nationalisation and localisation, the government formulated national development policies that increasingly played an important role in attracting and maximising the potential for trade and FDI for economic development, and ensured political stability for the continued implementation of these policies. Other factors that now give Malaysia its competitive advantage include its professional human resources and skilled labour force, physical and commercial infrastructures as well as investment incentive schemes.

After Independence, pro-business policies and legislation in the late 1950s, in the shape of the five-year development plans and the Investment Guarantee Agreement, stimulated a new wave of FDI, particularly from the US. However, since the 1970s the tendency among Malaysian leaders has been for the state to intervene in capital formation and development programmes, as well as to play a key role in empowering local elite and, in so doing, to reduce the power of foreign capital. The preference for state intervention initially came about after the race riots of 13 May 1969 when Tun Razak Hussein took over from Tunku Abdul Rahman (prime minister from August 1957 to September 1970), and whose administration local critics such as K.S. Jomo, Lim Mah Hui and Hua Wu Yin alleged had maintained Malaysia as a quasi-independent nation and a neo-colony.[1] While the NEP may be seen as a 'protectionist ideology' due to its preoccupation with transforming the Malay underclass into entrepreneurs by reducing the share of existing foreign capital, the Malaysian government did pursue a liberal economic policy by offering favourable conditions to export-led and import-substitution industries. The Free Trade Zone Act of 1971, for example, saw an increase in the participation of US MNEs in producing electronic goods for export purposes. The shift towards export-oriented and import-substituting industries and the incentives provided in the free trade zones (FTZs) brought new entrants across the manufacturing sector, including electronics and electronic components, telecommunications, textiles, chemicals, car assembly and the heavy industries of iron and steel.

The focus on FDI-driven export-oriented industrialisation made Malaysia the primary supplier of electrical and electronic goods, textiles and rubber products with the FTZs ensuring that US capital in-flows rose to new heights. This resulted in US MNEs contributing 11.1 per cent to the manufacturing sector in terms of output and value added products by 1973, the third largest foreign investor in the manufacturing sector after Singapore (29.9 per cent) and Britain (26.5 per cent).[2] The US MNEs involved in the electronics industry included National Semiconductor, Hewlett-Packard, Intel, Litronix (now Litronix Siemens), Monsanto Electronics, Motorola, Texas Instruments and Western Digital. The phenomenal growth in the manufacturing and high-technology industries transformed the Malaysian economy from an agriculture and mining base in the early 1970s to the world's major producer of the semiconductor chip in the 1980s, mainly due to the presence of top US semiconductor MNEs in Malaysia.[3]

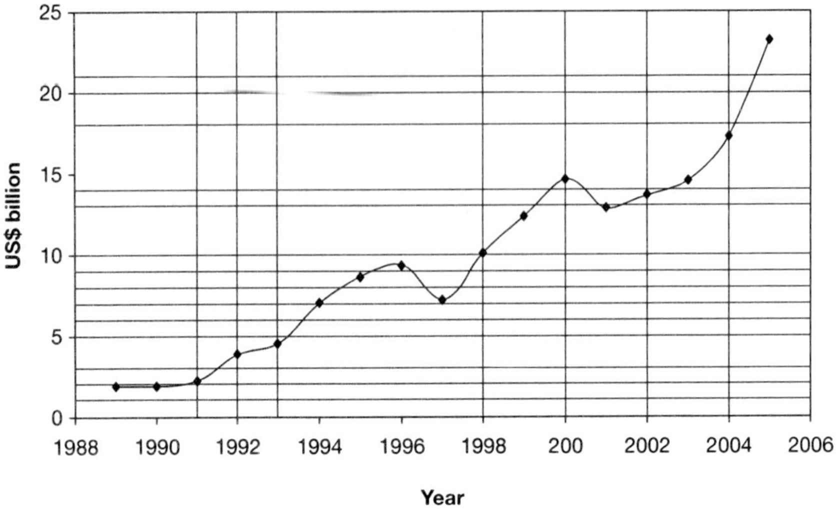

Figure 8.1 Malaysia's Trade Surplus with the US, 1988–2006

Source: TradeStats Express (http://tse.export.gov)

From the 1980s into 2006, the US remained Malaysia's largest trading partner as goods produced by US MNEs in the FTZs were largely exported to the US market. As had been the case when it had been a British colony, Malaysia enjoyed a rising trade surplus with the US (see Figure 8.1). In 2005, an increase of 8.4 per cent was seen from 2004 in US trade with Malaysia and which accounted for 16.6 per cent of Malaysia's total trade.[4] In the same year, bilateral trade between US and Malaysia exceeded US$44 billion. The announcement of negotiations towards a free trade agreement between the two nations in March 2006 has sparked mixed responses with concern that such a move may turn the trade balance in the US's favour. Others are more optimistic that such a move to forge closer economic relationships will increase trade flows.

Subsequently, the US remained the top source of FDI in the electronics industry, contributing 27 per cent from 1996 to 2002. In 2005, the Malaysian–American Electronics Industry Association with 18 US-based member companies in semiconductor and non-semiconductor industries, some operating in Malaysia for the previous three decades, contributed US$1 billion in investments, US$313.9 million in design and development, US$22.2 billion in exports (100 per cent of the goods exported, largely to the US market) with an employment of 55,000 workers.[5] US ICT companies, Microsoft, Oracle, Sun Microsystems, and certain high-profile personalities, such as Bill Gates, assumed a significant role in the development of Malaysia's Multimedia Super Corridor. In the year 2004 alone, these US MNEs that had Multimedia Super Corridor status invested US$38.2 million in Malaysia out of a total US FDI of US$20 billion.[6] By 2004, there were 19 US operational headquarters in Malaysia, with the major ones including Du Pont, Conoco,

American Express, PepsiCo, Amerada Hess, Intel, Agilent Technologies, Shields and Sara Lee. There were also 13 international procurement centres from the US including Gateway, Xircom, Flextronics and Dell. US regional service companies now include, Lifecore Biomedical, Parsons Global, Firecreek Global, Dell, Pepsico, Smart Modular, and American Express. Representative offices of US banks and financial institutions established in Malaysia include the Union Bank of California, Wachovia Bank and Visa International.[7]

At present, there are 350 US companies in Malaysia, including 130 listed in the US Fortune 500, and with investments worth US$28 billion. These are in the areas of manufacturing, trading and services sectors, as well as oil and gas exploration. US companies have participated significantly in Malaysia's growth initiatives, for example, in the areas of offshore financial services. Investment in these services by US companies has directly increased Malaysia's locational advantages, with, according to A.T. Kearney's Global Services Location Index 2005, Malaysia becoming the third most attractive location for 'offshoring services' after India and China. In the year 2004 alone, these MSC status US MNEs invested US$38.2 million in Malaysia.[8] More and more US companies are being awarded the MSC status and a recent example being Entellium (headquartered in Seattle, Washington), a global software company in business solutions (Customer Relationship Management). These US firms' core activities reflect the shift from low-intensity to high-intensity technology transfer in Malaysia.[9] There are currently 179 US MNEs operating in Labuan International Offshore Financial Services Centre. More significantly perhaps, US MNEs such as Intel, Monsanto and Hewlett-Packard, have indigenised their entire Malaysian operations and, importantly, over 78 per cent are now managed by Malaysian chief executive officers.[10]

US FDI has changed significantly from colonial to post-colonial Malaysia, necessarily adapting to economic and political challenges, but ultimately playing a significant role in Malaysia's development. It is probably right to assert that it is through the economic roadmap laid out by the Malaysian government which promoted these US investments. It is worthy of note that the NEP's concerns of localisation and Malaysianisation progressed relatively smoothly, and were embraced by these US newcomers.

8.2 US MNEs in post-colonial Malaysia: Pacific Tin, Uniroyal and Ford Malaysia

Pacific Tin Consolidated Corporation (PacTin): mutual prosperity

From the early 1970s, PacTin's management began discussing how they could fulfil the government's requirements on localisation. The company was concerned that future mining leases may not be renewed if they did not participate in the Malaysianisation or localisation process when the mining leases of Anglo-Oriental were rejected. In fact, PacTin was already assessing the candidates for local partners including a number of Chinese interests, Selangor Dredging and the Selangor State Development Corporation (SEDC). Other key concerns included Malaysian and US tax issues, stockholders approval and share pricing strategy.[11]

A landmark event occurred on 5 March 1979 when an agreement was signed between Kumpulan Perangsang Selangor Berhad (KPS), a Malaysian state-owned company and Perangsang Pasifik Sdn Bhd – formerly known as Timah Pasifik (Malaysia) Sdn Bhd – PacTin's wholly owned subsidiary. KPS was given a 10 per cent equity interest in Perangsang Pasifik and 10 per cent royalty on tin sales in exchange for a mining sub-lease on all the currently mined areas for a period of 15 years. Eventually, KPS acquired 30 per cent interest in Perangsang Pasifik, which in return was granted mining sub-leases subject to 5 per cent royalty on tin sales, and this equity arrangement continued until 1993.[12]

By 1985, tin output and prices had declined, partly due to imposition of export control by the International Tin Council as well as the October tin crisis in the world market in the same year and following the collapse of the tin price support system. Malaysia, however, remained the world's largest producer, accounting for 19 per cent of the world's tin mine production. With the transition of the tin industry to a free market in 1986, despite an increase of tin ore sales due to the removal of export control, Pacific Tin recorded a loss of US$198,000 compared with an income of US$222,000 in 1985. These losses can be attributed to the 47 per cent decline in tin prices from $5.19 per pound to $2.73 per pound. With the decline of tin prices, production became uneconomic, causing many mines to stop operations around the world. Pacific Tin, however, persevered in its Malaysian mining operations although commercial production was halted.

In contrast to its continued losses in Malaysia in the tin sector, business in the US was very successful, and in line with its new corporate identity and expanded shareholder group, PacTin in 1986 became Zemex Corporation and was headquartered in Delaware. The name change reflected the diversification of the company's then current business into other areas of industrial minerals operations (feldspar, kaolin, industrial sand, mica and high purity silica), with tin, in contrast to the early 1930s, forming the smallest percentage of its business.[13]

Zemex's Malaysian head office continued to be Kuala Lumpur, although its subsidiary Perangsang Pasifik was located in Batang Berjuntai, Selangor, where most of its tin mining activities were located. The company continued to hold leases on all its mining acreage. A turnaround in profits occurred in 1987 due to an increase in the price of tin, improvements in operating productivity, cost reductions and sale of accumulated mine by-products, when Perangsang Pasifik reported an operating income of US$229,000 in contrast to an operating loss of US$697,000 in 1986.[14]

In 1993, Zemex Corporation disposed of the remaining 70 per cent share held by Perangsang Pasifik because of their shift in strategic direction, which relegated tin mining properties as non-core assets. This was not surprising in light of Zemex's earlier selling off of its Thai stake in the Sierra Mining Company. Although there were undoubtedly localisation pressures exerted through the NEP, the combined external factors, such as the declining global tin market and the shift in business priorities, probably carried greater weight in the company's decision to sell its stake in Perangsang Pasifik, particularly when considering that Zemex's selling of its mining stake in Thailand.

UniRoyal: goodwill through knowledge sharing

The United States Rubber Company formerly changed its name to Uniroyal Inc in 1967, registered in New Jersey, and there followed a name change in Malaysia from Malayan American Plantation Sdn Bhd to Uniroyal Malaysia Plantations Sdn Bhd in 1968. The firm's focus on manufacturing meant that activities in rubber production remained stagnant in the 1960s and 1970s, except for expansion into Liberia. Despite certain challenging policies of the new post-colonial government, such as the requirements of localisation, as it had only a marginal role as a producer and buyer of its own output, the firm was largely unaffected.

Unlike the unconventional takeover of British plantation interests such as the Guthrie Corporation in 1981, Uniroyal itself decided to dispose of its Malaysian rubber plantation business in 1984. The company was keen not to work with a local partner in its plantation venture, and this led to its eventual divestment. This was made clear in a statement made by Uniroyal's then chairman, Joseph P. Flannery, when he cited the Malaysian government New Economic Policy (NEP) of giving Malaysians majority control of its rubber plantations venture as the reasons behind the sale of its Malaysian company.[15] In 1984 Kumpulan Guthrie Ltd acquired the entire assets of Uniroyal Malaysian Plantations for a total cash consideration of RM198,943,560. The principal assets of Uniroyal, later renamed Kumpulan Jerai Sdn Bhd, comprised the five estates acquired since the 1920s. That spelled the end of Uniroyal's romance with rubber in Malaya. The company continued to produce rubber at its Indonesian and Liberian plantations secured through concession agreements with the respective local governments.[16] Yet, in 1985, because of lower rubber prices, Uniroyal sold its Liberian plantation.

For Uniroyal, the sale of its Malaysian stake was much needed to offset large losses incurred in the early 1980s, although there was sizeable gain in profits in 1983 and 1984 because of the rise of automobile sales in the US.[17] In the early 1980s, with the wave of mergers and acquisitions starting to hit the US tyre industry, the low rubber prices, and because of the urgent need for capital injection for the survival of its tyre manufacturing operations, Uniroyal was forced to agree to a joint-venture with Goodrich. In 1986, Uniroyal Goodrich Tire Company (UGTC) was formed and in 1990, UGTC was acquired by Michelin. This development is not surprising as control of 'traditional' US tyre manufacturers, such us Firestone, Goodrich, Armstrong, and General Tire, fell into the hands of foreign companies leaving US tyre manufacturers representing only 17 per cent of world production in 1991, as compared to 59 per cent in 1971.[18]

Thus, these developments demonstrate that the localisation process was not the sole, or even major reason for US capital flight in the case of Uniroyal. While it was convenient to put the blame on the NEP requirements, as evident in the statement made by Uniroyal's chairman, clearly the poor performance of the manufacturing arm and low rubber prices also contributed to the divestment of the Malaysian subsidiary. By the 1980s, the transformed global economy led to widespread restructuring of US businesses, which compelled Uniroyal to focus on its core manufacturing activities. In fact, the Uniroyal Annual Report of 1985 listed the company's Indonesian rubber plantations among its non-strategic assets being offered for sale. In retrospect, the decision to integrate backwards into rubber plantation did not serve the long-term interests of the MNE, which drew its main source of income from rubber manufacturing. Unlike United Plantations, for example, which focused on plantation enterprise, Uniroyal was not able to diversify and reinvest in new ventures such as coconuts and palm oil to offset the unreliability of rubber profits. By the 1980s, Uniroyal's leading role in R&D and its contribution to technological innovations was significantly diminished when funds dwindled to just 2 per cent of total sales.[19]

As the sole US corporation which continued to invest in rubber plantations in Malaya, Uniroyal had remained steadfast in the face of challenges to the local rubber industry. However, since its rubber plantations produced only a small percentage of its manufacturing requirements, it should be remembered that rubber production remained marginal to its performance as a rubber manufacturer.

Ford-Malaysia: the spirit of resilient capitalism

Ford continued its investment in post-colonial Malaysia, and retained its ties with Wearne Brothers, which remained Ford's biggest Malaysian representative. Up until Singapore was ousted from Malaysia in 1965, Ford's Singapore plant had been supplying the Malaysian market. However, Ford elected not to relocate its assembly facilities to Malaysia and submit to the Malaysian government's directive to allow sale of only locally assembled vehicles in Malaysia. In 1967, Ford, along with Chrysler and British Leyland, resolved this issue of 'local assembly' by having their vehicles assembled by Wearne Brothers, which had entered into the assembly business in independent Malaysia through its subsidiary, Associated Motor Industries. Meanwhile, the importation and distribution of European Ford vehicles was handled by another of Wearne's subsidiaries, Universal Cars. Ford's decision to deal exclusively with Wearne proved not to be a prudent business strategy because it failed to capitalise on its former alliances with large Chinese firms in the Malaysian car market when it secured the Toyota franchise (although some Chinese dealers continue to market Ford products today and United Motor Works, which had been selling Ford spare parts since 1916, became a major player in 1959).

In 1972, the Ford Motor Company of Malaysia Sdn Bhd (Ford Malaysia), a wholly owned subsidiary of Ford US, was set up following an injection of RM$23 million (US$8.2 million). Ford Malaysia was only a marketing operation that sourced its products from Ford England, because the Malaysian market required right-hand drive vehicles. The Wearne group concentrated on assembling. Earlier, in 1970, Ford US had set up Ford Asia Pacific Inc, headquartered in Australia, to co-ordinate manufacturing, marketing, sales and service in Malaysia as well as in Thailand, Vietnam, Indonesia, Philippines, Taiwan, China, India, Japan, New Zealand and Australia.

Through the 1970s, Japanese companies successfully elbowed Western cars from the Malayan automobile market and made the strategic choice of shifting their alliances from Western trading firms to local Chinese firms. While Western firms failed to develop such relationships or, like Ford, had let them languish, the Japanese MNE late-movers aggressively penetrated the local automobile market as they continued to form important alliances in the early 1980s. It is perhaps not surprising then that Japanese automobile manufacturers were the strategic choice of business partners when the Malaysian government embarked on a national car project with state-controlled enterprises in the early 1980s and into the 1990s. These projects, that included Proton, a joint venture between HICOM and Mitsubishi in 1985, and Perodua, a joint venture in 1994 between United Motor Works with the Toyota subsidiary, Daihatsu, came in the wake of the government's 'Look East' policy, a conscious turning away from Western investors and technologies to Japanese and Korean FDI and product innovations.

In 1981, following the Malaysian government's localisation demands, a joint venture was forged between Ford US and Pernas Sime Darby (a company taken over from the British), with the latter acquiring 49 per cent equity in Ford Malaysia, catapulting Ford from seventh to third position in the Malaysian automobile market. In compliance with the NEP in 1984, Ford reduced its equity to 30 per cent with Pernas Sime Darby becoming the majority shareholder. The affiliate's name was changed to AMIM Holdings Pvt Ltd in 1985. Already, by mid-1984, Ford had repositioned itself as the leader in the Malaysian light trucks market. Even as a minority shareholder, Ford US participated directly in the affairs of the firm, by setting up a representative office in Malaysia in 1996, and appointing a general manager from Ford US in 1997. In 2000, Ford US rescued AMIM Holdings from the debilitating effects of the 1997 Asian financial crisis when it increased its equity from 30 per cent to 49 per cent in AMIM Holdings with the latter subsequently renamed Ford Malaysia Pvt Ltd.

To protect the fledgling national car industry, high excise taxes and import duties were imposed on non-national or foreign cars, which made it extremely difficult for foreign automobile multinationals to compete, at least in terms of price, with the subsidised national cars quickly gaining monopoly position in car manufacturing and distribution in Malaysia. In addition, a perceived lack of transparency and inconsistency of the government national automotive policy, which seldom considered the views of foreign car companies with Malaysian interests, made it extremely difficult for these companies to plan their long-term investment strategies. This highlights the negative impact of economic nationalism on foreign car assemblers and distributors, such as Ford-Malaysia. The decision of the Malaysian government to joint venture with Japanese companies had alienated Ford US, which then chose Thailand to manufacture Ford products in 1996, retaining Ford Malaysia only as an assembly plant. In 2002, Ford Thailand became the headquarters of Ford's Asia-Pacific Marketing and Sales Division.

In the late 1990s, in reaction to declining passenger car sales, due largely to the dominance of national cars and Japanese assemblers as well as the economic turmoil surrounding the 1997 financial crisis in the region, Ford Malaysia concentrated their local assembly and sales operations in the relatively less competitive light truck and pickup segments. These segments remained relatively small, unlike in the surrounding markets of Thailand and Indonesia, again because of favourable government policy towards national cars, and also because of consumer preferences for passenger cars. Following increased competition from the Malaysian national car projects and other, mainly Japanese, automobile manufacturers, Ford's performance has continued to languish below 1 per cent of total industry sales in 2004 and 2005. However, Ford's performance in the segments in which it does compete, such as the pick-up vehicles, remains relatively strong, despite the entry of new models from Japanese and Korean manufacturers. It is notable that the Malaysian market enjoys the biggest passenger car market in the ASEAN region.

The contemporary position of Ford Malaysia is very much the legacy of how the company responded to Malaysia's decolonisation, as well as the shifting parent company-subsidiary relations, and the interplay between foreign MNEs and domestic firms as well as the post-independent government. Ford Malaysia, as an incumbent player in the local automobile sector, symbolises the spirit of resilient capitalism by the MNE's capacity to reinvent and survive the challenges of localisation and heavy industrialisation. Ford stayed the course in spite of all the odds stacked against it because the company recognised Malaysia's competitive advantage in the ASEAN region. However, it is probably true to say that the national car industry would probably have benefited from competition with another car manufacturer, for example, if Ford US had decided to set up its plant in Malaysia instead of Thailand. The case study of Ford US, nonetheless, shows that the US MNE experience in colonial Malaya and post-colonial Malaysia could be a mutually beneficial venture with local firms in terms of management method, dealership networks, employment opportunities and technological innovation.

8.3 Summary

The three case studies included in this work challenge the assertion that economic nationalism must necessarily be unfavourable to the economic growth of developing countries such as Malaysia. The introduction of the NEP and the process of localisation sustained and localised the imperial legacy of the Western enterprises by building on their capital assets, managerial expertise, technological innovations and the culture of R&D. Malaysia's experience in localising foreign businesses evoked varied responses ranging from conventional to unconventional takeovers. It should be noted that Malaysia did not practice 'narrow' nationalism based on confiscation of foreign assets, but relied on open market transactions as in the case of the acquisitions of British firms.

This work has provided a foundation from which to re-assess Malaysian government policies in the years since Independence. At first glance, it certainly appears that the NEP brought few benefits to Malaysia as efforts to reduce foreign ownership largely failed. The great leap forward for Malaysia in its quest to be an industrialised nation has continued to be dependent upon foreign MNEs, with the significant difference being that the main participants are no longer the former colonialist British, but from the US whose limited FDI pre-Independence is the subject of intense scrutiny here.

Appendix A

Straits settlements exports to the United States, 1902

Items	*(silver dollars)*
Coffee	690,158
Dried fruits	387,483
Rice	20,181
Malt liquor	381
Prepared opium	212,560
Sago	126,218
Sago pearl	9,860
Casia	18,030
Cinnamon	90
Cloves	22,100
Cubebs	13,987
Mace	94,199
Nutmegs	584,066
Black pepper	2,486,855
Pepper long	3,813
Pepper white	647,441
Spirits	120
Gin	19
Whisky	32
Tapioca flake	132,715
Tapioca flour	108,489
Tapioca pearl	805,403
Tea	50
Wine	13
Textile cotton	34,004
Tin	24,136,996
Tin ore	200
Canes	2,916
Copra	850
Gambier	4,019,565
Gums	11,133

Borneo rubber	202,674
Gum copal	894,990
Gum damar	61,423
Dragon's blood	1,476
Gambodge	15,207
Gutta inferior	970,964
Gutta percha	148,913
India rubber	670
Hides	103,613
Horns	6
Oil cajeput	6,880
Oil coconut	93,603
Oil essential	90
Wood	3,726
Rattans	1,562,192
Shell green-snails	5,529
Shells other sorts	6,517
Shells tortoise	14,660
Wood	1,640
Textile apparel	260
Cotton goods	60
Guns	180
Oil cakes	44
Machinery	250
Mats & matting	1,080
Musical instruments	1,500
Soap	500
Sundries	1,800
Silver dollars	3,500
Total	1,807,630

Source: American Consulate General, Singapore, 3 April 1905. Dispatches from the United States Consuls in Singapore 1833–1906.

Appendix B

US firms and selected agencies held by US, British and Chinese firms in Malaya, 1931–1939

(a) US firms in Malaya

1. Dollar Steamship Lines Inc Ltd (Inc USA).
2. American Express Co Inc (Travel Banking and Shipping) S'pore.
3. National City Bank of New York (Inc USA)
4. Union Oil Co of California (Inc in California, USA), S'pore.
5. Singer Sewing Machine Co (Inc New Jersey, USA), S'pore, Penang, K.L, Ipoh, Seremban.
6. Standard-Vacumm Oil Co S'pore, K.L. Penang.
7. United Artists Corp (Inc NY) S'pore.
8. Metro Goldwyn Mayer (MGM).
9. Remington Rand Inc (Dealers in typewriters & office appliances).
10. Universal Pictures Corp. (of S'pore)
11. Western Electric Co of Asia (Inc USA).
12. Firestone Tire and Rubber Co (S.S) Ltd S'pore.
13. General Rubber Co Inc USA, S'pore.
14. Goodyear Orient Sales Co Ltd S'pore.
15. Fisk Tire & Export Company.
16. United States Steel Corp NY McAllister & Co Ltd S'pore.
17. American Asiatic Underwriters Ltd (AAU).
18. American Lloyd Agency Ltd (Inc SS).
19. American Foreign Insurance Association (fire, marine, car)
    Agents for:
    a. The American Insurance
    b. The Fidelity-Phoenix Fire Insurance
    c. Great American Insurance Co
    d. Home Insurance Co
    e. St. Paul Fire & Marine Insurance Co

(b) Selected US agencies held by US trade intermediaries

1. Getz Bros Co (Inc USA) (Import/Export)
2. Connell Bros Co Ltd (Inc USA), (Import/Export)

3. American & Co (Imports/Export)

4. Muller & Phipps – Agents for:
   a. Cheesebrough Mfg. Co NY ("Vaseline"), Muller & Phipps (Malaya) Ltd S'pore.
   b. Phoenix Hosiery Co Milwaukee, USA, Muller & Phipps (Malaya) Ltd S'pore.
   c. The Quakers Oats Co Chicago, USA Muller & Phipps (Malaya) Ltd S'pore.
   d. John B. Stetson Co, Philadelphia USA, Muller & Phipps (Malaya) Ltd S'pore.

5. Dodge & Seymour – Agents for:
   a. Cleveland Twist Drill Co, Dodge & Seymour Ltd S'pore.

6. Jacks & Co – Agents for:
   a. American Asphalt Paint Co Chicago, USA, Jacks & Co (Malaya) Ltd.
   b. Caterpillar Tractors Co USA, Jacks & Co (Malaya) Ltd. S'pore.
   c. Master Builders Co Cleveland, Ohio, (concrete colouring powder), Jacks & Co S'pore.
   d. Page Steel & Wire Co USA, Jacks & Co S'pore.
   e. Rumsey Pump Co Ltd NY (hand and powered pumps), Jacks & Co S'pore.
   f. Stanco Inc NY (flit insecticide), Jacks & Co S'pore.
   g. Texas Co NY (Texaco petroleum products), Jacks & Co S'pore.
   h. Witte Engine Co USA (Kerosene oil engines), Jacks & Co S'pore.

(c) Selected US agencies held by British merchant firms

---

1. Boustead & Co – Agents for:
   a. American Screw Co.
   b. American & Oriental Line.
   c. California Corrugated Culvert Co.
   d. American Pulley Co, Borneo Co Ltd S'pore.
   e. Fairbanks Morse & Co NY.
   f. International General Electric Co of America.

2. Sime Darby – Agents for:
   a. US Playing Cards Co.
   b. Aberthaw & Bristol Channel Portland Cement Co.
   c. California Ink Co.
   d. Cleveland Pneumatic Tooth Co.
   e. Hawaiian Cane Products Ltd.
   f. Union Oil Co of California.

3. John Dickinson – Agents for:
   a. The Chandler and Price Co Cleveland, Ohio.

   b. The Intertype Corp Brooklyn USA.
   c. The Bates Mfg Co NY, John Dickinson & Co.

4. Mc Allister & Co – Agents for:
   a. American & Manchurian Line, USA.
   b. Isthmian Steamship Co (Inc USA).
   c. United States Steel Products Co.

5. Paterson, Simons & Co – Agents for:
   a. Chicle Development Co NY.

6. Harper Gilfillan & Co – Agents for:
   a. Colgate-Palmolive Peet Co.

7. Henry Waugh & Co – Agents for:
   a. The Standard Textile Co of NY.

8. Travers & Sons Ltd – Agents for:
   a. William R. Warner & Co NY.
   b. The Knox Co Kansas City, USA.

(d) Selected agencies held by Chinese firms

---

1. Cycle & Carriage Co Ltd KL – Agents for:
   a. US Light & Heat Corp.
   b. Singer.
   c. Brockway Motor Truck Co, NY.
   d. Hudson Motor Car Co, Detroit, Michigan.

2. Lee Rubber – Agents for:
   a. The Home Insurance Co Ltd of NY.

3. Boon Seng & Co Ltd S'pore – Agents for:
   a. Goldwell Lawn Mower Co, NY.
   b. Champion Motors Co, Minneapolis.

4. Low Tan Chong – Agents for:
   a. S.C. Johnson & Sons, Inc Racine, USA.
   b. Liberty Gold Fruit Co San Francisco, USA.
   c. Sunset Produce Co Ltd San Francisco, USA.
   d. General Export Co, San Francisco, USA.

5. United Motor Works Ltd S'pore – Agents for:
   a. North East Appliance Corp NY.
   b. Fisk Tire Export Co.

Source: *The Singapore and Malayan Directory*, 1932–1939.

Appendix C

Mining technology

Gravel Pumping

This method was more popular among small-scale entrepreneurs due to its low operating costs. It takes place in an open pit and the tin ore is broken down by high-speed water jets directed along a pipe through a monitor creating high pressure. The liquid ore and mud is sucked up from the bottom of the pit by gravel pumps and elevated onto a sluice for primary concentration. Jigs are used for further concentration. A gravel pump mine can operate to a depth of 150 feet.

Dredges

Dredging was more popular among European companies due to its heavy capital expenses. Dredges operates on man-made ponds or on the sea. They are ship-like structures consisting of a floating barge or hull which digs the ore from the bottom with a continuous bucket chain. Dredges can work to a depth of 150 feet and with this depth, 130 buckets would be in line.

Underground mining

This method is similar to coal mining methods in Europe. It was used to mine hard rock deposits.

Open-cast mining

This is dry mining where no use is made of hydraulic methods. Excavators are used to mine richer deeper and more concentrated deposits.

Dulang Washing

This method is the working of surface tin deposits by panning.

Source: Thoburn, *Multinationals, Mining and Development*, pp. 39–40.

Appendix D

Pacific Tin mining properties, 1957

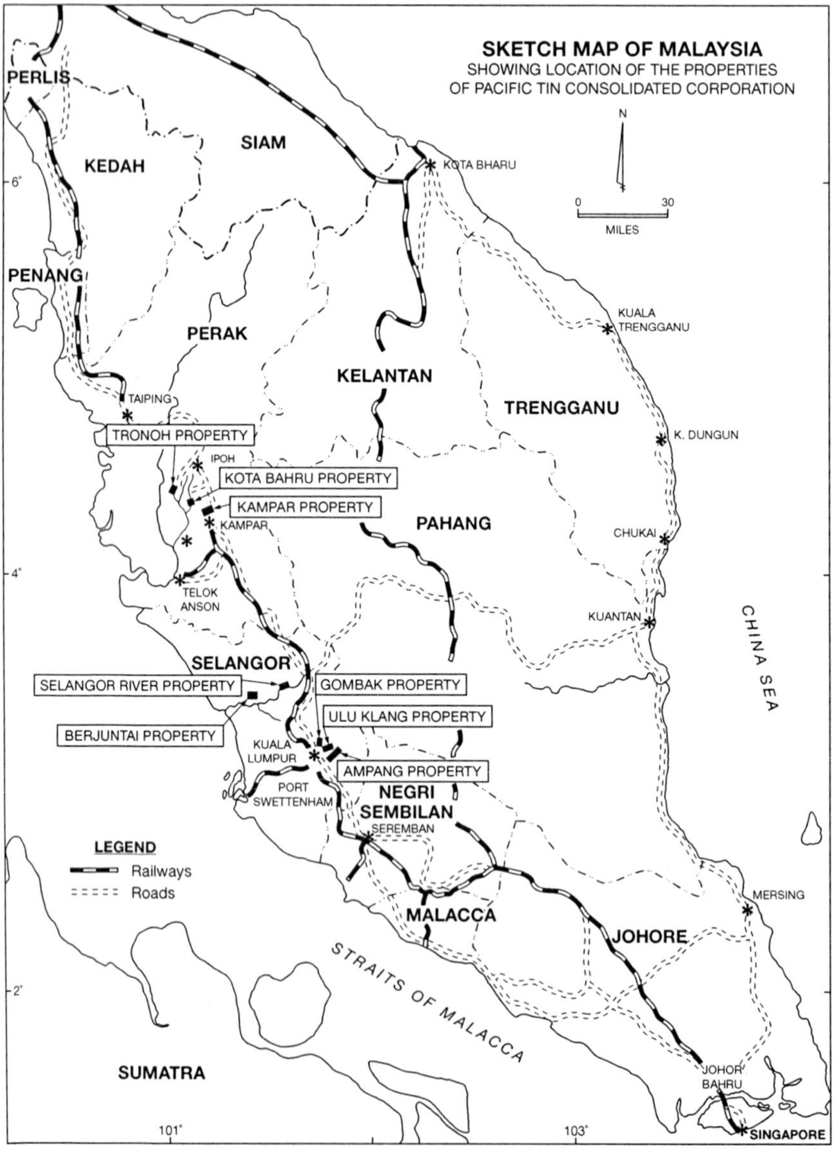

Source: Adapted from Annual Report Pacific Tin, 1958.

Notes

1 Introduction: The United States, Colonial Rule and the Malayan Economy

1 'Opening the door to new possibilities', *fDi Magazine*, 5 December 2006, www.fdimagazine.com/news/fullstory.php/aid/1877/Opening_the_door_to_new_possibilities_.html, accessed 16 January 2007.
2 UNCTAD World Investment Report, 2006, www.un-ngls.org/site/article.php3?id_article=146, accessed 18 April 2007.
3 *The Star*, 11 April 2007.
4 Volume one outlines the evolution of traders into investors and presents the evolution of US MNEs abroad until 1914. While this volume did not detail the existence of US traders and investors in the South East Asian region, the second volume is much more relevant to this work as it gives some detail on the history of US MNEs in Malaya. M. Wilkins, *The Emergence of Multinational Enterprise: American Business Abroad from the Colonial Era to 1914*, Cambridge, Mass.: Harvard University Press, 1970; *The Maturing of Multinational Enterprise: American Business Abroad from 1914 to 1970*, Cambridge, Mass.: Harvard University Press, 1974.
5 M. Wilkins, *The History of Foreign Investment in the United States to 1914*, Cambridge, Mass.: Harvard University Press, 1989; *The History of Foreign Investment in the United States, 1914–45*, Cambridge, Mass.: Harvard University Press, 2004.
6 J.H. Dunning, *Multinational Enterprises and the Global Economy*, Wokingham, Berkshire: Addison-Wesley, 1993, p. 3; G. Jones, *Multinationals and Global Capitalism*, Oxford: Oxford University Press, 2005, pp. 4–5.
7 J.H. Dunning, 'The Eclectic (OLI) Paradigm of International Production: Past, Present and Future', *International Journal of the Economics of Business* 8, 2001, pp. 173–90; 'Trade, Location of Economic Activity and the MNE: A Search for an Eclectic Approach', in B. Ohlin et al. (eds), *The International Allocation of Economic Activity*, London: Macmillan, 1977, pp. 395–418; 'Explaining Changing Patterns of International Production: In Defence of the Eclectic Theory', *Oxford Bulletin of Economics and Statistics* 41, 1979, pp. 269–95.
8 S. Hymer, *The International Operations of National Firms*, Cambridge: Mass, 1976, p. 34; R. B. Cohen, Nadine Felton, Morley Nikosi and Jaap van Liere (eds), *The Multinational Corporation: A Radical Approach*, Papers by S. Hymer, Cambridge: Cambridge University Press, 1979; Mohammad Yamin, 'Reassessment of Hymer's Contribution to the Theory of the Transnational Corporation', in C.N. Pitelis and R. Sugden (eds), *The Nature of the Transnational Firm*, London: Routledge, 1991, pp. 64–80.
9 Jones, *Multinationals*, pp. 7–9.

10 R.E. Caves, 'International Corporations: The Industrial Economics of Foreign Investment', *Economica* 38, 1971, pp. 1–27; C.P. Kindleberger, *American Business Abroad – Six Lectures on Direct Investment*, New Haven: Yale University Press, 1969.

11 R.H. Coase, 'The Nature of the Firm: Influence', in O.E. Williamson and S.G. Winter (eds), *The Nature of the Firm: Origins, Evolution and Development*, Oxford: Oxford University Press, 1993.

12 O. Williamson, *Markets and Hierarchies – Analysis and Antitrust Implications*, New York: Free Press, 1975; *The Economic Institutions of Capitalism*, New York: Free Press, 1985.

13 P. Buckley and M. Casson, *The Future of the Multinational Enterprise*, London: Macmillan, 1976; Jean-Francois Hennart, 'The transaction cost theory of multinational enterprise', in C.N. Pitelis and R. Sugden (eds), *The Nature of the Transnational Firm*, London: Routledge, 1991, pp. 81–116.

14 H. Demsetz, 'The theory of the firm revisited', *Journal of Law, Economics and Organisation* 4, 1988, pp. 141–61.

15 J.H. Dunning, *Explaining International Production*, London: Unwin Hyman, 1988; 'Forty Years On: American Investment in British Manufacturing Industry Revisited', *Transnational Corporations* 8, 1999, pp. 1–34.

16 A.D. Chandler, *Strategy and Structure*, Cambridge, Mass.: MIT Press, 1962; *The Visible Hand: The Managerial Revolution in American Business*, Cambridge, Mass.: Harvard University Press, 1977; *Scale and Scope*, Cambridge, Mass.: Harvard University Press, 1990.

17 A.D. Chandler, 'The Emergence of Managerial Capitalism', *Business History Review* 58, 1984, pp. 368–70.

18 Chandler, *Scale and Scope*, pp. 236–7.

19 M. Wilkins, "Defining a Firm: History and Theory", in P. Hertner and G. Jones (eds), *Multinationals: Theory and History*, Aldershot: Gower, 1986.

20 M. Wilkins, 'The Free Standing Company, 1870–1914: An Important Type of British Direct Foreign Investment', *Economic History Review* 41, 1988, pp. 259–85; M. Wilkins and H. Schröter (eds), *The Free-Standing Company in the World Economy 1830–1996*, Oxford: Oxford University Press, 1998.

21 K.E. Sluyterman, *Dutch Enterprise in the Twentieth Century: Business Strategies in Small Open Country*, London: Routledge, 2005, pp 41–45; Laura Stanciu, "Free Standing Companies in the Oil Sector in Romania and Poland before 1948: Typologies and Competencies", *Business History* 42, 2000, pp. 27–66.

22 G. Jones, 'Great Britain: Big Business, Management, and Competitiveness in Twentieth Century Britain', in A. D. Chandler Jnr, F. Amatori, and T. Hikino (eds), *Big Business and the Wealth of Nations*, Cambridge: Cambridge University Press, 1997, pp. 105–112.

23 Jones, *Multinationals*, pp. 21–22; *Merchants to Multinationals: British Trading Companies in the Nineteenth and Twentieth Centuries*, Oxford: Oxford University Press, 2000.

24 G. Jones and M.B. Rose (eds), *Family Capitalism*, London: Frank Cass, 1993.

25 R.R. John, 'Elaborations, Revisions, Dissents: Alfred D. Chandler Jr.'s the Visible Hand after twenty years', *Business History Review* 71, 1997, pp. 151–200; Maury Klein, 'Coming Full Circle: The Study of Big Business since 1950', *Enterprise and Society* 2, 2001, pp. 425–60.

26 For different perspectives on entrepreneurship, see, J. A. Schumpeter, *The Theory of Economic Development*, Cambridge, Mass.: Harvard University Press, 1959; F. H. Knight, *Risk, Uncertainty, and Profit*, Boston: Houghton Mifflin, 1967; I. M. Kirzner, *Competition and Entrepreneurship*, Chicago: University of Chicago Press, 1973; M. Casson, *The Entrepreneur. An Economic Theory*, Oxford: Martin Robertson, 1982.

27 Kirzner, *Competition and Entrepreneurship*, p. 39.
28 Schumpeter, *The Theory of Economic Development*, pp. 93–4.
29 Casson, *The Entrepreneur*, p. 23.
30 P.J. Cain and A.G. Hopkins, *British Imperialism: 1688–2000*, Harlow: Longman, 2002; D.K. Fieldhouse, *The West and the Third World: Trade, Colonialism, Dependence, and Development*, Oxford: Blackwell Publishers, 1999.
31 For examples of the various ministers and their role in the Malayan policy formulation see, E. Thio, *British Policy in The Malay Peninsula, 1880–1910*, Singapore: University of Malaya Press, 1969, pp. xii–xv.
32 K.M. Stahl, *The Metropolitan Organization of British Colonial Trade*, London: Faber and Faber, 1951, pp. 71–3.
33 The association was seen championing Malay rights during the decentralisation debate in 1922 and was also against the imposition of Japanese quota of textile imports. Stahl, *Metropolitan Organization*, pp. 76–8; Yeo Kim Wah, *The Politics of Decentralisation: Colonial Controversy in Malaya 1920–29*, Kuala Lumpur: Oxford University Press, 1982, pp. 340.
34 Other rubber agencies included the Malayan-based United Planting Association of Malaya formed in 1934. N.J. White, *Business, Government, and the End of Empire: Malaya, 1942–1957*, Kuala Lumpur: Oxford University Press, 1996, pp. 30–3.
35 Ibid., pp. 30–3.
36 The Straits Settlements were governed from India until 1866. It became a Crown Colony in 1867 and administration was transferred to the Colonial Office. The Governor, based in Singapore, was the highest authority in the Straits Settlements and was assisted by an Executive and a Legislative Council.
37 R. Emerson, *Malaysia: A Study in Direct and Indirect Rule*, Kuala Lumpur: University of Malaya Press, 1964.
38 With the introduction of the residential system, each state had a ruler, state council, British resident, civil service and professional departments dominated by Europeans. The residents were assisted by the state councils, which dealt with all administrative matters.
39 The Malay States were called protectorates, not colonies. Britain took charge in the Malay States but the Malay rulers were acknowledged legally as sovereign rulers. J.M. Gullick, *Malaya*, London: Ernest Benn, 1964, p. 41. For an assessment of British–Malay relations, see J.M. Gullick, *Rulers and Residents: Influence and Power in the Malay States, 1870–1920*, Singapore: Oxford University Press, 1992.
40 Sir Frank Swettenham became the first resident general. The resident general was the high commissioner's executive representative and was the chief executive officer in charge of the Federated Malay States' administration. For further readings on Swettenham, see E. Chew, 'Swettenham and British Residential Rule in West Malaya', *Journal of the Malaysian Branch of the Royal Asiatic Society* 5, 1974, pp. 165–78.
41 Before 1909, Siamese commissioners (these officers were Europeans) were appointed to Perlis, Kedah and Kelantan. British advisors were appointed after 1909. Terengganu, however, accepted a British advisor only in 1919. Between 1909 to 1919, there was a British agent in Terengganu.
42 The British military administration took over the Malayan administration from 15 August 1945 until 1 April 1946 (with the inauguration of the Malayan Union). See M. Rudner, 'The Organization of the British Military Administration in Malaya, 1946–48', *Journal of South East Asian History* 9, 1968, p. 97.
43 A. Thurston, *Records of the Colonial Office, Dominions Office, Commonwealth Relations Office and Commonwealth Office*, London: HMSO, 1995, p. 207.
44 C.H. Ding's *History of the Straits Settlements Foreign Trade, 1870–1915* (1978) and W.G. Huff's *The Economic Growth of Singapore: Trade and Development in the*

Twentieth Century (1994) forefront the economic importance of Singapore during the colonial period and its relations with US MNEs.

45 He was assisted by a Federal Legislative and Federal Executive Council. A chief minister was appointed to administer the nine Malay States, which remained under the respective rulers. A resident commissioner was appointed for Penang and Malacca.

46 T.N. Harper, *The End of Empire and the Making of Malaya*, Cambridge: Cambridge University Press, 1999, p. 376.

47 For further readings on the emergency, see K. Ramakrishna, '"Transmogrifying" Malaya: the impact of Sir Gerald Templer (1952–54)', *Journal of South East Asian Studies* 32, 2001, p. 79; A.J. Stockwell, '"A Widespread and Long-concocted Plot to Overthrow the Government in Malaya?": The Origins of the Malayan Emergency', *Journal of Imperial and Commonwealth History* 21, 1993, pp. 66–88.

48 N. Tarling, *Imperialism in South East Asia: A Fleeting, Passing Phase*, London: Routledge, 2001, p. 94.

49 According to Allen, 'the affairs of the Straits Settlements were very small fry in London.' He noted that the Colonial Office was heavily dependent on the governors in Malaya for information and policy execution in the Straits Settlements and the Malay States. This was due to ignorance about the region, communication delays and strong personalities that do not 'promote the meek subordination of the men-on-the-spot to directives from Whitehall'. J. de Vere Allen, 'The Colonial Office and the Malay States, 1867–73', *Journal of the Malaysian Branch of the Royal Asiatic Society* 36, 1963, pp. 3–7.

50 Abdullah Zakaria Ghazali, 'Diplomasi Kapal Perang: Pembedilan Ke atas Terengganu, 1862', *Malaysia Dari Segi Sejarah* 13, 1984, pp. 72–84. Regardless of the formal Whitehall policy of non-intervention, there was indeed increased evidence of intervention by British administrators in the Malay States. For discussions on British interferences in the Malay States of Terengganu and Pahang, see L.A. Mills, 'British Malaya 1824–1867', *Journal of the Malaysian Branch of the Royal Asiatic Society* 33, 1960, pp. 196–8.

51 E. Sadka, 'The Colonial Office and the Protected Malay States', in J. Bastin and R. Roolvink (eds), *Malayan and Indonesian Studies*, Kuala Lumpur: Oxford University Press, 1964, p. 188.

52 Sadka, *Protected Malay States*, pp. 339–40.

53 Tarling, *Imperialism*, p. 210.

54 S. Sundara Raja, 'British Economic Involvement in the Agriculture and Mining Sectors in the Federated Malay States, 1896–1909', Ph.D. Thesis, University of Malaya, 2004.

55 Thio, *British Policy*, p. xv.

56 Sundara Raja, 'British Economic Involvement', p. 48.

57 Tarling, *Imperialism*, p. 210.

58 Drabble, 'Economic Development', pp. 204–5; *Rubber in Malaya, 1876–1922, The Genesis of the Industry*, Kuala Lumpur: Oxford University Press, 1973, pp. 192–7. Lim Teck Ghee, however, may have some justification in arguing that on various occasions, the colonial administrators were supportive of British planters. Lim Teck Ghee, *Peasants and their Agricultural Economy in Colonial Malaya, 1874–1941*, Kuala Lumpur: Oxford University Press, 1977, p. 91.

59 White, *Business, Government, and the End of Empire*; 'Government and business divided: Malaya, 1945–57', *Journal of Imperial and Commonwealth History* 22, 1994, p. 252; 'The frustrations of development: British business and the late colonial state in Malaya, 1945–1957', *Journal of South East Asian Studies* 28, 1997, pp. 103–19.

60 White, *Business, Government, and the End of Empire*, p. 35.

61 Ibid., p. 44

62 P. Clegg and T. Shaw, *The Caribbean Banana Trade: From Colonialism to*

Globalization, Basingstoke: Palgrave, 2002, Chapters 2 and 3. M. Moberg, 'Crown colony as Banana Republic: the United Fruit Company in British Honduras, 1900–1920', *Journal of Latin American Studies* 28, 1996, pp. 357–82. For a wider discussion on the cultural, political, economic and agricultural processes of the banana industry in Latin America and the Caribbean which also includes several essays on the operations of UFC, see M. Moberg and S. Striffler (eds), *Banana Wars: Power, Production and History in the Americas*, Durham: Duke University Press, 2003. There is a wide literature on the United Fruit's political intervention in the countries in which it operated. See for example, R.J. Barnet and R.E. Muller, *Global Reach: The Power of the Multinational Corporations*, New York: Simon and Schuster, 1974; P. Dosal, *Doing Business with the Dictators: A Political History of United Fruit in Guatemala, 1899–1940*, Wilmington, DE: Scholarly Resources, 1993.

63 M. Wilkins, 'Comparative Hosts,' *Business History* 36, 1994, pp. 18–50.

64 G. Jones and F. Bostock, 'U.S. multinationals in British manufacturing before 1962', *Business History Review* 70, 1996, pp. 207–9. See also Jones, *Multinationals*, p. 7.

65 H.G. Callis, *Foreign Capital in South East Asia*, New York: Institute of Pacific Relations, 1942, pp. 1–4; Library of Congress, Washington D.C. (hereafter LoC), American Direct Investments in Foreign Countries, 1936, Economic series no. 1, US Department of Commerce, 1938, pp. 2–3; American Direct Investments in Foreign Countries, 1936, Economic series no. 1, US Department of Commerce, 1938; Census of American-Owned Assets in Foreign Countries, US Department of Treasury, 1947; C. Lewis, *America's Stake in International Investment*, Washington DC, 1938, pp. 281–88.

66 Wilkins, *Maturing*, p. 184.

67 Callis, *Foreign Capital in South East Asia*, p. 11.

68 US National Archives, College Park, Maryland (hereafter NARA), RG84, Singapore Consulate, 1950–52, Box 16, 'Imports into Malaya of United States Goods via Hong Kong', 1950.

69 In a speech given by Mr H.B. Phillips, vice president of General Motors Export Company for the Far East, he described GM as an international institution using its vast resources to promote the products of Vauxhall Motors Ltd 'all over the world and in so doing is participating in the development of British export trade'. Vauxhall Motors Ltd was taken over by GM in 1925. *Straits Times*, Singapore, 15 November 1929.

70 NARA, US Department of Commerce, Bureau of Foreign and Domestic Commerce, Automobile, Straits Settlements, File Number 531, 'Automotive Statistics in Middle Asia', 2 April 1928.

71 NARA, RG 151, File No. 531, 'Imports of automobiles and parts under the heading of 'British Possessions' in Malaya originated chiefly from Canada'; 'Listing of Imports of Motor Vehicles', 14 May 1935.

72 This work makes a distinction between automobiles made by British-owned firms in Britain, automobiles made by US-owned firms in Britain and automobiles made by US-owned firms in Canada.

73 R.A. Brown, *Capital and Entrepreneurship in South East Asia*, London: Macmillan, 1994.

2 US and Malaya Connetions, 1870–1918

1 The closure of the British West Indian Islands to New England traders began when the American colonies gained independence from Britain. The Peace Convention signed in 1781 between America and Britain was perceived as a violation of the French–American Alliance signed in 1778. As a result, the French also closed their

islands to American trade. S. Ahmat, 'Joseph B. Balestier: The First American Consul in Singapore 1833–1852', *Journal of the Malayan Branch of Asiatic Society* 39, 1966, p. 108.

2 J.W. Gould, 'American Imperialism in South East Asia before 1898', *Journal of South East Asian History* 3, 1972, p. 307.

3 C.M. Turnbull, *The Straits Settlements (1826–1867): Indian Presidency to Crown Colony*, Kuala Lumpur: Oxford University Press, 1972, p. 160; J.W. Gould, 'Sumatra-America's Pepperpot 1784–1873', *Essex Institute Historical Collections* 112, 1956, p. 31; R.H. Fifield, *Americans in South East Asia: The Roots of Commitment*, New York: Thomas Y. Crowell Company, 1973, pp. 16–7.

4 Article 5 of the treaty signed on the 6 February 1819 stipulated that the Sultan of Johore and his representative at Singapore, Dato Abdul Rahman, 'will not enter into any treaty with any other Nation and will not admit or consent to the Settlement in any part of their Dominion of any other power European or American'. C.B. Buckley, *An Anecdotal History of Old Times in Singapore, 1819–67*, Vol. 1, Singapore, 1902, p. 39; Gould, *United States and Malaysia*, p. 58.

5 In 1825, the *HMS Larne*, in strict accordance of the 1815 Convention, detained an American bark *Governor Endicott* within the vicinity of Singapore. The British commander ordered it to sail to Calcutta to stand trial. Since she was not caught trading at Singapore, the court acquitted the ship. Despite the acquittal, this incident deterred US traders from coming to Singapore due to the time and expenses incurred during the trial. S. Ahmat, 'American Trade with Singapore, 1819–1865', *Journal of Malayan Branch of Royal Asiatic Society* 38, 1965, p. 243; C.B. Buckley, *An Anecdotal History of Old Times in Singapore*, 1819–67, Vol. 1. Singapore, 1902, p. 272. For a detailed account of the US exclusion from the trade in Singapore see, R.E.A. Hackler, 'Americans in Singapore, 1819–1850', B.A. dissertation, University of Malaya, Singapore, 1961.

6 S. Ahmat, 'Joseph B. Balestier', *Journal of Malayan Branch of Royal Asiatic Society* 39, 1966, p. 111.

7 S. Ahmat, 'American Trade with Singapore, 1819–1865', *Journal of Malayan Branch of Royal Asiatic Society* 38, 1965; 'Some Problems of the Rhode Island Traders in Java, 1799–1833, *Journal South East Asian Studies* 6, 1965, p. 104.

8 J.M. Callahan, *American Relations in the Pacific and the Far East*, Baltimore: John Hopkins Press, 1901, pp. 10–11.

9 R.H. Miller, *The United States and Vietnam, 1787–1941*, Washington DC: National Defense University Press, 1990, p. 41.

10 P. Sodhy, 'Passage of Empire', p. 19.

11 S. Ahmat, 'Joseph B. Balestier', p. 117.

12 J.C. Jackson, *Planters and Speculators: Chinese and European Agricultural Enterprise in Malaya, 1786–1921*, Kuala Lumpur: University of Malaya Press, 1968, pp. 135–7.

13 K.G. Tregonning, 'American Activity in North Borneo, 1865–1881', *Pacific Historical Review* 23, 1954, pp. 358–9. See also, N. Tarling, *Britain, The Brookes and Brunei*, Kuala Lumpur: Oxford University Press, 1971, pp. 71, 169–70.

14 Gould, *United States and Malaysia*, p. 62.

15 D.S. Ranjit Singh, *The Making of Sabah 1865–1941*, Kuala Lumpur: University of Malaya Press, 2000, p. 114; *Brunei 1839–1983: The Problems of Political Survival*, Singapore: Oxford University Press, 1984, pp. 65–6.

16 PRO, CO 144/37, 'Intentions of United States Government to form a Naval Station', 17 August 1872.

17 The grant of 3 February 1877 executed by Sultan Ali, ruler of Muar, held nearly 50 square miles or about 30,000 acres of land. ANM, CO273/264, 'Adolph Gottwald Studer against the State of Johore', 1877.

18 The US government pursued this matter with the British government to claim the

grant on behalf of Studer's descendant and this lasted until 1912. ANM, CO 273/414; CO 270/390, 'Studer vs. Johore', 1877.

19 Sodhy,'Passage of Empire', p. 14.

20 C.H. Ding, A History of Straits Settlements Foreign Trade, 1870–1915, Singapore: National Museum Singapore, 1978, p. 39.

21 C.H. Ding, *Straits Settlements Foreign Trade*, pp. 52–4.

22 Ibid., pp. 103–4, 124–5, 135–43.

23 Huff, *Economic Growth of Singapore*, pp. 50, 82.

24 Gutta percha is the condensed juice of trees used in the manufacture of gum. W.L. Ken, 'The Trade of Singapore, 1819–1869', *Journal of Malayan Branch of Royal Asiatic Society* 33, 1960, pp. 1–315.

25 Drabble, *Rubber in Malaya*, Appendix VII, p. 220.

26 Ibid., p. 224.

27 Huff, *Economic Growth*, pp. 80–1.

28 Ibid., pp. 50, 82.

29 C.H. Ding, 'Malaysian Currency System', pp. 1–18. The dollar was established as the official currency in the Straits Settlements in 1867, and the silver dollars of Hong Kong, Spain, Mexico, Peru and Bolivia were specified as legal tender in the colony at various times. The year 1867 marked the transfer of Straits Settlements administration from the India Office to the Colonial Office, when prior to this transfer, as a dependency of the British Empire in India, the official currency of was the Indian rupee. The US silver dollar and the Japanese yen were declared legal tender in Malaya in 1874.

30 G. Jones, *The State and the Emergence of the British Oil Industry*, London: Macmillan Press, 1981, pp. 20–3; Huff, *Economic Growth*, p. 237.

31 For an overview of French trade and investment activities in Malaya see, J. Sig. D. Rawlins, 'French Enterprise in Malaya', *Journal of the Malayan Branch of Royal Asiatic Society* 39, 1966, p. 55.

32 Several scholars suggested that the German factor played a role in British intervention in Malaya. K.G. Tregonning, 'How Germany made Malaya British', *Asian Studies* 2, 1964, pp. 180–7; C.D. Cowan, *Nineteenth-Century Malaya*; D. MacIntyre, 'Britain's Intervention in Malaya: the origin of Lord Kimberley's instructions to Sir Andrew Clarke in 1873', *Journal of South East Asian Studies* 2, 1961, pp. 47–69.

33 K.K. Kim cites economic motives for British intervention in Malaya. K.K. Kim, 'The Origin of British Administration in Malaya', *Journal of Malayan Branch of Royal Asiatic Studies* 39, 1966, pp. 52–91.

34 Other important firms include Rautenberg, Schimdt & Co. (1849), which expanded in 1878 by taking over ten new European agencies; Zapp, Bauer & Co. (1854); Heiber, Katz & Co. (1867), which was re-established in 1878 as Katz Brothers, Brinkman, Kumpers & Co. (1867) and E.H. Hinnekindt (1868). H. Kellenbenz, 'German Trade Relations with the Indian Ocean from the end of the Eighteenth Century to 1870', *Journal of South East Asian Studies* 13, 1982, p. 145; Tareq Abd. El-Hamid Ahmed Amin, 'Anglo-German Rivalry in the Malay Peninsula and Siam, 1870–1909', Ph.D. thesis, University of Malaya, 1995, pp. 195–216.

35 C.H. Ding, 'Sino-British Mercantile Relations in Singapore's Entrepot Trade, 1870–1915', in J. Chen and N. Tarling (eds), *Studies in the Social History of China and S.E. Asia*, Cambridge: Cambridge University Press, 1970, pp. 247–66; S.O. Siang, *One Hundred Years' History of the Chinese in Singapore*, Singapore: University Malaya Press, 1967.

36 Although there were rampant abuses of the credit system, it remained an important means of disposing of goods. W.L. Ken, 'Trade of Singapore', p. 163; C.M. Turnbull, *The Straits Settlements 1826–67: Indian Presidency to Crown Colony*, Kuala Lumpur: Oxford University Press, 1972, pp. 181–2.

37 NARA, Records of the Department of State Relating to the Internal Affairs of British Asia, 1910–1929, (encl.) *Straits Budget*, 7 January 1915; Turnbull, *The Straits Settlements*, pp. 180–1; Huff, *Economic Growth*, pp. 265.
38 Jones, *British Multinational Banking*, pp. 70, 89.
39 In 1915, the Singapore Chamber of Commerce struck off the memberships of several German firms including Behn, Meyer & Co. Ltd; Deutsche Asiatic Bank; R. Forwerg, Franzen & Co; Kumpers & Co; Rautenberg, Schmidt & Co; Siemens Brothers, and Dynamo Works Ltd. Chiang Hai Ding, *Straits Settlements Trade*, pp. 37 and 37n.
40 The imports from Japan, for instance, amounted to S$7.3 million in 1913, declined slightly in 1914 (figures not available) and later increased to S$8.4 million in 1915. In 1916, imports from Japan increased further to S$12.9 million and went upward to S$19.7 million in 1917. University of Malaya Main Library (hereafter UML), Records of the Department of State Relating to the Internal Affairs of British Asia, 1910–1929, 'Political, Economic, Commercial, and Financial Information', US Consulate General Singapore, Quarterly Report, 31 March 1919.
41 V.P. Keong, *Western Rubber Planting Enterprise in South East Asia, 1876–1921*, Kuala Lumpur: University Malaya Press, 1976, p. 65; Jones, *Merchants*, pp. 69–70; Huff, *Economic Growth*, pp. 257–63.
42 J.H. Drabble and P.J. Drake, 'The British Agency Houses in Malaysia: Survival in a Changing World', *Journal of South East Asian Studies* 12, 1981, pp. 308–9.
43 Ibid.
44 L.W. Fong, 'The Singapore Houses of Agency, 1819–1900, B.A. dissertation, University of Malaya, Singapore, 1958, p. 45.
45 S. Nicholas, 'Agency Contracts, Institutional Modes and the Transition to Foreign Direct Investment by British Manufacturing Multinationals Before 1939', *Journal of Economic History* 43, 1983, pp. 675–86; 'The Overseas Marketing Performance of British Industry, 1870–1914', *Economic History Review* 37, 1984, pp. 489–506; S.D. Chapman, *The Rise of Merchant Banking*, London: George Allen and Unwin, 1984, pp. 9–15; *Merchant Enterprise in Britain: From the Industrial Revolution to World War I*, Cambridge: Cambridge University Press, 1992, pp. 54–5; Jones, *Merchants*, Chapter 8.
46 D.C. Bliss, *Market for Machinery in British Malaya*, Washington: GPO, 1931, p. 3.
47 A.C. Harper and Co was among the earliest agents in the motor trade when motorcars and accessories were their chief import line around 1910. Drabble and Drake, 'British Agency Houses', pp. 310–1.
48 Fyfe, *Wheels in Malaya*, p. 27.
49 *Singapore Free Press*, 21 June 1905.
50 For a complete list, see NARA, Dispatches from the US Consuls in Singapore 1833–1906, US Consulate General, Singapore, 9 December 1905.
51 UML, Dispatches from the United States Consuls in Singapore 1833–1906, (encl.) *Straits Times*, 22 June 1905.
52 UML, Dispatches from the US Consuls in Singapore 1833–1906, US Consulate General, 21 December 1905; Wong Sin-Kiong, 'The Genesis of Popular Movements in Modern China: A study of the Anti-American Boycott of 1905–1906', Ph.D. thesis, Indiana University, 1995, pp. 186–94.
53 The British American Tobacco Company was a joint venture formed in 1902 between the UK's Imperial Tobacco Company and the American Tobacco Company of the US. Initially the US firm held two-thirds of the equity even though BAT was British-registered. However, in 1911, American Tobacco divested its shares as a result of an anti-trust action, and over the next decade the firm became effectively British. This boycott created problems for British American Tobacco although the decline in sales was arrested when the company's main dealers continued trade.

H. Cox, *The Global Cigarette: Origins and Evolution of British American Tobacco, 1880–1945*, Oxford: Oxford University Press, 2000, p. 274.

54 Ibid.

55 L.A. Mills, *British Rule in Eastern Asia*, London: Oxford University Press, 1942, pp. 117–18.

56 *Malay Mail*, 7 May 2002.

57 *Perak Pioneer*, 1 September 1894, 5 September 1894, 12 September 1894 and 15 September 1894.

58 R.H. Wright, 'Marketing Foodstuffs in Malaya and the East', *Crown Colonist* 6, 1936, p. 533.

59 S.M. Martin, *The UP Saga*, Copenhagen: NIAS Press, 2003, p. 23.

60 Y.C. Leng, 'Japanese Rubber and Iron Investments in Malaya', *Journal of South East Asian Studies* 5, 1974, p. 21.

61 NARA, Reports made by the US Consul in Singapore in Dispatches from the US Consuls in Singapore, 1833–1906 and Records of the Department of State Relating to the Internal Affairs of British Asia, 1910–1929.

62 Huff, *Economic Growth*, pp. 237–9.

63 SOCONY attempted to gain a footing in the Dutch East Indies oil production since 1898. *Straits Budget*, 4 March 1898, 9 January 1902, 12 March 1902 and 18 November 1903. PRO, POWE 33/1714, 'British North Borneo Arbitration, Report of Mr. Thomas Dewhurst on Petroleum Prospects in British North Borneo', 3 May 1949.

64 W. Makepeace, G.E. Brooke and R.S.J. Bradell (eds), *One Hundred Years of Singapore*, Vol. II, London: John Murray, 1921, p. 98.

65 Arkib Negara Malaysia (hereafter ANM), CO 273/465, No. 55201, 'Tin for USA', 9 December 1917.

66 Sodhy, *The US-Malaysian nexus*, p. 12.

67 This US rubber firm was sold to a British concern in 1920. NARA, Records of the Department of State Relating to the Internal Affairs of British Asia, 1910–1929, US Consul General Singapore, 'American Capital in Rubber Production in British Malaya', 30 October 1922.

68 Huff, *Economic Growth*, p. 197; Huff did not include BFGoodrich, which set up a purchasing agency in Singapore in 1918. See M.G. Blackford and K.A. Kerr, *BFGoodrich: Tradition and Transformation, 1870–1995*, Columbus: Ohio State University Press, 1996, p. 56.

69 W.G. Huff, 'The development of the rubber market in pre-World War II Singapore', *Journal of South East Asian Studies* 24, 1993, pp. 285–307.

70 'Things That Interest Firestone Shareholders', The Firestone Tire and Rubber Co, Akron, Ohio, 1919.

71 ANM, CO 273/290, Government House, Singapore, 28 January 1903.

72 Wilkins, *Maturing*, p. 20.

73 Wilkins, *Emergence*, pp. 37–47; A. Godley, 'Pioneering Foreign Direct Investment in British Manufacturing', *Business History Review* 73, 1999, pp. 394–429; F.V. Carstensen, *American Enterprise Abroad: Case Studies of Singer and International Harvester in Imperial Russia*, Chapel Hill: University of North Carolina Press, 1984; R.B. Davies, *Peacefully Working to Conquer the World: Singer Sewing Machines in Foreign Markets, 1884–1920*, New York: Arno Press, 1976.

74 This Chinese firm was founded by Chua Cheng Bok and his four brothers in Kuala Lumpur with branches in Ipoh (1906), Penang (1914) and Singapore (1916). E. Jennings, *Wheels of Progress: 75 Years of Cycle & Carriage*, Singapore: Meridien Communications, 1975, p. 24.

3 Strengthening Ties, 1919–1957

1 PRO, CAB 58/149, 'Economic Advisory Council Reports, Proceedings and Memoranda of Committee on Empire Trade', 1930.
2 Huff, *Economic Growth of Singapore*, pp. 77–9.
3 It should be noted that the Federated Malay States figures include drinks and tobacco – despite being branded manufactured goods – in foodstuff imports. The term 'manufactured goods' refers to articles wholly or mainly manufactured, such as machinery, cotton yarn, electrical goods and apparatus etc. In 1920, total Federated Malay States import figures showed foodstuffs commanding 55.5 per cent, as compared to 35 per cent for manufactured products. In 1940, manufactured articles commanded 53.3 per cent while foodstuffs commanded 42.1 per cent. A. Azmi Abdul Khalid, 'The Federated Malay States: Growth and Development of the Import Trade, 1900–1940' in Muhammad Abu Bakar, Amarjit Kaur and Abdullah Zakaria (eds), *Historia*, Kuala Lumpur: University of Malaya, 1984, pp. 326–7.
4 J.V. Jesudason, *Ethnicity and the Economy*, Singapore: Oxford University Press, 1989, p. 32; R. Emerson, *Malaysia: A Study in Direct and Indirect Rule*, Kuala Lumpur: University of Malaya Press, 1964, p. 42; P.P. Courtenay, *Geography of Trade and Development in Malaya*, London: G. Bell & Sons, 1972, p. 109.
5 Drake and Drabble, 'Agency Houses in Malaysia', p. 311; W.G. Huff, 'Monetization and financial development in South East Asia before the Second World War', *Economic History Review* 2, 2003, p. 328.
6 Jones, *Merchants*, p. 293.
7 *British Malaya: Trade and Commerce*, London: Malay States Information Agency, 1924, pp. 55–73; *British Malaya: Production and Trade*, London: Malay States Information Agency, 1932, pp. 16–19.
8 PRO, CO 852/178/1, 'Commercial relations with the USA – Tariff Negotiations', 1938.
9 Ibid.
10 The slightly higher figures for the Philippines during the Depression period of 1931 to 1935 were due to increased efforts by the US to bolster the Philippine economy. M.S. Farley, 'America's Stake in the Far East – 1: Trade', *Far Eastern Survey* 5, 1936, p. 168.
11 Jones, *Multinationals*, p. 45.
12 Cain and Hopkins, *British Imperialism*, Chapter 20, pp. 464–78; D.K. Fieldhouse, *The West and the Third World: Trade, Colonialism, Dependence and Development*, Oxford: Blackwell Publishers, 1999, pp. 92–7; 'British Exporters Prospects in the United States', *The Manchester Guardian Commercial*, February 1938.
13 M.B. Rose, *Firms, Networks and Business Values: The British and American Cotton Industries since 1750*, Cambridge: Cambridge University Press, 2000, pp. 214–16.
14 Huff, *Economic Growth of Singapore*, p. 266.
15 B.C. Butler, 'Economic Conditions in British Malaya', *Commercial Intelligence Journal* 51, 1934, p. 375.
16 However, with the introduction of the quota system, this turnaround was abruptly ended. These European merchant firms received only a small share of quota rights due to their lack of previous dealings with Japan. Huff, *Economic Growth of Singapore*, p. 267; Fieldhouse, *The West and the Third World*, p. 95.
17 ANM, General Advisor Johore (hereafter GAJ), 355/1934, CO to Governor, 7 May 1934.
18 R. Emerson, *Malaysia: Direct and Indirect Rule*, pp. 369–73.
19 The textile quotas were rendered irrelevant with the outbreak of the World War II.
20 ANM, CO 273/527/3753, Circular No. 13, 11 September 1923; Governor to CO, 12 April 1923.
21 In 1939, a tender was awarded by the colonial authorities to a British firm although

the price was more than S$57,420 higher as compared to the Japanese tender for cement. *British Malaya* 14, 1939, p. 84.

22 Boulter, *Economic Conditions*, p. 17; Beale, *Review of Trade*, p. 29.

23 ANM, CO 717/73/72410, HM Trade Commissioner, Federated Malay States to Comptroller-General, Department of Trade, 23 April 1930; Mills, *British Rule*, p. 138.

24 Li Dun Jen, *British Malaya*, p. 54.

25 UML, Records of the Department of State Relating to the Internal Affairs of British Asia, 1910–1929, US Consulate General, Singapore, 12 December 1928.

26 'British Malaya is Market for American Goods', *The Far Eastern Review*, June 1940, p. 230.

27 By contrast, Huff suggested that Guthrie was the only merchant house involved in motor distribution. Huff, *Economic Growth of Singapore*, p. 263.

28 Ibid, p. 260.

29 Jennings, *Wheels of Progress*, p. 23.

30 Chia Yee Soh founded this firm in 1902. This Chinese family firm evolved from bicycle to motorcycle and finally automobile repair works. NARA, RG84, Singapore Consulate, 1950–1952, Box 19, United Motor Works Limited to Department of Commerce, Washington DC, 20 March 1951.

31 NARA, RG84 Foreign Service Posts of the Department of State, Singapore Consulate, General Records, Box 19, 'Annual administrative report on activity in behalf of American trade interests for the period from July 1, 1938 to June 30, 1939'.

32 UML, Records of the Department of State Relating to the Internal Affairs of British Asia, 1910–1929, US Consulate General Singapore, 'Prosecution Regarding Infringement of American Trademark', 12 June 1919. See also, US Consulate General, Penang, 24 January 1922. A Trade Marks Bill with the purpose of providing registration of trade marks in the Colony was introduced in the SS Legislative Council in April 1938 and was finally enforced on 1 February 1939. A. Hartland, *Report on Economic and Commercial Conditions in Malaya*, London: HMSO, 1937, p. 8.

33 F.R. Eldridge, 'Trading with Malaysia', Trade Info Bulletin No 377, Department of Commerce, Bureau of Foreign and Domestic Commerce, Washington DC: GPO, 1925.

34 In 1926 a Californian company, Van Camp Sea Food selling canned sardines, forwarded their labels to the US Consulate in Penang and Singapore to find out if it was necessary to translate the 'Number 1' on their label into a native vernacular. The labels were later shown to principal sardine importers in Singapore and were found that no alterations were needed, as it was acceptable for the local markets. The US consul in Penang made some comments regarding the importance of distinctive brand symbols in the Asian market. He reiterated that the figure 1 on the label fulfilled the requirement, as the figure was readily comprehended as being top quality by all classes in Malaya. Records of the Department of State Relating to the Internal Affairs of British Asia, 1910–1929. For the importance of brand symbol in an Asian market see, R.H. Wright, 'Marketing Foodstuffs in Malaya and the East', *Crown Colonist* 6, 1936, pp. 533–4.

35 NARA, RG84, Foreign Service Posts of the Dept of State, Box 6, Singapore Consulate General Record 1936.

36 The Japanese were allowed to gain a monopoly in the iron industry mainly due to the lack of interest among British firms in investing in the backwater states of Johore, Terengganu and Kelantan, but also due to the revenue which was seriously lacking in the Unfederated Malay States as compared to the Federated Malay States. Y.C. Leng, 'Japanese Rubber and Iron Investments in Malaya', p. 27; Brown, *Capital and Entrepreneurship*, pp. 92–4.

37 V.P. Keong, *American Rubber Planting Enterprise in the Philippines, 1900–30*, London: SOAS, 1977, p. 26.

38 No mention was made about the British firm. National University of Singapore Library (hereafter NUSL), Records of the Department of State Relating to the Internal Affairs of British Asia, 1910–1929, 'Dublin Estate – The New Plantation of the United States Rubber Company in Kedah', 29 October 1923.

39 NUSL, Records of the Department of State Relating to the Internal Affairs of British Asia, 1910–1929, 'American Capital in Rubber Production in British Malaya', US Consulate General, Singapore, 29 October 1923.

40 Wilkins, *Maturing*, p. 109. For details on Japanese iron-ore ventures in the Unfederated Malay States, see Y.C. Leng, 'Japanese Rubber and Iron Investments in Malaya'.

41 This tyre company was taken over by USRC in 1940. Babcock, *History of the United States Rubber Company*, pp. 314–19.

42 'British Malaya Buys More American Goods', *Commerce Reports* 27, 7 July 1930, p. 5.

43 The stock holding banks were: Anglo & London Paris, National Bank of San Francisco, Bankers Trust Company (New York City), Continental & Commercial National Bank of Chicago, First National Bank of Portland (Oregon), Guaranty Trust Company of New York, Guardian Savings & Trust Company (Cleveland), Mercantile Bank of Americas (New York City), National Bank of Commerce (Seattle, Washington), and National Shamut Bank (Boston). UML, Records of the Department of State Relating to the Internal Affairs of British Asia, 1910–1929. US Consulate General, Singapore, 20 October 1920.

44 Wilkins, *Maturing*, Chapter 3.

45 Library of Congress, Washington DC (hereafter LoC), 'The Balance of International Payments of the US in 1933', (United States Department of Commerce, Bureau of Foreign and Domestic Commerce: Washington, 1934); *A New Estimate of US investment Abroad*, United States Department of Commerce, Bureau of Foreign and Domestic Commerce: Washington, 1931.

46 Wilkins, *Maturing*, pp. 155, 213.

47 Ibid, Chapter 9; Jones, *International Business*, p. 45.

48 Ibid, p. 155.

49 Among reasons for the small amount of foreign investment in Indochina other than French were: the French tariff policy, wide fluctuations between the franc and the local currency (piastre), fiscal restrictions, and limitations on acquisition of land and mining rights to foreigners. Callis, *Foreign Capital in South East Asia*, p. 11.

50 Ibid, p. 22.

51 The Philippine Act of 1902 gave control of the public domain to the Philippine government. In 1916, the Jones Act was approved by the American Congress granting total control of legislation to the Filipinos. J.W. Wheeler-Bennett, 'Thirty years of American-Filipino Relations, 1899–1929', *Journal of the Royal Institute of International Affairs* 8, 1929, pp. 503–21.

52 In Malaya, land was granted in perpetuity of 999 years, while a 75-year lease was provided in Java and Sumatra. Meanwhile, realising the crucial need of cheap labour for the successful development of the rubber industry, the British and Dutch authorities had promoted unrestricted entry of foreign labour. V.P. Keong, 'American Rubber Planting Enterprise', p. 17.

53 Filipino labour was insufficient and unskilled (thus the ban would protect the Filipinos, who would not be able to compete with Chinese labour).

54 Moreover, the amendment of both these laws would be insufficient unless American sovereignty was established in the Philippines. V.P. Keong, 'American Rubber Planting Enterprise', pp. 30–3.

55 C. Porter, 'The Philippines as an American investment', *Far Eastern Survey* 9, 1940, pp. 220–5.
56 Callis, *Foreign Capital in South East Asia*, p. 94.
57 M. Falkus, 'Early British Business in Thailand' in Davenport-Hines and Jones (eds), *British Business*, p. 123.
58 Callis, *Foreign Capital in South East Asia*, p. 82.
59 This figure refers to Peninsular Malaya (including Penang). Huff, 'Monetization and financial development', p. 304.
60 Sharp, 'Colonial Regimes', p. 438.
61 Drabble, *Economic Growth*, p. 113.
62 'British Malaya is Market for American Goods', *The Far Eastern Review*, June 1940, pp. 230–1.
63 Jones and Bostock, 'U.S. multinationals in British manufacturing before 1962', pp. 256–7.
64 The same matter was brought to the attention of James Griffiths (Colonial Secretary) during his ministerial visit to Malaya in June 1950. White, *Business, Government, and the End of Empire*, p. 54.
65 Jones, *International Business*, pp. 45–6.
66 N.J. White, *Decolonisation: The British Experience Since 1945*, Seminar Studies in History, London: Longman, 1999, p. 7; F.V. Meyer, *Britain: The Sterling Area and Europe*, London: Bowes & Bowes, 1952, p. 23.
67 These controls were intensified in 1940 due to the speculative accumulation of import licences and excessive stocks in 1939. A quota system was designed to restrict imports from non-sterling countries. 'British Malaya is Market for American Goods', *The Far Eastern Review*, June 1940, p. 230.
68 Sodhy, *US-Malaysian Nexus*, p. 25.
69 'Malayan Basic Industries Respond to American Demand during 1940', *Foreign Commerce Weekly*, 19 April 1941; Thompson, *Postmortem on Malaya*, New York: The Macmillan Company, 1943, p. 217.
70 LoC, 'British Malaya Offers Opportunity for American Goods', *Commerce Reports* 50, 16 December 1939, pp. 1167–70.
71 LoC, 'Malayan Basic Industries Respond to American Demand during 1940', *Foreign Commerce Weekly*, 19 April 1941.
72 Sodhy, *The US-Malaysian Nexus*, p. 65.
73 LoC, 'Malaya: Economic Conditions', *Foreign Commerce Weekly*, 27 February 1950, pp. 17–18.
74 Sodhy, *The US-Malaysian Nexus*, p. 65.
75 PRO, 'An Economic Review of Malaya, 1945–1949', London: Central Office of Information, 1950, p. 221.
76 NARA, RG84 Foreign Service Posts of the Department of State, NARA, College Park, Box No 3, Malaya Consulate, Kuala Lumpur, 1950–1955.
77 The expansion of US exports to Malaya after the war was based chiefly on the increased trade in cotton textiles, which, prior to World War II, had formed a small part of US exports.
78 Max Seitelman, 'Malayan Trade Restrictions', *Far Eastern Survey*, August 1948, pp. 181–2; Fyfe, *Wheels in Malaya*, p. 181.
79 PRO, CO 852/1134/5, 'UK Trade Commissioner in Malaya', 15 March 1950.
80 NARA, RG84, Foreign Service Posts of the Department of State, Box 16, 'Imports into Malaya of United States Goods via Hong Kong', Singapore Consulate, 1950–52.
81 For example, the price paid by Singapore for goods was also higher. Before the devaluation, sterling was officially valued at US$ 4.03 but it was worth as little as US$2.25 on the open market. *Straits Times*, 12 March 1948.
82 PRO, CO 852/1134/5, 'Control of Imports – Dollar Ceilings (Malaya/Singapore)', 11 December 1950.

83 *Far East Trader* 7, 1952.
84 NARA, RG 84, Foreign Service Posts of the Department of State, KL Consulate General, Box No. 12, 'Commercial Intelligence: Hong Kong Company Buys Controlling Interest in Large Malayan Agency House', 1953–55.
85 Guildhall Library, London (hereafter GHL) MS 27259, Borneo Company Limited in-letter from the branches in Singapore and Malaya 1955–58, Borneo Company Limited, Singapore, 2 May 1955.
86 GHL, MS27297, Letter from Acting General Manager, Borneo Co Ltd, Singapore to Revlon International Corporation, New York, 25 January 1956.
87 GHL, MS27297, 'Trade and development correspondence with branches in Malaya, Sarawak, Singapore & Thailand', Borneo Co. Ltd, London to Borneo Co Ltd, Singapore, 2 October 1956.
88 Sodhy, *US-Malaysian Nexus*, 64; White, 'The forgotten case of Malaya', pp. 179–82.
89 van Helten and Jones, *British Business*, p. 181.
90 A cautionary note from Lord Milverton in a February 1952 House of Lords debate on the importance of Malayan economic resources to the British economy. M. Curtis, 'The ambiguities of power: British foreign policy since 1945', *The Ecologist* 26, 1996, pp. 5–12.
91 Sodhy, *US-Malaysian Nexus*, p. 185n.

4 Mining: Yukon Gold Company to Pacific Tin

1 J.H. Davis, *The Guggenheims: An American Epic*, New York: William Morrow & Co, 1978, p. 117.
2 L.L. Fermor, *Report Upon the Mining Industry of Malaya*, Kuala Lumpur: Federated Malay States Government Press, 1940, p. 72.
3 K.G. Tregonning, 'Straits Tin: A brief account of the first seventy-five years of The Straits Trading Company, Limited', *Journal of the Malayan Branch of Royal Asiatic Society* 36, 1963, p. 81.
4 For most of the nineteenth century, Cornish mines in England were the world's largest tin producers. However, Cornish tin output reached its maximum in 1871. In the 1880s, Australia became the largest world producer of tin but by the 1890s, its tin resources were depleting. J.F. Hennart, 'The Tin Industry' in M. Casson (ed.), *Multinationals and World Trade*, London: George Allen & Unwin, 1986, pp. 226–7.
5 The Chinese, for instance, were able to control the employment of labourers through the clan system and secret societies. The Societe de Etains de Kinta, a French company, attempted to avoid labour problems by hiring Tamils but found them not as efficient as the Chinese. Rawlins, 'French Enterprise', pp. 73–4.
6 W.L. Ken, *Malayan Tin Industry to 1914*, pp. 146–9; Tregonning, 'The Straits Trading Company', pp. 83–4.
7 F.D. Birch, 'Tropical Milestones: Australian Gold and Tin Mining Investments in Malaya and Thailand 1880–1930', M.A. thesis, University of Melbourne, 1976, p. 17.
8 Y.Y. Hoong, *Tin Mining Industry of Malaya*, pp. 97–9.
9 In 1912 known as Gopeng Consolidated Ltd. Fermor, *Mining Industry of Malaya*, pp. 24–5.
10 Birch, 'Tropical Milestones', p. 81.
11 J.F. Hennart, 'Internalization in Practice: Early Foreign Direct Investments in Malaysian Tin Mining', *Journal of International Business Studies* 17, 1986, p. 135.
12 The Straits Trading Company Ltd was initiated by two Straits businessmen, a German, Herman Muhlinghaus, and a Scot, James Sword, in 1886. It was registered as a public company on 8 November 1887 with an initial capitalisation of S$150,000 with five additional British shareholders. Both Muhlinghaus and Sword disposed

of all their shares in 1901. STC's shareholders eventually included most of the European business leaders in Singapore. Tregonning, 'The Straits Trading Company', pp. 26, 90–101.

13 Huff, *Economic Growth of Singapore*, pp. 61–2.

14 The firm's proposal to pay duties based on 60 per cent (later increased to 65 per cent) of the gross weight of ores was accepted by the local British authorities. However, the fair average of duties was 70 per cent. W.L. Ken, *Malayan Tin Industry*, pp. 163–6, 228.

15 J.F. Hennart, 'Free-standing firms and the internalization of markets for financial capital: a response to Casson', *Business History* 36, 1994, pp. 118–32; Allen and Donnithorne, *Western Enterprise*, p. 160.

16 W.L. Ken, *Malayan Tin Industry*, pp. 227–9; Y.Y. Hoong, *Tin Mining Industry*, pp. 108–9; I. Brown, *Economic Change in South-East Asia c.1830–1980*, Oxford: Oxford University Press, 1997, pp. 206–7.

17 O.T. Hong, 'The Straits Trading Company 1887–1937', B.A. dissertation, University of Malaya, Singapore, 1958; W.L. Ken, *The Malayan Tin Industry to 1914*, p. 228; Tregonning, 'The Straits Tin Trading Company', p. 103; Y.Y. Hoong, *Tin Mining Industry of Malaya*, p. 229.

18 *Straits Times*, 30 March 1900.

19 Amalgamated Copper Company, incorporated in Montana, was floated in April 1899 with a capital outlay of US$75 million (increased to US$155 million in 1901). This company was active in silver, lead, gold and copper mining in Montana. R.F. Pearce, the president of ITC, took charge of their mining and smelting industries in Montana for three years prior to setting up ITC in 1902. By June 1915, the Amalgamated Copper Company was fully controlled by Anaconda Mining Company. ANM, CO 273/304, R.F. Pearce, President of ITC to William H. Treacher, Resident General Federated Malay States, 20 April 1904; C. Schmitz, 'The Rise of Big Business in the World Copper Industry 1870–1930', *Economic History Review* 39, 1986, p. 396.

20 ANM, CO 273/304, R.F. Pearce to Frank Swettenham, High Commissioner, Singapore, 6 May 1904.

21 Hennart, 'The Tin Industry', pp. 227–9; PRO, CO 852/430/17, Mr E.V. Pearce, Chairman of Consolidated Tin Smelters, 'Memorandum on the History of Differential Export Duties', Vol II, 1907.

22 In August 1902, the Manager of ITC, R.F. Pearce was given verbal assurance through his interview with Swettenham and Venning (acting resident of Selangor) that ITC would receive the same consideration as other firms in the Malay states. This, however, was refuted by Swettenham. According to him, he was not made aware that the tin-ore would be smelted in the US. ANM, CO 273/304, R.F. Pearce to Frank Swettenham, High Commissioner, Singapore, 6 May 1904.

23 K.E. Knorr, *Tin Under Control*, California: Stanford University, Food Research Institute, 1945, p. 61.

24 The US consulate general in Singapore in his dispatch to the Department of State, Washington, stated that the introduction of the legislation had 'a sting in the tail' as STC was the sole beneficiary representing a monopoly not only to the detriment of the labourers and middlemen but also to the Federated Malay States as competition could have brought more revenue. He further provided an analogy:

> Suppose the USA which produces 80 per cent of the world cotton should enact a law that no raw cotton should be exported, all should first be made into yarn in USA before export. Such a measure would within five years close one half of the cotton mills of Britain and Europe and give USA the monopoly of the cotton yarn and cloth market of the world. And England would but get a dose of her own patent medicine as advertised here.

UML, Despatches from United States Consuls in Singapore, 1833–1906, US Consulate General, Singapore. 'Present Condition of Tin Market Reflect Local Opinion and Comments', 25 October 1903.

25 W.L. Ken, *Malayan Tin Industry*, p. 229; Li Dun Jen, *British Malaya*, pp. 75–6; V. Purcell, *Malaya: Outline of a Colony*, p. 110.

26 W.L. Ken, *Malayan Tin Industry*, p. 230.

27 ANM, CO 273/294, 'Export of Tin from FMS: Reports on the imposition of Export Duty', Frank Swettenham, Governor of Straits Settlements to Joseph Chamberlain, 3 June 1903.

28 PRO, CO 852/434/7, Mr E.V. Pearce, Chairman and Managing Director of Consolidated Tin Smelters Ltd to G.L.M. Clausen, 19 August 1941; PRO, CO 852/430/17, Mr E.V. Pearce, Chairman of Consolidated Tin Smelters, Memorandum on the History of Differential Export Duties on Tin Ore Exported from Malaya and Nigeria, Recorded 24019/1903 – Govt 16172/1907 in Straits Settlements Vol II, 1907.

29 STC went to the extent of offering the Malayan Federal government a large interest in the company for fear that the ITC might acquire its shares in the open market. Despite the support of the high commissioner (Federated Malay States), the resident general was not in favour of the move. He was supported by the secretary of state who opposed the move but agreed to the necessity of keeping the firm British. ANM, CO 273/294, 'Export of Tin From Federated Malay States: Reports on the Imposition of Export Duty', Resident General to High Commissioner, 12 May 1903; W.L. Ken, *The Malayan Tin Industry*, p. 230.

30 Huff, *Economic Growth of Singapore*, pp. 62–3.

31 The British authorities in fact feared the consequences of allowing ITC to smelt ores in the Straits Settlements or Federated Malay States as:

> with the command of capital and the exercise of American ingenuity for the formation of large trusts and combinations it would in time control or buy up the shares of the Straits Trading Company or effectively compete with it, and by the offer of high prices for tin ore shut down the local Chinese smelters and to obtain the command of the tin export trade of the Federated Malay States, and ship direct to America in American vessels; for I doubt if any law could be passed by a British legislature lending to prevent a smelter from exporting his product to any particular country to which he desired to send it.

ANM, CO 273/294, Resident General to High Commissioner, 12 May 1903.

32 ITC then collaborated with William Harvey & Company in Britain and R.F. Pearce was appointed as manager. This firm was smelting Nigerian ores in Britain.

33 Lord Curzon was the viceroy of India (the highest position in the Indian administration) from 1899 to 1905. ANM, CO 273/294, 'Export of Tin from FMS', 17 April 1903; Resident General to High Commissioner, 12 May 1903; High Commissioner to Resident General, Federated Malay States, 16 May 1903.

34 Jones, 'The State and Economic Development', pp. 353–75.

35 L. Vogelstein & Co was set up in 1897. Its president, Ludwig Vogelstein, became a naturalised American; however, the German parent, Aron Hirsch & Sohn, one of the great German metal traders prior to 1914, maintained its interests in the company. ANM, CO 273/448, No.18753, 'L.Vogelstein & Co', 19 April 1916; Wilkins, *Emergence*, pp. 272–3.

36 PRO, FO 371/5475, 'Erection of tin smelting works by Mr Hothorn in Malaya', 12 November 1920; CO 273/501/48674, Governor to CO, 25 August 1920.

37 Wilkins, *Maturing*, p. 10n.

38 NARA, Records of the Department of State Relating to the Internal Affairs of British Asia, 1910–1929, US Consulate General Singapore, 4 May 1923.

39 Sodhy, *US-Malaysian Nexus*, p. 63.
40 E.S. Hedges, *Tin in Social and Economic History*, New York: St. Martin's Press, 1964, pp. 25–6.
41 ANM, CO 273/477, No 5510, 'Export of Tin from the Straits Settlements', 14 December 1918.
42 Y.Y. Hoong, *Tin Mining Industry of Malaya*, pp. 97–9; Wong Lin Ken, *The Malayan Tin Industry*, p. 143.
43 Birch, 'Tropical Milestone', p. 17
44 Allen and Donnithorne, *Western Enterprise*, pp. 156–7.
45 By 1900, this technique was examined by gold producers from all over the world including British and Americans who congregated at New Zealand to cash in on this new technology. Birch, 'Tropical Milestone', pp. 84–9.
46 J.W. Cushman (ed. Craig J. Reynolds), *Family and State: The Formation of a Sino-Thai Tin Mining Dynasty 1797–1932*, Singapore: Oxford University Press, 1991, pp. 69–71; T.A. Miles, 'Diamond Jubilee of Tin Dredging', *Tin International*, January 1967, pp. 3–7; 'World's First Tin Dredging Facing Failure?', *Tin International*, February 1967, pp. 31–8; 'The World's Tin Dredges Start Building', *Tin International*, March, 1967, pp. 70–3.
47 Gould, *The United States and Malaysia*, p. 72.
48 Y.Y. Hoong, *Tin Mining Industry*, p. 134.
49 Birch, 'Tropical Milestone', p. 164.
50 J. Thoburn, *Multinationals, Mining, and Development: A Study of the Tin Industry*, Hampshire: Gower, 1981, p. 42.
51 Bliss, *Market for Machinery*, p. 1.
52 Hennart, 'Internalization in Practice', p. 138.
53 Y.Y. Hoong, *Tin Mining Industry*, p. 158.
54 Annual Report YGC 1916.
55 T.F.O. Brien, 'Rich beyond the dreams of avarice: the Guggenheims in Chile', *Business History Review* 63, 1989, pp. 122–60; Schmitz, 'The Rise of Big Business in the World Copper Industry 1870–1930', p. 396; J.H. Davis, *The Guggenheims: An American Epic*, New York: William Morrow and Company, 1978, pp. 109–134.
56 The Guggenheims were actively involved in the management of Pacific Tin. Interview notes with A.E. Thiele, chairman of the board, Pacific Tin, New York, 26 April 1965. The author is grateful to Professor Mira Wilkins, Department of Economics, Florida International University, for providing access to the interview notes. Wilkins, *Maturing*, p. 144.
57 In Selangor, they filed for a prospecting licence covering 85 acres of land in Batu Mukim, and a prospecting licence filed at the Ulu Langat District Office for over 500 acres at Mukim Ulu Langat and Cheras in July 1920. ANM, Selangor Secretariat File (hereafter SSF), 3822/1920, 25 July 1920.
58 In support of their application, they attached a letter from the minister of interior, Canada addressed to the chief secretary of the Federated Malay States in May 1920 signifying the good relationship between the company and the Canadian government and their business acumen in the mining ventures at western Canada. ANM, SSF 3822/1920, 29 May 1920.
59 Munro spent four months in Malaya from January to April 1920 investigating the mining conditions and reviewing the details provided by YGC engineers. Special Report YGC 1920.
60 According to Yip, this policy gave foreign firms (with their heavy investments in fixed capital) an advantage over small Chinese miners. Y.Y. Hoong, *Tin Mining Industry*, pp. 20–1. With the introduction of the Federal Mining Enactment of 1899, a uniform mining land policy in the Federated Malay States came into existence. This act was repealed by the Mining Enactment 1904 and subsequently by the Federal Mining Enactment 1911. W.L. Ken, *Malayan Tin Industry*, pp. 173–4.

61 J. Hillman, 'The Impact of the international tin restriction schemes on the return to equity of tin mining companies, 1927–39', *Business History* 39, 1997, p. 8n.
62 For various case studies on British authorities inconsistencies in approving mining leases, see, Sundara Raja, 'British Economic Involvement'.
63 Charles Alma Baker, was a New Zealander who moved to Perak in 1890 and in the next three decades made a considerable fortune in contract surveying, tin mining and rubber planting. He planned to introduce the dredging system by an Australian and New Zealand process in Perak and in 1901, he was granted a 400 acre mining concession in Perak. In 1902, another application for a bigger concession (800 acres) was submitted over the original concession to economise on the use of large-scale dredging operations. Although the prospecting licence was approved and having spent S$7,000, he failed to secure the mining leases. His application was held for more than a year at the Kinta Land Office when it was finally rejected on the grounds that the land belonged to the Sakai aborigines and had to be handed back to them. Sundara Raja, 'British Economic Involvement', pp. 116–17. See also, Barrie MacDonald, *Imperial Patriot: Charles Alma Baker and the History of Limestone Downs*, Wellington: Bridget William Books, 1993, pp. 30–2.
64 British authorities in Pahang, for instance, turned down three applications for tin prospecting by British investors in 1921 as they were suspected to be speculators. ANM, CO 717/14/55528, The High Commissioner to CO, 6 October 1921.
65 The Anglo Oriental (Malaya) in 1938 applied for a prospecting licence to prospect the entire Malayan coast up to a distance of three miles from the shore. The chief inspector of mines in the Federated Malay States, upon consultation with local authorities in the Malay States, granted instead an insignificant area not exceeding 200 square miles. ANM, GAJ 224/1939, Chief Inspector of Mines, Federated Malay States to Anglo-Oriental (Malaya) Ltd, 29 April 1940.
66 Wilkins, *Maturing*, p. 109.
67 G.E. Greig, *Mining in Malaya*, London: Malay States Information Agency, 1924, p. 42.
68 'Plan of Mining and Agricultural Leases between Tronoh and Siputeh', ANM, Kinta Land Office (hereafter KLO) 551/19, 1919.
69 'Status of the Yukon Gold Company's Holdings in Selangor', 1922, ANM, SSF 5481/22; N. Cleaveland, *Bang! Bang! in Ampang: Dredging Tin during Malaya's Emergency*, San Pedro, California: Symcon Publishing Company, 1973.
70 ANM, KLO, 37/20, 'Application for prospecting license onto plan no.s 13473 and 1929 area about 62.1.35 in Kampar Mukim', 21 December 1920. The same requirements were stated two years later on 25 May 1922, when an agreement was signed between YGC and the British resident of Perak. The fulfilment of these requirements must satisfy the chairman of Kinta Sanitary Board. ANM, SSF, 5223/1922 'Agreement made by YGC with the British Resident in Perak', 25 February 1922.
71 Annual Report YGC 1919.
72 ANM, SSF5481/1922, YGC to Warden of Mines Office, Selangor, 'Status of the YGC Holdings in Selangor', 11 December 1922.
73 N. Cleaveland, 'The most travelled Dredge in the World', *Malaya in History* 5, 1959, pp. 26–7.
74 Annual Report YGC, 1923; ANM, SSF5481/1922, 'Status of the Yukon Gold Company's Holdings in Selangor', 11 December 1922.
75 Annual Report YGC, 1925.
76 Special Report to Stockholders, YGC, 10 December 1920.
77 Annual Report YGC, 1922.
78 Special Report to Stockholders, YGC, 10 December 1920.
79 Annual Report YGC, 1925.
80 Y.Y. Hoong, *Tin Mining Industry*, p. 302n.

81 United Engineers Limited, one of the largest European engineering enterprises in Malaya, had its origins in two partnerships formed by Britons. In 1912, both these well-established firms merged. Huff, *Economic Growth*, p. 216.

82 The Yuba Construction Co (founded in 1906) co-owned by Wendell P. Hammon and Newton Cleaveland had operated the first successful gold dredge in California. The Special Collections, Meriam Library, California State University, Chico carries papers on the Yuba Manufacturing Company from 1898–1957. See also, S.P. Johnston, *Gold Dredges: The Part Played by the Yuba Manufacturing Company in the Great Romance of Dredging for Placer Gold, Platinum and Tin*, San Francisco: John Henry Nash, 1927.

83 Patino was the owner of the Patino Mines and Enterprises Consolidated registered in the US with an initial capital of US$50 million. By 1910, this company was the largest Bolivian producer of tin concentrates. In 1916, Patino obtained control of a British smelter – Williams Harvey of Liverpool in partnership with the National Lead Company, a major consumer of tin from the US. Hillman, 'Malaya and the International Tin Cartel', pp. 239–40; Hennart, 'The Tin Industry', pp. 231–2.

84 Cleaveland, *Bang! Bang! in Ampang*, pp. 43–5.

85 Ibid.

86 YGC, President's Report, 21 April 1924.

87 Cleaveland, *Bang! Bang! in Ampang*, p. 55.

88 Annual Report YGC 1930.

89 Y.Y. Hoong, *Tin Mining Industry*, p. 160. See also, Allen and Donnithorne, *Western Enterprise*, p. 157.

90 Birch, *Tropical Milestone*, p. 231.

91 Ibid, pp. 241–2.

92 PRO, BT 64/2162, 'International Cartels – Tin Control', 5 January 1945.

93 Hennart, 'The Tin Industry', pp. 232–3, 250. Similarly, a process of consolidation occurred in the Malayan tin smelting industry in the 1920s. In 1929, Patino with Howeson formed a British-registered holding company, the Consolidated Tin Smelters, which acquired the Malayan tin smelting company Eastern Smelting Company. With this acquisition, Consolidated Tin Smelters had 40 per cent of world smelting capacity. Patino also took an equity stake in London Tin Corporation (in the region of £700,000) and this alliance was 'favoured by the British government which was anxious to counter the strong American influence in the world's metals industry'. By the 1930s, there were two large holdings in the Malayan tin smelting industry: the Consolidated Tin Smelters and the Straits Trading Company. Van Helten and Jones, *British Business*, pp. 168–9; Knorr, *Tin under Control*, p. 57.

94 Wilkins, *Maturing*, pp. 192–3.

95 Annual Report YGC 1931.

96 Annual Reports YGC 1933 and 1934.

97 NARA, RG59, State Department, 1930–1939, 846d.6354/50, 'On Tin Restriction', US Vice Consul, Singapore, 12 June 1935.

98 Annual Reports YGC 1938–1941.

99 PacTin Annual Report 1941.

100 PacTin Annual Report 1941.

101 PacTin Annual Reports 1946–49.

102 PacTin Annual Report 1945.

103 Sodhy, *US-Malaysia Nexus*, p. 62.

104 NARA, RG84, Foreign Service Post of the Department of State, Singapore Consulate, 1945–47, 31 October 1945.

105 However, efforts to import rice from California were not given import permits by the military government in Malaya as it was considered unfair that PacTin's employees would be better fed than other members of the Malayan population. Cleaveland, *Bang! Bang! in Ampang*, pp. 87–9.

106 Ibid.
107 PacTin Annual Report 1946.
108 Francis Loh Kok Wah, *Beyond the Tin Mines: Coolies, Squatters, and New Villagers in the Kinta Valley, Malaysia c.1880–1890*, Singapore: Oxford University Press, 1988, p. 10.
109 Norman Cleaveland was born in Oakland and had an engineering degree from Stanford University. He was involved in mining operations for several years in Burma, Thailand and Malaya. He came to Malaya in 1930 with his cousin W.M. Warren to work on the installation of two dredges for the Anglo-Oriental (M). He then left Malaya in 1932 to pursue his graduate study for a year at Stanford's Mining School. During the war, he was a pilot in the Army Air Corps and travelled extensively in Central America and the Far East. He was also a member of the Pauley Reparations Mission observing first hand the post-war conditions in Manchuria and Korea. The objective of the Pauley Reparations Mission was to appraise Japanese assets for reparation purposes and Cleaveland's primary role was to deal with mining machinery. Cleaveland, *Bang! Bang! in Ampang, passim.*
110 He was appointed on the Selangor War Executive Committee to represent the mining industry during the early days of the Emergency. However, he was dropped from the committee and was then elected as a member of the Selangor War Advisory Committee. Cleaveland, *Bang! Bang! in Ampang, passim.*
111 Annual Report PacTin 1947.
112 These pre-war tin control schemes (referred to as the International Tin Restriction Scheme), which involved tin producing countries, differed from the post-war International Tin Agreements. The latter agreements, renewed every five year, involved the world's major tin producing and consuming countries, except the US and USSR. The supply and demand of tin was controlled through its own tin buffer stockpile involving export quotas and the fixing of floor and ceiling prices. John Hillman, 'Malaya and International Tin Cartel', *Modern Asian Studies* 22, 1988, pp. 242–57.
113 Cleaveland, *Bang! Bang! in Ampang*, pp. 119–20.
114 Sodhy, *US-Malaysia Nexus*, p. 114.
115 N.J. White, *British Business in Post-Colonial Malaysia, 1957–70: 'Neo-colonialism' or disengagement'?*, London: RoutledgeCurzon, 2004, pp. 144–7.
116 Cleaveland, *Bang! Bang! in Ampang*, pp. 92–3.
117 A temporary licence to work a plot of land less than 10 acres to be registered with the district office and can be renewed annually upon good maintenance of crops.
118 Cleaveland, *Bang! Bang! in Ampang*, pp. 91–7.
119 Population control, according to General Sir Harold Briggs, was a competition between the government and the MRLA for control of the local population, namely Chinese rural population which include squatters, miners and plantation workers. J. Newsinger, 'Counter Revolution: The Malayan Example', *Monthly Review* 45, 1994, pp. 19–29.
120 Cleaveland, *Bang! Bang! in Ampang*, pp. 110–11.
121 Ibid, p. 113.
122 Sir Henry Gurney, then the British high commissioner of the FMS was killed by the communists while on his way to Fraser's Hill in 1951.
123 On the origins of Emergency, see A.J. Stockwell, '"A Widespread and Long-concocted Plot to Overthrow the Government in Malaya"?: The Origins of the Malayan Emergency', *Journal of Imperial and Commonwealth History* 21, 1993, pp. 66–88; R. Stubbs, 'The Malayan Emergency and the development of the Malaysian state', in P.B. Rich and R. Stubbs (eds) *The Counter-Insurgent State: Guerrilla Warfare and State Building in the Twentieth Century*, Houndmills: Macmillan, 1997; A. Short, *In Pursuit of Mountain Rats: The Communist Insurrection in Malaya*, Singapore: Cultured Lotus, 2000; Ramakrishna, 'Transmogrifying' Malaya, p. 79;

K. Hack, '"Iron Claws on Malaya": The Historiography of the Malayan Emergency, *Journal of Southeast Asian Studies* 30, 1999, p. 99.

124 NARA, RG84, Kuala Lumpur, Malaya, 1950–1955, Box 4, PacTin to the US Consulate, Ampang, 8 July 1948.

125 He then requested 24 US army-type Winchester automatic carbines with 2000 rounds of ammunition. His request was immediately put forward by the US consulate to the secretary of state, US. NARA, RG84, Kuala Lumpur Malaya, 1950–1955, Box 4, Cleaveland to US Consulate, Kuala Lumpur, 28 June, 1948; US Consulate, Kuala Lumpur to the Secretary of State, US, 29 June 1948; Interview notes with A.E. Thiele, chairman of the board, Pacific Tin, New York, 26 April 1965.

126 PacTin Annual Report 1958.

127 NARA, RG 84, Malaya, Kuala Lumpur, 1950–1955, Box No. 12, No. 501.62, 'Investment of Capital', 1953–55.

128 Interview notes with A.E. Thiele, chairman of the board, Pacific Tin, New York, 26 April 1965.

5 Plantation: United States Rubber Company

1 Annual Report USRC 1905–6.

2 In 1907, Davis first heard about the production of 'shilling a pound' rubber on Asian plantations. He decided to visit Ceylon (now Sri Lanka) with his friend, Walter B. Mahony, a Wall Street lawyer. Both of them were amazed at the low cost of producing plantation rubber in Asia and were impressed by the growing importance of rubber cultivation. R. Chalk, 'The US and the International Struggle for Rubber, 1914–1941', Ph.D. thesis, University of Wisconsin, 1970, p. 6.

3 J.H. Drabble, *Rubber in Malaya 1876–1922: The Genesis of the Industry*, Kuala Lumpur: Oxford University Press, 1973, p. 61.

4 Annual Reports USRC 1910–11.

5 G. Babcock, *History of the United States Rubber Company*, Indiana: Indiana University, 1966, p. 22.

6 Ibid, p. 83.

7 Drabble, *Rubber in Malaya*, p. 125.

8 Ibid.

9 Robert, *Struggle for Rubber*, 1970, p. 20.

10 ANM, CO 273/459, 'Disposal of State Land to Aliens', E.L. Brockman, Chief Secretary to Government, Federated Malay States, 24 January 1917.

11 In 1907, US Rubber sent H. Stuart Hotchkiss to survey the possibility of rubber production in South East Asia. *Between US*, March 1922.

12 ANM, CO 273/446, No 55810, 'Introduction of American Capital Into Rubber Estates', 20 October 1917; HCO 1861/1916, Chief Secretary to High Commissioner, 25 October 1916; CO 273/459, No 27642, 'Land Grant to Mr. Ch. M Naested', 19 April 1917; CO 273/463, No11210, 'American Rubber Interest In Malaya', 28 February 1917.

13 Due to World War I, there was a lack of young British planters since those available in Malaya were recruited by the army. Due to the scarcity of young British planters, US capitalists might offer any terms to secure the services of experienced men. ANM, CO 273/452, No 59749, 'General Rubber Company of USA', 12 December 1916.

14 ANM, CO 273/459, No 27642, 'Land Grant to Mr. Ch. M. Naested', 19 April 1917. The British vice consulate in Medan reported that there was no local evidence of strained relations between British and US planting organisations with regard to unfair methods in respect of labour. The 'crimping' (snatching) of time-expired labourers had never happened. According to him, The Hollandsch-Amerikaansche Plantage Maatschappij, as a member of the Planters Association of the East Coast

of Sumatra (AVROS), which was under the strict control of the DEI government, was allowed to import labour from Java. At present, there was no American interest in establishing a recruiting organisation in Java; therefore, there was no danger of American and British interests coming into conflict. ANM, CO 273/462, No 38833, 'American Interference with Labours of British Planters', 2 August 1917.

15 ANM, HCO 1861/1916, Chief Secretary to High Commissioner, 25 October 1916.

16 Brockman argued that the Federated Malay States policy of considering land applications based on individual merits should be upheld as the present laws were the outcome of many years of experience designed to promote productive cultivation on the land and not for it to be 'held up for speculative purposes'. ANM, CO 273/459, No 11659, Brockman's Memo, 24 January 1917.

17 Ibid.

18 Drabble, *Rubber in Malaya*, p. 106n.

19 Lim Chong Yah, *Economic Development of Modern Malaya*, Kuala Lumpur, 1967, p. 350.

20 The secretary of state for the colonies, Sir Walter Long, described the attitude of the FMS government towards the American danger as 'unduly complacent'. ANM, CO 273/459, No 11659, 'Grindle's Minute', 24 January 1917.

21 ANM, CO 273/459, No 4234, Telegram to High Commissioner, 30 January 1917.

22 Drabble, *Rubber in Malaya*, p. 136.

23 Ibid.

24 Drabble, 'Investment in the Rubber Industry in Malaya, c. 1900–1922', *Journal of Southeast Asian Studies* 3, 1972, p. 257.

25 Drabble, *Rubber in Malaya*, p. 133.

26 ANM, CO 273/462, 'Alienation of Rubber Lands', 16 August 1917, 'Land Grant to Mr. Ch. M Naested'; Drabble, *Rubber in Malaya*, p. 136; Jomo, *A Question of Class*, p. 184.

27 Y.C. Leng, 'Japanese Rubber and Iron Investments in Malaya', p. 21.

28 *New York Times*, 19 January 1917.

29 Robert, 'International Struggle for Rubber', pp. 17–9.

30 Drabble, 'Investment in Rubber', p. 258.

31 Robert, 'International Struggle for Rubber', p. 29.

32 Drabble, *Rubber in Malaya*, p. 3.

33 Tate, *RGA History*, pp. 346–7.

34 NARA, File 846d 6176, Secretary of Commerce to the Secretary of State, Washington: Department of Commerce, 26 October 1922; Robert, 'International Struggle for Rubber', pp. 30–1.

35 Robert, 'International Struggle for Rubber', pp. 30–1.

36 A supreme court of directors composed of five Americans, ten Englishmen, three Dutchmen, one Dane, one Belgian and one Japanese would be based in London and routine matters would be handled by an executive council consisting of four Englishmen, two Americans, and one Dutchman. Robert, 'International Struggle for Rubber', pp. 28–9.

37 Under this plan, rubber exports were controlled through the distribution of export coupons to plantation owners.

38 Sodhy, *Passage of Empire*, p. 249.

39 Although it seemed that the Colonial Office acted in support of the various rubber interests, mainly the RGA, Drabble argues that the decision was made to preserve Britain's imperial interests by preventing the Americans from taking control of British rubber plantations and 'was not made in the narrow interests of British capital'. Drabble, *Economic Development*, p. 128; *Rubber in Malaya*, pp. 192–7.

40 ANM, CO 717/26/45256, Chairman of Amalgamated Rubber Estates to British Prime Minister, 4 September 1922.

41 Drabble, *Rubber in Malaya*, p. 193; L.C. Yah, *Economic Development*, p. 76; L.T. Ghee, *Peasants and their Agricultural Economy in Colonial Malaya*, Kuala Lumpur: Oxford University Press, 1977, p. 142.
42 By the beginning of the 1920s, the American rubber industry comprised of 477 individual firms employing around 160,000 workers. However, four large corporations produced 55 per cent of the rubber goods sold in the US. USRC, Goodrich, Goodyear and Firestone dominated the decision-making process. By 1929, these companies produced three-quarters of the tyres sold in the US. Blackford and Kerr, *BFGoodrich*, p. 77; Tate, *RGA History*, pp. 361–3.
43 *Bulletin of RGA*, August 1926, p. 374.
44 The Goodrich Corporation was also sympathetic to the Stevenson Scheme, reiterating that Americans 'should be thankful that they [the British] had the foresight and courage to create the present supply rather than find fault with them for seeking to make their investments profitable'. V.P. Keong,'American Rubber Planting', p. 32.
45 *India Rubber Journal* 65,1923, p. 11–12. *Malayan Tin and Rubber Journal* 15, 1926; *Rubber Age* 12, 1923; H.S. Firestone, *Men and Rubber: The Story of Business*, New York: Doubleday, Page & Co, 1926; V.P. Keong, 'American in Rubber Planting', p. 22.
46 Sir Eric Geddes of the Dunlop Rubber Company took the opposite stance when he resisted the restriction scheme. For him, the restriction would penalise the efficient producer and those who were not bound under the restrictions, particularly Indonesian smallholders, would gain and prosper. This was one of the major factors that led to the scheme's failure. *Dunlop Estate Berhad News* 1976, p. 8.
47 V.P. Keong, 'American Rubber Planting', p. 24.
48 Babcock, *United States Rubber Company*, pp. 175–9.
49 Ibid.
50 Tate, *RGA History*, p. 363.
51 'Rubber in Malaya, Singapore, and Borneo territories, 1942–60', BoE, OV 65/3, London, UK; Drabble, *Economic History of Malaysia*, pp. 28–9; C. Whittlesey, *Governmental Control of Crude Rubber*, New Jersey: Princeton University Press, 1931, pp. 142–4.
52 PRO, CO 273/539/12, 'British Imperialism in Malaya', London: The Labour Research Department, 1926; Robert, 'International Struggle for Rubber', p. 108.
53 *Rubber Age* 27, 1930, p. 417.
54 M.J. French, 'The Emergence of US MNE: the Goodyear Tire and Rubber Company, 1910–1939', *The Economic History Review* 40, 1987, pp. 64–79.
55 *The Rubber Age* 27, 1930, p. 417.
56 French, 'Goodyear Tire and Rubber Company, 1910–1939', pp. 64–79.
57 V.P. Keong, 'American Rubber Planting', p. 24.
58 Drabble, *Malayan Rubber*, p. 42.
59 Ibid. See also, J.H. Drabble and P.J. Drake, 'More on the financing of Malayan Rubber, 1905–1923', *The Economic History Review* 27, 1974, p. 116.
60 M. Falkus, 'Early British Business in Thailand', in Jones and Davenport-Hines (eds), *British Business in Asia*, p. 122.
61 Wilkins, *Maturing*, pp. 100–1.
62 V.P. Keong, 'American Rubber Planting Enterprise in the Philippines, 1900–1930', Occasional Papers, London: SOAS, 1977, p. 31.
63 Wilkins, *Maturing*, pp. 99–102.
64 ANM, CO273/446, Letter from Edgar B. Davis, Vice President of the General Rubber Company, New York to AB Milne of Ipoh, 12 October 1916.
65 French, 'Goodyear Tire', p. 68.
66 Annual Reports USRC 1912–1913.
67 Annual Report USRC 1915.
68 Babcock, *United States Rubber Company*, p. 22.

69 Annual Report USRC 1917; *New York Times*, 20 April 1917.
70 Annual Reports USRC 1915–19; *New York Times*, 21 May 1919.
71 Annual Report Dunlop Rubber Company 1919 (encl.) *India Rubber Journal* 58, 1919.
72 In the early twentieth century, Sumatra attracted considerable foreign investments in the rubber industry as rubber firms in the Federated Malay States had to pay higher land rents and premium due to popular demand for land in the boom years as well as a 2.5 per cent *ad valorem* duty on the gross value of rubber.
73 *The Planter* 1921, p. 51; Drabble, *Rubber in Malaya*, p. 24.
74 Annual Report USRC 1923.
75 Annual Report USRC, 1922; Lewis, *America's Stake*, pp. 281–8.
76 Annual Report USRC 1927; *Bulletin of RGA*, August 1926, p. 374.
77 Babcock, *United States Rubber Company*, pp. 170–1.
78 'American Planting Companies', *India Rubber World*, 1 September 1928, p. 57.
79 Babcock, *United States Rubber Company*, p. 308.
80 Blackford and Kerr, *BFGoodrich*, p. 111.
81 Drabble, *Malayan Rubber*, p. 306.
82 Babcock, *United States Rubber Company*, p. 353.
83 The plan prohibited planting of rubber trees in additional areas, placed tight controls on stocks of crude rubber held in the controlled area, limited replanting to 20 per cent of existing areas and restricted the exportation of planting materials to territory not covered by the agreement.
84 Robert, 'International Struggle for Rubber', p. 170.
85 French, 'Goodyear Tire', p. 67.
86 Blackford and Kerr, *BFGoodrich*, pp. 130–1; V.P. Keong, 'American Rubber Planting', p. 32.
87 Babcock, *United States Rubber Company*, p. 356.
88 Ibid, 357.
89 Ibid.
90 Ibid, 356–9.
91 USRC Prospectus 1946.
92 Annual Reports USRC 1941–46.
93 NARA, RG 84, Records of the Foreign Service Posts of the Department of State, 1945–55, Singapore Consulate – 1945–47, Office of Strategic Services IB Theater, 27 September 1945, Box 4, Report of Mr Inglis, Manager of Linden Estates, Malayan–American Plantations Ltd, 3 October, 1945.
94 *Financial Times*, 17 November 1995.
95 Bicknell wrote to Sir Gerard Clauson in London to enquire about the status of the land titles owned by the MAP in Malaysia. Since, the Malayan plantations of MAP were located in the states of Kedah, Johore and Selangor, information was needed regarding action by the states of Kedah, Johore and Selangor as well as action by the British government or the Federated Malay States. According to Bicknell, the Dutch East Indies government had, as opposed to inaction in Malaya, issued a Royal Decree in 1942 vesting title in the Crown to all property in the Dutch East Indies for the protection of the persons entitled to protection during the war. ANM, CO 852/605/8, United States Rubber Company, NY, USA, 21 March 1946.
96 H.E. Smith (president USRC) at Annual Meeting of Stockholders, New Jersey, 16 April 1946.
97 Annual Report USRC 1952.
98 Annual Report USRC 1955.
99 Annual Report USRC 1952.
100 The report of the director of agriculture, Federated Malay States and Straits Settlements, for 1920 on soil deterioration was sent to Grantham, *The Planter* 3, April 1922, p. 98.

101 R. Froh, *Edgar B. Davis and Sequences in Business Capitalism: From Shoes to Rubber to Oil*, New York: Garland Publishing Incorporated, 1993, p. 42.
102 *Straits Times*, 15 December 1933; *Dunlop Estate Berhad News*, December 1976; Tate, *RGA History*, p. 417.
103 Schwinges, 'America's Greatest Stake in Rubber', p. 157.
104 *The Planter* 6, January–February 1922, p. 4.
105 Froh, *Edgar B. Davis*, pp. 44–45.
106 In Malaya, conditions vary in the Federated Malay States and Unfederated Malay States, but in the case of land concessions, the grant was usually for longer periods and in some cases actual ownership was possible. The State government received a specified price per acre which was continually increased, as available lands became limited. NARA, Records of the Department of State Relating to the Internal Affairs of British Asia, 1910–1929, Assistant Vice Consul, Penang, Straits Settlements, 22 August 1923.
107 ANM, Kedah Secretariat Files (hereafter KSF) 767/43, 1924.
108 Schwinges,'America's Greatest Stake', pp. 156–8.
109 Among works on corporate welfarism include, L. Baritz, *The Servants of Power: A History of the Use of Social Science in Industry*, Middletown, CT: Wesleyan University Press, 1960; S. Meyer, *The Five Dollar Day: Labor, Management, and Social Control in the Ford Motor Company, 1908–1920*, Albany: State University of New York Press, 1981; O. Zunz, *Making America Corporate, 1870–1920*, Chicago: University of Chicago Press, 1990.
110 S.D. Brandes, *American Welfare Capitalism, 1880–1994*, Chicago: University of Chicago Press, 1970; D. Brody, *Workers in Industrial America: Essays on the Twentieth Century Struggle*, Oxford: Oxford University Press, 1980.
111 Welfare capitalism was also implemented by employers in Britain such as Lever Brothers and Cadbury. See J. Griffiths, '"Give my regards to Uncle Billy . . .": The Rites and Rituals of Company Life at Lever Brothers, c1900–c1990', *Business History* 37, 1995, pp. 25–46; C. Smith, J. Child and M. Rowlinson (eds), *Reshaping Work: The Cadbury Experience*, Cambridge: Cambridge University Press, 1990.
112 S.M. Jacoby, *Modern Manors: Welfare Capitalism since the New Deal*, New Jersey: Princeton University Press, 1997.
113 The rapid development of the Malayan rubber industry came with state protection and patronage. L.Y. Fong, *Labour and Trade Unionism in Colonial Malaya: A Study of the Socio-economic and Political Bases of the Malayan Labour Movement 1930–1957*, Penang: Universiti Sains Malaysia Publisher, 1999, p. 95.
114 ANM, CO 273/446, No 61128, 'American Interest in Malay States Rubber Estates', 14 November 1917.
115 This estate was named after the first manager and his assistants who were from Dublin. Tate, *RGA History*, Appendix 1, p. 602.
116 For a detailed study on the paternalistic practices of USRC at its Malayan and Indonesian subsidiaries see, Shakila Yacob, 'Model of Welfare Capitalism? The United States Rubber Company in Southeast Asia, 1910–1942', *Enterprise and Society* 8.1, 2007, pp. 136–74.
117 ANM, Records of the Department of State relating to the internal affairs of British Asia, 1910–1929, 'Dublin Estate – The New Plantation of the United States Rubber Company in Kedah', Vice Consul, Penang, 29 October 1923.
118 *The Planter* 4, 1925–1926, p. 231.
119 Further details on the profit-sharing and bonus system are, unfortunately, not available.
120 Jones, *Merchants*, pp. 216–18.
121 In Malaya (the Straits Settlements and Federated Malay States), the provision of hospital services had been the legal responsibility of the planters since 1886, which included the provision of hospital accommodation, medical supervision and

maintenance of sufficient good-quality medicines. L. Manderson, *Sickness and the State: Health and Illness in Colonial Malaya, 1870–1940*, New York: Cambridge University Press, 1996, pp. 116–17.

122 ANM, KSF 2505/44, 'Malayan-American Plantations Ltd.', 25 March 1926.

123 S. Hotchkiss, 'Operations of an American Rubber Company in Sumatra and the Malay Peninsula', *The Annals of the American Academy* 112, 1924, p. 160; ANM, KSF 2505/44, 1926.

124 Martin, *The UP Saga*, pp. 58–9, 76–80.

125 For details on the human resources policies and procedures of British firms in Malaya and elsewhere see Jones, *Merchant Firms*, Chapter 7.

126 In 1911, the RGA research station was established, and by 1924 it had spent more than S$600,000 (£70,000) on research. This research station operated until 1926. The much-awaited Rubber Research Institute (RRI), proposed in 1921, was finally set up in September 1925. Khoo Kay Kim, 'Malayan Agriculture, 1920–21', *Journal of the Malaysian Branch of the Royal Asiatic Society* 72, 1999, pp. 30–1.

127 Bauer, *The Rubber Industry*, p. 274.

128 Ibid, p. 43.

129 A short write-up on Dunlop's company history was published in *Dunlop Estate Berhad News*, December 1976.

130 A.L. Stoler, *Capitalism and Confrontation in Sumatra's Plantation Belt, 1870–1979*, Ann Arbor: University of Michigan Press, 1985, p. 21.

131 Tate, *RGA History*, pp. 402–4.

132 Gould, *Americans in Sumatra*, p. 87

133 Ibid.

134 'How to Grow High Yielding Rubber Trees', *India Rubber World* 77, 1927.

135 *The Planter* 7, 1924, p. 347.

136 Herbert Ashplant, 'Recent Developments in the Rubber Planting Industry with Special Reference to Budding, Brown bast treatment, manuring of rubber etc.', Government Mycologist, South India, September 1924, p. 23.

137 Major H. Gough, the pioneer of bud grafting in Malaya in 1921, points out that in Malaya there was very little literature on the subject nor was there any research station to which a planter can turn to for advice and instruction. *The Planter* 7, 1927, p. 156.

138 Jones and Wales, 'Diversification Strategies', pp. 74–5.

139 Babcock, *History of the United States Rubber Company*, p. 186.

140 Tate, *RGA History*, pp. 416–21.

141 *The Planter* 10, August 1929; 'American Planting Companies', *India Rubber World*, September 1928, p. 58; 'Rubber Plantations Owned by the United States Rubber Company', *Bulletin of RGA* 8, 1926, p. 373.

142 Annual Report USRC 1957.

143 Drabble points out that by 1941 in Malaya, 'only about 14 per cent of the estate acreage and a mere two per cent of small-holdings had been planted with specially developed trees capable of yields per hectare three to four times that of the unselected types planted in the early 1900s'. Drabble, *Economic History*, p. 132.

144 Schwinges, 'America's Greatest Stake in Rubber', p. 158.

145 NARA, Records of the Department of State Relating to the Internal Affairs of British Asia, 1910–1929, American Consulate General, Singapore, Monthly Review of Economic Condition, August 1923.

146 *The Planter* 6, September 1925, p. 46.

147 *The Bulletin of RGA*, August 1926, p. 374.

148 Babcock, *History of the United States Rubber Company*, p. 235

149 Babcock, *History of the United States Rubber Company*, pp. 236–8.

150 The second synthetic plant, the largest plant operated by any one rubber company during World War II, was set up at Institute, West Virginia. The third synthetic

rubber plant facility in Los Angeles, California, was already producing in 1943. By 1944, the three plants represented 20 per cent of the 916,000 tonnes of synthetic rubber produced in the US, amply meeting the requirements of American, British and associated armies. C. Barlow, *The Natural Rubber Industry: Its Development, Technology, and Economy in Malaysia*, Kuala Lumpur: Oxford University Press, 1978, pp. 76–7.

151 Annual Report USRC 1945.

152 Report by Herbert E. Smith, President USRC, Annual Meeting of Stockholders, 20 April 1948.

153 Annual Report USRC 1945.

154 Tate, *RGA History*, pp. 563–4.

6 Taking the High Road: Ford Malaya

1 Elsewhere around the world, there was a lack of British automobile FDI because British automobile manufacturers opted for exporting.

2 A yearly publication of statistical data by the British colonial government in Singapore.

3 LoC, US Department of Commerce, Bureau of Foreign and Domestic Commerce, William I. Irvine, 'Automotive Markets in China, British Malaya and Chosen', Special Agent Series, No 221, Washington DC, 1923, p. 89.

4 LoC, US Department of Commerce, Bureau of Foreign and Domestic Commerce, J.A. Fowler, 'Motor Vehicle Market in Netherlands East Indies and British Malaya', Trade Info Bulletin 25, Washington DC, 1922; Fyfe, *Wheels in Malaya*, p. 99.

5 D.M. Phelps, *Effect of the Foreign Market on the Growth and Stability of the American Automobile Industry*, Ann Arbor: Michigan, 1931, p. 683.

6 In 1925, Ford was operating an assembly plant in Japan and the company's application to set up a manufacturing plant was refused by the Japanese government in order to protect the local Japanese car manufacturers; the Nissan Jidosha Kaisha and Toyoda Motor Car Manufacturing Company. Wilkins and Hill, *Ford on Six Continents*, pp. 150, 254–5.

7 NARA, RG 151 Records of the Bureau of Foreign and Domestic Commerce, 1914–58, Box No: 2405, 'Automotive Chart of Malaya', Office of Trade Commissioner, Singapore to Director, 22 April 1929.

8 The Borneo Company Ltd was registered in London in 1856 mainly to conduct a range of business in Sarawak under the rule of Sir James Brooke. In 1868, new branches were established at Calcutta, Singapore, Batavia, HK, Shanghai and Bangkok. In Singapore, BCL became owners of the Teluk Blanga Singapore wharves. GHL, MS 27186, Borneo Company Archives, The Borneo Company Ltd Centenary Celebrations (encl. *Indian Daily Mail*, 28 October, 1956).

9 Fyfe, *Wearne Brothers*, passim.

10 Their main business concerns were general shipping merchants and agents, mines and estates agencies, insurance agencies and general imports business.

11 GHL, MS 271371, Borneo Company Archives, Borneo Company Ltd, Report on the Finances of Borneo Motors, Ltd, of Singapore and its subsidiaries with related correspondence 1955–56. Peat, Marwick, Mitchell & Co, 5 December 1955.

12 However, Guthrie's motor department closed in 1929. Jones, *Merchants*, pp. 109–10; Fyfe, *Wearne Brothers*, passim.

13 The Straits Motor Garage was later acquired by Cycle & Carriage in 1926.

14 Fyfe, *Wearne Brothers*, passim.

15 GHL, MS 27186, Borneo Company Archives, The Borneo Company Ltd Singapore Branch, Accounts for the year ended 31 March 1940.

16 This was proposed at its annual meeting in December 1926. The action allowed Wearne to be an entirely automotive financial concern providing hire purchase and

lending facilities with reasonable rates of interest, inadvertently promoting the sales of Ford automobiles. Annual Report *Wearne Brothers*, 1926.

17 NARA, RG 84, Singapore Consulate, 1950–1952, Box 19, United Motor Works Limited to Bureau of Foreign and Domestic Commerce, Department of Commerce, 20 March 1951. Most of the agencies held by UMW matched the listing in the *Singapore and Malayan Directory*, 1933, p. 495. See also, Jennings, *Wheels of Progress*, passim.

18 'Marketing of Parts and Accessories in British Malaya', *Commerce Reports* 48, 1930, p. 551.

19 United Motor Works Limited to Bureau of Foreign and Domestic Commerce.

20 Ibid.

21 In 1921 the US share of Malayan automobile sales dropped to 52 per cent: the 22 per cent difference was caused by a large surplus from 1920 being carried over into 1921. Irvine, 'Automotive Markets', p. 73.

22 This study makes a distinction between automobiles made by British-owned firms in Britain, automobiles made by US-owned firms in Britain, and automobiles made by US-owned firms in Canada.

23 PRO, CO 323/1005/2, 'Motor Cars: Position of Canadian Manufactured Ford Cars', 1928.

24 NARA, Records of the Department of State Relating to the Internal Affairs of British Asia, 1910–1929, US Consulate General Singapore, Monthly Report, March 1924 (encl. *Singapore Free Press*).

25 I. Sharp, *Wheels of Change: The Borneo Motors Story*, Singapore: Borneo Motors, 1993.

26 Ibid.

27 According to the British government in London, the best advertisement was the usage of British cars by government officials, which would, in turn, encourage private users to follow suit. ANM, HCO 259/1922, Circular by Winston S. Churchill, 'Encouragement of the purchase of British cars in the place of those of American make', 28 December 1921.

28 However, the 'Cubitt' five-seater petrol consumption was the same as the 'Ford' five seater though less for 20 mpg for 'Dodge' and 'Hupmobile.' ANM, HCO 259/1922, The Crown Agents for the Colonies to the Under Secretary of State, 22 November 1921.

29 Wilkins and Hill, *Ford on Six Continents*, p. 145. Carl H.A.C. Dassbach, *Global Enterprises and the World Economy*, New York: Garland, 1989, p. 279; Ray Batchelor, *Henry Ford: Mass Production, Modernism and Design*, Manchester: Manchester University Press, 1994, p. 73.

30 Wilkins and Hill, *Ford on Six Continents*, pp. 142, 287.

31 An editorial (the publication was not stated) criticised the taxation policy, saying that it was an antiquated policy abandoned by most other countries which adopted petrol tax. The writer further argued:

> Why should Malaya adopt a tax based on horse-power which is most unfair and unjust when there is at hand a means of taxation which is easy to collect and is both fair and just, under which motorists pay in proportion to the use they make of the roads?

NARA, Records of the Department of State Relating to the Internal Affairs of British Asia, 1910–1929, (Encl.) US Consulate General Singapore, Monthly Report, 1929.

32 NARA, Records of the Department of State Relating to the Internal Affairs of British Asia, 1910–1929, US Consulate General, 'New Taxes in Straits Settlements and Federated Malay States designed to aid British Motor Manufacturers', 30 October 1928.

33 Ibid.
34 Ibid.
35 NARA, Records of the Department of State Relating to the Internal Affairs of British Asia, 1910–1929, US Consulate General Singapore, Monthly Report, March 1924.
36 Wilkins and Hill, *Ford on Six Continents*, p. 18.
37 Ibid.
38 Ibid.
39 C.F.F. Wearne Brothers was founded by brothers Charles and Theodore J.B. Wearne on 1 April 1906 with initial capital of S$700. In 1912 they formed Wearne Brothers Ltd with initial capital of S$275,000. GHL, MS 27236, Borneo Company Archives, Borneo Company Ltd (encl.) '50 years progress celebrated by Wearne's', *Straits Times*, 16 December 1955.
40 Fyfe, *Wheels in Malaya*, p. 27.
41 Ibid, p. 28.
42 Ibid.
43 Not to be confused with the two Dodge brothers, makers of the popular Dodge cars. Wilkins and Hill, *Ford on Six Continents*, pp. 44–5.
44 Wilkins and Hill, *Ford on Six Continents*, p. 44.
45 Annual Report, Wearne Brothers, 1926; Fyfe, *Wheels in Malaya*, pp. 59–60.
46 NARA, Records of the Department of State Relating to the Internal Affairs of British Asia, 1910–1929, US Consulate General, Singapore, Monthly Report 24 February 1924.
47 Dodge & Seymour Exports Shipments. Ford Motor Company of Canada Ltd, Oakville, Ontario, Canada.
48 Director's Minutes, Ford Malaya 1926–27, Ford Motor Company of Canada Ltd, Oakville, Ontario, Canada; Wilkins and Hill, *Ford on Six Continents*, p. 44.
49 As explained by Nicholas in terms of the internalisation theory, opportunism and contract monitoring were the major transaction costs for manufacturing MNEs, thus encouraging the shift from intermediate modes (such as employing agents) to hierarchical modes. Stephen Nicholas, 'Agency Contracts, Institutional Modes, and the Transition to Foreign Direct Investment by British Manufacturing Multinationals before 1939', *Journal of Economic History* 43, 1983, pp. 675–86; 'The Theory of Multinational Enterprise as a Transactional Mode,' in P. Hertner and G. Jones (eds) *Multinationals: Theory and History*, Aldershot: Gower, 1986.
50 S. Tolliday, 'The rise of Ford in Britain: From sales agency to market leader, 1904–1980', in H. Bonin, Y. Lung and S.Tolliday (eds) *Ford, 1903–2003: The European History*, Volume Two, Paris, 2003, pp. 8–11.
51 Ford Motor Company of Canada Ltd, Oakville, Ontario, Canada, Director's Minutes, Ford Malaya, Singapore, 12 November 1926.
52 As announced in the *Straits Times*, 20 November 1926. Ford Malaya was a few months behind Ford India, which was set up in July 1926.
53 Ford Malaya Historical Album, A Henry Ford Centennial Publication, Public Relations Office, Ford Motor Company of Malaya Ltd, Nanyang Printers Ltd: Singapore, 1963.
54 Ford Motor Company of Canada Ltd, Oakville, Ontario, Canada, Director's Minutes, Ford Malaya, Singapore, 22 December 1926 and 30 December 1926.
55 *Straits Times*, 20 November 1926.
56 Wilkins and Hill, *Ford on Six Continents*, pp. 129–30.
57 F. Bostock and G. Jones, 'Foreign Multinationals in British Manufacturing, 1850–1962', *Business History* 36, 1994, p. 117.
58 A.D. Chandler Jr (ed.), *Giant Enterprise: Ford, General Motors, and the Automobile Industry: Sources and Readings*, New York: Harcourt, Brace and World, 1964, p. 14.
59 Chandler, *Giant Enterprise*, p. 14.
60 Fyfe, *Wearne Brothers*, p. 97.

61 Wilkins and Hill, *Ford on Six Continents*, p. 205.
62 Ford Motor Company of Canada Ltd, Oakville, Ontario, Canada, Director's Minutes, Ford Malaya 1927–33 and Ford Malaya's Ordinary General Meeting of Shareholders 1930–31.
63 Fyfe, *Wearne Brothers*, p. 103.
64 Borneo Motors did make a satisfactory profit declaring a small dividend in 1926; however, dividends were not paid between 1929 and 1933. GHL, MS 2785, Borneo Company Archives, Directors Reports: 6 October 1926, 9 October 1929 and 8 October 1930; Jones and Wale, 'Merchants as business groups', pp. 367–70. Cycle & Carriage paid a dividend of 8 per cent for preference shares and 10 cents on the S$1 ordinary shares in 1927. However, the latter experienced capital reduction in 1931 and in 1932. This led to the closure of their Penang and Ipoh branches with further reduction of capital in 1933 amounting to S$540,000. Jennings, *Wheels of Progress*, p. 34.
65 Ford Motor Company Canada Ltd, Oakville, Ontario, Canada. Overseas Shipments, Sales Division 1935.
66 *Straits Times*, 2 May 1936. For advertisements on new Ford models, see *Straits Times*, 7 May 1936.
67 Fyfe, *Wheels in Malaya*, pp. 111–12.
68 Ibid.
69 Wilkins and Hill, *Ford on Six Continents*, pp. 321–2.
70 Cited from Anthony Ooi Kwee Yang, 'A Study of Marketing in the Ford Motor Company of Malaysia, Ltd in Singapore 1966', (Academic Exercise, Department of Economics, National University of Singapore, 1967), pp. 17–19. This study relies on the above secondary work as the Malaysian Automotive Association (established in November 1960 and was known as the Federation of Malaya Motor Traders Association, later Motor Traders Association of Malaysia) unfortunately had destroyed earlier records on the Malayan automobile sales figures. However, records on the Malaysian automobile sales figures were available from the mid-1970s onwards.
71 General Accounting and Financial Analysis, Overseas Division, Ford Motor Company of Canada Ltd, Oakville, Ontario; Wilkins and Hill, *Ford on Six Continents*, p. 442.
72 Ford Malaya Historical Album.
73 *After the Battle*, Singapore 31, 1981, pp. 3–10.
74 Wilkins and Hill, *Ford on Six Continents*, pp. 350–1
75 Fyfe, *Wearne Brothers*, p. 170.
76 Ibid, pp. 170–1.
77 Annual Reports of the Road Transport Department, 1947, 1948 and 1949, Federation of Malaya, Kuala Lumpur: GPO, 1948, 1949 and 1950.
78 GHL, MS 27186, The Borneo Company Archives, The BCL Singapore Branch, Accounts for the year ended 31 March 1940; White, *Business and Government*, pp. 233 and 247.
79 Ford placed an advertisement in *Straits Times* dated 4 September 1953 to announce the arrival of this new Ford product and its marketing agent, Sime Darby & Co.
80 These agents were listed in its advertisements, see *Straits Times*, 19 September 1953; Jones, *Merchants*, p. 142.
81 *Ford Graphic*, 15 December 1952, p. 22. At that time the Australian Ford programme remained under the auspices of Ford Canada in Windsor, and Ford Australia continued to control the Ford subsidiaries in Malaya, New Zealand, South Africa and India. Wilkins and Hill, *Ford on Six Continents*, pp. 351–2.
82 The scout cars were covered with heavy armour plate for protection from the Communist attack. *Ford Graphic*, 15 December 1952, p. 22.
83 The vice president of the Studebaker Corporation, who was in Singapore in October

1950, registered a protest about the policy and suggested that the imposition of quotas would be more acceptable. Fyfe, *Wearne Brothers*, p. 181.

84 Wilkins and Hill, *Ford on Six Continents*, p. 398n.

85 Ibid, p. 398.

86 According to Robert Scruton, Ford Malaya assistant managing director, because of the ban, large numbers of Ford England products were assembled for the Malayan market, while the small number of Ford Canada products assembled in Singapore during this period were exported to Thailand. *Ford Graphic*, 2 March 1951, p. 3.

87 Ford Motor Company Canada Ltd, Oakville, Ontario, Canada, Director's Report, Ford Malaya 1954–1957.

88 *Far Eastern Economic Review* 91, 1960, pp. 455–7.

89 In 1931, General Motors Australia (established in 1926) had merged with Holden's Motor Body Builders Ltd to form General Motors-Holden Ltd. Wilkins and Hill, *Ford on Six Continents*, pp. 124–5n.

90 Ibid, p. 398n.

91 *Far East Trader* 7, 1951, p. 676.

92 *Straits Times*, 15 November 1929.

93 In 1930, Ford Canada assembled automobile units imported in semi-knocked down conditions – to reduce freight charges on the parts which came from Canada and from Ford England in Dagenham.

94 *Ford Graphic*, 2 March 1951, p. 3.

95 Interview script with Gordon Withell (managing director of Ford Malaysia 1947–1951, and 1957–1964), 1985. Ford Malaysia, Shah Alam, Selangor, Malaysia.

96 Ford Motor Company Canada Ltd, Oakville, Ontario, Canada, Directors Minutes, Ford Malaya, 28 December 1928 (encl.) Cable from Ford Canada approving the amount of dividends declared for the year 1927. Minutes of General Meeting of Directors, Ford Malaya, 1 December 1933 (encl.) Letter from President, Ford Canada to Ford Malaya, 2 October 1933 stating the amount of remuneration for Stevenson at S$1,500 per month. Wilkins and Hill, *Ford on Six Continents*, pp. 299–300.

97 *Ford Graphic*, 15 December 1952, p. 13; interview script with Gordon Withell.

98 Ford Motor Company Canada Ltd, Oakville, Ontario, Canada, Minutes of General Meeting, Ford Malaya, Singapore, 23 April 1955.

99 For examples of managerial appointments at Ford affiliates worldwide and overseas operations chart, see *Ford Graphic*, 15 December 1952, p. 13.

100 Wilkins and Hill, *Ford on Six Continents*, p. 363; Jones and Bostock, 'Foreign Multinationals in British manufacturing', p. 124.

101 ANM, HCO 259/1922, Letter from British Adviser, Kelantan to the Secretary to the HC, 22 March 1922.

102 The five-seater Ford compared to the popular British model 'Cubitt.' Ibid.

103 ANM, HCO 259/1922, Letter from British Representative in Unfederated Malay States to Winston Churchill, Colonial Office, 9 September 1922.

104 *Straits Times*, 8 April 1950.

105 Ford Motor Company Canada Ltd, Oakville, Ontario, Canada, Directors Minutes, Ford Motor Company of Malaya Ltd, 21 April, 1956. In the mid-1950s, Ford sold its Indian operations. Wilkins and Hill, *Ford on Six Continents*, p. 402.

106 M. Wilkins, 'Ford among multinational companies', in H. Bonin, Y. Lung and S. Tolliday (eds) *Ford, 1903–2003: The European History*, Volume One, Paris: P.L.A.G.E., 2003, pp. 73, 81–3. For further reading on Fordism, see J.M. Rubenstein, *Making and Selling Cars: Innovation and Change in the US Automotive Industry*, Baltimore: The Johns Hopkins University Press, 2001. See also, K. Starkey and A. McKinlay, *Strategy and the Human Resource: Ford and the Search for Competitive Advantage*, Oxford: Blackwell Business, 1993.

107 *Malay Mail*, 26 November 1926.

108 This could be seen in Britain too. By 1914, Ford, as compared to other British automobile manufacturers, was able to produce motor vehicles at an unbeatable price range of between £125 to £135. D.G. Rhys, *The Motor Industry: An Economic Survey*, London, 1972, p. 5.

109 'Automotive Markets', pp. 89–90.

110 Comparison can be made with Ford four/five seaters which were sold at S$1650 (non-self-starter) and S$1900 (self-starter) whilst an 8 HP Rover landed in Singapore cost S$2200 in 1920–1921. ANM, HCO 259/22, British Representative, State Secretary to Winston Churchill, Colonial Office, 29 March 1922.

111 Rhys, *Motor Industry*, pp. 13–15.

112 In the early 1950s, Ford and General Motors' Vauxhall in comparison with British manufacturers made higher profits per vehicle. Wilkins and Hill, *Ford on Six Continents*, p. 384.

113 Ford Malaya Historical Album; Directors Report, Ford Malaya 1956.

8 Epilogue: The Future Looks Bright

1 K.S. Jomo, *A Question of Class: Capital, the State and Uneven Development in Malaya*, Monthly Review Press, 1988; 'Whither Malaysia's New Economic Policy?' *Pacific Affairs* 63, Winter 1990–91; Hua Wu Yin, *Class and Communalism in Malaysia*, Kuala Lumpur: Zed Books, 1983; Lim Mah Hui, *Ownership and Control of the One Hundred Largest Corporations in Malaysia*, Kuala Lumpur: Pelandok Publications, 1986.

2 Sieh Lee Mei Ling, *Taking on the World: Globalisation Strategies in Malaysia*, Kuala Lumpur: McGraw-Hill (M) Sdn. Bhd., 2000.

3 'Investment from U.S.A. in the Manufacturing Sector in Malaysia', Malaysian Industrial Development Authority (hereafter MIDA), 1987.

4 'Performance of the Manufacturing and Related Services Sector 2005', MIDA, p. 10.

5 'Business Opportunities in Malaysia', MIDA, 2006.

6 'Performance of the Manufacturing and Related Services Sector, 2004', MIDA, 2005.

7 'Performance of the Manufacturing and Related Services Sector, 2004', MIDA 2005.

8 Ibid.

9 Multimedia Development Corporation (MDeC), Industry Development Division, MSC Malaysia, Cyberjaya, 2007; 'Entellium Awarded Malaysian Super Corridor Status', *Asia Pulse*, 5 December 2006.

10 'Business Opportunities in Malaysia', MIDA, 2006.

11 PacTin Annual Reports 1976–78.

12 PacTin Annual Reports, 1992–93.

13 LoC, Zemex Annual Reports 1985–87.

14 LoC, Zemex Annual Report 1987.

15 'Uniroyal Sells Natural Rubber Company to Malaysians, Cites Government Policy', *Chemical Market Reporter*, 31 December 1984; LoC, Annual Report Uniroyal Inc 1984.

16 LoC, Annual Report Uniroyal Inc 1984.

17 *Modern Tire Dealer* 65, August 1984.

18 R. Rajan, P. Volpin and L. Zinghales, 'The Eclipse of the U.S. Tire Industry', available online: http://gsbwww.uchicago.edu/fac/luigi.zingales/research/PSpapers/tie.pdf, accessed 15 June 2006.

19 M.G. Blackford and A.K. Kerr, *BFGoodrich: Tradition and Transformation, 1870–1995*, Columbus: Ohio State University Press, 1996, p. 374.

Bibliography

PRIMARY SOURCES

Malaysia

Arkib Negara Malaysia (ANM), Kuala Lumpur, Malaysia

Secretariat Files

HCO	High Commissioner's Office, 1922–40.
GAJ	General Advisor Johore, 1920–1940.
KSF	Kedah Secretariat Files, 1919–1957.
SSF	Selangor Secretariat Files, 1919–1957.

District/Land Office

KLO Kinta Land Office, 1919–1957.

Rubber Research Institute, Kuala Lumpur

This organisation carries a vast collection of materials on the development of the rubber industry in Malaya. Old issues of rubber journals include: Malayan Tin and Rubber Journal, Rubber Age and Bulletin of RGA. Also available were annual reports of selected rubber firms from various years.

The Incorporated Society of Planters, Kuala Lumpur

This organisation's library carries various issues of its official organ, *The Planter*, from 1921 to 1957.

Published Records

Report on the trade of Straits Settlements for the years 1890–1903.

Annual Reports of the Road Transport Department, Federation of Malaya, Kuala Lumpur: GPO, 1947–1950.

Federated Malay States Annual Reports, Selangor: GPO, various years.

Federated Malay States Chamber of Commerce Year Book, Kuala Lumpur: Federated Malay States Chamber of Commerce, various years (1941–1957).

Hume, W.J.P. and Dykes, F.J.B., Report and Proceedings of the Mining Conference, Taiping: Perak GPO, 1902.

Fermor, L.L., Report Upon the Mining Industry of Malaya, Kuala Lumpur: Federated Malay States Government Press, 1940.

Malaya, Foreign imports and exports (Singapore), annual series, 1921–1937.

Malaya, The foreign trade of Malaya (Singapore), annual series, 1929–39.

Straits Settlements, Blue Book (Singapore), annual series, 1870–1939.

Straits Settlements, Return of imports and exports (Singapore), annual series, 1900–1927.

Singapore and Straits Directory, 1900–1908.

Singapore and Malayan Directory, 1922–1948.

Straits Times Directory of Singapore and Malaya, 1949–1957.

Malaysian Industrial Development Authority (MIDA)

'Investment from USA in the Manufacturing Sector in Malaysia', MIDA, 1987.

'Investment from USA in the Manufacturing Sector in Malaysia', MIDA, 1986.

Reports on the Performance of the Manufacturing Sector, 1997–2004.

'Malaysia into an Era of High Technology', MIDA Report 1997.

'Performance of the Manufacturing and Related Services Sector 2004', MIDA, 2004.

'Performance of the Manufacturing and Related Services Sector 2005', MIDA, 2005.

'Business Opportunities in Malaysia', MIDA, 2006.

Multimedia Development Corporation (MDeC), MSC Malaysia.

Malaysia External Trade Development Corporation (MATRADE)

United Kingdom

UK National Archives (Public Record Office), Kew, London

Board of Trade

BT 11 Commercial Department, Correspondence and Papers. Commercial Relations and Treaties Department, 1919–1949.

BT 59 Department of Overseas Trade: Overseas Trade Development Council: Minutes and Papers, 1930–39.

BT 64 Industrial and Manufacturers Department, Correspondence and Papers, 1919–1942.

BT 70 Board of Trade: Statistical Department, 1918–1945.

Colonial Office

CO 144 Labuan Original Correspondence, 1844–1906.

CO 273 Straits Settlement, Original Correspondence, 1870–1945.

CO 323 Colonies, General: Original Correspondence, 1870–1952.

CO 717 Federated Malay States, Original Correspondence, 1920–1951.

CO 740 British Malaya, Annual Returns of imports and exports, 1921–1937.

CO 825 Eastern Department, Original Correspondence, 1935–1957.

CO 852 Far Eastern Reconstruction, Original Correspondence, various years.

Foreign Office

FO 371 Political Departments, General Correspondence, 1939–1947.

Cabinet Papers

CAB 58 Nature of Empire Trade

Ministry of Technology, Petroleum Division

POWE 33 North Borneo: Petroleum Development, 1934–1957.

The Bank of England Archive, Threadneedle St. London

EC 5 Exchange Control Act: Files, 1947–60.
EID 12 Commodities, 1947–1957.
OV 44 Sterling and Sterling Area Policy, 1947–1951.
OV 65 Malaya, Singapore, and Borneo Territories, 1929–1941.

The Guildhall Library, London

Inchcape Archives (IA)
Ms. 27178–442 Borneo Co Ltd (various years between 1910 to 1957).

Published Records

Nathan, J.E., The Census of British Malaya, 1921, London: Dunstable & Watford, 1922.
British Malaya: Trade and Commerce, London: Malay States Information Agency, 1924.
British Malaya: Production and Trade, London: Malay States Information Agency, 1932.
Malayan Trade Facts and Figures, Kuala Lumpur: Malayan Information Agency, 1929.
Beale, L.B., A Review of the Trade of British Malaya in 1928, London: HMSO, 1929.
Boulter, R., Economic Conditions in British Malaya, London: Department of Overseas Trade, 1931.
Hartland, A., Report on Economic and Commercial Conditions in Malaya, London: HMSO, 1937.
Willmot, R.B., Report on Economic and Commercial Conditions in Malaya, London: HMSO, 1939.
British Imperialism in Malaya, London: The Labour Research Department, 1926.
An Economic Review of Malaya, 1945–49, Central Office of Information, London, 1950.

United States

US National Archives, College Park, Maryland, USA

Department of State, Despatches from United States Consuls in Singapore, 1833–1906, (microfilm).
Department of State, Records relating to internal affairs of British Asia 1910–1929, (microfilm).
Record Group 59: General Records of the Department of State

Consular Correspondence, Decimal Files, 1945–49, Diplomatic Correspondence, General Administrative Records, Intelligence Reports, Lot file, Malaya, Numerical Files.

Record Group 84: Records of the Foreign Service Posts of the Department of State, 1945–55.

Record Group 151: (Records of the Bureau of Foreign and Domestic Commerce, Department of Commerce).

Annual Reports

The annual reports of the Yukon Gold Company (and its successor, Pacific Tin Consolidated Corporation and Zemex Corporation) and the United States Rubber Company (and its successor Uniroyal) deposited at the Library of Congress and the Baker Library, Harvard Business School, were especially useful. Annual reports of the former were analysed from the period 1919–1993 whilst for the latter 1898–1985. For Ford Malaya, the minutes of the board of directors and of stockholders' meetings (for various years between 1926 and 1957) including correspondence related to the agenda of the meetings deposited at the headquarter's of Ford Motor Company of Canada, Oakville, Ontario, proved especially valuable. Factory sales figures for Ford Malaya were available for the period 1911–1957 at the General Accounting and Financial Analysis Overseas Division, Ford Canada. The various materials, reports and minutes of Ford Malaysia were provided with courtesy by Mr Mike Pease, former managing director, Ford Malaysia, Shah Alam, Selangor.

Private Papers

Papers of duPont, Hagley Museum and Library, Wilmington, Delaware.

James D. Mooney Papers, Lauinger Library, Georgetown University, Washington DC.

Norman Cleaveland Papers, Rio Grande Historical Collections, New Mexico State University Library.

Company Publications

'Things That Interest Firestone Shareholders', The Firestone Tire and Rubber Co, Akron, Ohio, 1919.

Between US, United States Rubber Company, New York, 1922–1923.

Ford Malaya Historical Album, A Henry Ford Centennial Publication, Public Relations Office, Ford Motor Company of Malaya Limited, Singapore: Nanyang Printers Limited, 1963.

Published Records

Bureau of Foreign and Domestic Commerce, US Department of Commerce, Washington DC

The Bureau of Foreign Commerce was established in 1897 by the Department of State and for the first time approved the public distribution of diplomatic, consular, and other commercial reports. In 1912, the Bureau of Foreign and Domestic Commerce was created in the Department of Commerce and Labor. It acted as a major fact-finding organisation and soon became the centre for promoting and protecting US business interests around the world. Its publications, Trade Information Bulletins, Commerce Reports and Foreign Commerce Weekly, provided vital information on trade and investment opportunities in Malaysia and the South East Asian region.

Bliss, D.C., Market for Machinery in British Malaya, 1931.

Bruins, J.H., Market for Canned Foods in British Malaya, Trade Info Bulletin No. 534, 1928.

Dickens, P., American Direct Investments in Foreign Countries, Trade Info Bulletin, No 731, 1930.

---- A New Estimate of American Investments Abroad, 1931.

---- American Direct Investments in Foreign Countries, 1936, Economic series no. 1, 1938.

Eldridge, F.R., Trading with Malaysia, Trade Information Bulletin No. 377, 1925.

Figart, D.M., The Plantation Rubber Industry in the Middle East, Trade Promotion Series, No. 2, 1925.

Fowler, J.A., Motor Vehicle Market in Netherlands East Indies and British Malaya, Trade Information Bulletin No. 25, 1922.

Irvine,W.I., Automotive Markets in China, British Malaya and Chosen, Special Agent Series, No. 221, 1923.

Martin, C.D., Foreign Markets for Tractors, Trade Information Bulletin No. 502, 1927.

Odell, R.M., Cotton Goods in the Straits Settlements, 1916.

Sammons, R.L. and Abelson, M., American Direct Investments in Foreign Countries – 1940, Economic series, no. 20, 1942.

The Balance of International Payments of the US in 1933, 1934.

Commerce Reports

'British Malaya Buys More American Goods', Commerce Reports 27, 1930.

'Marketing of Parts and Accessories in British Malaya, Commerce Reports 48, 1930.

'British Malaya Offers Opportunity for American Goods', Commerce Reports 50, 1939.

'Marketing of Parts and Accessories in British Malaya – Part II, 49, 1930, 631–4.

Foreign Commerce Weekly

'Malayan Basic Industries Respond to American Demand during 1940', Foreign Commerce Weekly, 19 April 1941.

US Department of Treasury

Census of American-Owned Assets in Foreign Countries, 1947.

US Census Bureau

Foreign Trade Statistics, Data Dissemination Branch, Foreign Trade Division, 2003.

US Census Bureau, "Foreign Trade Statistics", available online: www.census.gov/foreign-trade/balance/c5570.html, accessed 16 January 2006.

Canada

Published Reports

Ford Motor Company of Canada Ltd, Oakville, Ontario.
General Accounting and Financial Analysis Overseas Division, Ford Canada.
Ford Motor Company of Malaya Ltd, Annual Reports, 1926–1957.

SECONDARY SOURCES

Abdul Khalid, A.A., 'The Federated Malay States: Growth and Development of the Import Trade, 1900–1940', in Muhammad Abu Bakar, Amarjit Kaur and Abdullah Zakaria (eds), Historia, Kuala Lumpur: University of Malaya, 1984, pp. 325–56.

—— 'The Import Trade of the FMS, 1900–1940: Some Preliminary Observations', in Mohd. Amin Hassan, Nik Hassan Shuhaimi Nik Abdul Rahman (eds), Eighth Conference, International Association of Historians of Asia, Malaysia: Universiti Kebangsaan Malaysia, 1993, pp. 565–70.

Ahmat, S., 'American Trade with Singapore, 1819–1865', Journal of Malayan Branch of Royal Asiatic Society 38, 1965, pp. 241–57.

—— 'Some Problems of the Rhode Island Traders in Java, 1799–1833, Journal Southeast Asian Studies 6, 1965.

—— 'Joseph B. Balestier: The First American Consul in Singapore 1833–1852', Journal of Malayan Branch of Royal Asiatic Society 39, 1966, pp. 108–22.

Allen, G.C. and Donnithorne, A.G., Western Enterprise in Indonesia and Malaya: A Study in Economic Development, London: George Allen & Unwin, 1957.

Allen, J. de V., The Malayan Union, New Haven: Yale University Press, 1967.

—— 'The Colonial Office and the Malay States, 1867–73', Journal of the Malaysian Branch of the Royal Asiatic Society, 36, 1963.

Amarjit Kaur, Bridge and Barrier: Transport and Communications in Colonial Malaya 1870–1957, Singapore: Oxford University Press, 1985.

Babcock, G.D., History of the United States Rubber Company, Indiana: Indiana University, 1966.

Baritz, L., The Servants of Power: A History of the Use of Social Science in Industry, Middletown, CT: Wesleyan University Press, 1960.

Barlow, C., The Natural Rubber Industry: Its Development, Technology, and Economy in Malaysia, Kuala Lumpur: Oxford University Press, 1978.

Barnet, R.J. and Muller, R.E., Global Reach: The Power of the Multinational Corporations, New York: Simon & Schuster, 1974.

Batchelor, R., Henry Ford: Mass Production, Modernism and Design, Manchester: Manchester University Press, 1994.

Bauer, P.T., The Rubber Industry: A Study in Competition and Monopoly, London: Longman, 1948.

Blackford, M.G., The Rise of Modern Business in Great Britain, the United States, and Japan, Chapel Hill: The University of North Carolina Press, 1998.

—— and Kerr, A.K., Business Enterprise in American History, Boston: Houghton-Mifflin Co, 1994.

—— and Kerr, A.K., BFGoodrich: Tradition and Transformation, 1870–1995, Columbus: Ohio State University Press, 1996.

Bliss, D.C., Market for Machinery in British Malaya, Washington: GPO, 1931.

Bonin, H., Lung, Y. and Tolliday, S. (eds) Ford, 1903–2003: The European History, Vol. 2, Paris, 2003.

Bottomley, A., 'The role of Foreign Branch Plants in the Industrialisation of Singapore', The Malayan Economic Review 7, 1962.

Brien, T.F.O., 'Rich beyond the dreams of avarice: the Guggenheims in Chile', Business History Review 63, 1989.

Brown, I., Economic Change in South-East Asia c. 1830–1980, Oxford: Oxford University Press, 1997.

Brown, R.A., Capital and Entrepreneurship in Southeast Asia, London: Macmillan, 1994.

Buckley, C.B., An Anecdotal History of Old Times in Singapore, 1819–67, Vol. 1, Singapore, 1902.

Buckley, P. and Casson, M., The Future of the Multinational Enterprise, London: MacMillan, 1976.

Butcher, J.G., The British in Malaya 1880–1941: The Social History of a European Community in Colonial Southeast Asia, Kuala Lumpur: Oxford University Press, 1979.

Cain, P.J. and Hopkins, A.G., British Imperialism, 1688–2000, Harlow: Longman, 2001.

Callahan, J.M., American Relations in the Pacific and the Far East, Baltimore: Johns Hopkins Press, 1901.

Callis, H.G., Foreign Capital in South East Asia, New York: Institute of Pacific Relations, 1942.

Cartensen, F.V., American Enterprise Abroad: Case Studies of Singer and International Harvester in Imperial Russia, Chapel Hill: University of North Carolina Press, 1984.

Casson, M., The Entrepreneur. An Economic Theory, Oxford: Martin Robertson, 1982.

Caves, R.E., 'International Corporations: The Industrial Economics of Foreign Investment', Economica 38, 1971, pp. 1–27.

Chandler, A.D., Strategy and Structure, Cambridge, Mass.: MIT Press, 1962.

—— Giant Enterprise: Ford, General Motors, and the Automobile Industry: Sources and Readings, New York: Harcourt, Brace and World, 1964.

—— The Visible Hand: The Managerial Revolution in American Business, Cambridge, Mass.: Harvard University Press, 1977.

—— 'The Emergence of Managerial Capitalism', Business History Review 58, 1984, pp. 473–503.

—— Scale and Scope, Cambridge, Mass.: Harvard University Press, 1990.

—— Amatori, F. and Hikino, T. (eds), Big Business and the Wealth of Nations, Cambridge: Cambridge University Press, 1997.

Chapman, S., The Rise of Merchant Banking, London: George Allen & Unwin, 1984.

—— Merchant Enterprise in Britain: From the Industrial Revolution to World War I , Cambridge: Cambridge University Press, 1992.

Chew, E., 'British Intervention in Malaya: A Reconsideration', Journal of Southeast Asian History 5, 1965, pp. 81–93.

—— 'Swettenham and British Residential Rule in West Malaya', Journal of the Malaysian Branch of the Royal Asiatic Society 5, 1974, pp. 165–78.

Chiang H.D., 'The Statistics of the Straits Settlements Foreign Trade, 1870–1915', Malayan Economic Review 9–10, 1964–1965, pp. 73–83.

—— 'The Origin of the Malaysian Currency System (1867–1906)', Journal of Malayan Branch of Royal Asiatic Society 39, 1966, pp. 1–18.

—— 'Sino-British Mercantile Relations in Singapore's Entrepot Trade, 1870–1915', in Jerome C. and Nicholas T. (eds), Studies in the Social History of China and S.E. Asia, Cambridge: Cambridge University Press, 1970, pp. 247–66.

—— A History of Straits Settlements Foreign Trade 1870–1915, Singapore: National Museum Singapore, 1978.

Cleaveland, N., 'The most travelled Dredge in the World', Malaya in History 5, 1959.

—— Bang! Bang! in Ampang: Dredging tin during Malaya's Emergency, San Pedro, Calif.: Symcon Publishing Company, 1973.

Clegg, P. and Shaw, T., The Caribbean Banana Trade: From Colonialism to Globalization, Basingstoke: Palgrave, 2002.

Coase, R.H., 'The Nature of the Firm', Economica 4, 1937, pp. 386–405.

—— 'The Nature of the Firm: Influence', in O.E. Williamson and S.G. Winter (eds), The Nature of the Firm: Origins, Evolution and Development, Oxford: Oxford University Press, 1993.

Cohen, R.B., Felton, N., Nikosi, M. and van Liere, J. (eds), The Multinational Corporation: A Radical Approach, papers by Stephen Hymer, Cambridge: Cambridge University Press, 1979.

Constantine, S., The Making of British Colonial Development Policy, 1914–1940, London: Frank Cass, 1984.

Courtenay, P.P., Geography of Trade and Development in Malaya, London: G. Bell & Sons, Ltd, 1972.

Cowan, C.D., Nineteenth Century Malaya, London: Oxford University Press, 1961.

Cox, H., The Global Cigarette: Origins and Evolution of British American Tobacco, 1880–1945, Oxford: Oxford University Press, 2000.

Curtis, M., 'The ambiguities of power: British foreign policy since 1945', The Ecologist 26, 1996, pp. 5–12.

Cushman, J.W. (ed. Reynolds, C.J.), Family and State: The Formation of a Sino-Thai Tin Mining Dynasty 1797–1932, Singapore: Oxford University Press, 1991.

Dassbach, C.H.A.C., Global Enterprises and the World Economy, New York: Garland, 1989.

Davies, R.B., Peacefully Working to Conquer the World: Singer Sewing Machines in Foreign Markets, 1884–1920, New York: Arno Press, 1976.

Davis, J.H., The Guggenheims: An American Epic, New York: William Morrow and Company, 1978.

Demsetz, H., 'The theory of the firm revisited', Journal of Law, Economics and Organisation 4, 1988, pp. 141–61.

Ding, C.H., History of the Straits Settlements Foreign Trade, 1870-1915, Singapore: National Museum, 1978.

Dosal, P., Doing Business with the Dictators: A Political History of United Fruit in Guatemala, 1899–1940, Wilmington, DE: Scholarly Resources, 1993.

Drabble, J.H., 'Investment in the Rubber Industry in Malaya, c. 1900–1922', Journal of Southeast Asian Studies 3, 1972.

—— Rubber in Malaya 1876–1922: The Genesis of the Industry, Kuala Lumpur: Oxford University Press, 1973.

—— 'More on the Financing of Malayan Rubber 1905–23', Economic History Review 27, 1974, pp. 108–20.

—— 'Some Thoughts on the Economic Development of Malaya under British Administration', Journal of Southeast Asian Studies 5, 1974, pp. 199–208.

—— Malayan Rubber: The Interwar Years, London: Macmillan, 1991.

—— Economic History of Malaysia, c.1800–1990: The Transition to Modern Economic Growth, London: Macmillan, 2000.

—— and Drake, P.J., 'The British Agency Houses in Malaysia: Survival in a Changing World', Journal of Southeast Asian Studies 12, 1981, pp. 297–328.

Drake, P.J., 'The Economic Development of British Malaya to 1914: An Essay in Historiography with Some Questions for Historians', Journal of Southeast Asian Studies 2, 1979, pp. 262–90.

Drummond, I.M., Imperial Economic Policy 1917–1939: Studies in Expansion and Protection, London: G. Allen & Unwin, 1974.

Dunning, John H., 'Trade, Location of Economic Activity and the MNE: A Search for an Eclectic Approach', in B. Ohlin et al. (eds), The International Allocation of Economic Activity, London: Macmillan, 1977, pp. 395–418.

—— 'Explaining Changing Patterns of International Production: In Defence of the Eclectic Theory', Oxford Bulletin of Economics and Statistics 41, 1979, pp. 269–95.

—— International Production and the Multinational Enterprise, London: George Allen & Unwin, 1981.

—— Explaining International Production, London: Unwin Hyman, 1988.

—— Multinational Enterprises and the Global Economy, Wokingham, Berkshire: Addison Wesley, 1993.

—— 'Forty Years On: American Investment in British Manufacturing Industry Revisited', Transnational Corporations 8, 1999, pp. 1–34.

—— 'The Eclectic (OLI) Paradigm of International Production: Past, Present and Future', International Journal of the Economics of Business 8, 2001, pp. 173–90.

Emerson, R., Malaysia: A Study in Direct and Indirect Rule, Kuala Lumpur: University of Malaya Press, 1964.

Falkus, M., 'Early British business in Thailand', in R.P.T. Davenport-Hines and Geoffrey Jones (eds), British Business in Asia since 1860, Cambridge: Cambridge University Press, 1989.

Farley, M.S., 'America's Stake in the Far East, I: Trade', Far Eastern Survey 5, 1936, pp. 161–70.

Ferguson, N., Empire: The Rise and Demise of the British World Order and the Lessons for Global Power, New York: Basic Books, 2003.

Fieldhouse, D.K., The West and the Third World: Trade, Colonialism, Dependence and Development, Oxford: Blackwell Publishers, 1999.

Fifield, R.H., Americans in Southeast Asia: The Roots of Commitment, New York: Thomas Y. Crowell Company, 1973.

Firestone, H.S., Men and Rubber: The Story of Business, New York: Doubleday, Page & Co, 1926.

French, M.J., 'The Emergence of US MNE: the Goodyear Tire and Rubber Company, 1910–1939', Economic History Review 40, 1987, pp. 64–79.

Froh, Riley, Edgar B. Davis and Sequences in Business Capitalism: From Shoes to Rubber to Oil, New York: Garland Publishing Incorporated, 1993.

Fui K. Soong, 'A Profile of US Companies in Malaysia', Ekonomika 16, 2004, pp. 1–3.

Fyfe, C., Wheels in Malaya: The Wearne Brothers and Their Company, Claremont, Western Australia: Lana Press, 2002.

Gatrell, V.C.G., The Entrepot Trade of Singapore, Singapore, 1945.

Ghazali, A.Z., 'Diplomasi Kapal Perang: Pembedilan Ke Atas Terengganu, 1862', Malaysia Dari Segi Sejarah 13, 1984.

Ghosh, K.K., Twentieth Century Malaysia: Politics of Decentralization of Power 1920–29, Calcutta: Progressive Publishers, 1977.

Godley, A., 'Pioneering Foreign Direct Investment in British Manufacturing', Business History Review 73, 1999.

Goodlad, G., British Foreign and Imperial Policy, 1865–1919, London: Routledge, 2000.

Gould, J.W., 'Sumatra-America's Pepperpot 1784–1873', Essex Institute Historical Collections 112, 1956, pp. 203–49.

—— 'The First American Contact with Asia', Claremont Asian Studies 7, 1960, pp. 1–11.

—— Americans in Sumatra, The Hague: Martinus Nijhoff, 1961.

—— The United States and Malaysia, Cambridge, Mass.: Harvard University Press, 1969.

___ 'American Imperialism in South East Asia before 1898', Journal of Southeast Asian History 3, 1972.

Greig, G.E., Mining in Malaya, London: Malay States Information Agency, 1924.

Griffiths, J., 'Give my regards to Uncle Billy . . .': The Rites and Rituals of Company Life at Lever Brothers, c1900–c1990', Business History 37, 1995, pp. 25–46.

Gullick, J.M., Malaya, London: Ernest Benn, 1964, p. 41.

—— Malay Society in the Late Nineteenth Century: The Beginnings of Change, and Rulers and Residents: Influence and Power in the Malayan States 1870–1920, Singapore: Oxford University Press, 1992.

Hack, K., '"Iron Claws on Malaya": The Historiography of the Malayan Emergency', Journal of Southeast Asian Studies 30, 1999.

Hannah, L., The Rise of the Corporate Economy, London: Methuen, 1976.

Harper, T.N., The End of Empire and the Making of Malaya, Cambridge: Cambridge University Press, 1999.

Havinden, M. and Meredith, D., Colonialism and Development: Britain and Her Tropical Colonies, 1850–1960, London: Routledge, 1993.

Hayes, S.P., The Beginning of American Aid to Southeast Asia: The Griffin Mission of 1950, Toronto, Canada: Heath Lexington Books, 1971.

Hedges, E.S., Tin in Social and Economic History, New York: St Martin's Press, 1964.

Hennart, J-F., A Theory of Multinational Enterprise, Ann Arbor, Mich.: University of Michigan Press, 1982.

—— 'Internalization in Practice: Early Foreign Direct Investments in Malaysian Tin Mining', Journal of International Business Studies 17, 1986, pp. 131–43.

—— 'The Tin Industry', in Mark Casson (ed.), Multinationals and World Trade, London: Allen & Unwin, 1986.

—— 'The transaction cost theory of multinational enterprise', in C. N. Pitelis and R. Sugden (eds), The Nature of the Transnational Firm, London: Routledge, 1991, pp. 81–116.

—— 'Free-standing firms and the internalization of markets for financial capital: a response to Casson', Business History 36, 1995, pp. 118–132.

Higgins, B., 'Western Enterprise and the Economic Development of Southeast Asia', Pacific Affairs 31, 1958, pp. 74–87.

Hillman, J., 'Malaya and International Tin Cartel', Modern Asian Studies 22, 1988, pp. 237–61.

—— 'The impact of the international tin restriction schemes on the return to equity of tin mining companies, 1927–39', Business History 39, 1997, pp. 65–81.

Hotchkiss, S.H., 'Operations of an American Rubber Company in Sumatra and the Malay Peninsula', The Annals of the American Academy 112, 1924.

Hua Wu Yin, Class and Communalism in Malaysia, Kuala Lumpur: Zed Books, 1983.

Huff, W.G., 'The development of the rubber market in pre-World War II Singapore', Journal of Southeast Asian Studies 24, 1993, pp. 285–306.

—— The Economic Growth of Singapore: Trade and Development in the Twentieth Century, Cambridge: Cambridge University Press, 1994.

—— 'Monetization and financial development in South East Asia before the Second World War', Economic History Review 2, 2003, pp. 300–45.

Hyam, R., Britain's Imperial Century 1815–1914, A Study of Empire and Expansion, London: B.T. Batsford, 1976.

Hymer, S., The International Operations of National Firms, Cambridge, Mass.: MIT Press, 1976.

Jackson, J.C., Planters and Speculators: Chinese and European Agricultural Enterprise in Malaya, 1786–1921, Kuala Lumpur: University of Malaya Press, 1968.

Jacoby, S.M., Modern Manors: Welfare Capitalism since the New Deal, New Jersey: Princeton University Press, 1997.

Jennings, E., Wheels of Progress: 75 years of Cycle & Carriage, Singapore: Meridien Communications, 1975.

Jesudason, J.V., Ethnicity and the Economy, Singapore: Oxford University Press, 1989.

John, R.R., 'Elaborations, Revisions, Dissents: Alfred D. Chandler Jr.'s the Visible Hand after twenty years', Business History Review 71, 1997, pp. 151–200.

Johnston, S.P., Gold Dredges: The Part played by the Yuba Manufacturing Company in the Great Romance of Dredging for Placer Gold, Platinum and Tin, San Francisco: John Henry Nash, 1927.

Jomo, K.S., A Question of Class: Capital, the State and Uneven Development in Malaya, New York: Monthly Review Press, 1988.

—— 'Whither Malaysia's New Economic Policy?', Pacific Affairs 63, Winter 1990–91.

Jones, G., The State and the Emergence of the British Oil Industry, London: Macmillan Press, 1981.

—— British Multinational Banking 1830–1990, Oxford: Clarendon Press, 1993.

—— The Evolution of International Business: An Introduction, London: Routledge, 1996.

—— 'US Multinationals in British Manufacturing before 1962', Business History Review 70, 1996, pp. 207–56.

—— 'Global Perspectives and British Paradoxes', Business History Review 71, 1997, pp. 291–8.

—— 'Great Britain: Big Business, Management, and Competitiveness in Twentieth Century Britain', in A.D. Chandler Jnr, Franco Amatori, and Takashi Hikino (eds), Big Business and The Wealth of Nations, Cambridge: Cambridge University Press, 1997.

—— (ed.) The Multinational Traders, London: Routledge, 1998.

—— Merchants to Multinationals: British Trading Companies in the Nineteenth and Twentieth Centuries, Oxford: Oxford University Press, 2000.

—— 'Control, Performance, and Knowledge Transfers in Large Multinationals: Unilever in the United States, 1945–1980', Business History Review 76, 2002, pp. 435–78.

—— Multinationals and Global Capitalism, Oxford: Oxford University Press, 2005

—— and Bostock, F., 'U.S. multinationals in British manufacturing before 1962', Business History Review 70, 1996, pp. 207–9. Kellenbenz, H., 'German Trade Relations with the Indian Ocean from the End of the Eighteenth Century to 1870', Journal of Southeast Asian Studies 13, 1982.

—— and Frances B., 'Foreign Multinationals in British Manufacturing, 1850–1962', in G. Jones (ed.), The Making of Global Enterprise, London: Frank Cass, 1994.

—— and Franco-Amatori (eds), Business History Around the World, Cambridge: Cambridge University Press, 2003.
—— and Galvez-Munoz, L. (eds), Foreign Multinationals in the United States: Management and Performance, London: Routledge, 2002.
—— and Hertner, P. (eds) Multinationals: Theory and History, Aldershot: Gower, 1986.
—— and Kirby, M. (eds), Competitiveness and the State Government and Business in Twentieth-Century Britain, Manchester: Manchester University Press, 1991.
—— and Rose, M.B., Family Capitalism, London: Frank Cass, 1993.
—— and Van Helten, J.J., 'British Business in Malaysia and Singapore Since the 1870s', in R.P.T. Davenport-Hines and Geoffrey Jones (eds) British Business in Asia Since 1860, Cambridge: Cambridge University Press, 1989.
—— and Wale, J., 'Merchants as Business Groups: British Trading Companies in Asia before 1945', Business History Review 72, 1998, pp. 367–406.
—— and Wale, J., 'Diversification Strategies of British Trading Companies: Harrisons & Crosfield c. 1900–c.1980', Business History 41, 1999, pp. 69–101.
Khasnor, J., The Emergence of the Modern Malay Administrative Elite, Kuala Lumpur: Oxford University Press, 1984.
Khoo Kay Kim, 'The Origin of British Administration in Malaya', Journal of Malayan Branch of Royal Asiatic Studies 39, 1966.
—— 'Malayan Agriculture, 1920–21', Journal of the Malaysian Branch of the Royal Asiatic Society 72, 1999.
Kindleberger, C.P., American Business Abroad – Six Lectures on Direct Investment, New Haven: Yale University Press, 1969.
Kirzner, I.M., Competition and Entrepreneurship, Chicago: University of Chicago Press, 1973.
Klein, M., 'Coming Full Circle: The Study of Big Business since 1950', Enterprise and Society 2, 2001, pp. 425–60.
Knight, F.H., Risk, Uncertainty, and Profit, Boston: Houghton Mifflin, 1967.
—— 'The Pangkor Engagement of 1874', Journal of the Malaysian Branch of the Royal Asiatic Society 41, 1974.
Knorr, K.E., Tin under Control, California: Stanford University, Food Research Institute, 1945.
Koehn, N.F., Brand New: How Entrepreneurs Earned Consumers' Trust from Wedgwood to Dell, Boston, Mass.: Harvard Business School Press, 2001.
Kumar R., '"Transmogrifying" Malaya: the impact of Sir Gerald Templer (1952–54)', Journal of Southeast Asian Studies 32, 2001, pp. 79–92.
Legge, J., 'The Colonial Office and Governor Ord', Journal of Southeast Asian Studies 29, 1998, pp. 1–8.
Leong Yee Fong, Labour and Trade Unionism in Colonial Malaya. A Study of the Socio-economic and Political Bases of the Malayan Labour Movement 1930–1957, Penang: Universiti Sains Malaysia Publisher, 1999.
Lewis, C., America's Stake in International Investment, Washington DC: The Brookings Institution, 1938.
Li Dun Jen, British Malaya: An Economic Analysis, Kuala Lumpur: Institut Analisa Sosial, 1982.
Lief, A., The Firestone Story: A History of the Firestone Tire and Rubber Company, New York: McGraw-Hill Book Company, 1951.
Lim Chong Yah, Economic Development of Modern Malaya, Kuala Lumpur: Oxford University Press, 1967.

Lim Mah Hui, Ownership and Control of the One Hundred Largest Corporations in Malaysia, Kuala Lumpur: Pelandok Publications, 1986.

Lim Teck Ghee, Peasants and their Agricultural Economy in Colonial Malaya, Kuala Lumpur: Oxford University Press, 1977.

Lockwood, W.W., 'America's Stake in the Far East, II: Investments', Far Eastern Survey 5, 1936, pp. 175–85.

Loh Kok Wah, F., Beyond the Tin Mines: Coolies, Squatters, and New Villagers in the Kinta Valley, Malaysia c. 1880–1890, Singapore: Oxford University Press, 1988.

Loh Wei Leng, 'The colonial state and business: the policy environment in Malaya in the inter-war years', Journal of Southeast Asian Studies 33, 2002, pp. 243–57.

Lomask, M., Seed Money: The Guggenheim Story, New York: Farrar, Straus and Co., 1964.

MacDonald, B., Imperial Patriot: Charles Alma Baker and the History of Limestone Downs, Wellington: Bridget William Books, 1993.

Macintyre, D., 'Britain's Intervention in Malaya: the origin of Lord Kimberley's Instructions to Sir Andrew Clarke in 1873', Journal of Southeast Asian Studies 2, 1961, pp. 47–69.

Martin, S.M., The UP Saga, Copenhagen: Denmark, NIAS Press, 2003.

Meyer, F.V., Britain: The Sterling Area and Europe, London: Bowes & Bowes Publishers, 1952.

Meyer, S., The Five Dollar Day: Labor, Management, and Social Control in the Ford Motor Company, 1908–1920, Albany: State University of New York Press, 1981.

Miller, A.R., 'American Investments in the Far East', Far Eastern Survey 29, 1950, pp. 81–9.

Miller, R.H., The United States and Vietnam 1787–1941, Washington DC: National Defense University Press, 1990.

Mills, L.A., British Rule in Eastern Asia, London: Oxford University Press, 1942.

—— 'British Malaya 1824–1867', Journal of the Malaysian Branch of the Royal Asiatic Society 33, 1960.

Moberg, M., 'Crown colony as Banana Republic: the United Fruit Company in British Honduras, 1900–1920', Journal of Latin American Studies 28, 1996, pp. 357–82.

—— and Striffler, S. (eds), Banana Wars: Power, Production and History in the Americas, Durham: Duke University Press, 2003.

Mohammad Yamin, 'A Reassessment of Hymer's Contribution to the Theory of the Transnational Corporation', in Pitelis, C.N. and R. Sugden (eds), The Nature of the Transnational Firm, London: Routledge, 1991.

Newsinger, J., 'Counter revolution: the Malayan example', Monthly Review 45, 1994, pp. 19–29.

Nicholas, S., 'Agency Contracts, Institutional Modes and the Transition to Foreign Direct Investment by British Manufacturing Multinationals before 1939', Journal of Economic History 43, 1983, pp. 675–86.

—— 'The Overseas Marketing Performance of British Industry, 1870–1914', Economic History Review 37, 1984, pp. 489–506

Nonini, D.M., British Colonial Rule and the Resistance of the Malay Peasantry, 1900–1957, New Haven: Yale University Southeast Asian Studies, 1992.

Parkinson, C., British Intervention in Malaya 1867–1877, Singapore: University of Malaya Press, 1960.

Phelps, D.M., Effect of the Foreign Market on the Growth and Stability of the American Automobile Industry, Ann Arbor: University of Michigan, 1931.

Porter, B., Critics of Empire, London: Macmillan, 1968.

Porter, M.E., Competitive Advantage: Creating and Sustaining Superior Performance, New York: Free Press, 1985.

Purcell, V., Outline of a Colony, Thomas Nelson, London, 1946.

Puthucheary, J., Ownership and Control in the Malayan Economy, Singapore: Eastern Universities Press, 1960.

Ramakrishna, K., 'Transmogrifying' Malaya: the impact of Sir Gerald Templer (1952–54)', Journal of South East Asian Studies 32, 2001, p. 79.

Ranjit Singh, D.S., Brunei 1839–1983: The Problems of Political Survival, Singapore: Oxford University Press, 1984.

—— The Making of Sabah 1865–1941, Kuala Lumpur: University of Malaya Press, 2001.

Rasiah, R., Foreign Capital and Industrialization in Malaysia, London: MacMillan, 1995.

Rawlins, J. Sig. D., 'French Enterprise in Malaya', Journal of the Malayan Branch of Royal Asiatic Society 39, 1966.

Rhys, D.G., The Motor Industry: An Economic Survey, London, 1972.

Rose, M.B., Firms, Networks and Business Values: The British and American Cotton Industries since 1750, Cambridge: Cambridge University Press, 2000.

Rostow, W.W., The Stages of Economic Growth, Cambridge: Cambridge University Press, 1960.

Rubenstein, J.M., Making and Selling Cars: Innovation and Change in the US Automotive Industry, Baltimore: Johns Hopkins University Press, 2001.

Rudner, M., 'The Organization of the British Military Administration in Malaya, 1946–48', Journal of Southeast Asian History 9, 1968, pp. 95–106.

—— 'Rubber Strategy for Post-War Malaya, 1945–48', Journal of Southeast Asian Studies 1, 1970, pp. 23–36.

—— 'Malayan Rubber Policy: Development and Anti-Development during the 1950s', Journal of Southeast Asian Studies 7, 1976, pp. 235–59.

Sadka, E., 'The Colonial Office and the Protected Malay States', in Bastin, J. and R. Roolvink (eds), Malayan and Indonesian Studies, Kuala Lumpur: Oxford University Press, 1964.

Schmitz, C., 'The Rise of Big Business in the World Copper Industry 1870–1930', Economic History Review 39, 1986, pp. 392–410.

Schumpeter, J.A., History of Economic Analysis, New York: Oxford University Press, 1954.

—— The Theory of Economic Development, Cambridge, Mass.: Harvard University Press, 1959.

Schwinges, C., 'America's Greatest Stake in Rubber: Modern Industry in the Midst of the Sumatra Jungle', The Outlook 146, 1927, pp. 156–8.

Sharp, I., Wheels of Change: The Borneo Motors Story, Singapore: Borneo Motors, 1993.

Sharp, L., 'Colonial Regimes in South East Asia', Far Eastern Survey 15, 1946, pp. 49–53.

Short, A., In Pursuit of Mountain Rats: The Communist Insurrection in Malaya, Singapore: Cultured Lotus, 2000.

Sieh Lee Mei Ling, Taking on the World: Globalisation Strategies in Malaysia, Kuala Lumpur: McGraw-Hill (M) Sdn Bhd, 2000.

Sluyterman, K.E., Dutch Enterprise in the Twentieth Century: Business Strategies in Small Open Country, London: Routledge, 2005.

Smith, C., Child, J. and Rowlinson, M. (eds), Reshaping Work: The Cadbury Experience, Cambridge: Cambridge University Press, 1990.

Sodhy, P., 'United States Consuls in Singapore 1859–1880', Journal of Malayan Branch of Royal Asiatic Society 56, 1983, pp. 12–33.

—— The US-Malaysian Nexus: Themes in Superpower-Small State Relations, Kuala Lumpur: ISIS, 1991.

Song Ong Siang, One Hundred Years' History of the Chinese in Singapore, Singapore: University Malaya Press, 1967.

Sopiee, M. N., From Malayan Union to Singapore Separation, Kuala Lumpur: University Malaya Press, 1974.

Stahl, K.M., The Metropolitan Organization of British Colonial Trade, London: Faber and Faber, 1951.

Stanciu, L., 'Free Standing Companies in the Oil Sector in Romania and Poland before 1948: Typologies and Competencies', Business History 42, 2000, pp. 27–66.

Starkey, K. and McKinley, A., Strategy and the Human Resource: Ford and the Search for Competitive Advantage, Oxford: Blackwell, 1993.

Stockwell, A.J., British Policy and Malay Politics during the Malayan Union Experiment, 1942–1948, Kuala Lumpur: Malayan Branch of Royal Asiatic Society, 1979.

—— '"A Widespread and Long-concocted Plot to Overthrow the Government in Malaya"?: The Origins of the Malayan Emergency', Journal of Imperial and Commonwealth History 21, 1993, pp. 66–88.

Stoler, A.L., Capitalism and Confrontation in Sumatra's Plantation Belt, 1870–1979, Ann Arbor: University of Michigan, 1985.

Stubbs, R., 'Malaya's Rubber Smallholding Industry: Crisis and the search for stability,' Pacific Affairs 56, 1983.

—— 'The Malayan Emergency and the development of the Malaysian state', in Paul B.R. and Richard S. (eds), The Counter-Insurgent State: Guerrilla Warfare and State Building in the Twentieth Century, Houndmills: Macmillan, 1997.

Sunderland, D., '"Objectionable Parasites": The Crown Agents and the Purchase of Crown Colony Government Stores, 1880–1914', Business History 41, 1999.

Tarling, N., Britain, the Brookes and Brunei, Kuala Lumpur: Oxford University Press, 1971.

—— Imperialism in Southeast Asia: A Fleeting, Passing Phase, London: Routledge, 2001.

Tate, D.J.M., The RGA History of the Plantation Industry in the Malay Peninsula, Kuala Lumpur: Oxford University Press, 1996.

Thio, E., British Policy in The Malay Peninsula, 1880–1910, Singapore: University of Malaya Press, 1969.

Thoburn, J., Multinationals, Mining, and Development: A Study of the Tin Industry, Hampshire: Gower, 1981.

Thompson, V., Postmortem on Malaya, New York: Macmillan, 1943.

Thurston, A., Records of the Colonial Office, Dominions Office, Commonwealth Relations Office and Commonwealth Office, London: HMSO, 1995.

Tolliday, S., 'The rise of Ford in Britain: From sales agency to market leader, 1904–1980', in H. Bonin, Y. Lung and S. Tolliday (eds), Ford, 1903–2003: The European History, Vol. 2, Paris, 2003.

Tregonning, K.G., 'American Activity in North Borneo, 1865–1881', Pacific Historical Review 23, 1954.

—— 'Straits Tin: A brief account of the first seventy-five years of The Straits Trading Company, Limited', Journal of the Malayan Branch of Royal Asiatic Society 36, 1963.

—— 'How Germany made Malaya British', Asian Studies 2, 1964, pp. 180–7.

Turnbull, C.M., The Straits Settlements (1826–1867): Indian Presidency to Crown Colony, Kuala Lumpur: Oxford University Press, 1972.

Vernon, R., Sovereignty at Bay: The Multinational Spread of United States Enterprises, New York: Basic Books, 1971.

Vila, George R., The Story of UNIROYAL, New York: The Newcommen Society, 1968.

Voon Phin Keong, Western Rubber Planting Enterprise in Southeast Asia, 1876–1921, Kuala Lumpur: University Malaya Press, 1976.

—— American Rubber Planting Enterprise in the Philippines, 1900–30, London: School of Oriental and African Studies, 1977.

Wardley, Peter, 'The Anatomy of Big Business: Aspects of Corporate Development in the Twentieth Century', Business History 33, 1991.

—— and Gemmell, N., 'The Contribution of Services to British Economic Growth, 1856–1913', Explorations in Economic History 27, 1990.

Webster, A., Gentlemen Capitalists, British Imperialism in South East Asia, 1770–1890, London: Tauris Academic Studies, 1998.

White, Nicholas J., British Business in Post-Colonial Malaysia, 1957–70: 'Neo-colonialism' or disengagement'?, London: RoutledgeCurzon, 2004.

—— 'Government and business divided: Malaya, 1945–57', Journal of Imperial and Commonwealth History 22, 1994, pp. 251–74.

—— Business, Government, and the End of Empire: Malaya, 1942–1957, Kuala Lumpur: Oxford University Press, 1996.

—— 'The frustrations of development: British business and the late colonial state in Malaya, 1945–1957', Journal of Southeast Asian Studies 28, 1997, pp. 103–20.

—— Decolonisation: The British Experience since 1945, Seminar Studies in History, London: Longman, 1999.

—— 'Gentlemanly capitalism and empire in the twentieth century: the forgotten case of Malaya, 1914–1965', in R.E. Dumett (ed.), Gentlemanly Capitalism and British Imperialism: The New Debate on Empire, London: Addison Wesley, 1999, pp. 175–95.

—— 'The business and the politics of decolonization: the British experience in the twentieth century', Economic History Review 3, 2000, pp. 544–64.

Whittlesey, C.R., Governmental Control of Crude Rubber, New Jersey: Princeton University Press, 1931.

Wilkins, M., The Emergence of Multinational Enterprise: American Business Abroad from the Colonial Era to 1914, Cambridge, Mass.: Harvard University Press, 1970.

—— The Maturing of Multinational Enterprise: American Business Abroad from 1914 to 1970, Cambridge, Mass.: Harvard University Press, 1974.

—— 'Defining a Firm: History and Theory', in P. Hertner and G. Jones (eds), Multinationals: Theory and History, Aldershot: Gower, 1986, pp. 80–95.

—— 'Business History as a Discipline', Business and Economic History 17, 1988, pp. 1–7.

—— 'Free Standing Company, 1870–1914: An Important Type of British Direct Foreign Investment', Economic History Review Series 41, 1988, pp. 80–95.

—— The History of Foreign Investment in the United States to 1914, Cambridge, Mass.: Harvard University Press, 1989.

—— 'Comparative Hosts', Business History 36, 1994, pp. 18–50.

—— 'The Free-Standing Company Revisited', in M. Wilkins and H. Schroter (eds), The Free-Standing Company in the World Economy, 1830–1996, Oxford: Oxford University Press, 1998.

—— 'Ford among multinational companies', in H. Bonin, Y. Lung and S. Tolliday (eds), Ford, 1903–2003: The European History, Vol. 1, Paris: P.L.A.G.E., 2003.

—— The History of Foreign Investment in the United States, 1914–1945, Cambridge, Mass.: Harvard University Press, 2004.

—— and Frank Hill, American Business Abroad: Ford on Six Continents, Detroit: Wayne State University Press, 1964.

Williamson, O., Markets and Hierarchies – Analysis and Antitrust Implications, New York: Free Press, 1975.

—— The Economic Institutions of Capitalism, New York: Free Press, 1985.

—— and Winter, S.G. (eds), The Nature of the Firm: Origins, Evolution and Development, Oxford: Oxford University Press, 1991.

Wilson, J.F., British Business History 1720–1994, Manchester: Manchester University Press, 1995.

Wong Lin Ken, The Malayan Tin Industry, Tucson: The University of Arizona Press, 1965.

—— 'The Trade of Singapore, 1819–1869', Journal of Malayan Branch of Royal Asiatic Society 33, 1960, pp. 1–315.

—— 'Singapore: It's Growth as an Entrepot Port, 1819–1941', Journal of Southeast Asian Studies 9, 1968, pp. 50–85.

Yacob, Shakila, 'Model of Welfare Capitalism? The United States Rubber Company in Southeast Asia, 1910–1942', Enterprise and Society 8.1, 2007, pp. 136–74.

Yeo Kim Wah, The Politics of Decentralisation: Colonial Controversy in Malaya 1920–29, Kuala Lumpur: Oxford University Press, 1982.

Yip Yat Hoong, The Development of the Tin Mining Industry of Malaya, Kuala Lumpur: University of Malaya Press, 1969.

Yuen Choy Leng, 'Japanese Rubber and Iron Investments in Malaya', Journal of Southeast Asian Studies 5, 1974, pp. 18–35.

Zunz, O., Making America Corporate, 1870–1920, Chicago: University of Chicago Press, 1990.

Thesis

The following are dissertations written at the University of Malaya, Singapore which could be found at the National University of Singapore (NUS) Library.

Hackler, Rhoda E.A., 'Americans in Singapore, 1819–1850' (B.A. dissertation, University of Malaya, Singapore, 1961).

Loh Wen Fong, 'The Singapore Houses of Agency, 1819–1900' (B.A. dissertation, University of Malaya, Singapore, 1958).

Ong Theng Hong, 'The Straits Trading Company 1887–1937' (B.A. dissertation, University of Malaya, 1958).

Ooi Kwee Yang, Anthony, 'A Study of Marketing in the Ford Motor Company of Malaysia, Ltd. In Singapore 1966', (B.A. dissertation, Department of Economics, University of Singapore, 1967).

Other Thesis

Birch, F.D., 'Tropical Milestones: Australian Gold and Tin Mining Investments in Malaya and Thailand 1880–1930', M.A. thesis, University of Melbourne, 1976.

Robert, C.F., 'The US and the International Struggle for Rubber, 1914–1941', Ph.D. thesis, University of Wisconsin, 1970.

Sivachandralingam S.R., 'British Economic Involvement in the Agriculture and Mining

Sectors in the Federated Malay States, 1896–1909', Ph.D. thesis, University of Malaya, 2004.

Smith, G.B., 'Rubber for Americans: The Search for an Adequate Supply of Rubber and the Politics of Strategic Materials, 1934–42', Ph.D. thesis, Bryn Mawr College, 1972.

Sodhy, P., 'Passage of Empire: US-Malayan relations to 1966', Ph.D. thesis, Cornell University, 1982.

Stoler, A.L., 'In the Company's Shadow: Labor Control and Confrontation in Sumatra's Plantation History, 1870–1979', Ph.D. thesis, Columbia University, 1983.

Sundara Raja, S., 'British Economic Involvement in the Agriculture and Mining Sectors in the Federated Malay States, 1896–1909', Ph.D. thesis, University of Malaya, 2004.

Tareq Abd. El-Hamid Ahmed Amin, 'Anglo-German Rivalry in the Malay Peninsula and Siam, 1870–1909', Ph.D. thesis, University of Malaya, 1995.

Wong Sin-Kiong, 'The Genesis of Popular Movements in Modern China: A study of the Anti-American Boycott of 1905–1906', Ph.D. thesis, Indiana University, 1995.

Newspapers, Journals and Magazines

Asia Pulse
British Malaya (Malaya after 1952)
Bulletin of the Association of British Malaya
Chemical Market Reporter
Commerce Reports
Crown Colonist
Far East Trader
Far Eastern Review
Far Eastern Survey
Financial Times
Ford Graphic
Foreign Commerce Weekly
Fortune
Malay Mail
Malayan Tin and Rubber Journal (various issues 1923–28)
Manchester Guardian Commercial
Modern Tire Dealer
New York Times
Pacific Affairs
Perak Pioneer
RGA Bulletin (various issues)
Rubber Age
Singapore Free Press
Straits Budget
Straits Times
The Daily Mail and Planters and Miners Gazette
Tin International
Wall Street Journal

Websites

'Opening the door to new possibilities', fDi Magazine, 5 December 2006, www.fdimagazine.com/news/fullstory.php/aid/1877/Opening_the_door_to_new_possibilities_.html, accessed on 16 January 2007.

R. Rajan, P. Volpin, L. Zinghales, 'The Eclipse of the U.S. Tire Industry', available online: http://gsbwww.uchicago.edu/fac/luigi.zingales/research/PSpapers/tie.pdf, accessed 15 June 2006.

UNCTAD World Investment Report, 2006, available online: www.un-ngls.org/site/article.php3?id_article=146, accessed on 18 April 2007.

Index